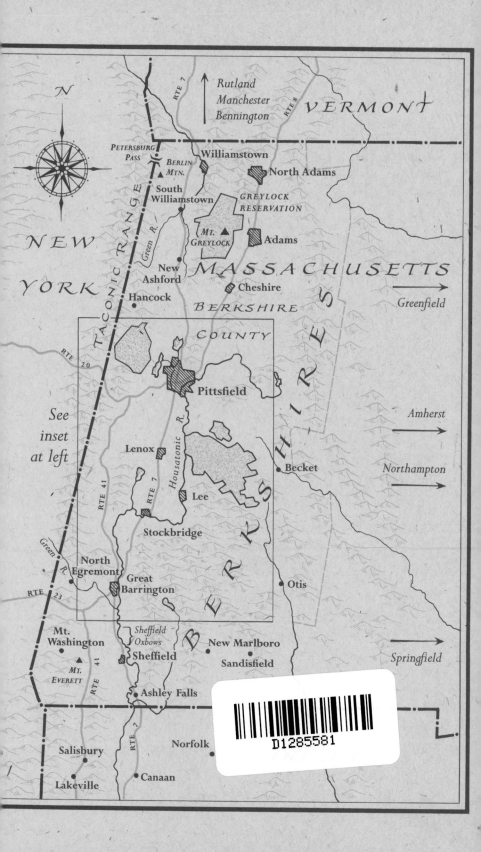

FIRST JOB

The Greylock massif from the west. (William H. Tague)

First Job

A MEMOIR OF GROWING UP
AT WORK

Rinker Buck

PublicAffairs
NEW YORK

Copyright © 2002 by Rinker Buck.

Map copyright © 2002 by Anita Karl and Jim Kemp.

Illustration of Royal typewriter copyright © 2002 by Michael Gellatly.

Newspaper collage on pages 320 and 321 by Amelia de Neergaard.

Published in the United States by PublicAffairs™,

a member of the Perseus Books Group.

All rights reserved.

Printed in the United States of America.

No part of this book may be reproduced in any manner whatsoever without written permission except in the case of brief quotations embodied in critical articles and reviews. For information, address PublicAffairs, 250 West 57th Street, Suite 1321, New York NY 10107. PublicAffairs books are available at special discounts for bulk purchases in the U.S. by corporations, institutions, and other organizations. For more information, please contact the Special Markets Department at the Perseus Books Group, 11 Cambridge Center, Cambridge MA 02142, or call (617) 252–5298.

BOOK DESIGN BY JENNY DOSSIN

Cataloging-in-Publication information is available
from the Library of Congress.

First Job
ISBN 1-891620-73-8

First Edition
1 3 5 7 9 10 8 6 4 2

This book is dedicated to three men
who together built a great newspaper
and "saved the mountains" of western Massachusetts,
Lawrence K. "Pete" Miller,
his brother Don,
and their most illustrious colleague,
Roger Bourne Linscott

CONTENTS

AUTHOR'S NOTE

ALL OF THE EVENTS in this account are as accurate as I could make them, relying upon interviews with participants from that time, newspaper files, letters, diary entries, and my own memory. However, I did change the names and alter a few identifying features of several women with whom I was involved at the time, for reasons that will be obvious to the reader once they reach those scenes. Romantic intimacy and how it contributes toward the development of character is an important aspect of my tale, and I wanted to be free to describe the richness and variety of that experience without causing embarrassment to the former partners involved. In this way, of course, books that change the names of a few characters can be more truthful than books that do not. Everything else, right down to the afternoon that Roger Linscott's donkey attacked his llama, is recreated just as it occurred.

I

The Eagle

CHAPTER ONE

LATER, AFTER I landed in New York and had worked for twenty years, people frequently asked how I had managed to begin my career at that mythic country newspaper in western New England's purple-black rim, *The Berkshire Eagle*. Oh, I said, cocking my head and letting out a self-confident sigh, it was all quite deliberate, the supremely rational choice of a promising young man on his way. Everyone dreamed then of starting out at *The Berkshire Eagle*, and I had merely been persistent.

This was, of course, a huge crock, one of those fabulous fibs I told while fitting out my personal rigging for life. As a matter of fact, there was nothing deliberate at all about my arrival at the *Eagle*. My first job was just another accident that happened along the gorgeous train wreck of youth.

Early one morning in April 1973, when I was twenty-two years old and had just finished up my course work at Bowdoin College in Maine, I rose at dawn and retrieved my motorcycle out of winter storage in a barn, loaded it up with camping gear and some books, and roared out of town for an aimless wander down through the southern states. A certain diffidence about the future and ambivalence about success was fashionable among college students then, and I was typical for the times. I had spent the past four months hanging

3

around the campus, desultorily adding to the slagheap of footnotes at the bottom of my senior thesis, chopping wood for my professors to pay my off-campus rent, mooning over a girlfriend who had decamped for Arizona. Now, a welcome break in the New England mud season had finally arrived. It was time to make my escape.

I've always remembered that day and that dawn departure because the weather and the signs in the sky so auspiciously fit my prevailing mood of freedom. Sixteen wearying years of my life—more than two-thirds of it—had been consumed by schooling of some kind, and for the last two years the amalgamated uproar over Vietnam, the draft, and Watergate had worn my generation down. Now the nirvana of being out and alone in the world, with no obligations to anyone, was finally mine. As I rumbled south on the Maine Turnpike, high, fleecy banks of cirrus clouds glowed amber and cobalt along the ocean horizon, and farther down near Portland, the snow squalls and rain I could see from the hills miraculously parted as I reached the valleys below. Coursing over the asphalt, my BMW cruising bike hummed from the stainless steel tailpipes and bucked gently over the frost heaves, the engine vibrating up through the handlebars to my arms. I emerged in bright sunlight just below the New Hampshire line. On the road ahead, a month of new sights and unplanned days seemed to open before me like a blissful mirage.

I was running away from myself and from life. A few weeks earlier, in mid-March, the college had announced that my senior thesis had won the coveted Class of 1873 History Prize, and I had also been selected as a graduation speaker. I should have been able to graciously accept these accolades as the fitting end of an academic career, one so studious and focused that ever since high school my friends had called me the "Book Turd." But there was no satisfaction for me in achievement, and the Book Turd was miserable about this. The prospect of public speaking filled me with dread, and the history prize seemed doubly embarrassing because the bright future that I had always imagined would instantly materialize as soon as I finished school was, if anything, more evanescent than ever. Indeed, I was emerging from college a unique, premature failure— the academic star who had run out of steam. Graduate school, which my professors were encouraging me to consider, sounded like a prison term to me. I was exhausted by the obsequious drill of gathering footnotes, kissing professorial ass, and making the Dean's List. All I wanted to do was wander around for a while and seek some new country, returning to my life as a boy. At the age of fifteen, I had flown coast-to-coast with my brother in a Piper Cub, and after that I had explored the West and the South on

The "Book Turd" from Bowdoin College, performing his commencement address.

motorcycles and in light planes. My summer jobs had always been a lot more romantic than practical—I had worked at horse farms, on a Maine lobster boat, and at an airport on Cape Cod. Reviving a life like that was a lot more enticing than planning a career.

Besides, I didn't have the foggiest notion about how to go about finding a job and hadn't lifted a finger in that direction yet. Indeed, the very prospect of making a living and all that it implied—bosses, a daily routine, real-life expectations— left me terrified and depressed.

So, I fled. I would visit my parents in northern Pennsylvania, and then make a leisurely tour of the Civil War battlefields along the Mason-Dixon line before roaming down the Blue Ridge and the Mississippi Delta to New Orleans. Journeys to nowhere and romantic illusions about life on the road were quite the rage then. Out there on the mythical blacktop, I thought, I would be "finding myself," clearing my head before

I returned north to Maine and faced the trauma of graduation in June.

By ten o'clock that morning I had already cut off the bottom of New Hampshire on back roads, crossed the Connecticut River at Brattleboro, Vermont, and now I was downshifting through the hairpin turns and over the granite summits of the Mohawk Trail, a lovely, familiar stretch of road that courses through the Berkshires and the Green Mountains along the Massachusetts state line. Below me the endless, purple-black folds of the high terrain fell to the Hudson and Lake Champlain, with tendrils of fog lifting off the lakes, and to the west the jagged, moody peaks of the Adirondacks filled the horizon like blackplate engravings. The sun rising behind me warmed my shoulders and back, and I felt refreshed and healed by the balsam vastness of interior New England, suffused by the euphoria of first-day travel.

I stopped to rest at the gravel pullout atop the Hoosac Gorge, enjoying the spectacular vistas west over the mountains. Looking straight down, I could see the orange-tile roof of my usual pit stop before I exited New England through the Petersburg Pass, the Howard Johnson's on Route 2 in Williamstown, Massachusetts. Shooting down through the twisting, shadowy ravines, with the tall stands of hemlock and birch swaying in the wind beside me, and the waterfalls and new ferns flashing white and pale green from the forest, I coasted into the valley below and swung into the Howard Johnson's.

It was there, while standing in line and waiting to be seated at a booth, that my future found me. The Williamstown Howard Johnson's was run by a local couple and had a folksy, unpretentious atmosphere, its menu dominated by meatloaf and fried chicken specials. Its interior was attractively littered with overflowing coatracks, bad watercolors by local artists, and a large bulletin board near the door jammed with thumbtacked business cards and stories about maple-sugaring from the pages of *The Old Farmer's Almanac*. That morning, two recent additions to the bulletin board caught my eye. The first was a full-page story from a recent issue of *Time* magazine, with the headline "The Eagle Tradition," about *The Berkshire Eagle*, a daily newspaper based in nearby Pittsfield. The second was a clipping from the *Eagle* itself about how the newspaper's chief editorial writer, Roger Linscott, had just won the Pulitzer Prize. I was intrigued. This was the sort of local curio I liked to indulge on my wanders. Removing the thumbtacks, I took the two clips along to read when I was seated for breakfast.

Time was one of the few national magazines that devoted much space to media coverage, and what it had to say about the *Eagle* was impressive. The newspaper was described as "40 freelance writers working under the same roof," reminding me of what I'd read about the early *New Yorker* under the legendary Harold Ross or the flinty, highbrow warrens of *The Nation*. Accompanying the story was an attractive black-and-white portrait of the paper's tall, aristocratic-looking publisher, Lawrence K. "Pete" Miller, who was leaning against his presses with a bemused, detached grin on his face. It was evident from the coverage that other newspapermen regarded the *Eagle* as exceptional. One prominent press critic, Ben Bagdikian, called the *Eagle* "one of three great newspapers in the world." (The other two were *Le Monde* and *The New York Times*.) *Boston Globe* editor Tom Winship called the *Eagle* the best newspaper "of its size in the country."

Time depicted the *Eagle* as existing in a rarefied realm of country newspapers—*The Ellsworth American* in Maine and William Allen White's old *Emporia Gazette* in Kansas—that had achieved outstanding quality in an out-of-the-way setting, defying the stereotype of rural newspapering as a bastion of mediocrity. Two of my book-turd heroes at the time, Roosevelt biographer James MacGregor Burns and the legendary foreign correspondent and author William L. Shirer, were regular contributors to the paper. Under the benevolent leadership of the Miller family, the *Eagle* had spent several decades patiently building quality and pioneering such concepts as liberal use of white space and generous photo displays, all the while championing aggressive news coverage and pithy, graceful editorial writing. Because of its fame and the scenic beauty of the Berkshire mountains, the *Eagle* was known as an important

The Olympian Lawrence K. "Pete" Miller (right) and his fun-loving brother Don (above) spent the post-war years building something unique. The Berkshire Eagle *was considered the best small newspaper in America.*

"feeder" for the big, prestigious dailies, a place where young journalists received three or four years of seasoning before they were ready for jobs at *The New York Times* or *The Washington Post*. Every year, graduates of the country's top journalism schools and Ivy League colleges competed fiercely for the one or two openings in the *Eagle* newsroom.

I liked one other quote in the *Time* piece. At the time, independent, family-run newspapers were under siege across America. Large, avaricious chains like Gannett and Thomson were snapping up dozens of small dailies, replacing local character with cookie-cutter dreariness. But the *Eagle* had managed to defy this trend and still maintain a large editorial staff of thirty-five full-timers and more than twenty local stringers covering the hill towns of western New England.

Time had asked Pete Miller how he and his brother Don, who had died the previous fall, could afford such largesse, and I liked the blunt Yankee charm of his reply.

"Neither of us has any expensive interests, like keeping a yacht or a woman on the side," Miller told *Time*.

Miller sounded interesting in a lot of other ways, a clarion out of the mountains of New England, the kind of figure that had always appealed to me. In the 1950s, he had gained national attention for a particularly brave stand against an ugly outbreak of McCarthyism at the mighty General Electric Company, which ran a big plant in Pittsfield, and several times he'd resisted attempts by powerful politicians and publishing industry titans to sway the editorial policies of the *Eagle*. An ardent land conservationist, Miller had regularly siphoned off a portion of the *Eagle*'s profits to preserve the historic vistas and open forests of the Berkshires—an astounding 20,000 acres in all. His legendary battles with mall developers and ski resort owners—unusual for a newspaper publisher—had made him a hero in the nascent environmental movement.

A compelling mental association occurred to me as I read the *Time* story. One of my favorite books then was a short, witty gem by John McPhee, *The Headmaster,* which enjoyed something of a cult status in the early 1970s. McPhee profiled the legendary Frank Boyden, who over a period of forty years had transformed a flea-bitten, third-rate local academy in Deerfield, Massachusetts, into one of the country's most prestigious prep schools. Nobody really understood Boyden very well or could fathom the secret of Deerfield's success. Boyden was cantankerous and short, maniacally fussy about details, notoriously impatient with academic theory or written rules. In its early years Deerfield was so short on resources and students that the headmaster filled in by playing on the baseball and football teams. Nevertheless, Boyden possessed a magic knack for infusing his students with his ferocious energy and passion for excellence, and so Deerfield thrived. *Time* depicted Miller as the same personality type: the craggy, inscrutable New Englander, a man of ideals whom everyone followed without quite knowing why. Pete Miller, it seemed to me, was the Frank Boyden of print.

Time's brief reference to the lyrical beauty of the Berkshires appealed to me for another reason. I wasn't particularly self-aware at that age, but I did appreciate that I was inordinately addicted to the outdoors and couldn't remain happy very long without gazing on a moody landscape, a result, I guess, of my motorcycle and flying junkets. When I was trapped in a city or on a college campus for too long, I appeased this need for natural surroundings by omnivorous reading—the travelogues of Wilfred Thesiger, the journals of Edward Weston or Ansel Adams—and I also got my weekly fix by visiting museums and obsessing on a Winslow Homer sky or the swirling pastel mists of J.M.W. Turner. I couldn't live without attractive country around me.

I knew a little bit about western Massachusetts already and had formed a dreamy impression. Biographers and historians had long called the poetic landscapes and comely oxbows along the Housatonic River the "American Lake District." For a time, in the mid-nineteenth century, the Berkshires had been the seat for America's Golden Age of writing. In 1850, the reclusive Nathaniel Hawthorne had moved west from Salem, Massachusetts, shortly after the publication of his masterpiece, *The Scarlet Letter*, and settled into a cottage on the shores of Stockbridge Bowl, where he wrote his *Tanglewood Tales* and parts of *The House of Seven Gables*. Just a few miles away, at his farm in Pittsfield, Herman Melville was wrestling his personal demons into the immortal *Moby Dick*. Melville was place-obsessed about the Berkshires, but delightfully so. From the palazzo porch he built on the north side of his house, and from the third-floor writing room where he finished his great novel, Melville had an unobstructed view to the state's highest peak, majestic, purple-black Mount Greylock, and he endlessly described it in his letters and poems. He dedicated his novel *Pierre* to the mountain out his north window, calling it the "Most Excellent Purple Majesty of Greylock."

Later on, Edith Wharton joined the migration of old blue-blood families and robber baron clans moving into the mountains from Newport and New York. It was the beginning of an epochal burst of house building, as Berkshire "cottagers" such as Andrew Carnegie and George Westinghouse turned Lenox and Stockbridge into the Versailles of the Gilded Age. Mansions grew on hillsides and river oxbows, plentiful as granite outcrops—by the turn of the century there were more than seventy-five in all. Carnegie's spread above Stockbridge Bowl, Shadowbrook, had 100 rooms and a crenellated facade that stretched 410 feet. The construction of gargantuan hotels and resorts soon followed, the most sumptuous of which was the 400-room Aspinwall Hotel atop a hill in Lenox. Aspinwall had its own orchestra and more than 30 chefs and grandly boarded the global rich and famous until it burned in a spectacular fire in 1931.

Wharton's relatively modest thirty-roomer in Lenox was called The Mount. It was good that she was there. Her classic, brooding tale of tragic romance, *Ethan Frome*, was based on a local folktale. Over the years the "secluded paradise" of western New England had drawn many others—Henry Wadsworth Longfellow, William Cullen Bryant, Edna St. Vincent Millay, James Gould Cozzens, William L. Shirer, and now even Thomas Pynchon and Norman Mailer—and they had turned the Berkshires into one of the most renowned writers' colonies in the country, immortalizing its scenery in prose.

Now, reading the *Time* piece over a late breakfast, I suddenly regretted that I had never seen the Berkshires. Racing in and out of New England along the Mohawk Trail, I was always too hurried to dip south into the fabled country below. My lack of initiative seemed almost pathetic. The alluring haunts of Hawthorne and Melville were so close, but I'd never ventured beyond the breakfast counter at Howard Johnson's.

I don't remember dwelling very long on whether I'd drive down to see the *Eagle* that day, mostly because there wasn't any reason not to make the trip. The coincidence of the *Time* piece seemed overpowering, and this was supposed to be a mythical motorcycle journey to nowhere, spontaneous and free-form, during which I could follow wherever the road and the points of interest led me. I was close—just thirty miles away—and I was fascinated by Pete Miller and his vaunted *Eagle*.

It never occurred to me that I might apply for a job at the *Eagle*. The *Time* article had made it abundantly clear that I wouldn't have a chance, and besides, I was the most unlikely prospect imaginable for a newspaper reporter. I could barely type thirty words a minute, didn't own a car, and my experience in journalism was limited to a handful of articles I'd written for the college paper. No one at the *Eagle* could possibly take me seriously. But I wasn't going to take *myself* that seriously either, spoiling my wander south. I hadn't jumped on my motorcycle that morning to conduct a job search. College was over, my girlfriend had bolted, and I was running away.

This was just a detour, a way to stretch out the day. In Pittsfield, I would park my motorcycle by the curb, quickly dip in and out of the *Eagle* offices, and if I happened to be feeling especially ambitious, I could always ask the receptionist for a job application, which I would quickly toss out. Nobody would have to know that I was even there.

And so, charmed by the diversion, I paid my bill at Howard Johnson's and returned the clippings to the bulletin board. Stepping outside, I kick-started my motorcycle and pulled out of the lot. Turning right just below the Williams College campus, I glided down the winding stretch of road that follows the oxbows of the Green River into South Williamstown. I was impressed by the beauty of the land unfolding below, astonished that I hadn't taken this route before. Stately rows of sugar maples and stone walls, glistening with lichen and wet moss, crowded right up to me along the shoulders of the road. Along the ridges, stands of birch and shaggy-bark cherry had burst with spring buds, receiving the sunlight as watery fringes of pink and green. From the road above the meandering river there were pretty vistas of cobbled fields and dairy farms. Deer and Guernseys browsed the grass together beside the racing white water.

And Greylock, Greylock finally viewed from a racing motorcycle on the first warm day of spring, its vast forested dome arching skyward as a pastel mosaic of lavender, pink, and blue. There it is, I thought, shifting down to slow my bike and enjoy the view. Herman Melville's mountain. And everything that Melville had written about Greylock seemed to be true. It was a magnificent piece of earth, a benign, endlessly fascinating massif, etching its elegant profile against hard blue sky.

Delighted with my decision and my route, I pushed on south toward Pittsfield, through some of the loveliest hill country I'd ever seen, a comely, purple-black rim that seemed to wall out the rest of the world. I was free and on the road, enjoying my first spontaneous detour of the trip, and all qualms about my future seemed to evaporate in the charmed landscape around me. There was even something vaguely familiar and rapturous about reaching this terrain, as if I were coming home to a place I already knew so well from books. At last I had entered the valleys that Nathaniel Hawthorne had described as "bright with heavenly gold."

CHAPTER TWO

WHEN I GOT into Pittsfield, the *Eagle* wasn't hard to find. The newspaper's offices occupied the only building on Eagle Street, a narrow, one-way street that ran off the main commercial thoroughfare, North Street. The building was an attractive, unpretentious affair, three stories of brick with tall transom windows all around, constructed as a triangle in the style of the famous Flatiron Building on 23rd Street in New York. Over the main entrance, beneath an art deco clock, hung a stainless steel logotype with the newspaper's name and an American eagle perched on talons between "Berkshire" and "Eagle." In the upstairs lobby I would discover an original oil painting by Norman Rockwell, inconspicuously hung among a dusty collection of photographs of turn-of-the-century Berkshire blizzards and floods. In the painting, a curmudgeonly, ruddy-faced geezer in red suspenders was contentedly snoring in his rocking chair beside a glowing woodstove, with a copy of *The Berkshire Evening Eagle* crumpled in his lap. The painting created an aura of repose about the familiar ritual of closing out the day with a newspaper for a companion. The first impression that it created, of the *Eagle* as a quaint, musty archetype of New England, a subject fitting for Norman Rockwell, never left me.

There was a side entrance right where I parked on Eagle Street, so I kicked out the stand on my motorcycle, threw my crash helmet under my arm, and stepped over to the large glass door.

As I opened the door, an attractive, middle-aged couple, laughing merrily about something, bounded down the stairs and breezed past me through the open door.

The woman was quite tall and Irish-looking, with a perfect aquiline nose and mouth, rosy cheeks, and a short bob of

The "Flatiron" style of the Eagle Building expressed the distinct but unpretentious values of its proprietors.

dark brown hair with shiny auburn highlights. The man was also quite tall and angular, with classic blue-blood good looks and a bemused Emersonian glow. He wore a dark gray herringbone jacket so worn down at the elbows that the lining showed underneath, pressed wool trousers, and scuffed cordovan shoes. He had a striking personal resemblance to a famed public figure of the day, the Watergate special prosecutor, Archibald Cox.

The only thing I could do was stand there politely and hold the door.

"Well gosh, thanks," the woman laughed.

"Hah!" the man said. "Quite a gentleman, I see."

I immediately recognized him from the picture in *Time*. Nervous shivers crawled up my back and I could feel my face turning red. This was supposed to be the quick in-and-out. No one would even know I was there. Now I'd practically had a head-on collision with *Eagle* publisher Lawrence K. Miller.

The door was awkwardly hung, with the hinges facing south, and I had to stand there like a hotel bellhop, meekly clinging to the handle while Miller and his companion swung around me and started down the sidewalk.

Miller was an immensely curious man to watch. Courtly and eccentric, he reminded me of one of those slightly dazed characters in a Washington Irving novel. Seven or eight steps down the sidewalk, he danced up high on the balls of his feet, twirled a full circle, and gazed skyward. With his right hand he scratched his forehead, and with his left hand he reached down underneath the flaps of his herringbone jacket, and then, artfully, thoughtfully, as if something tremendously worthwhile would result from the effort, he scratched his rump.

Miller stood erect and stared due west into the sky, at nothing in particular, as if he were about to declaim to the heavens.

"Ah, Pat. . . . Pat."

"Yes, Pete?"

"Pat. Who is that young man? Am I supposed to know him?"

"Pete," she laughed. "How am I supposed to know if you're supposed to know him? He's a young man. With a motorcycle."

"Gad. I can see that! But who is he? What's his name? What's he doing at the *Eagle*? Could you please determine these facts and report back to me?"

Apparently, Pat was used to this.

She turned on her heels and strode back toward me with her shoulders sloped forward and her arms swinging wide. When she noticed me watching her, she turned her head to one side, giggled, and blushed, and then abruptly threw back her head and straightened her shoulders, which reminded me of my sisters, who were also Irish and quite tall. My mother and the Catholic school nuns were forever pestering them to remember their posture.

Pat also had the most wonderful, open smile, which caused the skin at the corner of her eyes and her mouth to quiver slightly. I could tell that she was very shy, but had worked bravely at conquering that, which made me feel comfortable. So obvious and touching a deficit in someone else helped erase my own.

"Hi, I'm Pat Faucett," she said, blushing some more as she extended her hand. "Pete Miller's secretary. Ah, Pete. Well, see, Pete."

"Mr. Miller wants to know my name."

"Right! But you can't call him Mr. Miller. It's Pete. Everybody just calls him Pete."

"All right. Pete."

As affirmatively as I could, I told her my name and where I was from, because I didn't want her to suspect the truth, that I was just passing through and had stopped at the *Eagle* on a whim.

"Okay, good," she said. "I suppose you're looking for a job as a reporter."

Jesus. Things were getting out of hand. How could she just look at me and suspect that? But I knew that I had to say what she expected. I was too rattled about bumping into her and Pete Miller like this and didn't know a way out. Besides, if I did return later and apply for a job, I didn't want to look like some loser who changed his mind a lot.

So, I would just have to be polite about it. I took a deep breath, spooled up the charm, and then heaved off this immense bag of Eddie Haskell bullshit for Pat Faucett.

"Oh yes, Pat," I said. "As a matter of fact, I've been considering *The Berkshire Eagle* for some time. But I wanted to finish my college education first."

"Okay," Pat said. "But look, we're terribly flooded with applications right now. You've probably heard that we just won a Pulitzer Prize. But I'll tell Pete."

She marched back for Pete Miller, who continued to stand on the sidewalk as erect as a drill sergeant, gazing at a point in the Berkshire sky a few degrees above an American flag fluttering on the roof of City Hall. While he stood there, he ponderously scratched his forehead and rump, and then he reached over to massage the ragged sleeve at his elbow while Pat told him my name.

"*Rinker?* Oh my Lord. That's his name, huh? Rinker Buck. Hah! Jeez. Ah, Pat, are you sure you're not joking? No. It's probably not a joke."

The publisher of *The Berkshire Eagle* arched up again on the balls of his feet, pirouetted around on the sidewalk with this terribly intent and contemplative look on his face, and then came to a halt after a full rotation of 360 degrees. This street ballet seemed to have produced a decision.

"Oh, all right, Pat," Miller said. "Two o'clock. We haven't had one riding a motorcycle for a while. Tell him to come back at two o'clock."

Pat came marching back up.

"Listen, Pete and I are just going out to lunch, and probably no one else has time to see you today without an appointment. Go upstairs, ask for a man named Bob Rose, and fill out a job application. Tell him to send it over to me. Then I'll see you at two o'clock. We're on the second floor."

"Great," I said. "Two o'clock. Back here."

I must have looked astonished, which made Pat uncomfortable, because I could see the crow's-feet at her eyes and the corners of her mouth quivering again. She smiled sympathetically and reached over and touched my shoulder.

"Oh! Please," she said. "Relax. This is Pete. He does this all the time. Pete likes meeting people. He doesn't have anything else in his life except the newspaper. His hobby is young people."

Pat turned to go and breezed down the sidewalk past Pete Miller. At the corner of the *Eagle* parking lot, she wedged herself into the passenger seat of a faded blue Volkswagen Bug.

Scratching his forehead and his rump, Pete Miller hesitated for a moment or two, twirled back around on the balls of his feet, and faced me up the block. Then, in that peculiar way he seemed to have of addressing someone while staring up into the heavens, he spoke up in his high-pitched voice.

"Ah. . . . Ah. . . . . Young man. What's that name again?"

"Rinker," I called down the street. "Rinker Buck."

"Hah! Rinker. What a nameplate! Jeez. All right. I'll see you at two o'clock!"

With that, he turned for the parking lot, serenely scratching his rump a few more times and bobbing this way and that, like some big old mule deer in the rut season that wasn't sure which way to turn in the woods.

Down at the Volkswagen, Miller contorted his lanky frame into the driver's seat, rolled down the driver's window, and stuck out his arm. His legs were so long that they jutted up almost to the middle of the steering wheel, and I noticed that the VW's radio antenna had broken off and been replaced with a coat hanger. As the Bug skittered around the corner in a haze of white exhaust smoke, the coat hanger-cum-antenna wobbled crazily from side to side, and the tattered fabric on Miller's elbow flapped in the breeze. This was one aspect of the great and saintly Pete Miller that *Time* seemed to have neglected. The man was a total coot.

I stood there for a moment watching them go, amazed at my dunderhead behavior.

Oh you complete nincompoop, I said to myself. How utterly typical and asinine a stunt. A day that began in joyful vagabondage was ending in this, a job interview with the publisher of the famous *Berkshire Eagle*. I was terrified about what might happen if Pete Miller actually liked me and sent me to see his editors. They would instantly discover that I had absolutely no qualifications for the job. Across the table there would be long, embarrassed silences and amazed grins aimed in my direction, an orgy of humiliation for the Book Turd. Just out of college, girlfriend bolts, hops onto the motorcycle to escape, and then flunks his first job interview. This would be the opening gambit of my brilliant career.

Still, I felt entranced by the queer visage of Lawrence K. Miller. He was such an odd, beguiling figure to encounter for the first time that I felt I couldn't resist him. So, I climbed the stairs, took a job application from Bob Rose and filled it out, attached it to the file folder they gave me, and left the whole pile for Pat Faucett. Back on the sidewalk, I fished a jacket and tie out of my motorcycle sidebags and decided to fill the time until my interview with a stroll around town.

I liked Pittsfield—the imaginary "Bettsfield" in *Ethan Frome*—more than I expected. By the early 1970s industrial abandonment had given most other New England cities a gritty, derelict look, and you couldn't drive through Portland or Worcester without being depressed by the obvious economic decline of the Northeast. But Pittsfield threw off a refreshingly different ambience. It was a tidy, low-slung urban center, caught somewhere between small city and big town, and didn't look as if it had changed much since the turn of the century. Between two facing rows of brick Federal-style facades, a lively lunchtime crowd was bustling in and out of the restaurants and stores on North Street. The main commercial area emptied onto a classic, New England green, the Berkshire Commons, at one end of which stood a stone Congregational church and at the other an old-fashioned red popcorn wagon.

And from every sidewalk and street corner, it seemed, there were breathtaking views of the Berkshire peaks. Granite escarpments, shimmering purple and yellow under the noon sun, hemmed in the city on three sides. I felt that I had stumbled upon a well-swept, architecturally pristine remnant of the nineteenth century, an image out of a Currier and Ives print, charmingly framed by a mountain landscape. I pleasantly whiled away the time until my interview inspecting the collection of Melville memorabilia at the Berkshire Athenaeum, and then took a stroll out behind the high school along shady streets lined with well-porched Victorian houses, large backyards, and Catholic churches with elaborate flower beds and green lawns. My stomach raged with butterflies as I left for the *Eagle*, timing my arrival for precisely two o'clock.

.   .   .

Pete Miller was then sixty-five, with close-cropped, possum-white hair, smooth, pink cheeks, and an expression so inquisitive and cherubic that he seemed completely ageless. His large, second-floor office in the *Eagle* building reminded me of the inner sanctum of a university library, or a musty old museum devoted to literature and natural history. Elegant, glass-fronted bookcases ran the length of the room on three sides, and above them there were daguerreotype portraits of Abraham Lincoln, Walt Whitman, and Henry David Thoreau. A large map of Berkshire County dating back to 1856 hung above an oak roll-top desk.

I sat opposite Pete in one of those green aluminum chairs that were the popular style in office furniture in the 1940s, with a long grimy table of the same design between us. Every flat surface was covered with piles of newspapers, photos, reference books, and several coffee cans stuffed with pencils, some of them sharpened right down to the eraser. But the clutter and clash of styles was pleasing and purposeful, as if the occupant of the office was too preoccupied with the weighty issues of the world to fuss with a trivial matter like decor.

As I had already noticed out on the street, Pete had one disconcerting habit. While he spoke with me he either stared out the window to the mountains or looked at a fly buzzing up on the ceiling—anything, it seemed, to avoid eye contact. But this air of supreme detachment, taken in with his craggy good looks—he had a face, really, that belonged on Mount Rushmore—only added to his appeal. I immediately found him wonderful to be around, a genuine presence. An interview with him was more like a conversation.

Miller casually perused my job application and we talked a little about my background and travels, and he seemed genuinely fascinated by the fact that I had a pilot's license and that I was driving aimlessly through New England on a motorcycle,

Pete Miller was a man who seemed to have everything—strong instincts as an editor, a legendary reputation as a pioneering environmentalist, and some of the best mental baggage in New England.

on my way south to visit the Civil War battlefields. Cupping his hands behind his neck and leaning back in his chair, he looked out again to the purple-black rim of mountains at the edge of town, lost in reverie. He seemed so completely at home with himself, confident of his status and position, that he could allow long, silent lapses in conversation. Finally, he spoke.

"I've never actually, well, hah!" he said, pausing as if he needed to build up a head of verbal steam. "I've never actually *done* anything like that. Just taken off and seen the world. On a motorcycle no less. I envy you, young man. I actually do."

Then, abruptly, he swiveled back in his chair. I could sense that he was impatient with small talk. Conversations should move swiftly toward some higher purpose or idea.

"All right, young man," Miller said, pointing his finger at a line on my job application. "You are the one gadding off on a motorbike for our national battlefields, and it says here that you're from Bowdoin College in Maine. I do have one question for you. I can't imagine that you won't be able to answer it."

"Yes sir."

"Pete! Please, Pete. Everyone calls me Pete."

"Okay. Pete."

Miller leaned forward in his chair, formed the fingers of both hands into a steeple under his chin, and then stared intently at my face before he spoke.

"Do you happen to be familiar with a gentleman by the name of Joshua Lawrence Chamberlain?"

"Yes, of course," I said. "Joshua Chamberlain was a professor of natural and moral philosophy at Bowdoin College. When the Civil War broke out, he formed a regiment called the 20th of Maine, which fought with distinction during the Virginia campaigns. He returned a war hero and became the governor of Maine."

"Hah! Yes! Yes-yes-yes-yes. I can see you've read your history!"

The change in Pete Miller's demeanor was dramatic. Under arching eyebrows, his eyes brightened and danced, and then he began vigorously wagging the steeple of fingers underneath his chin.

"Hah! Old Joshua. More, young man. Tell me more. What was Joshua Chamberlain's finest hour?"

"Well, that would have to be Gettysburg."

"Yes? Ah, what day?

"The second."

"Ah-huh. Morning? Noon? Night?"

"Afternoon, late."

"Where?"

"Little Round Top."

"Hah! Yes. All right. We're getting somewhere. Now, tell me all about it. In your own words, could you please just describe for me this, ah, little, well, this engagement at Little Round Top?"

I couldn't believe my good fortune here. Apparently the publisher of *The Berkshire Eagle* was a Civil War buff. And he had just served me the easiest cream puff of all, Joshua Chamberlain at Little Round Top. I didn't consider myself a very able Civil War scholar. All those trans-Mississippi campaigns and Red River battles down in Texas, even Sherman's March to the Sea, didn't interest me very much. But the four years of bloodletting between Washington and Richmond—the endless bumbling of Lincoln's generals, the tactical brilliance and resourcefulness of Stonewall Jackson and Robert E. Lee—had never ceased to fascinate me. The Book Turd couldn't possibly screw the pooch on this.

"Well, sir," I said.

"Pete! Call me Pete. I already told you that."

"Right, Pete! Well, before dawn on the second day General Meade and General Sedgewick came up, and they were appalled to learn that the entire left flank of the Union position was exposed. Chamberlain and the 20th of Maine were dispatched to the high ground on the extreme left of the Union army, Little Round Top, and told to hold it at all costs. Meanwhile, the rebels were massing in the fields below."

"Who were they?" Pete interrupted. "Which corps?"

"Longstreet. Directly in front of Chamberlain was the 15th Alabama—the best fighters there were."

"Okay, good. Now, what happened?"

"Well, Pete, over the next two hours Longstreet's men charged six times. It was awful fighting, with heavy losses on both sides—I think Chamberlain lost a third of his men. His own brother was injured. But he had the advantage of high, angled ground, and Little Round Top was heavily forested, with all these natural rock outcrops. Actually, I've been up there. It's a very protected hill."

"Good. Good . . . good. What did old Joshua do next?"

"He was desperate, down to 250 men. He had already bent his line back as far as it could go, and now he was out of ammunition. Before the rebels could charge a seventh time, Chamberlain ordered his men to fix bayonets, raced forward himself, and in a sweeping, clockwise motion, he led the 20th of Maine in a magnificent downhill charge that chased Longstreet's regulars all the way back past their positions. There was massive confusion at the bottom of the hill, with bodies and wounded men everywhere, and the rebels never had a chance to regroup."

When I reached the part about Chamberlain's men fixing bayonets and charging downhill, Miller had softly muttered "Hah!" several times and begun this ridiculous little wiggle with his arms and feet, jabbing into the air with an imaginary musket and bayonet, as if he were cantering downhill himself with the 20th of Maine.

And he was pleased, extravagantly so, which I could tell by the way he quickly reached over and pulled a note card from the corner of his desk, underscoring with a flourish as he wrote a few words in pencil. Reading upside down, I could just make out the words from where I sat.

KID FROM MAINE = MOTORCYCLE = KNOWS JOSHUA CHAMBERLAIN

"Splendid," Pete said, expansively, folding his arms over his chest and breaking out into a benign smile. "So, it was the element of surprise, the unexpected, that proved decisive?"

"No, Pete," I said. "Chamberlain said after the war that he'd never thought of that. Little Round Top saved Gettysburg for the North, but it was almost a mistake."

Pete bristled and curled his face up in mock surprise.

"An *accident?* Joshua Chamberlain an *accident?*" Miller said, scratching at his elbow. "Oh my Lord. But all right. Tell me about that."

I explained to him that Chamberlain was a complete amateur at war, with no military training. He had boned up for the war by reading tactics manuals in the college library, most of which were horribly obsolete and dated back to the eighteenth century. Up on Little Round Top, Chamberlain remembered that one of the manuals said that a bayonet charge was effective when facing an entrenched force downhill. Chamberlain was desperate and didn't have any other choice, so he gave it a try.

That aspect of the Civil War—how necessity, even serendipity, had forged tactics—had always impressed me a lot more than the conflict's vaunted pageantry and bravery. Chamberlain's famous charge at Gettysburg was, in essence, an act of foolhardy daring, antiquated by mid-nineteenth-century standards. Most of the regimental commanders who heard about it afterward considered Chamberlain a lunatic. Yet Chamberlain's tactic had worked and held the Union left, decisively setting the stage for Pickett's charge and the fateful Confederate disaster the next day.

"Jeez. I'm actually learning something here," Miller said. "What irony, though. Chamberlain's disadvantage, in other words, was his advantage."

"Exactly," I said. "No West Pointer would ever have thought to do it."

"Well, splendid," Miller said again, arching up his eyebrows as if surprised. "You've actually thought about this!"

"Well, Pete," I said, mustering as much modesty as I could, "I guess I have thought about it."

This was pure bull. I hadn't spent five minutes thinking about old Joshua and his bayonet charge. I'd made up all this palaver on the spot. But I was enjoying myself up there in the *Eagle* sanctum with Pete Miller, and there was one particular revelation from that first session with him that stayed with me for years. For the first time in my life, I was overwhelmed with complete, unalloyed happiness about being the Book Turd.

It had always been an immense problem for me, something that divided me from my surroundings and my friends. All through high school and college, I had been stuffing into the back alleys of my memory this immense lode of trivia—Civil War notes, arcane literary and religious facts, assorted phenomena of weather, wildlife, and exploration. I obsessed on maps, old daguerreotypes, and the designs of nineteenth-century locomotives and paddle wheel steamers. Most of this was completely useless, knowledge that I didn't need for any of my school courses, but still I couldn't prevent myself from acquiring this cerebral claptrap, the way most people couldn't prevent themselves from gorging on movies and sports. I was aware that my reading was compulsive, even delusional, because I tended to identify with the characters and far-off places that I visited in books, fantasizing that I would lead one of these lives myself. I considered myself an oddball for this, but I knew that I couldn't stop doing it.

Now, in a flash, I realized that I could think completely differently about myself. Undeniably, I was still that Book Turd, but for the first time I liked myself for it. Old Joshua and his bayonet charge had sure saved my ass with Pete Miller.

Pete Miller spent the next fifteen or twenty minutes delivering a long, discursive homily on the *Eagle* and its values, turning sideways in his swivel chair and staring out at the rim of mountains out the window. "Localism," he said, was the concept that drove the paper. Miller was so high-minded and inspired by his own vision that I couldn't prevent myself from being charmed by him and also intellectually charged by his sense of mission.

"Localism," Pete said, stabbing the table. "That's what we practice here. We pay a lot of money every week for all these wire services and correspondents in Boston and New York, and they bring the world in for us. We've got this Pulitzer Prize–winning editorialist upstairs, the great Roger Linscott, who tells us what it all means. But I care most about what happens right here in these mountains. We're looking for reporters who understand that, people who get involved in their surroundings and look first to the things happening immediately around them. That's why I asked you this question. Can you imagine anyone graduating from Bowdoin College in Maine and not knowing about Joshua Chamberlain? Hah! That would be pathetic."

"Yes," I said. "Pathetic. And that would just about cover 80 percent of my graduating class."

"Hah!" Miller laughed, linking his palms behind his neck again and leaning back in his chair.

"And you're a cynic too! A wiseacre. Hah! Ah, ah, Pat! Pat!"

It appeared that we were done. Miller abruptly stood up, scratched his forehead and rump, and did another one of those queer little jigs of his across the linoleum floor. From behind me I heard the rustle of skirts and the click of heels as Pat Faucett came in to retrieve me.

Standing to go, I extended my hand toward Pete. Adroitly, as if he were horrified by the spectacle of physical contact and had devised a whole body language to avoid it, Pete swung his shoulders around and stared out the window to the mountains. As a sort of consolation prize, Pat grabbed my hand and vigorously pumped it instead. Then she gently pushed me out the door.

When I got out to the hall, safely out of range for hand contact, Miller wheeled again and faced me through the open door, jabbing his index finger up in the air.

"Young man, I've enjoyed this. Enjoyed it! Let us know if you get up into the mountains again."

.   .   .

Without really meaning to, I pulled a nice one over on Pat Faucett as she walked me down to my motorcycle. As we descended the stairs, she asked me how many children there were in my family. I decided just to go with my instincts about Pat. She was a dead ringer for Irish Catholic, and all of these Irish Catholic gals got hooked by the same line. All I had to do was exploit the truth.

"Eleven children," I said. "I've got ten brothers and sisters."

"Eleven! Oh my God," Pat said. "You're joking. Eleven!

Your mother's a saint—just a pure saint. Oh! A big family must be so much fun. You're close, right? I mean, are you close and do everything together?"

"Oh, sure," I said. "I mean, you know, all the usual stuff. Christmas, Easter, family reunions over the Fourth of July. Right now, I'm heading home to help my mother turn over her vegetable garden."

This was utter horseshit. I had been at war with my father for years, skipped the last two Christmases at home, and not once in my life had I set foot in my mother's garden. I didn't even know if my mother had a goddamn garden. Mostly, I "headed home" to the bosom of my family for free meals and to do my laundry, always making certain that my parents accurately relayed any messages from girlfriends that might have come in while I was off scouring the countryside for still more girl-friends. I considered my family a total pain in the ass.

But I obviously couldn't say that to Pat.

"Yeah, well, you know, Pat," I said. "It's great having a big family like ours. When I'm home on Sundays? I let my mother sleep in late and take all the little kids to Mass."

"Oh that's so *nice*," Pat said. "That's really nice. I can't wait to tell Pete."

Pat was ecstatic, red-faced and bubbly all over, a good Catholic lady jubilant over meeting genuine big-family issue. It was one of those rare moments when I worshiped my parents for being so thought-less about birth control. As

Pat Faucett, Pete Miller's secretary, was an ideal power behind the throne at the Eagle. She was devoted to her boss, well-briefed on the latest office gossip, and always fun.

regards the putative joys of growing up in a large family, another sucker is born every minute.

Before we said good-bye, Pat scribbled out the *Eagle*'s phone number on a note, handed it to me, and I stuffed it into my shirt pocket. She told me that it was all right to call. There weren't any openings at the *Eagle,* but she wouldn't mind telling me if any came up. I kick-started my motor, pulled on my helmet, and gunned my engine a few times.

I sounded my horn as I pulled out from the curb, squealed my tires up through the gears, and leaned over hard as I took the corner off Eagle Street. I was pleased with this first-day detour of my trip. Nothing would come of this job interview, of course, but I'd met the redoubtable Pete Miller of *The Berkshire Eagle* and acquitted myself well. It had been a nice time.

.   .   .

The country south of Pittsfield was less rugged and almost too pretty to look at, as stylized and pristine as a landscape painting. Along Route 7, Lenox, Stockbridge, and Great Barrington went by, tidy collections of white clapboard saltboxes, gingerbread Victorians, and country inns with broad porches that reached right down to the road. The low afternoon light turned the hard purple and black up on the peaks into pastel embers, suffusing the meadows and the Housatonic oxbows I could see from the road with lavender and beige. After Sheffield I turned west for New York State, reluctant to leave the hill country behind. Motoring down through Millbrook and Poughkeepsie, I crossed the Hudson and began the weary, up-and-down ride over the Catskills.

At dusk, heavy rain stopped me just short of the Delaware River, and I pulled into one of those seedy, 1940s-era motels with a long row of small bungalow cabins built under pine trees. Edward Hopper country. The nearest diner was too far to reach in the rain, so the woman who ran the motel lent me a hotplate, a saucepan, and a can of beef stew. After I cooked and ate the stew, I sat out on the porch, listening to the rain ping onto the tin roof and smoking my pipe, brooding about myself and the surprising events of the day.

I felt a little ridiculous and confused, because I realized that I was allowing myself to get excited about the possibility of landing a job at the *Eagle*. How typical and silly of me, I thought. Yesterday I was petrified about the very idea of finding a job. I hadn't even heard of Pete Miller and his *Eagle* before I reached Williamstown this morning, and now I was distracted by the remote chance of an opportunity there, even obsessing on it. I was impetuous by nature, often depressed about it, and this reminded me of how unrealistic I always was.

But I couldn't worry about that now. Tomorrow I would reach my parents' place in Pennsylvania, and a few days after that I would be crossing the Mason-Dixon line in fine spring weather, enjoying the long southern wander I had promised myself.

I turned in from the rain feeling exhausted, my arms and the small of my back aching from the motorcycle ride, but enjoying the fleabag warmth of my bungalow room. It had been a long day, Maine to the Delaware River with the purple-black rim of the Berkshires wedged in between. Time seemed implausibly stretched out, a welcome road-trip sensation.

As I pulled off my shirt to collapse into bed, the note Pat Faucett had scribbled out for me fell from my shirt pocket. I was surprised to see that she had written a short message below the phone number. As I picked up her note to read it, I could see in my mind's eye Pat's bright, impish face, the dimples quivering beside her mouth.

"Rinker. Relax. You did great with Pete. The last guy from Bowdoin didn't know who Joshua Chamberlain was."

CHAPTER THREE

I WAS ALL THE way down in Front Royal, Virginia, and had just finished a canoe trip down the Shenandoah River when I called home one night and my mother told me that a woman had phoned from a newspaper in Massachusetts. It was Pat Faucett. She wanted to set up interviews for me with several *Eagle* editors the following week. By now I had spent ten days roaming the lush, green countryside of Maryland and Virginia and hiking up along the Blue Ridge, and my interest in a country newspaper back in New England seemed like a distant, passing fling.

When I called her back, Pat made the interviews sound routine. There still weren't any openings at the *Eagle*, but Pete Miller thought that his editors should look me over anyway, "just in case." I was reluctant to move north again so quickly, but I knew I couldn't wiggle out of these interviews now. I spent the rest of that week dawdling my way back up the Appalachians, and a few days later I was seated at a conference table in Pittsfield facing managing editor Tom Morton and city editor Bill Bell, unaware that my mating dance with the *Eagle* had begun at a moment of considerable change for the paper.

Morton had grown up in Adams in a blue-collar family and joined the *Eagle* as a labor reporter after World War II. His tough pieces on price-fixing and labor disputes at the local General Electric plant had regularly enraged GE executives and led to several government investigations, contributing to the *Eagle*'s reputation for fearless reporting. Morton was plucky and blunt, effortlessly confident about slapping together a story at the last minute, the embodiment of the ad hoc style of a lifelong reporter. But Morton didn't have a lot of editing experience and he was still feeling his way after being appointed managing editor that spring. Bell, a cautious, detail-oriented former teacher from Indiana, was also new to his position. Together, they represented a sharp break from *Eagle* tradition.

Since the late 1950s, the *Eagle*'s editorial policies and recruitment practices had been largely determined by three men—Pete Miller, editorial writer Roger Linscott, and managing editor Rex Fall—a crusty, informal threesome who flew by the seat of their pants. Miller had gone to Williams College, Linscott was a Harvard man, and Fall was a graduate of Dartmouth. Essentially, they were old-fashioned New England Brahmins, and there was a mystique about what they had achieved at the *Eagle*. To them, newspapering was an extension of personal taste, a quiet confidence about who they were and the beliefs they wished to project to the world. They trusted themselves, their instincts. If they met a college hockey goalie that they liked, or a local dairy farmer's son who could turn a sentence well, they hired him on the spot. To them, a newsroom was supposed to be clamorous and fun, full of inquisitive minds, and the last thing they were concerned about was "professional standards" or formal training.

Early in 1973, however, just before I found the *Eagle*, Rex Fall decided to retire. Pete Miller had assumed the title of publisher after his brother Don had died of cancer the previous fall and was slowly withdrawing from day-to-day editorial affairs. Linscott, whose editorials had won the *Eagle*'s Pulitzer, was still loosely involved in the news operation, but notoriously overworked, moonlighting across town at a trade publishing company to put his daughters through college. The old triumvirate was breaking up, but its Olympian outlook would continue to influence the paper for years.

Morton and Bell had never been a part of Pete Miller's inner circle, and they made no secret of their wish to scrap the paper's Waspy executive style. They felt that the *Eagle* should take advantage of its growing prestige and the flood of applications that had come in since the paper had won the Pulitzer Prize by professionalizing its standards, hiring more specialists in business, finance, and health and more journalism school graduates. The *Eagle* had always placed a great deal of emphasis on visual quality and had spent lavishly on staff photographers. Morton and Bell felt that they should hire more reporters capable of illustrating routine stories with their own photographs, which would free up the staff photographers to take better "scenics" for the front page and major feature stories. The news business, they thought, was changing, and they were intent on dragging the *Eagle* into the modern age and away from the seat-of-the-pants operating style of Pete Miller.

Sitting down with Morton and Bell, I could see right away that they had little in common with the lofty Pete Miller. They were all business. They didn't want to talk about Joshua Chamberlain up on Little Round Top. Had I ever written photo captions under deadline? Was I interested in business or natural gas prices? They made newspapering sound gloomy and morbid. The only assignments a cub reporter received, they said, were obituaries, car wrecks, and the weather.

Morton was particularly easy to read, and I felt comfortable around him right away. He was short, plump, and bald, prone to wearing brown suits with color-coordinated brown ties and brown socks, but very open and likable. He spoke a lot in clichés, the clichés of an upwardly mobile blue-collar man intent on adopting the Waspy vernacular, or what he considered to be the Waspy vernacular, of his blue-blood predecessors in the *Eagle* newsroom. Titles and pedigrees, the slightest suggestion of privilege, seemed to annoy and fascinate him at once.

It was amazingly simple to buffalo Morton and Bell. They were supposed to be these hard-assed newsmen, with fifty years of experience between them, but as far as I could tell, their bullshit detectors had shut down years ago. Morton was particularly impressed, for example, that I had spent a year abroad studying at the London School of Economics.

"So, you're a gentleman and a scholar, I can see," Morton said. "The London School of Economics. Good show. In other words, you actually know economics?"

This was laughable. I had spent my year in England living in pubs, falling in love with beautiful Australian girls, learning aerobatics in gliders at the old Royal Air Force base in Lasham. But I'd picked up all I needed to know about economics listening to the nerdy graduate students from Hong Kong and Perth discuss their courses as they rode up and down the elevators to classes at LSE.

"Yes, I know economics," I assured Morton. "Macro, micro, monetary policy, interest-rate theory, the doctrine of competitive advantage, and so forth. Those were my courses."

"Budgets? Do you know budgets?" Morton asked. "For example, if we sent you down to south county to cover the annual town meeting in North Egremont, could you read the budget?"

"Oh, budgets," I said. "Well, my thesis in London was on postcolonial agrarian reform in East Africa. I analyzed a lot of budgets for that. You know—Kenya, Tanzania, Uganda. Probably, I can handle North Egremont."

I felt a little guilty about this. In fact, my thesis on East Africa was written by a friend, a graduate student from Ghana, in exchange for a new L.L. Bean down parka that I'd brought over from America but found that I didn't need over the mild London winter. It was an excellent paper and I received an honors grade for my friend's work. Morton seemed to like the way the nations of east Africa effortlessly rolled off my tongue.

"Well, good," Morton said. "Good. That's what we're looking for here. A gentleman and a scholar."

Morton was obsessed with another subject, his big "reform" at the paper. He was determined to hire a reporter who could illustrate his own stories by taking pictures. Dabbing his forehead with his pudgy hand, Morton launched into this earnest, long-winded homily about how newspapers today were training a new generation of "visually adept" journalists, "multidisciplined types" who could both write and photograph their own stories. I didn't have an objection to this approach, since it was all theory anyway. The only problem I could foresee was purely practical. I was about as visually adept as a toad, and I had never taken a picture in my life.

But I wasn't going to let a technicality like that spoil my chances at the *Eagle*. I would have to improvise, but fortunately I was in a pretty good position to do that. My girlfriend in college had been this big, tall gal with a Gaston Lachaise body, long, thick brown hair, a lovely face, and a rapturous laugh. She was a photography major. Sure, she'd ditched me late in the winter to travel to Arizona and study with a famous photographer, but I never blamed her for that because the mind-fuck part of our relationship had been so good. On snowy Maine nights, after we'd studied together for a few hours, she and I would cuddle up into the bed of this romantic little ratshack apartment that she had and pore through all of her photography books—Paul Strand, Dorothea Lange, Harry Callahan, I knew them all. My girlfriend adroitly explained to me the work of each of these photographers, and then she would laminate that new knowledge to my brain with great all-night sex. That was the best course I took at Bowdoin College. A one-hour lecture every night on the history of photography, from Matthew Brady to Todd Papageorge, and then high honors extra credit in fucking. She was the best, that girl, but it had never occurred to me that she was also readying me to face the world.

So, it was gratifying, listening to Morton drone on with his homily on photography, realizing that he didn't know half of what I knew on the subject. When Morton was done, I palavered away for five or ten minutes about Edward Weston's daybooks, Walker Evans, and all the wonderful things going on down at the Light Gallery in New York. Morton sat there with this amused, quizzical grin on his face while Bell furiously scribbled notes.

"Sounds good to me," Morton said when I was done.

"Yeah, but wait a minute here, Tom," Bell interjected. "Rinker, can you actually take a picture?"

"Oh sure, Bill," I said. "That's the easy part. It's figuring out a good image that makes it hard."

"But we need proof," Bell said. "I don't see any photos in your application. We need proof."

Jeez. This guy Bell seemed like a pain in the ass. I didn't even have the job yet, and he was already putting on the heat. It was clear to me what the division of labor was here. Morton was trusting and fun and just wanted to draw the best out of me. Bell was the cleanup man who attended to details. His demand for "proof" of my photography skills irritated me, but I knew that I had to satisfy his request.

"Done," I said, in the crisp, businesslike tone that I assumed was required for all reporters. "I'll send you some prints right away."

The next day, I called one of my closest friends from high school, John Bermingham, who was just finishing his final year in the photography program at Pratt Institute in New York. Berm sent me a pile of his best photographs. Most of them were way too abstract for my purposes—studied, composed images of Hispanic kids staring out of tenement windows, or teenage drunks with funny hats on at the St. Patrick's Day parade, the sort of ersatz Diane Arbus look that everyone at Pratt was into then. But the faces were crisp and well-exposed, the printing excellent, and overall the effect was very professional. Anyone could look at that stack of John Bermingham prints and tell that Rinker Buck was a darn good photographer.

Neatly arranging Bermingham's photographs into an attractive portfolio, I wrote "Copyright: Rinker Buck" on the back of each print, typed up a nice note, and sent the pile off to Morton.

I let a week go by before I called Morton about the pictures. My first instinct about Morton—that I liked him a lot—seemed to be accurate. He was irrepressibly cheerful, laughing all the time and murdering his cliches, delightfully easy to please.

"Tom," I said, "Did you get my pictures?"

"Kiddo, you're a renaissance man. These shots you sent us aren't exactly news photos yet—they're, you know, college-level work. But I can see that you're a real ace with the camera. We can always knock that artsy-fartsy stuff out of you later."

"Great, Tom. Thanks."

Now that my photography requirement was out of the way, Morton was recommending that I take one further step in the interview process.

"Now look," Morton said. "I'm not promising anything yet, see? We don't have any openings. But I don't think it's a bad idea for you to meet, just as a formality, our redoubtable editorial writer, Roger Linscott. He just won the Pulitzer Prize, you know. We call him "the Great Linscott.""

I decided to act dumb and breathless about this.

"Mr. Linscott?" I said. "Wow. You mean I get to meet him?"

"Throttle back, pal," Morton said. "The Great Linscott is, well, shall we say, a tough cookie. He's a bit of an eccentric and an egghead, and he'll probably throw you out of his office within five minutes. But like I said, it's just a formality."

"Okay, Tom."

"Give me three days to get my arms around this," Morton said. "Then call Pat Faucett."

.   .   .

One week later, I rumbled up into the mountains again and met Pat Faucett on the upstairs landing at the *Eagle*, in front of the Norman Rockwell painting. She led me down the hall to a triangular, glassed-in office formed by the apex of the building, just down from the newsroom. Pat stuck her head around the corner of the door and started making all these hand signals, as if she was communicating with the person inside in Indian sign language, and then swung back around.

"This is Roger Linscott," she said. "He's on the phone right now, so just wait. He'll call you in when he's done."

Before she breezed down the hall Pat reached out for my

shoulder, squeezed it, and smiled weakly, as if I were a prisoner being delivered to the scaffold.

"Don't be discouraged," she said. "Roger can be a little gruff. But everybody gets the same treatment, and deep down, he really likes people."

I felt uncomfortable standing there in the busy hallway, resumé and job application in one hand and my motorcycle helmet in the other, as reporters and editors streamed by, trailing long sheets of copy and discussing their stories, stealing sideways glances in my direction. Finally I heard the phone receiver drop on its cradle and Linscott called from within. His was at once the most melodious and intimidating voice I had ever heard.

"For God's sake. It's extremely annoying to have security, a night watchman, lurking outside my door. Whoooo's out there?"

I stuck my head around the corner.

"It's me."

"Jeeez. I can see very well that it's yoooou. But who's yoooou?"

"Me. Rinker Buck."

"Preposterous. That's your name?"

"That's my name. I'm part Pennsylvania Dutch."

"Oh Christ. And what about that headgear? Are you an astronaut? Just arrived from the moooooon?"

His dialect sounded like a cross between a Boston accent and a thick Newfoundland brogue, with all sorts of nineteenth-century contractions like "'tisn't" and "shan't" thrown in, and then I remembered that there was a town called Linscott, Maine. He could be from there. Anyway, Linscott had a way of grandiloquently stretching out certain syllables and vowels.

I stepped into the room, placed my crash helmet on the floor, and handed Linscott the folder with my job application and clips.

"No sir," I said. "I ride a motorcycle."

"Doubly preposterous. Are you some kind of a fraaaaud? Pete Miller is always doing this to me. I get all the basket cases he doesn't know what to do with himself."

"Do you want me to leave?"

"No! Jeeeeez. Can't you take an insult?"

"Well, ..."

"Stop!" Linscott held up his hand and lit a cigarette. "Please, take a seat. Let me read this stuff, and then we'll talk."

I couldn't believe the hovel where this year's Pulitzer-winning editorials had been composed. Frisbees, broken snowshoes, fly-casting gear, the dismembered parts of several typewriters, and what appeared to be the broken taillight of a Dodge Dart lay in haphazard piles in the dusty corners. There were several pyramids of newspapers, dried glue pots encrusted with spider webs, and a coatrack overflowing with lumberjack caps, sweaters, and a trench coat. As he smoked and read, Linscott absentmindedly dumped a glowing butt into an ashtray still smoldering from the last one, and then he reached over and heaved the whole smoking mass into his wastebasket. When the papers in the waste basket ignited, he languidly kicked them a couple of times with his shoe, cursed, and then he reached over for a half-finished cup of coffee and doused the fire. Acrid, billowy plumes of smoke floated up from the wastebasket, joining several years' worth of nicotine residue that coated the windows and ceiling. Linscott's office was a landfill, a toxic waste site. Prisoners in the Soviet gulag wouldn't put up with this filth.

Linscott looked up from my pile of clips and took a long drag on his Kent.

"These aren't half baaaad" he said. "Of course, the competition isn't very stiff. Most of the clips I'm forced to read these days are perfectly execrable."

I wasn't sure whether I was supposed to reply to that, but Linscott didn't give me much of a chance.

"Another thing," he said, impatiently. "I have always thought that Bowdoin College in Maine occupies the very zenith, the tippety-top, the pinnacle—yes, yes, that is the word, the very pinnacle—I have always considered that Bowdoin College in Maine occupies the very pinnacle of the second-rate New England schools."

At this point it would have been a relief to get thrown out of his office, so I just blurted out the first thing that came into my head.

"Well, thank you, Mr. Linscott. This makes perfect sense. I might as well go straight from a second-rate school into a second-rate profession."

"Jeeeez! Touchéeee!" he said. "I can see that you're an incomparable pain in the aaass, but conceivably I could learn to enjoy this."

The man was lethal. I was so flabbergasted by my first few minutes with him that I didn't dare open my mouth again, which turned out to be useful. Linscott was a monologist, a raconteur, a festival of talk, brilliantly amusing and excessive, with all sorts of asides about books I couldn't believe anyone would think to read, ancient grudges, and digressions that lasted a full five minutes. Sonorously, with encyclopedic reach,

His was the most melodious but intimidating voice that I'd ever heard, but beneath the gruff exterior of the Great Roger Linscott dwelled a man of touching kindness and sensitivity.

Linscott discoursed about everything from the Hudson River school of painters to celestial navigation.

But Linscott did have an ounce of sympathy for me. His office was stuffy and hot, and his monologue had made me drowsy. When he could see that I was about to drop off to sleep, he suddenly interrupted himself, yawned, and stretched his long arms out behind his head.

"Gad, how foolish of me," he said. "I'm sorry. I detest these interviews. I'm not the least bit interested in your qualifications—you've probably just lied about them anyway. I suppose that's why I'm doing all the talking. Say, do you play pool?"

"Pool?"

"Billiards. Pockets. Chicago ball."

"Sure. A little. I'm not great."

"Fine," he said. "Normally at this time of the day it's my habit to take a constitutional about town. However, if someone mildly amusing shows up, I play pool."

Linscott led me out of the building and up North Street. He walked with a pronounced limp, but he carried this handicap well, swinging wide with his right foot and then lunging forward with his shoulders and chest to pull along his bad leg, a graceful, Ethan Frome lope. He stopped abruptly at an unmarked door near the Boy's Club and pushed through the door. Upstairs, there was a wonderful, 1940s-era billiard room, musty and dark, with big, regulation-size slate tables and shaded green lights.

Linscott's caustic side emerged again as soon we started to play. He seemed to be a man who defined himself by constantly testing how much goading someone could take.

"Preposterous! What hubris," he said every time it was my turn to shoot. "Only a jackass or a brilliant contortionist would essaaaay that shot."

But I enjoyed it. Linscott's quips gave me an edge of anger that improved my game.

As we cleared the tables together, I gradually sensed that Linscott had been bored back in his office, and that our real interview had begun here, up in the pool hall. As he played,

Linscott kept up his lively banter about politics, books, and the bizarre cast of characters he'd met while newspapering, and he told me a little about himself. After graduating from Harvard, he had served in the Navy during World War II. His own first job had been at *The New York Herald Tribune*, where, by the age of twenty-seven, he already had his own column in the book section. But he had given that all up in 1946 to follow his dream of raising his family in the country. Linscott's father, Robert Linscott, had been a distinguished book editor in New York—his authors included Conrad Aiken, Carson McCullers, William Faulkner, and Truman Capote, all of whom Roger had met and known pretty well as a teenager.

Linscott gulled me into believing that he was only an average pool player by letting me win a few games. Then he cleaned my clock several games in a row. When we got back to my motorcycle on Eagle Street, Linscott lit a cigarette and took a long drag.

"Well, listen," he said, "I've enjoyed this, moderately, but I'm not going to pull one over on you. The *Eagle* has become frightfully competitive lately. If anyone asks me, however, I shall tell them that you're a semi-interesting character who probably won't embarrass us *that* horribly."

I pulled on my helmet, kick-started my bike, and reached over to shake his hand.

"Well thanks, sir," I said. "I enjoyed the pool."

"Me toooo," Linscott said. "By the way, you look perfectly hideous in that headgear. If I were a cop I'd arrest you, just for the sport of it."

I waved, pulling out from the curb, and Linscott waved back, the burning end of his cigarette making orange circles in the dusky sky. Behind him, the dome of Greylock glowed lavender on the horizon, and Linscott, tall and angular, stood on the sidewalk alone, a figure out of Winslow Homer.

Once more, I rode west over the mountains, mesmerized by the conversation I had just had. Why was I drawn so to these men and their landscape? It had never occurred to me that such interesting people would be out there after I left school.

I didn't know what I was going to do with myself if I couldn't get onto *The Berkshire Eagle*.

.   .   .

That spring, every couple of weeks, I rode up into the Berkshires, camped overnight in a state park, and took a leisurely stroll through the newsroom after the noon deadline passed. I said hello to everyone I'd met so far, pestered Tom Morton about a job, and even went to lunch once or twice with Pat Faucett. I didn't think of this as persistence on my part or even appreciate its value in helping me find a job. By this time my heart was set on the *Eagle*, and I simply couldn't stay away.

In June, after I delivered my commencement address, I arranged for the college publicity office to send a press release and photo down to Tom Morton at the *Eagle*, and my timing proved useful. The young reporter who had written obituaries for the *Eagle* for the past four years had just been accepted at Columbia Journalism School and was leaving the paper in August. Morton considered me overqualified for that position, but I'd made such a nuisance of myself, he felt obligated to let me know about the opening. When he tracked me down in New York, I got the impression he was trying to talk me out of the job.

"Kiddo," Morton said on the phone, "nobody wants to spend the next year of their life covering the stiffs. Weather and church news are also part of the beat. But you'll have your afternoons free to work on other stories. You won't offend me by saying no."

"Tom," I said, "I'll take the job."

"Oh, Christ. Don't you know the script here? You're supposed to ask for a week to think about this, and then I play hardball and tell you we need a decision in twenty-four hours."

"Okay, Tom. I'll call you back in the morning and say yes."

"Oh Jeez," Morton said. "Hey, what about money? Do I have to tell you everything? You haven't even asked me about your salary."

I was so magnificently stupid about financial matters that I had never even considered this, that jobs generally arrive with a paycheck attached.

"Oh, I don't know Tom," I said. "I just figured you'd pay me whatever you wanted."

"Oh my God," Morton groaned. "You're hopeless. But in that case, I'm prepared to tell you that the House of Miller is offering you the princely sum of $130 a week."

Wow. One-hundred and thirty dollars a week. I was really going to be on Easy Street now. The extent of my financial stupidity didn't dawn on me until several months later, when I was assigned a "local angle" story on a new federal report on income distribution in the United States. The report classified

I wasn't ready yet for the hustle of the big city. The great outdoors and the therapeutic value of lyrical scenery were something that I intuitively sensed that I needed.

individuals living on less than $7,500 a year as "marginal households." As I worked on the story, I realized that I was living $800 below the national poverty line.

.   .   .

I wasn't scheduled to begin work at the *Eagle* until August, but I decided to get settled in the Berkshires right away. In early June I hurriedly left New York and moved into the southern Berkshire town of Great Barrington, where I rented a furnished room in a Victorian house on Dresser Avenue, a quiet, tree-lined street just down from the Episcopal church. Within a few days I found a summer job, pumping diesel fuel at an all-night truck stop out on the Berkshire Spur of the New York State Thruway.

Before leaving New York, I had made an important purchase. Strolling into a Ninth Avenue pawnshop one day, I bought a used Nikon camera. Over the summer, I was determined to use my free time learning photography. By night I pumped diesel out at the truck stop, scrambling from truck to truck while I filled several tanks at once, enjoying the boastful, ribald talk of the truckers against the distant whine of the highway. By day, after a few hours of sleep in the morning, I ranged out over the hills, shooting several rolls of practice film with my camera, then racing to the Brooks Pharmacy in town to get the film developed overnight. The next day I flipped through the envelopes of prints, checking my progress toward becoming the "visually adept" reporter-photographer that the *Eagle* expected in two months' time.

One morning I went into the pharmacy for my prints and then stepped outside to the bench near the curb. An attractive, casually dressed woman about my age was sitting there, waiting for the bus that ran south into Canaan, Connecticut. When she saw me wincing as I examined that day's batch of prints, she leaned over and asked to look at my pictures and then frowned.

"You don't have a clue about what you're doing here, right?" she said.

"Well, I wouldn't necessarily say that," I said. "I'm just learning, you know?"

"Look," she said, "Nobody wants to look at these boring compositions of cows in a field or ferns growing out of boulders, okay? You need to start with simple images. Single people in neutral backgrounds. Just a face. That's best."

"Oh, all right," I said. "I guess I could try that."

"Yeah, you better," she said. "By the way, my name's Sheila."

"Oh, good," I said. "My name is Rinker."

"Whoa, dude. Rinker, huh? Maybe we can work on that too."

Sheila was a junior at Vassar College in Poughkeepsie who had just dropped out after deciding to change her major from biology to art. She was taking courses at the Yale Summer School down in Norfolk, a lovely, historic village in the Connecticut Berkshires, until she left for California in a couple of months to enroll in drawing classes at UCLA. Sheila wasn't extravagantly beautiful, but she had this immense mane of frizzy brown hair with blonde highlights, an easy, familiar smile, and I liked the way she tried to hide her figure with a mannish outfit of baggy chino pants, work boots, and a faded plaid shirt.

Sheila told me that she had taken photography courses at Vassar and she sounded very knowledgeable. It was Sheila who introduced me to the fundamentals of bracketing f-stops, so that I was always assured of at least one decently exposed frame, and shooting fast so I could focus for both faces and depth of field. She also taught me to shoot a lot of film, perhaps the best lesson she provided. Images are just random opportunities of reality out there. You have to have the confidence to leave a lot to chance.

I wasn't much of a pickup artist, but Sheila did have a legitimate transportation issue that day. After she took the bus down to Canaan, she said, she hitchhiked across Route 44 into Norfolk. As a favor, I offered to run her straight down to Norfolk on my motorcycle instead, and she accepted. On the way out of town, she suggested, more or less to return the favor, that we detour over to the Green River, out by the airport. There was a good swimming hole there where kids were always frolicking around on inner tubes and rafts. Farther up, where the oxbows started, trout fishermen liked to work the riffles and still pools formed by the rocks. It was a good place, Sheila said, to concentrate on shooting simple images of people.

So, we ended up spending a couple of relaxed hours down on the river together. While I scrambled along the banks looking for pictures and focusing my camera lens, languidly expending my film on shirtless boys spinning around on inner tubes, Sheila lounged in the shade of a large oak and called out suggestions.

"Dude, you're not shooting enough. Here's the thing: Think, compose, recompose, then shoot, shoot, shoot. Fill the frame with a good image and then shoot it, a lot. Got it?"

"Okay, okay. I'm trying here."

It was a sunny day and we both felt lazy together down on the river. It was easy graduating toward feelings of familiarity with Sheila because the mind-fuck between us was so good. I liked taking orders from a strong, confident woman, being goaded into taking better pictures by a babe, and she enjoyed doing it to me. *Guy, you're not listening to me. Fill the whole lens with that kid's face, and then shoot, shoot, shoot. Okay?* As the sun beat down on the river banks, Sheila perspired nicely between her breasts. She was fun, and sexy.

"Wow, look at this. It's two o'clock already," she said. "My day is shot. But who cares? This is art, you know."

"Yeah, what the hell," I said. "We're doing art."

After that we rode south and ate a late lunch at the Snack Shack in Canaan, talking about ourselves and goofing off at a picnic table in the shade, and by the time we got back to Norfolk all of the students at the Yale Summer School were heading off for their afternoon activities. So that her day wouldn't be completely lost, I ran Sheila down into Winsted for art supplies. Our excuse after that was that we both needed a beer. We ended up at this fleabag country-western bar out on the other side of the Mad River, quite drunk, dancing with all these bearded and tattooed shit-kicker types who drove dairy tankers all night or worked at the bowling ball factory in Tor-rington.

I was the sort of person who never made fast moves on a date, mostly because I was bashful that way to begin with. But I was also repulsed by the inebriate and predatory male behavior toward women I'd witnessed over the past four years at fraternity parties and college bars. But Sheila was very self-confident and intuitive, and didn't trouble herself a lot about what somebody else might think.

"Listen, dude. I'm leaving for California in two months. You're starting this new gig at the Berkshire Bird, or whatever that place is that you can't shut up about. We'll never see each other again. It's perfect. We define summer fling."

I had no objection to this definition of us. I liked Sheila's bad-girl way of throwing her leg out to mount my bike, the way she grabbed my belt to hang on with a strong arm, and she liked the way that I was willing to just lounge along a river bank somewhere, listening to her chat away about her art and her dreams. It would have been a complete waste of bodies and awesomely boring to sit around and wait, so we started making love right away.

Sheila and I had a nice routine that summer. Some nights, after my shift was over at the truck stop, I raced down over moonlit roads through West Stockbridge and Mill River, exultant with the black peaks towering into the clouds all around me, the brisk night air and the deer spooking in my headlights. Our assignation place was the seventh green of the Norfolk Country Club. I carried sleeping bags on my bike and we slept there together until dawn. Other times I went back to my room after work, showered and slept, and then swung down for Sheila in the afternoon.

Toward the middle of July, Sheila and I found another spot that we liked a great deal, in the undisturbed hill country north of the village of Norfolk, Doolittle Pond.

Doolittle was a pristine, upland lake carved into a bowl among the mountains, about 200 acres of water in all, as quiet as any spot in the Adirondacks. Its shoreline and surround-ing forest had been meticulously preserved by an association of millionaire landowners, whose discreet summer "camps" were hidden in the trees well off the lake. The association maintained a small swimming beach and boathouse, built in the Adirondack style, on the eastern end of the lake. There were always a couple of canoes and sets of paddles stowed in the bushes beside the boathouse. Sheila and I borrowed those. Arriving well after dark, we hid my motorcycle in the woods, loaded up a canoe with sleeping bags, sandwiches, and wine, and then we paddled noiselessly down to the far end of the lake where a rundown camp lay secluded in the hemlocks.

Nobody ever seemed to be around. On nights when it was clear we slept on the swimming dock out in the middle of the lake, spinning dizzily around as we picked out Venus and Orion. Black water merged with black sky, obliterating all horizon, so that we felt we were floating up with the stars. We chatted and smoked, made love, critiqued my pictures in the beam of a flashlight, and then made love again. One night we discovered that the door on the screen porch of the camp was open. There was an old sleeping mattress on a metal cot parked in the corner. If it rained, we slept and made love in there.

Doolittle was the secluded paradise I'd come into the Berkshires to find. The nights out there were still and cold and utterly quiet. At two or three in the morning we'd hear loons splash down, and then they filled the sky with their eerie, anguished wails. After that, the whippoorwills got started, and then the great horned owls hooted down from the ridges like bassoons.

The surreal, mournful screeching of the loons was quite sexual, a kind of tortured, orgasmic keening. Woken by this, Sheila and I would drink some more wine, hold each other tightly while we listened to the birds, and then make love again, enjoying the chilly, sensual moistness that gushed between our legs after repeated acts of sex. Sheila seemed ideal as a sexual partner. She was quite aggressive and didn't sit around waiting for me to make a move, which was necessary with me because I still possessed a lot of residual

Catholic guilt about sex. I liked being with a woman who unilaterally just grabbed me by the neck and ramped things up.

It was a romantic, carefree summer. The wine and the sex, mixing with the creamy reflections of moon on the water, filled me with expectations for the future. In a few weeks' time, Sheila would be leaving for California. I would be starting my first job. My dreams of becoming a writer someday had assumed new form. I would get carried away some nights and imagine myself being old Joshua up on his hill, fixing bayonets and calling to his men. It was a magnificent charge downhill, and I was planning on making one of my own at *The Berkshire Eagle*.

CHAPTER FOUR

I HAD SPENT the summer listening to the loons, deliriously making love to Sheila out on the raft at Doolittle Pond, rumbling back and forth between Great Barrington and my night job over lovely, moonlit roads black with new rain. The brisk mountain air and the scenic wealth of the Berkshires inspired many exaggerated visions about my new life as a cub reporter. These fantasies, however, evaporated almost as soon as I pushed through the swinging double doors to the newsroom in early August. I had completely forgotten that I'd signed on as an obituary writer. And the Book Turd knew absolutely nothing about his own country and its dismal practices at death.

Anne-Gerard Flynn, my predecessor on the obit desk, was remaining in the newsroom for three weeks to break me in before she decamped for Columbia Journalism School. Anne-Gerard was a cheerful, round-faced young reporter with long, wavy brown hair, freckles, and a perfect pug nose, so Irish she could have been cast as a stewardess in an Aer Lingus ad. She was very earnest, kind to everyone, and virginal, and following her around for three weeks to learn my new job was monumentally depressing. I knew that I could never approach my work as virtuously as she did, and I felt as if I'd been hired to replace a nun.

The first and practically the only thing I had to know about writing obituaries, Anne-Gerard informed me, was the strict ethnic divisions in the local bodies trade. In an old, blue-collar industrial town like Pittsfield, people were very dogmatic about this. Irish bodies always went to the Irish funeral homes, Italians to the Italians, and so forth, with the occasional, exotic cadaver from a smaller ethnic group—a random Croat, say, or maybe a Chinese or a Greek—up for grabs. I wasn't to be deceived by how obvious all of this sounded, Anne-Gerard said. On busy days, when a lot of people were dying all over town, the obit desk could get swamped with a dozen or more obits right on top of the noon deadline. It was very easy, Anne-Gerard said, to get your notes mixed up and send a body or two to the wrong funeral home, which would only get you into grievous trouble with Bill Bell. He hated running corrections for something as annoyingly straightforward as an obit.

None of this made any sense to me. I had grown up in the green, rolling horse country of northern New Jersey, just outside New York. Everyone there worked at swank jobs in publishing and banking in Manhattan, and our neighbors were nouveau riche Italians and Irish who had recently escaped the lower-middle-class wards of Patterson and Newark. They were devoted to their swimming pools and their children's pony meets, and they mostly spent their days aping the dressing style and Republican values of the old blue-blood Protestant families they were rapidly displacing. Nobody wanted anything to do with something as embarrassingly proletarian as an ethnic past. For several years I had been an altar boy at our local Roman Catholic church, and of course I'd worked a lot of funerals, swinging the old brass incense burner or carrying this big heavy cross as I followed the procession behind a casket. When somebody croaked in my town, it didn't matter whether their name was Giordano or Gallagher. They all got the same treatment: lots of flowers and a motorcade of Cadillac limousines, a requiem High Mass sung in hideous falsetto by a priest, and then out at the cemetery, a ludicrously expensive white tent. Now I had to shed all of that cultural baggage for the gritty mores of an industrial town up in the hills of New England.

So, grimly but naïvely, I went to work. I soon prided myself on the no-nonsense manner with which I cradled the phone on my shoulder and spooled copy paper into my battered Royal typewriter as the first obits came in. The *Eagle* was an afternoon paper with a noon deadline, and I could easily rack up a dozen or more stiffs in a single day—my record was eighteen. I also learned to enjoy the perverse, gallows humor of the funeral directors, most of whom I never met and got to know only by phone. They were men with names such as Remo Dagnoli, Fran Devanny, Terry Munevich, and Ray Haughey, and they couldn't seem to prevent themselves from peppering their dry recitations of basic obituary details with bitter little asides and wisecracks about their deceased clientele. Their jargon was unique. No conceivable death scenario, it seemed, escaped a label from the funeral directors.

Early one morning, Terry Munevich called in to feed me an obit on what he called a "Led Zeppelin." I considered myself absolutely brilliant for immediately picking up what he meant.

"Oh, great," I said. "You've got a rock star."

"Ah, Jesus," Terry moaned. "You don't know anything, do you?"

The deceased, as it turned out, was a 300-pound retired GE worker who had died in his attic over on Appleton Avenue, necessitating a cumbersome, time-consuming removal down four flights of stairs. That's what Terry called a "Led Zeppelin." As far as he was concerned, people should die only in hospitals, where by design the wide swinging doors, wheeled gurneys, and inclined halls made it easy to whisk a heavy body from the morgue to the cement hearse bays outside. Terry's customers were forever forgetting about the undeniable convenience of hospitals and keeling over in the worst places—the "Led Zeppelins" up in their attics, the "floaters" who had heart attacks in their swimming pools, the "Daniel Boones" way the hell up in October Mountain State Forest, where they'd died from overexertion while on deer-hunting trips. The funeral directors particularly resented "Jet-setters." These were people who died far away from home while visiting relatives or on a business trip, requiring complicated arrangements with the airlines to fly their bodies home.

"That's gratitude for you," Terry would say. "None of my customers ever thinks ahead."

Sarcasm this rich made writing obituaries almost bearable, and there were other things that I was learning. An amazing number of people died from acute alcoholism, but the *Eagle* was always careful to observe the polite fiction that they had passed on after a "long illness." The funeral directors absolutely wallowed in the disease and couldn't seem to prevent themselves from telling me that they'd just reeled in another drunk. In the trade, deceased drinkers were either called "White Russians" or "Liver on the rocks." The undertakers, however, seemed to reserve their deepest contempt for the mostly unknown, financially pressed residents of several seedy trailer-home parks hidden by high stockade fences up along Route 7 just north of town. Trailer-home residents tended to die intestate or broke, which annoyed the hell out of the funeral directors because the estates would have to be attached in probate court before the funeral homes could collect their fees. These were called "DOAs," for "Debt on Arrival."

By late August, as the long Labor Day weekend approached, one other change in my outlook surprised me. All through high school and college I had been an inveterate wanderer, undisciplined and spontaneous about everything except my studies. I had always dreaded finishing college because I doubted that I could ever adopt a regular schedule that even remotely resembled work. Now, miraculously, that was happening all by itself.

I loved rising early every morning in my grimy little rented room in Great Barrington, with the breezes rolling off the mountains and lifting the window shades, the lawns outside filled with the chorus of songbirds. The ride north, up past Monument Mountain and the vast wetland at Stockbridge, with the purple and gray cirrus clouds scudding overhead, was a beguiling romp through Winslow Homer terrain. Reaching North Street in Pittsfield, I dipped into the Friendly's restaurant for take-out coffee and doughnuts, then walked across the bridge over the railroad tracks to the newsstand for the Boston and Springfield papers, finally reaching the *Eagle* building precisely when I was supposed to be there, 7 A.M.

Besides, the *Eagle* newsroom was a wonderful old place, out of an earlier century, almost exactly fitting my romantic preconception of what a country newspaper should be like. The mixed olfactory sensation of grease pencils, glue pots, tobacco smoke, and photo development chemicals greeted me as I reached the third floor every day. By nine in the morning a dozen or more reporters were clattering away on old Royal typewriters along several rows of grimy, gunmetal gray desks dating from the 1940s. Tom Morton and Bill Bell were running around in several directions, trailing long sheets of paper glued together from the separate "takes" of each story, and querying reporters on their copy.

The pace—and the sounds—intensified as the *Eagle*'s noon deadline neared. Bells chimed on the rumbling teletype machines, the phones rang more often, and the long pneumatic *whoooosh* as copy was sent down the composing room tube throbbed constantly in the background. The din and the

During my drive toward work through the mountains every morning, the clusters of Eagle *delivery tubes on country lanes and street corners reminded me of the paper's strong regional presence.*

clutter and the confusion of it all seemed purposeful and exciting. It was true that I occupied the bottom rung of the newsroom, the dreaded and humiliating obit desk, but there was no place I wanted more to be. Occasionally, as I banged away on my Royal in the morning, my head would inexplicably flood with the happiest of thoughts, so intense that my heart fluttered and I could feel my arms momentarily weaken from the loss of blood pressure.

"God, this is nice," I would think. "I'm out of college and actually doing something with my life."

.   .   .

It didn't take me very long to screw up. At the end of my first week as the obit man, just as I was beginning to feel confident about the way I had handled the busy midweek rush of stiffs, a fellow by the name of Danny Ruggerio died. There was nothing remarkable about Danny. He had the typical curriculum vitae of a Berkshire cadaver—born in Pittsfield, fought (no medals) in World War II, thirty-year veteran of the ordnance division of the General Electric Company, beloved member of the Knights of Columbus, the Onota Sportsmen's Club, and the East Side Bowling League. Mount Carmel Church. Left behind a wife, several children, and grandchildren. Most of these obits were so formulaic I could have written them in my sleep.

Normally, a body attached to a name like Ruggerio would automatically be dispatched to the Bencivenga-Dagnoli Funeral Home out by the high school, which enjoyed the local monopoly on the Italian dead. But this was one of my first Italian obits and Dagnoli's wasn't an automatic reflex for me yet. For some reason the Devanny Funeral Home kept cropping up in my notes. I was unfamiliar with the surname Devanny. To my tin ear for the ethnics, Devanny was just another one of those names, like Clohessy or Sudarsky, that could crop up almost anywhere, but its vaguely Latinate cadence sounded more Italian than anything else. I was pretty sure of it, even confident. Devanny had to be an Italian name. Ergo, Devanny's was an Italian funeral home.

The noon deadline was fast approaching and Bill Bell was glowering over at me from the city desk, calling for the last of the obits so he could close the paper. Nobody gave a shit about a guy named Danny Ruggerio—he was just another thirty-year veteran of GE who had kicked the bucket on time for the Friday deadline, a last-minute obit to be crowbarred onto the page.

So, fuck it. On the obit page that day, old Danny got a one-way ticket to the Devanny Funeral Home.

Three o'clock in the afternoon, I would soon learn, was a lethal hour for me. That is when the building stopped rumbling

While bells chimed on the rumbling teletype machines, and a dozen old Royals clattered around me, my head was usually buried in a phone book, checking middle initials for an obit.

from the presses running in the cellar and the first editions of the *Eagle* hit the street. I was amazed that the funeral directors and *Eagle* readers took obituaries as seriously as they did, and how quickly and often they would call to complain about the most inconsequential mistakes. The screwup with Danny Ruggerio's obit, of course, was hardly inconsequential, and the ink was barely dry on the paper when I got the call from funeral director Fran Devanny.

"Hey, now you've done it! Get the hell over here and clear these guineas off my porch!"

"Guineas? What guineas?" I said.

"The Ruggerio guineas, you dummy. You sent an Italian body to an Irish funeral home."

"Ah shit," I said. "Isn't Devanny's an Italian funeral home?"

"Eye-talian? Jesus, we kicked the Romans out of Ireland 2,000 years ago. This is Fran! Remember me? I called in the O'Neil obit."

"Yeah, but I did the O'Neil obit, right?"

"Yeah!" Fran said. "You sent me the O'Neils, and then you sent me these guinea Ruggerios too. What's your background anyway? Where are you from?"

"New Jersey."

"Oh Christ. You're helpless. Your *background*, dumbbell. The old country. Where's your family from?"

"Oh. Ireland," I said. "I'm mostly Irish, with a little Swiss-German."

"Oh, Mother of Christ," Devanny said. "Pete Miller is so goddamn cheap he went out and found the only Irishman in the country who doesn't know the Devannys. Now I've got all these guineas on my porch."

Fran was one of four Irish funeral directors in town. He was a mirthful, inveterately cynical man with a raspy, asthmatic voice and a ready quip every day about local politics or an article that he'd read in the *Eagle*. He berated me for a full five minutes, because a number of Danny Ruggerio's friends had shown up for the wake at his funeral home, and he'd had to steer them to the right funeral parlor across town, which was Bencivenga-Dagnoli.

But Fran was too good an Irishman to take it beyond that. Now that he'd vented, he just wanted to become my friend.

"How about if I cut you a deal?" Fran said, toward the end of his call. "Bill Bell doesn't get to hear about this Ruggerio fuckup if you let me take you out to dinner. We'll go to the Highland and I'll explain your new beat."

I met Fran a few nights later at the Highland, a big, dark, jukeboxy dive that opened onto a narrow street behind City Hall, and we had a nice time together drinking beer and eating heaping plates of baked ziti and chicken parmigiana. It was Fran's opinion that the only truly smart funeral directors in town were the Derys. Years ago, through smart politicking at Notre Dame Church, the Derys had locked up all of the French Canadian stiffs in town and had a monopoly on that ethnic group. ("If you're French, unless you're nailed to the floor," Fran said, "you go straight to Derys'.") The Irish, himself included, were just "too frigging stupid" to establish a monopoly for their bodies. Even the "Eye-talians" had the sense to send all of their stiffs to Remo Dagnoli, Fran said. There wasn't a bit of dirt about the local bodies trade that Fran wasn't willing to share with me.

"Okay now, kid, you got it?" Fran said as we emerged from the smoky warrens of the restaurant and said good night on the street. "No more guineas for me now, all right? Remo Dagnoli is all yours."

Remo Dagnoli, as it happened, was my biggest problem on that beat. Remo was a short, squat man with shiny, slicked-back hair, heavily starched collars, and a thick black woolen suit. He was utterly humorless and stupid, and he had this one enormously annoying habit. He always called in his obits while he was working on a body in his cellar mortuary, leaving the sink running and the embalming apparatus on while he talked on the phone. The embalming machine gave off these strange pneumatic sighs and whooshes, like a milking machine hissing on a dairy floor, and in the middle of dealing with some particularly dense organ or body part the pumping mechanism would suddenly begin to labor and groan. Then Remo would put down the phone and step over to the corner to fiddle with his tubes and dials.

Italian obits were a little bit different. Remo and his customers insisted that death notices include the name of the
province in Italy where the deceased was born. I found this
interesting, because the Irish or the French Canadians could-
n't have cared less about their birthplaces, but the Italians
were fanatical about this. Remo carried his devotion to the
correct spelling of these locales to the point of fetishism. He
lived in perpetual fear that the *Eagle* was going to misspell
some miniscule village in Tuscany or Sicily, which the Italian
Daily Faithful would blame on him.

When he was back from adjusting the controls on the
embalming machine, Remo would yell over the pneumatic
background noise to make sure I got the spelling right.

"Born in Catania" (*pump, whoosh, whoosh*).

"That's C (*whoosh, pump*) as in Cat."

"A as in Ajax" (*whoosh, whoosh, whoosh*).

As the embalming machine strained and the occasional
pumps gave way to a constant, groaning *whooooosh*, I could
hear Remo sighing with annoyance as he reached over to
adjust the hardware once more while he yelled into the
phone.

"Catania! This old lady was born in east Sicily."

Remo Dagnoli, however, was a cupcake compared to city editor Bill Bell. I was certain during my first few months at the
Eagle that his only job was the identification of each and every
one of my personal defects. Bell was a short, jumpy man with
fastidiously parted gray hair and this froggy little potbelly that
he refused to acknowledge by buying a pair of pants that were
let out at the waist. There was something vaguely ecclesiastical
about his temperament that I couldn't quite put my finger on.
Inevitably, I made a lot of small mistakes on the first obits and
the church news stories that I was assigned. I didn't know
much, for example, about the differences between the Eastern
Orthodox and Roman Catholic rites, or between Reform and
Conservative Judaism. This drove Bell insane. If I forgot to
include a middle initial on an obit, he treated me as if I had just
committed a mortal sin.

Bell had one curious habit. Every day, as soon as the noon

deadline passed, he rose with a dignified air from his desk, clasped his hands behind his back, and then, quaintly swaying back and forth with his shoulders, he exited for North Street and took this long ruminative stroll across town, as if he were some English country vicar escaping up among the hedgerows to read his breviary. Tom Morton found Bell's daily constitutional highly amusing. He and Bell were vastly different in temperament, and the tension between them was sometimes palpable, but Morton generally made an effort to ignore these conflicts. Sometimes, however, he couldn't resist.

"The Reverend Mr. Bell has now departed on his noontime walk," Morton would say, with mock veneration, as Bill left for his stroll. "Kiddo, it's time for you to pull out your rosary and recite a hundred Hail Marys."

In a lot of ways, I was my own worst enemy. Bill Bell did try to be kind to me, but I perpetually annoyed him by backsliding into an absurd verbosity. When there was a lull on the obit desk, Bell would assign me the sort of low-level, beginner stories that came with the beat—weather disasters, car wrecks, church suppers. I was completely unprepared for these assignments, wrecked in the head by four years of writing the kind of bullshit expected by college professors. In my hands, the Housatonic River, swollen by two nights of heavy rains, became a "perfervid, turbulent Euphrates." A moose that wandered down from Vermont and caused a pileup on the Massachusetts Turnpike became a "mercurial mammal gamboling across the exit at Lee." I am probably the only reporter in history who described a flipped-over car as coming to rest against a "meretricious guardrail."

There wasn't any particular reason that I chose "meretricious" that morning. I just liked the way "meretricious" sounded, and what the hell, it might just work with "guardrail."

Bell's metabolism simply couldn't process phrases like this. He kept beside his desk an immense, twelve-pound edition of the *Oxford English Dictionary*. Discovering in my copy another "mercurial mammal" or "meretricious guardrail," he would turn beet red, launch out of his chair, and then strut over to my desk with the giant OED in his hands. He dropped the volume on the file cabinet next to my desk with a bang that could be heard clear across the newsroom.

"I'm sure that you had a perfectly good reason for choosing a meretricious guardrail instead of the ordinary steel one," he said. "Why don't you look it up and make sure the usage is correct."

"Ah, Bill," I said. "C'mon. It's just a car wreck story. Bag the meretricious and just change it back to guardrail."

"No," Bell said. "I would like to be educated on this. It's entirely possible that meretricious is just the right word here."

City editor Bill Bell did try to be kind to me, but then I'd turn in another car-wreck story with a "meretricious guardrail" gaffe.

So, while the other reporters rolled their eyes and snickered behind their typewriters, I waded into the OED and then hauled it back to Bell's desk.

"Bill," I said. "Meretricious: Lewd and lascivious behavior. Or, acts of or relating to the occupation of a prostitute."

"Aha! Now we know," Bell said. "Now, tell me, would that meaning apply to a guardrail?"

"Well, probably not, Bill," I said. "Unless it's a guardrail where a lot of prostitutes hang out."

"Right, but that is highly unlikely along Route 102 in West Stockbridge, wouldn't you agree?" Bell said. "Please watch it next time. It's extremely annoying to confront these errors in your copy."

Tom Morton loved these encounters. He considered me a hero for butting heads with Bell over ridiculous questions like mercurial mammals or meretricious guardrails. Watching me fuck up was the best part of his day. As soon as Bell left for his noon constitutional, Morton would call me over. He sat there with his stubby wingtips propped up on his desk, rubbing his hand over his bald pate and stifling a mischievous grin.

"Kiddo," Morton said. "Mind if I make a suggestion regarding your relationship with the Reverend Mr. Bell?"

"Sure Tom. Shoot."

"Okay," Morton said. "Next time you've got a car wreck story? Try calling it a *fucking* guardrail, all right? I've always wondered what the Oxford English Dictionary has to say about that."

· · ·

One Friday afternoon, Remo Dagnoli called in a body that finally seemed to have some possibilities. That morning, a retired General Electric mechanic had died. His profile sounded pretty standard for Pittsfield—the fellow's memberships included the Knights of Columbus and the Pittsfield Ham Radio Club and he had been an usher at Mount Carmel Church. But then Remo said something else.

"Oh yeah, I almost forgot. The family said to tell you that this guy is the last surviving veteran of World War I in Berkshire County. But don't take my word for it. Check it out."

Curious about that, I checked the information in the *Eagle*'s clip morgue over in the corner of the newsroom and discovered that, in fact, the deceased had been the last remaining veteran of World War I. I was captivated by the possibilities of writing about this. It seemed to me that the passing of the last veteran of World War I was an important historic milestone, and I had always been fascinated by the way Americans were entranced by the events of World War II but found World War I relatively boring and insignificant. Stretching the obit to reflect on this question might be interesting, but I had a problem. There was only sketchy information about the battles that the deceased had participated in, Saint-Mihiel and Metz, and his life after returning home to Pittsfield was annoyingly pedestrian—the most that could be said about him was that he'd joined the Ham Radio Club.

Still, I was determined to do something with this obit, and there was another reason for that. I liked working Fridays and often felt inspired to write better pieces on that day. The *Eagle* split its staff on Fridays, one shift coming in until the noon deadline to turn out the Friday paper, the other working from late afternoon until midnight churning out copy for Saturday. With only half the staff around, the newsroom was refreshingly quiet and I could always pick up an extra story or two off the senior reporters' beats. I usually elected to work both shifts on Friday, enjoying the intensity and nervous exhaustion of working from dawn to well after ten o'clock at night.

Besides, on the Friday afternoon shift, Bill Bell's city desk slot was usually taken over by Charles Bonenti, a young, personable editor who also doubled as the *Eagle*'s art and architecture critic. Charles had a strong story sense and would spend hours fiddling around with typeface design and photo layouts to achieve the airy, spare look that the *Eagle* prized, and he loved sitting around for fifteen or twenty minutes pensively batting around a story concept, a collaborative sharing of ideas I rarely experienced with Bill Bell. When I told him about my idea of gussying up the veteran's obit with some history from World War I, I could see that Charles was skeptical but didn't want to discourage me from taking a stab at something new.

"Rinker, you probably can't pull this off," Bonenti said. "But at least when you're done, you'll know why."

When Pete Miller had moved downstairs after his brother's death to take over the publisher's job, most of the *Eagle*'s reference books on history had moved with him. I was still too in awe of the great Lawrence K. Miller to feel comfortable about barging into his office just to locate a book, but when I got down there Pat Faucett wasn't in her cubicle adjoining Pete's inner sanctum. The only thing I could do was poke my head around the corner and stare into the musty museum space of his office.

Pete was sitting at the long metal table that he used as a desk, reading a sheaf of copy from the Sunday supplement that he still edited, *UpCountry* magazine. When he saw my head poke around his doorjamb he looked up with that mirthful, quizzical grin he always wore.

"Hah! What can I do for you, young man?"

I told Pete about the veteran's death and my plans for writing about World War I. Pete rose from his chair, scratched his rump with satisfaction, and then danced back toward his bookshelves. He pulled down several ancient encyclopaedias and illustrated war histories, theatrically puffing up his cheeks to blow the dust off the spines as he placed them on the table.

"Young man, this is what we used to call a 'casual,'" Pete said. "Call the family and squeeze out any details they can remember about this fellow, and then stitch that in with some history of the Great War. Don't try and force the material, just write what you know. Do you think you can manage that?"

"Yeah, but Pete. There's almost no information about this guy. All I've got is an essay on World War I."

"What's wrong with *that*?" Pete said. "The family's not going to mind if you just use this fellow as your hook. It's a 'casual' about World War I."

While Pete scratched his bony elbows through his frayed shirt sleeves, we discussed the World War I casual for a bit more. Before I left, he asked me a question.

"Say, who's on the desk tonight?"

"Charles Bonenti," I said.

"Good," Pete said. "If you'd like to, you can show this to me first when you're done. Charles won't mind."

Writing that casual was immensely rewarding. After poring through the books Pete had lent me and then calling the veteran's family for more details, I sat down at my Royal, scrolled in a piece of copy paper, and effortlessly churned out what I knew was probably the most graceful and informative piece I had ever written. The sensation of writing quickly and well was both emotive and physical, and I was infused with feelings of intellectual power and personal well-being. My arms and legs quivered as I typed, and I felt energized, yet at rest, overwhelmed with profound satisfaction.

Another intellectual breakthrough occurred for me that night, a realization so powerful that I remembered that Friday in the newsroom for years. My book-turdism was paying off in spades. There were huge blocks of information stored within me, just begging to be released. Indeed, my compulsive reading and then meditating upon what I'd absorbed had an "unseen hand" effect. I'd done most of my reading about World War I two years before, while studying in England. But now that I needed that information, my mind seemed to have already worked out all the issues and formed clear ideas on the subject. My "take" on the Great War was sitting there, just waiting for me to use it someday.

Refreshed, swelling with feelings of confidence, I took my copy down and showed it to Pete Miller.

Pete cupped his forehead in his hand and furrowed his brow as he read my copy. He had this eccentric habit of lick-

Pete Miller's inner sanctum at the Eagle *was almost spiritually cluttered and eccentric, and every visit there felt special. "Hah! Young man, what can I do for you today?"*

ing the tips of his fingers and then applying the moisture to the sharpened end of a Number 2 copy pencil, so that the lead flew over the paper as he edited. With lightning speed, he raced through the copy, grimaced a few times, and then boldly scratched out several sentences at the beginning of my paragraphs. He finally looked up with that bemused Emersonian glow of his.

"You did fine, young man, just fine," Pete said. "Your sentences are crisp and to the point, and I very much like this business here of the soldiers pushing through the forests to Metz. But you made the usual mistake of a newcomer doing a casual. You wrote too much."

"Too much." I said dumbly.

I must have looked crestfallen because Pete suddenly beamed and cocked his head sideways.

"Whoa, young man, whoa," he said. "I said, you did just fine. Why, when I was your age, I never would have gotten even this far. You just need to learn the secret of what to leave out."

Pete then launched into a short lecture about the importance of brevity in writing. He swiveled my copy around to show me the material that he had excised. They were all "transition sentences" from one paragraph to the next, where I had worked too hard to make sure the readers were carried to the next point or been too insistent with my prose. Good writing, Pete reiterated, was an exercise in "what to leave out."

"Don't force your best conclusions on the reader," Pete said. "This is writing now, real writing—you're not in college anymore, proving your brilliance to these terribly erudite professors. Everyone has a father or a grandfather or an uncle who told them their war stories. You want the reader to just obliquely make that association. What you leave out and the reader places there themselves? That's the strongest part of every story."

Because it was Pete Miller saying this, and because I so enjoyed being alone with him in his office, Pete's suggestions about my copy had an enormous impact. I returned to the newsroom rushed with new excitement about my writing, but also with complicated feelings about Pete. He was such a graceful, avuncular man, but I was bothered by the intuitive sense that there was a terrible loneliness about him too.

But there wasn't much time to dwell on that now, because I had to retype my story to reflect Pete's edit and then hand it in to Charles Bonenti. While Charley read the story, I went out to Friendly's for dinner.

"Jeez, Rinker, this obit about the vet and World War I is really sweet," Bonenti said when I got back. "How did you manage to make it so smooth?"

"Oh, I don't know, Charley," I said. "I worked on it."

.   .   .

After that, working double-shifts on Friday became my favorite time of the week, an addiction for me. I enjoyed the relative quiet of the newsroom when only a half-shift was around, Charley Bonenti's collaborative style, and the challenge of taking on stories that I wouldn't normally be assigned. The variety and intensity of a sixteen-hour day made me feel romantic, all ramped up for a weekend of hiking or motorcycling up into Vermont.

Fixing bayonets and charging downhill. As I roared out of Pittsfield after ten o'clock, the blackplate peaks were etched in the sky, up against the bright canopy of stars. I raced down Swamp Road in Richmond for the Westbridge Inn in West Stockbridge. There were a number of fun-fun motorcycle gangs that hung out there, and they always seemed to be happy to see me when I pushed through the door. The biker babes lined me up for pool games and called me a "rich dumb fuck" every time I missed a shot, and then guffawed and tried to barge in when I flirted with the pretty daughters of wealthy weekenders up at the bar. At two in the morning, when the gang left the Westbridge, I rode south with them down Route 41. The mists rising off the Housatonic oxbows were inspiring and dreamy, and I felt comforted by the roar of a dozen Harleys all around me. Old Joshua at Gettysburg, I thought, never felt as good as this.

CHAPTER FIVE

EARLY ONE afternoon a couple of weeks later, just as I was beginning to calculate how many more obituaries it would take to turn me into a suicide case, Bill Bell strolled over and dropped a press release on my desk. The press release carried the logo of the big hospital in town, the Berkshire Medical Center, which had emerged in recent years as a regional medical powerhouse and Pittsfield's second-largest employer. BMC's hyperactive director of publicity was forever pestering the *Eagle* to write the sort of gushy "human interest" features considered a staple at other papers, but that the *Eagle* resolutely refused to publish. Now, as part of a continuing program to upgrade its stature in pediatrics, the hospital had just hired what it called a "nationally recognized pioneer" in the field.

Dr. Keith Mahoney was a specialist in the "fascinating and new" discipline of thanatology. I was unfamiliar with the word *thanatology* and, just guessing, figured that it probably had something to do with either foot surgery or maybe colon polyps. But Bell was impressed with the word. Before he came over, I'd noticed him monkeying around at his desk with the press release, checking several words against his *Oxford English Dictionary,* which was not a good sign. As he stepped over, Bell had a satisfied, portentous expression on his face.

Thanatology, Bell explained, derived from the Greek root

thanatos, "death," and was defined as "the science and psychology of death and dying." According to the press release, Dr. Mahoney would be coordinating the efforts of the BMC medical staff, parents, and social workers, helping to meet the medical and emotional needs of terminally ill children, and generally applying "thanatological principles" to the hospital's clinical program. Mahoney and his mysterious Greek science initially struck me as a bit of a medical hustle, but it was hard to question the man's credentials. He was a graduate of Notre Dame University and the Johns Hopkins Medical School in Baltimore, and before arriving in Pittsfield, he had served residencies and conducted clinical studies at several prestigious teaching hospitals across the country.

"Thanatology!" Bell said, warming to the subject. "Most of our readers have never heard of this. I mean, gosh, *I've* never heard of this!" Dr. Mahoney and his gospel of thanatology, Bell thought, would make an excellent Name in the News.

The Name in the News was a small monument to the *Eagle's* lofty purpose. It was a carefully written, detailed personal profile on some interesting politician or national writer on tour who had made the news that week, and was prominently displayed every Saturday on the first page of the local section. The feature embodied Pete Miller's ideal of guaranteeing an interesting read and raising the paper's profile among the New York literary types and affluent vacationers who swelled Berkshire County's weekend population, one of those Waspy sleights of hand that the *Eagle* pulled off to earn its outsized reputation.

An amusing newsroom comedy was required every week, however, to get the Name in the News done. Bell often relied on Rory O'Connor, a tall, devilishly funny reporter with a fine ear for the subtleties and cadences of country life, who was one of the *Eagle's* most elegant wordsmiths. Rory sat along the back wall a short distance away from me, at a desk piled so high with notebooks and stacks of yellowing newspapers that I could barely see the top of his head. Like many gifted stylists, Rory was both monstrously overworked and a notorious procrastinator. On Tuesday or Wednesday afternoons, when Bell wandered over to pester him about a Name in the News, Rory squinted sideways, stroked his salt-and-pepper goatee, and stifled a yawn.

"Bill, I don't have anything yet," Rory would say. "But let me sleep on it, okay?"

With that, Rory would strip off his faded seersucker jacket, neatly fold it into a pillow on top of his typewriter, and then drop his head down onto the top of his Royal with a heavy metallic plunk. Rory was almost instantly asleep and spent the next hour contentedly snoring on top of his Royal.

Rory's biorhythms drove Bill Bell insane. It was only Tuesday, nobody else in the newsroom could give a shit about Saturday's paper, but Bell always required something to worry about in advance. Panicking, he scurried around the newsroom, his potbelly proceeding him like the prow of a boat, hitting up every reporter he could find for a "backup" Name in the News. Between Tuesday noon and Friday morning, all kinds of ridiculous subjects and crackpots—local fanatics obsessing on cable television hookups, landowners irate about a new Route 7 bypass, Czechoslovakian immigrants who were yoga instructors, any old dogmeat idea, really—got assigned as "backup" Names in the News. Then, on Friday afternoon, Rory calmly woke up from his nap, conceived and pumped out thirty peerless inches on a worthy subject, and blew the whole newsroom out of the water. Eight backup Names in the News assigned by Bill Bell went right where they belonged in the first place, straight into the crapper.

That's what was happening to me right now, and Bell laid it on quite thick. A Name in the News assignment, he said, was just about the toughest duty that the *Eagle* handed out. I should treat this like an exercise that would prepare me for the sort of high-toned profiles that the *Eagle* expected from its writers. I wasn't to be offended if he made me rewrite it several times. Bell told me to go out to the medical center and interview Mahoney, bone up on thanatology, and present this new and mysterious Greek medical science to readers of the *Eagle* in as interesting and simple a way as I could. I'd better get started right away—he wanted my first draft by tomorrow afternoon.

So, this would be my first big test. My rendezvous with destiny at the vaunted *Berkshire Eagle* would be a renowned thanatologist, Dr. Mahoney. When I dialed the hospital, Dr. Mahoney's secretary told me that I could come over right away. Stuffing a couple of notebooks and the press release into my jacket pocket, I bounded down the back stairs, kick-started my bike, and roared up North Street to the medical center, terrified that I was going to fumble my first backup Name in the News.

.   .   .

The interview with Dr. Mahoney didn't go well at all. He was a tall, extremely thin man with prematurely drooping shoulders, curly, swept-back hair, and black, darting eyes. His handshake was clammy and weak, and the fan humming behind his shoulder nearly asphyxiated me with the smell of his cheap, drugstore cologne. Every time I asked Mahoney a question, he nervously fished into his back pocket for a handkerchief and wiped the perspiration off his face. The man was gloomy, epicene, and strangely repressed. All he could do was endlessly palaver on about Socrates, Plato, and the seminal differences between Christian and Islamic "death motifs" during the Crusades. I wasn't worried merely because my interview was a total loss. I was bothered a lot more by who this man was. Who would hire a creepy geekster like this to work with sick and dying kids?

Then, all of a sudden, I had it. There were a number of things that tipped me. Mahoney just didn't have a doctor's demeanor, the crispness of speech and quiet confidence of a medical man. He was more conversant in theology than in medicine. But I think it was Mahoney's cheap cologne that activated my internal radar. To me, cheap cologne was always suggestive of shady characters and murky sexual identity.

That's how I solved the riddle bothering me about my Name in the News subject. Keith Mahoney wasn't a doctor. Without question, this guy was a goddamn ex-priest.

As it happened, I was one of America's leading authorities on ex-priests. I could smell one a mile away. It was one of those inadvertent, quirky traits, resulting from an unusual family background, a gift that I simply hadn't had the opportunity yet to exploit. But instead of appreciating this talent—that I could always smoke out an ex-priest—I was embarrassed about it.

My father had been a very successful business executive in New York and a weekend pilot, but in 1946 he spun in his plane and lost his leg, and after being released from the hospital he graduated from morphine to booze. He caught himself in time, just before I was born in 1950, and joined the burgeoning Alcoholics Anonymous movement. My father expressed his gratitude for being "saved" in a unique way. His subspecialty within AA became "recovering" Roman Catholic priests. With a close friend who was a priest, he had cofounded a private AA clinic in New Jersey, and many of its patients were alcoholic priests. My father's fondness for boozy clerics knew no bounds. When they had finished their month-long course of sobriety at his clinic, my father brought these sad, lonely men home to live with us for a while, and living beside priests in transition had become a defining complex of my youth.

We had a big old ramshackle farmhouse in rural New Jersey with extra bedrooms above the kitchen and a large, dormitory-style attic where the priests bunked down. I grew up to the familiar routines of these hushed figures in our lives—the sickly, saccharine smell of their breath mints and cheap aftershave when they joined us for meals, their shuffling around the living room in bedroom slippers while they read their breviaries. Priests annoyed me for another reason. I just couldn't stand the way that these unctuous ordained men seemed to crave the companionship and physical touch of little boys.

They were very creepy about it. Father Dan or Father Brendan were forever pestering me to take them for long horse-and-buggy rides out in the country, or asking me to play softball down in the backyard, after which they would stroke my perspiring back and hold my hand as we walked up to the house, offering delightful compliments about my personality.

One of my favorite pastimes as a child—a vital search for privacy away from my ten brothers and sisters—was sitting alone in a warm bathtub at night, reading a Hardy Boys mystery. But then Father Brendan would barge in, sit down on the toilet seat and fold his legs underneath his cassock, and give me these long boring lectures about the importance of studying hard in school and avoiding sin. I just didn't need that dipshit Father Brendan in my life right then. I was in the bathtub, trying to finish *Secret of the Old Mill*. Father, couldn't you just leave me alone right now? Priests were a pain in the ass in general, and I certainly didn't need one paying attention to me while I was taking a bath.

I was hardly alone in this—most Catholic schoolboys were aware that the priests up on the altar were emotional train wrecks, even if we couldn't quite articulate what was wrong with these strange men. But this truth collided with another marvelous instrument of repression, the Catholic Doctrine of Silence. If an uncomfortable subject was never discussed, it would simply go away. The issue of priests and their obvious difficulties—their boozing, their murky sexuality, their loneliness—was taboo.

Still, I had pretty good radar for these guys. Although I had no way of knowing about Mahoney's sexual identity, I was sure about one thing. Mahoney wasn't a doctor, and he was definitely some kind of weird, escaped priest. But there was no mention of his clerical past in the hospital press release, and that meant that everything else on his resumé was probably bogus. How could a reputable hospital have hired a quack like this and turned him loose on kids?

Screw Bill Bell. I wasn't going back to the newsroom to write a Name in the News. I was going back to the newsroom to check Mahoney out. I brought the interview to a close as gracefully as I could, and I even had the presence of mind to innocently ask for a copy of his resumé, which I knew I would need to investigate his academic credentials.

Little flickers of excitement and self-doubt coursed down through my arms and legs as I rode back down North Street. This was the time of that national primal scream called Watergate, and down in Washington, a pair of virtually unknown police reporters for *The Washington Post*, Bob Woodward and Carl Bernstein, had become heroes by uncovering the crimes of Richard Nixon's White House. All of a sudden everybody in the country wanted to become investigative reporters.

I had discussed this a lot with Peter Scheer, an Amherst graduate just my age who had joined the *Eagle* staff that summer after working for Pete Miller's beloved weekend supplement, *UpCountry*. Peter was instantly likable and we took to each other right away. He was extremely bright and intellectually earnest, and he had this wild Jewish afro and told hilarious stories about growing up in Poughkeepsie, New York, where his father was a doctor. At Amherst, he'd been a

Peter Scheer was brilliant, hilariously witty, and an automatic babe-magnet. Our friendship defined my Eagle *years and became an important sharing of vulnerabilities.*

protégé of historian Henry Steele Commager, and during *his* job interview, Peter had discussed with Pete Miller his senior thesis on the Cuban Missile Crisis, about which he was obsessed. Peter was an obvious comer in the newsroom and very popular. All of the women at the *Eagle*—Mary Jane Tichenor over on the social desk, the librarian Madeline Winters, and this hot little tightbody who wrote for *The Berkshires Week* entertainment section, Vicki Saunders—had crushes on him and were forever inventing reasons to hang around his desk. Peter loved Norman Mailer, hot chicks, and the films of Bernardo Bertolucci and François Truffaut.

Peter and I were convinced that Watergate was trashing our careers, because it would all be over before we could join the fray. We were obsessed about it, morose. While we were stuck in journalistic gulag way up here, covering the fight over the Route 7 bypass or the plans for a new Berkshire Athenaeum, Woodward and Bernstein were down there, pillorying the Nixon White House. But you didn't have to go all the way to Washington to find great investigative journalists. There were several right here at the *Eagle*. In the early 1960s, Tom Morton had unearthed evidence of a price-fixing scheme and its cover-up by General Electric, a series of stories that made national headlines and sent several GE executives to jail. In 1972 a brilliant and much-loved *Eagle* reporter, Dick Weil, had done it all over again when he revealed that GE executives had ordered the destruction of an unfavorable earnings forecast. Morton's and Weil's accomplishments covering GE were a part of the *Eagle* culture, the lore of its newsroom. Peter and I were wildly ambitious for ourselves. If we couldn't become Woodward and Bernstein overnight, at least we could emulate the adventures of Morton and Weil.

Of course, Pittsfield's bogus thanatologist, Dr. Keith Mahoney, hardly rated up there with price-fixing GE vice presidents or the malfeasant Richard Nixon. Still, I knew I had a good story here, and I was now at least marginally practicing the craft of investigative reporter. The local medical center, one of the largest in New England, had hired a quack.

I couldn't wait to get back to the newsroom and trump Scheer with this.

.   .   .

The story proved remarkably easy after that. As soon as I got back to the newsroom I picked the richest academic plum on Mahoney's resume, Johns Hopkins University Medical School in Baltimore, located and dialed the proper area code, and tracked down the registrar's office. The associate registrar I spoke with, a woman, exhaled what sounded like a familiar sigh of frustration when I mentioned Keith Mahoney, and it only took her a minute or two to locate his records, as if they were sitting right there on her desk. Yes, she told me, Keith Mahoney had been briefly associated with Johns Hopkins, back in the late 1960s, but he'd been nowhere near the medical school. His sole credential was enrollment in a brief suicide-prevention course.

After that, most of the entries on Mahoney's resume fell like tenpins. The distinguished clinical studies, the internships and residencies, the deliciously professorial and important-sounding International Symposium on the Thanatological Sciences, were all a crock.

I was perplexed about what to do next. I didn't know how I was going to explain this to Bill Bell. Somehow, when *Washington Post* editor Ben Bradlee queried Woodward and Bernstein about how they had cracked the Watergate break-in, I couldn't imagine them telling their editor that they didn't like the quality of Richard Nixon's cologne.

Uncertain, I kicked the wheels of my swivel chair over to Peter Scheer's desk and told him what I'd found.

"You've got to be dicking me," Scheer said. "The guy's a phoney?"

"Phoney Mahoney," I said. "Legally, he's probably not even licensed to drive the ambulance."

"But Rinker, that's a great story! Morton and Bell will give you a medal for this."

"Bell?"

"Okay. Morton will give you a medal. But just go over and tell them. They're not going to bite your head off."

When Bell finally came over, I was sitting with my feet up on the desk, smoking my pipe, still trying to figure out what I was going to tell him.

"So, how's the Name in the News coming?" Bell said. "Was the doctor at all interesting?"

"Well, ah, Bill, the guy *was* interesting. More interesting that we expected. But I don't think we can do a Name in the News."

"What do you mean?" Bell said. "This is an *assignment*. An interesting assignment. You just said so yourself."

Bell seemed annoyed when I explained my suspicions about Mahoney and described the calls I had made. He was more concerned about mistakes that he said I'd committed than about Mahoney. First of all, I'd failed to alert my superior that I was launching an investigation, failed to alert Mahoney about my suspicions, failed to call the hospital to get them to straighten out the problem. As he ticked off this litany of errors on his fingers, Bell was turning red around the collar. I was astonished that he could boil himself up into such a rage over this and amused by my own reaction. The angrier he got, the more cheerful I became. I was determined to enjoy this.

"By the way, Rinker," Bell said. "Why do you suspect this guy? Why didn't you just come back and write a Name in the News?"

"Oh, that's the easy part Bill," I said. "The guy's an ex-priest."

"*What?*"

"An ex-priest, Bill. You can always smell an ex-priest."

The veins on Bell's neck expanded to the size of garden hoses.

"Now Rinker, that is just outrageous," Bell fumed. "I am your editor and I am telling you that you cannot *smell* an ex-priest. And even if you could, no one would say such a thing. This is egregious prejudice. Against ex-priests. Besides, how do you know you can even prove it?"

Oh. I hadn't thought about that. I could easily document

that Mahoney wasn't a doctor. But it might be difficult to prove that he *was* an ex-priest.

"Bill, that's my next step," I said. "I'm going to prove to you that I can smell an ex-priest."

"Stop saying that, will you?" Bell said. "You're making me repeat myself. You cannot smell an ex-priest."

"Bill, that's the wonderful thing about it. You can smell an ex-priest!"

"No! You cannot smell an ex-priest!"

Jesus. He was really screaming at me now. The whole newsroom was watching. And it was just the best damn thing, fascinating for me to observe in myself. The madder he got, the calmer I became.

"Bill, you can smell an ex-priest. I've been doing it my entire life"

"You can't," Bell insisted.

The conversation was ridiculous, an infinite regress of ex-priests. I had obviously touched a raw nerve with Bell. As he and I argued, the newsroom fell silent around us. Peter Scheer lit a cigarette and leered hilariously out of the corner of his mouth. Rory O'Connor gleefully stroked his goatee and gave me a thumbs-up over the top of the foxhole of newspapers on his desk. I was fast becoming Rory's favorite addition to the newsroom. Anybody who could draw mortar fire from Bell was definitely his kind of guy.

Tom Morton strolled over in the middle of this.

"Hey, fellas, c'mon now," Morton said. "White priest, black priest, ex-priest, what the hell? I thought this damn story was about a doctor."

As Bell and I started going back at each other again, Morton yanked his thumb over his shoulder, pointing to the conference room out past the clip morgue. As soon as we got there, Bell started right back in again, I objected, and Morton held up his hands.

I would learn to love Tom Morton at such moments. He never lost his sense of humor or his plucky, blue-collar style. When challenged, the mixed metaphors flowed out of him as a cascade.

"Hey guys, whoa, whoa, whoa. Let's just pipe down, hold our horses here, and pull in our sails. Nobody wants to throw a rod over a Name in the News. Throttle back, wil'ya?"

Morton made us go one at a time. I told him what had happened with Mahoney so far, then Bell dug in his spurs about all the mistakes I'd made, not the least of which was my egregious bias toward ex-priests. I could see that Morton was amused about all this but, for Bell's sake, was trying not to laugh. That calmed me down. I was naturally drawn toward people with a sense of humor, and Morton had that in bags. Maybe the dynamic in the room would fall toward me if I just tried to enjoy myself and remain calm.

Morton swiped his bald pate with an authoritative pat of his hand.

"Okay fellas, here's what we're going to do," he said. "Rinker, you get on the phone and get Johns Hopkins to send us a letter stating that Mahoney's not a graduate of their medical school. The *Eagle*'s not going to run a story without proof. When we get that letter, I'll call the medical director over there, Dr. Barnaba. Old Vince is going to shit a brick on this one, but we've got to be fair. The hospital deserves at least a heads-up."

"But Tom," I said. "Then they'll fire Mahoney and we won't have a story."

"That's none of your business," Bell snapped. "*We'll* decide when stories get placed in the paper."

Morton dabbed his head again.

"Bill, please," he said. "Rinker, you're right on that. They probably will fire Mahoney, but we'll still have a story. The reputation of the *Eagle* doesn't depend on slamming people before they've had a chance to reply."

I couldn't believe this. The *Eagle* was wimping out on the story. My hopes of becoming the next Bob Woodward were fading fast.

"Jesus, Tom," I said. "Don't you think we should run the story *first*? To show people in town that we check resumés?"

"No, I don't," Morton said. "Now look. You're all piss and vinegar on this thing. I happen to respect what you've just done here. But we're going to show some restraint."

Morton's respect for my piss and vinegar was more than Bill Bell could bear. Leaning forward against the table, he stared first at me and then to Morton.

"But Tom, ah Tom," he said, "we need to review Rinker's reporting methods here."

I could see that Morton was annoyed by that, but he'd triumphed and become managing editor by tolerating a lot of personality differences in the newsroom, and now he was just going to let Bell be Bell. So, like some schoolboy caught with the spitball, I had to sit there and meekly listen to Bell's enumeration of all of my errors, right down to my egregious prejudice against ex-priests. It was humiliating. I had gone out and found a great story. Now Bell was backing over me with a truck.

When Bell was done, Morton thanked him and told him that he wanted to speak with me alone. Here we go, I thought. The big lecture from the managing editor. But as soon as Bell was gone Morton threw his stubby brown oxfords up on the table, clasped his hands behind his neck, and threw back his head and laughed.

"Way to go kiddo—great sleuthing job on this Mahoney fellow," he said. "This is exactly the sort of thing I expected from you. But look, you seem to have found just about every way there is to pull the chin hairs on Bill Bell's goat. Do you think you could work on that?"

"But Tom—"

Morton held up his hand.

"No. I'm not saying it's your fault. Just work on it, okay?"

"Okay, Tom. But, I mean, being accused of—"

Managing editor Tom Morton was plucky and blunt, and he murdered the English language every time he opened his mouth, but his management style was inspirational and fun.

"Whoa, stop right there son," Morton said. "You don't always get to pick who you work with, all right? It's not a date with Mary Poppins."

"Okay. Okay. I'll try to remember that."

Morton asked me one more thing before I stepped up to go.

"Hey, about this ex-priest stuff. Are you sure? Can you prove it?"

"I'm sure, but I can't prove it. Yet."

"Good," Morton said. "You've got forty-eight hours to prove it, to *me*."

Morton dabbed his head once more and his mouth was turned into a sly smile. He liked watching me squirm.

"Oh," I said. "What if I can't prove that Mahoney's an ex-priest?"

"Simple, kiddo," Morton said. "Your ass is grass."

.   .   .

I spent a couple of spooky, starlit nights up in the mountains after that, gumshoeing around the northern Berkshires in search of Mahoney. I knew that I had to prove to Morton that my initial instincts about Mahoney were correct, but this would involve some lurking around the woods at night. I treated this task as a romantic adventure up in the high purple-black rim. It was the one thing that I could always do well—losing myself and my cares up in the woods. So why not enjoy it?

I started out like any greenhorn reporter, naïvely dialing the Catholic diocese down in Springfield, but the priest who handled public affairs refused to help and even actively opposed my investigation. Instead, I decided to turn to the funeral directors for help, on the theory that there was one thing that the body haulers had to know about: local priests. They were actually quite enthusiastic about my search and seemed to vicariously enjoy the adventures of a reporter. It was Fran Devanny who suggested that I start poking around the half-dozen or so retreat houses and remote farms maintained by independent Catholic orders in and around the

Berkshires. Gradually, by guesswork and a process of elimi-
nation, I had the search narrowed down to a small seminary
run by the Carmelite Fathers in Williamstown, which was
located on a converted farm deep in a hollow underneath the
brow of Berlin Mountain. The Carmelites had an unlisted
phone number, so I decided to ride up there for a couple of
nights, stash my motorcycle in the woods, and wait in the
trees outside the seminary to see if Mahoney showed up.

I had a couple of great nights up there, bombing over the
hills through New Ashford and Hancock and then rambling
over the back roads that led west to the Carmelite place. I
found a small stand of hemlock that commanded a decent
view of the seminary's parking lot and drive and sat with my
back against a tree with a pair of binoculars hung around my
neck, reading, smoking my pipe, jotting down notes on some
other stories I was considering at the time. As an orange nimbus of sun sank behind Berlin Mountain, the air was bracing
and cool, and the eerie hoot of a great horned owl was carried
up by the breeze from the black canopy of pines behind me.

My wait was rewarded on the second night. From my perch
up in the hemlocks I saw a battered Volkswagen sedan bounce
up the drive and into the lot, trailing vortices of dust. The
familiar, stooped figure of Mahoney stepped out, wearing the
same dark slacks and poorly fitted jacket that he'd had on when
I'd met him three days earlier. After he disappeared inside a
farmhouse in the complex, I remained hidden in the pines for a
while longer. About twenty minutes later, floodlights suddenly
illuminated the seminary grounds and Mahoney emerged
again, this time in the long dark robes of a Carmelite, circuiting
the yards with a couple of other priests. They chatted amiably
and seemed to be enjoying themselves, and it was about as ordinary and peaceful a scene as you'd expect to see in a remote
mountain cloister.

I had my quarry now, I would be vindicated in the eyes of
Morton and Bell, but I could sense that there wouldn't be
much fun in the story now. Finding my way back through the
woods, I started my bike and bounced off, turning for the
route over the Petersburg Pass and riding south on the

Taconic side of the range, dodging the raccoons and possum crossing the road as I meditated on the sad, bizarre case of Mahoney.

In the morning, Tom Morton smiled when I described what I'd found, but he told me just to remain mum about things and start writing my story while we waited for the letter from Johns Hopkins. He would deal with Bell. Morton suggested that I call the national headquarters of the Carmelites and confront them with what I knew. Understandably, the Carmelite order wouldn't say much, except to confirm that Mahoney was indeed one of their priests—he even held the title of "director" at the Williamstown seminary. They couldn't explain why he was posing as a doctor. At the time, however, it was well known that the Carmelites were starved for vocations and money, the Williamstown seminary was shaky, and Mahoney might have cooked up his moonlighting gig in a desperate gambit to keep the place alive.

The Phoney-Mahoney caper became even more sad that day, after I called Johns Hopkins back and picked up the information that Mahoney had posed as a doctor in other towns across the country. Morton was particularly pleased to hear this because it established a larger agenda for my story—the *Eagle* was exposing someone who was more than just a local quack.

Even when nothing is happening, newsrooms are a cauldron of rumors, and now everyone had some genuine scuttlebutt to mull over. A lot of the younger reporters were appalled that the paper was holding my story and wandered over to whisper questions and to offer support.

Sportswriter Mike Meserole was the cutup of the newsroom, as antic as Lenny Bruce. Nothing got past him; every event could be turned into a prank. There was palpable tension in the newsroom now over the Phoney-Mahoney affair, which Meserole couldn't resist. He composed a theme song, which he sang out loudly to the tune of a British sailor's chantey, whenever I walked by his desk.

"Oh, Phoney Mahoney! But Rinker wouldn't swallow his baloney!"

Meserole even accosted Pete Miller about it. Once or twice a week, Pete made an appearance in the newsroom, absentmindedly strolling by on his way to the editorial department to fuss over a layout or consult with Roger Linscott about one of his beloved rustic columnists. He was an amusing but detached figure, his bony elbows sticking out through the holes in his shirt sleeves as he briskly gaited by, the pieces of colored yarn and string that he used to patch his shoelaces shining brightly from his scuffed cordovans.

Because of Pete's resemblance to Watergate Special Prosecutor Archibald Cox, Meserole called him "Archie." Only Meserole could get away with impudence like that. As Pete passed the sports department, Meserole performed a jig on the linoleum floor and sang his ditty.

"Hey! Archie!" Meserole called after Pete. "Whad'ya think about Phoney Mahoney?"

Pete stopped by the newsroom double doors, did the Miller twirl, and scratched his rump, declaiming toward the ceiling in his high-pitched voice.

"Hah! Phoney Mahoney! I like it! That'll teach those stuffed shirts over there how to hire a doctor!"

The ladies on the social desk all laughed, and there were guffaws from the sports department too.

"Phoney Mahoney!"

"Rinker doesn't eat baloney!"

I didn't know how to respond, and I felt the hair on the back of my neck going airborne and my face turning red. Were they laughing at me, or was I the hero? I just didn't know.

Rory O'Connor was another lunatic, but he kept my spirits up. Rory couldn't have cared less about the Phoney-Mahoney story. He was a long-distance feature man himself and didn't really follow the news that much. But he was fiendishly pleased about my dustup with Bill Bell. He refused to regard my screaming match over ex-priests as anything less than the epic farce of a young reporter.

"Psst! Hey, Rinker, found any ex-priests lately?" Rory would whisper into my ear as he passed my desk. "By the way, did you hear? The pope just won the Nobel Prize. For medicine!"

He was merciless about it. Rory just wouldn't let me forget what a jackass I was. Even though he sat just a few desks away, Rory would dial my phone extension a couple of times a day.

"Psst! Hey Rinker. This just in. The Associated Press is reporting that there are three ex-nuns working on the *Eagle* staff. You've got twenty-four hours to smoke 'em out!"

.   .   .

I hadn't spoken with Roger Linscott since our afternoon of pool a couple of months earlier, but I could hardly avoid his leonine presence in the newsroom. My desk sat right beside the pneumatically powered copy tube, which ran up from the composing room one floor below. It was a tall length of plumping pipe, shaped as an inverted J, not unlike the tube on an old navy ship through which the bridge communicated with the engine room. Linscott was the only writer on the paper who could bypass the copy desk and send his editorials directly to typesetting. Every morning at 10:30 and noon, when he was done with his main editorials for the day, Linscott loped into the newsroom and swung wide around the social desk. His limp made the change in his pocket jingle loudly, announcing his approach.

A slight hush fell over the newsroom as Linscott passed. Halting at the copy tube, Linscott reached out with a yellow No. 2 pencil hanging in his right hand and tapped loudly two times on the pipe. He stuffed a roll of copy paper into the clear plastic canister, and then, with the confidence of a seasoned pitcher, he swept back his arm and rammed the canister home with a brisk jab of his palm. He was an immensely satisfying figure to watch, but I was terrified that he might pause one day and say something, expecting me to come up with an intelligent reply.

One morning, in the middle of the Phoney-Mahoney fiasco, Mount Rushmore finally stopped and did just that. I

87

was in the middle of typing up an obit from Remo Dagnoli. Then I heard the pencil tap twice on the pipe, the copy slam home, and out of the corner of my eye I saw Linscott's elegantly panted leg and scuffed oxford come to rest on the corner of my desk.

Linscott towered above me, leaning with his arm against his knee.

"Say," he drawled. "Tom Morton has brought me up-to-date on this incomparable tale of your imposter, Dr. Mahoney. Bravo. But I'm astonished by this scarcely credible fiction of yours, this *outraaaageoouus booooaast*, that you can smell an ex-priest. Are you ecclesiastically clairvoyant? Speak in tongues? Where did you acquire this preposterous aura?"

At this point in our relationship, I was too bamboozled by Linscott to say much. Around him, English felt like a second language to me. So, all I could do was blurt out my personal history, telling Linscott all about my father, AA, and the priests around our house when I was a boy.

Linscott looked satisfied, and his jowls nodded with relief. He was impressively well read, experienced himself with drinking and with drunks, and nothing fazed him. Eccentricity appealed to him—his social circle included crazy Stockbridge millionaires and many madcap writers and playwrights. To Linscott, it made perfect sense that a young reporter who had grown up as an AA brat could smell an ex-priest.

"Yes, I've got this depressingly long roster of friends who have joined AA," Linscott said. "Actually, they are *ex-friends*. It's a nefarious organization. There's nothing more la-*gooob*-rious than coffee drinkers at a cocktail party. But say, one other thing? Are you afraid of this piece?"

I hadn't thought about the Mahoney story that way, but I realized with a start that Linscott was right. In a single word, he'd expressed how I felt.

"Yes, to tell the truth," I said, "I'm afraid of it. Right now, I wish I'd never heard of Keith Mahoney."

"Well, good," Linscott said. "A few weeks ago, I just happened to come across a few of the editorials that were submitted for my Pulitzer, and I realized that I was afraid of them when I wrote them, but I published them all the same. It's almost a measurement of worth. If you're afraid of the blasted thing, then unequivocally it's what you should write. Anyway, good show. This Mahoney business puts you in a good place."

"Oh," I said. "It does?"

"Indubitably," Linscott said. "You have only just arrived here. But already you're pointing the wind."

"Oh, okay," I said.

Linscott dropped his leg and turned to go. A few paces out he hesitated, did this Pete Miller–style whirligig on the floor, and turned back to face me, far enough away now so that everybody could hear.

"Say. What are you doing Friday after deadline?"

"Oh, I don't know. Nothing, I guess."

"Good. I should say that we could tolerably pass the time having lunch together."

"Sure, Roger," I said. "Thanks!"

Linscott loped back around the social desk, swinging wide with his bad leg and then disappearing through the double doors.

Jesus. I couldn't get over my performance here. Fuck up, be a hero. The Great Linscott had invited me to lunch.

.　　.　　.

The article on the Phoney-Mahoney case that finally appeared in the *Eagle* late that week, to be as charitable as possible about it, was a short, tight fart. It ran for about eight measly inches on the inside pages under an unremarkable headline:

Rehab "Psychiatrist" Dismissed Following Credentials Check.

The piece was just a bare recitation of the facts, containing none of the drama or personal quirks that I associated with the tale. Things had more or less worked out according to Morton's plan as soon as the letter from Johns Hopkins arrived. After Morton informed the hospital's medical director about our findings, Mahoney was quickly fired, and then I was forced to sit in the big conference room behind the newsroom with the medical director and his public relations flack, jotting down everything they had to say about the fiasco. By this time, the hospital's flunkies lacked all credibility and couldn't possibly defend their hiring of Mahoney, but they tried nonetheless.

"And this is the irony of the entire situation," Barnaba told me. "Everyone was very pleased with Mahoney's work. I would say, in fact, that his contribution in the last three weeks has been one of the most significant of anyone we have hired in a number of years."

I was disgusted with myself for including such unctuous drivel in my story. But Morton insisted that we needed it, for "balance and fairness."

.   .   .

On Friday morning, when he made his 10:30 lope through the newsroom, Roger Linscott tapped twice on the copy tube and then looked up, staring me down with a long, jowly smile.

"Noooooon. At the Rockwell painting."

When I got out there at noon, Linscott proposed that we drive down over South Mountain and eat at a "swanker place than usual," the Yellow Aster in Lenox. The restaurant was a spacious and well-appointed luncheon spot favored by country club ladies and retirees. Linscott didn't feel comfortable about eating there without first expressing his contempt.

"'Tis the Yellow Disaster," he said. "Rather too plush for my taste. However, they make tolerable martinis."

Out in the parking lot, Linscott stopped in front of a bright red, long-hooded Plymouth Duster. I was astonished by this, a car so out of keeping with Linscott's image. The Plymouth Duster was a popular muscle car of the time, right up there with the Camaro Z/28 or the Shelby Mustang, and this one had the works—the big 275-horse V-8, the three-speed

TorqueFlite transmission, dual mufflers, and shiny oval hub-caps.

"Roger," I said. "This is your car?"

"Yes. Preposterous wheels, wouldn't you say? My problem is elemental. I so intensely loathe car salesmen that I can't stand to spend more than five minutes with them. Ergo, the first vehicle they present to me, that is the one I instantly purchase, just to rid myself of the odious bastards. However, I assure you that in this case I plunked down my meager lucre for outstanding transport. This Duster is out-*rage*-ously fast."

We strapped ourselves in and the Duster trembled to life with an exotic, throaty roar. Dappled sunlight splashed down from Lenox Mountain and onto the hood of the car, highlighting Linscott's herringbone jacket. I was excited about going to lunch with the big man. Linscott dropped the TorqueFlite into gear and we burned rubber across the lot.

"Bravo! We're off."

As we squealed onto First Street, Linscott glanced sideways across his broad Mount Rushmore jowls.

"Say. There's something I ought to politely mention to you so we can get it out of the way and enjoy lunch. 'Tis about this ex-priest business. It's extremely offensive to a couple of people in the newsroom."

I would always remember that moment. We had just screeched to a halt at the Berkshire Commons light. A few shoppers were circuiting the green oval with baby strollers and the sun drenched the stone facade of First Church. It was right there that my internal radar belatedly locked on and I began to paint Bill Bell.

"Oh no," I said. "No. No-no-no-no. Roger please don't tell me this. Don't say that. Not Bill Bell."

"Oh yes," Linscott said. "Yes-yes-yes-yes, you infernal jackass. I'm told that Bill Bell is an ex-priest."

CHAPTER SIX

I WAS IN THE crapper with Bill Bell for the longest time after that. The story about his being an ex-priest was, in fact, inaccurate, but the *Eagle* rumor mill kept it alive because it fit Bell's image so well. It wasn't just his noonday stroll down North Street or his clerical, earnest demeanor. In fact, Bell was a convert to Catholicism, quite devoted to his adopted faith, quite fond of priests. My reflexive anticlericalism might have delivered me to the Phoney Mahoney story, but it hardly endeared me to the boss. After that, every dogmeat press release that came along fell on an inclined plane toward my desk. I became the *Eagle*'s writer of choice for such stellar stories as the Post Office's new batch of commemorative stamps, Berkshire County's first female phone linemen, or the new steeple atop the Evangelical Lutheran Church. The Romans were crucifying the Book Turd.

In late August, however, Bell's luck finally ran out, and I was redeemed by a stupendous act of God.

One afternoon that month a small hippie den down in south county, the Great Barrington Pottery, called with urgent news. A potter from Japan would be spending several days that week demonstrating the ancient art of ceramics by firing his work in a wood-fired kiln. Bell sent me down there to cover this marvelous event. I spent the afternoon watching a sallow, infirm Japanese potter stuff hideously ugly bowls into a homemade kiln, which, every time he fired it up with his Zippo lighter, quivered in the hazy Berkshire sky like a pathetic little phallus.

I was disgusted. The most salient entry in my reporter's notebook that afternoon was, "This story sucks." My job at *The Berkshire Eagle* was turning out to be career suicide. I felt reduced, humiliated, completely trapped by my foolish decision to join the Olympian Pete Miller at his acclaimed paper in the mountains. So, I quickly took a picture of the freakish Japanese potter and his smoldering penis of a kiln and got the hell out of there.

The road out of Great Barrington passed through a long, level tableau of attractive agrarian land, occasionally dotted with lovely Federal-style farmhouses, before disappearing into the hardwood forest as it climbed along the shady banks of the Williamsville River. Just before the road reached the trees, there was a clear prospect northeast, toward the long, purple-black brow of West Stockbridge Mountain. A single, cleared summit was distinctly visible over the lavender expanse of trees.

I was pretty sure that this was Maple Hill, a fabled resting spot where Nathaniel Hawthorne and Herman Melville had stopped in the wilderness while momentarily lost during their return from a visit to the Hancock Shakers in August 1851. While their buggy horse rested, the two writers lounged in the upland meadow, dipping into their picnic basket for ginger-bread and fruit and then, inspired by the awesome mountain views, they ruminated together about their shared literary demons. They were very restful and unplanned about it, very Byronic. You don't turn out novels like *The House of Seven Gables* by being in a hurry. Inspired by the breathtaking views, their dawdle up on Maple Hill had been one of their longest and most fruitful conversations. Places like that meant the world to me—I *had* to go there, make the pilgrimage, because it was a crime against literary nostalgia not to indulge the whim.

Earlier in the summer, Sheila and I had wasted whole after-noons searching for Maple Hill, exploring the vast and pretty heights along the Alford–West Stockbridge line, and never found it, but that was mostly because we were incredibly lazy about it and frequently elected just to pull over into an alluring bed of ferns and make love. Sheila was working on me. She considered me too "serious" and not "spontaneous enough." If we were out on the raft at night on Doolittle Pond in Norfolk, with the loons sounding, I considered that a romantic calling and was more than willing to become sexually engaged. But midafternoon carnal acts made me feel guilty and without purpose—it wasn't something that you were supposed to do.

But Sheila had done a fine job curing me of that. I liked the moist, fungal smell of ferns beside me as Sheila pulled my hands to her breasts, the splay of her plaid work shirt on the forest floor as we made love. The gritty mix of earth and bits of dried leaves scraping in the gushing between our legs was erotically abrasive, like a fine sandpaper, and bad-girl Sheila had a nice way of waking me after I'd dozed off with my face in the sun. *Whoa, Dude, we're not done yet.* Then, smiling and pursing her lips, she pushed my back up against a boulder, strode me on her knees, and with her spongy, heaving, bosomy body, gently and long she rode me to an orgasm. The Book Turd was extravagantly satisfied with this, of course. With Sheila I had learned to sensually linger in a forest, dawdling away the light with afternoon sex. As a consequence, however, I never found Maple Hill.

But now I was determined. Finding the high, hallowed Hawthorne-Melville ground was my afternoon mission. Maple Hill or bust. I would turn north on the Alford Road just ahead and dead reckon the dirt lanes from there, climbing high into the purple hills.

. . .

By this time I owned a new car, a Ford Pinto, which would prove to be quite a social embarrassment. I had handled that first, crucial out-of-college purchasing decision with my usual idiotic aplomb.

In early August several exceptionally crisp, autumnal nights in a row convinced me that I would soon have to be enclosed by a fuller, warmer piece of metal than my motorcycle. I was excited about having a paycheck now and associated moving up in the world with going out and splurging on a new car. Part of my problem then was that I was already under the thrall of Roger Linscott, and he had volunteered the information that he never spent more than five minutes with the "odious bastards" who sold cars.

So, that's how I handled it. Dropping by Great Barrington Ford one day, I allowed an unctuous former school principal by the name of Steve to sell me a new Pinto, which I could drive away that very day for only $400 down and a financing agreement calling for car payments of just $85 a month. God, did I love that new car smell. The hatchback Pinto had a tinny four-cylinder engine, shiny plastic hubcaps and was painted baby blue—"Robin's Egg Metallic," Ford called it. The seats were upholstered in real Naugahyde and—this was absolutely the best part, I assure you—my Pinto had an FM radio and a center console with round holes for a soda can and coins.

Peter Scheer was disconsolate when he saw me pull into the *Eagle* lot in my new car. He drove a boxy, battered white Subaru, wheels that had the advantage of being both cheap and possessing a bohemian, shitwreck appeal. Peter already seemed to believe that he could reform me. The practical details of my life, he seemed to feel, lacked savoir faire.

"Oh my God, Rinker," Peter said. "This is yours? A Pinto?"

"Yeah. Have you got a problem with that? Peter, it's new. Brand new. It has an FM radio."

"Hey look, man. No offense, okay? But a Ford Pinto is the biggest loser vehicle of all time. And this thing is baby blue."

"Robin's egg, Peter," I said. "Robin's egg. And it has a 50,000-mile warranty on all parts."

"The quintessential Detroit rip-off," Peter said. "They'll still charge you for labor. And now you have car payments. Car payments, Rinker! On an *Eagle* salary. Way to go."

But it was too late now. I would just have to drive the Pinto for a while and see.

So, those were the image-wrecking wheels that I was now negotiating over a rutted back road up along the Alford–West Stockbridge line. It was nothing more than a logging trail, really, with a tall hump in the middle and very little maneuvering room on the shoulders, so that I was constantly scraping the Pinto's tinfoil muffler on the granite outcrops. But it was beautiful up there, and my depression about the Japanese potter back in Great Barrington receded as I steadily climbed in elevation. Several times the road plunged off the ridge and passed through wetlands with tall, feathery walls of cattails and wood ducks and plovers browsing along the edges, land that seemed as vast and remote as the moose country of Maine.

Then the road climbed again, up through a series of cleared fields fenced with an attractive, geometric network of stone walls. Finally I reached a high point where I could just barely make out Mount Greylock and the Green Mountains in Vermont through the inclement afternoon haze. Pulling in beside a row of gnarled maples, I decided to hike up to the top of the highest field to enjoy the view and take some pictures. Maple Hill would be visible from there and I could figure out the remainder of my route.

As I climbed out of the car, a green, squally cloud was snarling up out the west, spitting off a rooster tail of rain and gray, gauzy mists as it boiled in over the Taconics to the west. I'd never seen a cloud quite like it before—it was smaller and more compacted than a thunderstorm and very menacing. But the dirty green mass seemed to be tracking due east and would probably pass several miles away.

I didn't worry very much about inclement weather. From flying, and from compiling the *Eagle*'s weather reports every day, I knew the regional weather patterns very well. The Berkshires were the first tall range to stop the massive summer weather systems spilling east across New York State from the Great Lakes, and these thunderstorm clusters frequently collided with drier, cooler fronts moving north off the Atlantic coast. The edges of the fronts would meet along Mohawk or Haystack Mountain down along the Connecticut line, furiously boil up trouble, and then rumble uprange. As a result, the Berkshires were well known for sudden, intense late-afternoon thunderstorms in the summer, and during the winter the same colliding fronts generated classic nor'easters and the county's legendary snows.

This would be the same kind of afternoon, I thought, as I left my car and climbed the hill, ignoring the black thunder cloud dropping down from the west. If it started to pour, I could always run back down for the safety of my car.

I could never account for what happened next, because the sensation of being ambushed from behind was so overwhelming. It was a cataract of sensation, a fury that struck quickly. Halfway up the field, I suddenly felt the lash of rain and hail on my back, as painful as bird shot, and when I turned to look behind me, I had to shield my face. I couldn't believe what was happening down there. The field below my car was already an immense green and black maelstrom of swirling branches and leaves, with these strange, airborne whitecaps skittering vertically and sideways from the moisture being thrown so hard against itself. The woods further down thundered with a deafening volley of sharp cracking sounds. It was Fredericksburg down there, Major Pelham blasting away with his brass Napoleons.

I couldn't believe what I was seeing now. Tree limbs, and then even whole tree trunks, were splintering to pieces and being carried up by the wall of wind. They were somersaulting all over each other now, a continuous wall of oak and shaggy-bark cherry crowns, broken occasionally by open black holes, moving uphill like surf to where I stood.

I had maybe four or five seconds left to do something. By now the fields all around me were featureless and black, with just a narrow aperture of light opened on the field and trees above. Turning for the light, I could just make out a large depression in the field slightly above me, surrounded by a natural cobble of boulders. Half running and crawling, I stumbled uphill and threw myself into the trench between the boulders, tossing my camera beneath me before I crouched with my hands over my head against the boiling sky. I could hear and see tree roots and splintered limbs passing right over my head. Airborne leaves plastered the sides of the trench and my back.

I lay face down in the trench as the green fury passed overhead. The thunderous artillery all around me was too much to take in. Now there was just the white-on-white implosion of noise, the scraping of branches and sheets of rain over my shoulders, and dozens of rivulets cascading down and flooding the cobble trench. The furious pools eddying around my waist, frigid and muddy, forced me to raise my head. I was genuinely panicked for a few moments, utterly helpless in the flash-flood basin of the trench. But it was panic beyond panic, a surreal, slow-motion sensation of transcendence and awe at a point where life and death seemed to merge. I was dying in here, trapped in an overturned boat, but, God, wasn't it a marvel. Then, almost as quickly as it had arrived, the storm seemed to dissipate and lift and all I was left with was stunning quiet and a feeling of deliverance. Grey and purple pulses of light—bizarre as heat lightning—flickered through the cobble and trench. Higher up and off to the east, I heard one last Fredericksburg volley as the storm crashed off over the mountain and splintered through more trees.

Drenched, my clothes plastered with matted grass and leaves, blasted sand and mud, I poked my head out over the top of the trench, amazed at the scene of devastation that fell down the hills in front of me.

It was an alien landscape, an extraplanetary vision. Everywhere I looked there were immense, twisted piles of trees, some of them lifted wholesale from the woods below and forked top-first into the ground, so that the craggy roots jutted crazily into the sky, blocking the horizon. The two stone walls that ran parallel to the road I had driven in on had acted as windbreaks, collecting long, irregular hedgerows of limbs and trunks. Whatever it was that had just blown through was powerful enough to lift trees 100, even 150 years old and toss them about like paper. A couple of amputated trunks had landed just a few yards from my position.

The twisted maze of trees below me was so impenetrable

that I couldn't see my car, and I had to walk in circles around the wreckage just to get down there. I had parked in just the wrong spot, and now, apparently, I was stranded. The hood of the Pinto was pinned by a fallen leader from a large maple tree, which had landed so hard that one of the tires was flat. Another limb blocked the car from behind. Prying back some branches, I wiggled in through the hatchback door in the back, dried off my camera with a sweatshirt and grabbed a couple of notebooks and my hiking boots. I would have to bushwhack out—straight northeast across the open parts of the meadows and then the woods to where I thought Route 102 was. The dirt road ahead of me was so choked with fallen trees I knew that I couldn't get through there.

It took me nearly an hour to scramble back to civilization, but it was a walk of rude beauty. Field after field were littered with the mangled detritus of trees, even bits of cardboard, roofing shingles, and plywood carried up from some homesite below. I knew that this was big and damaging, very wide, powerful enough to carry up building materials from far below. Several times I had to leap across leveled tree trunks to traverse the heavy slash in the woods, acres and acres of it. Jumping across the bridge of trees took forever, and from ten or fifteen feet up I could stare down through the tangled mass of wood to rushing streams cutting new routes on the forest floor. Huge gaping holes in ground, caves almost, had been formed where the root structures of ancient oaks and hemlocks were pulled out as one mass, and now they were filling up with muddy water. The air around the slash smelled of hemorrhaging sap and moist, freshly cut wood, the odor of a sawmill. The scenes of devastation were so vast, across such a broad stretch of mountain, that I began to realize that I was lucky just to be alive.

I was intrigued as well. I had seen large blowdowns before, whole sections of forest knocked over by a freak storm. But this was broader and more ferocious than anything I had ever witnessed, and the image of whole ash and maple trees skittering around like witches still frightened me.

Still, I was infinitely happy. As per my usual, I'd screwed

up on a story, run away in frustration, and then had my encounter with the airborne Niagara. I loved myself for this. Fuck up, run away, bump into the pandemonium of a major weather event. It was the ultimate storm chase. The House of Miller was actually paying me $130 a week to enjoy this.

.   .   .

When I got out to Route 102, a chain-saw crew from Western Massachusetts Electric was mowing through the debris of several trees hung up on a power line. Farther west on the road a long line of police cruisers, ambulances, and tow trucks was jammed up behind a temporary roadblock set up by the state police. Obviously the blow I'd just survived was huge—the devastation reached all the way out here, almost to the border with New York State. I was relieved to have reached the safety of an open road, but my hands and face felt raw and numb, beaten to a pulp by the limbs snapping back as I pushed through the slash.

I must have looked like a sojourner from hell. As I stamped the mud off my boots, one of the workers from the electric company truck stared incredulously in my direction, shut off his chain saw, and walked over to join me on the road. He handed me his water canteen, lit a cigarette, and offered me a smoke, which I gratefully declined, but I did need his help getting my pipe lit. The matches from my shirt pocket were soaked through.

"Jesus," he said. "Where'd you come from?"

"Up there," I said, pointing back over my shoulder. "Almost to the top of the ridge."

He let out a long, low whistle and shook his head.

"Well, you're damned lucky," he said. "Nobody would have thought to look for victims up there."

"What victims?" I said. "What happened anyway?"

"Tornado."

"Impossible. We don't have tornadoes in the Northeast."

"Yeah, that's what I thought," he said. "But they just had it on the radio. But hey, if you don't believe me, look at the truck stop down there. It took a direct hit. They've got fatalities down there."

Down the hill to the west, a long, low wetlands separated Route 102 from the four-lane spur that connected the Massachusetts Turnpike with the New York State Thruway, beside which stood the remains of the Berkshire Truck Stop. In the demolished parking lot, several semitrailers stood upended and tossed about like Lego blocks, and the roof of the truck stop diner was blown off, with a long triangular fantail of plywood, insulation, and roofing material splayed out on a southwest to northeast track. A glistening oil slick, throwing off strange iridescent rainbow reflections, spilled out across the asphalt and into the edges of the swamp. A filthy whiff of diesel hung in the air, blown uphill by the clearing breezes. I couldn't believe I was witnessing a scene like this in the hills of New England.

I was completely naïve in the way I handled everything after that. Exhausted and dazed by my own brush with the twister, I wasn't thinking very clearly. Drawn more out of curiosity and a sense of completing the day's adventure, I trudged downhill toward the roadblock. There, a state trooper stepped over and held up his hand.

"You can't go beyond here," he said. "Only rescue crews and media are allowed past this point."

"Oh," I said, feeling suddenly brilliant as I flashed the *Eagle* identification card from my wallet. "But I *am* media. I need to get through."

It was madness down at the truck stop. When I got there several ambulance crews and volunteer firemen were cutting through the wreckage of the restaurant with crowbars and chain saws. Three bodies had already been pulled from the restaurant, and a fourth victim would be found later, up on Dean Hill Road. Now the rescue teams were searching for more people inside while several jostling knots of reporters were racing between stunned truck drivers and the firemen, gathering whatever information they could. A couple of the *Eagle*'s south county reporters, whom I recognized but still didn't know very well, were already there, and they told me to just work the edges of the story as best I could. I could prepare a "feed" for the big wrap-up stories they would be writing once we all got back to the newsroom.

A few state troopers who had managed to work their way in on back roads from the New York side were throwing up temporary plastic fences around downed electrical lines. Even as this confusion boiled all around me, more was arriving. From as far away as Boston and New York, helicopters kept chomping in and out, delivering more emergency medical crews and television reporters, and then chattering back out with the injured and dead.

The tornado had arrived at the worst imaginable time, midafternoon, when a long line of tractor trailers was strung out at the diesel pumps. Six or seven pumps were running when the tornado hit. The force of the twister ripped the pump-stands off at ground level, but the underground electrical supply was not affected, and the pumps continued to feed fuel up through the severed pipes until the tanks under-

The scene at the West Stockbridge truck stop, where four people were killed during the Great Berkshire Tornado, was one of utter devastation and confusion.

neath ran dry. Thousands of gallons of diesel had sprayed up in geysers and then flowed south down the asphalt incline, pooling up into a lake at the entrance to the truck stop.

But that was only the beginning of the problem. Three of the semitrailers parked near the truck stop entrance were refrigerated units with Illinois plates. They were carrying a large shipment of bulk cottage cheese, transported in 100-gallon vats. When the tornado hit, the cottage cheese trailers got suctioned up, spun around several times in midair, and then slammed back down on top of each other, which blew off the rear doors and dislodged the lids on the vats. A thick, oleaginous wave of cottage cheese—thousands of gallons in all—exploded across the truck stop, where it soon mixed with the escaped diesel fuel.

Diesel cottage cheese, I learned that day, is an extremely noxious mixture. You feel like vomiting, just looking at and smelling the stuff, and diesel cottage cheese is quite slippery underfoot. Now there was a whole lake of it, a turd-brown effluent custard, blocking the truck stop entrance.

I was particularly impressed with one dramatic display shortly after I arrived at the tornado scene. As I walked down the hill below the roadblock, logging crews were clearing trees off the road so that the line of cop cars and ambulances could get through. Four state police cruisers, shiny Ford Custom 500s, parked bumper-to-bumper, were at the head of the line. The state troopers, like all cops antsy to get to the scene of the action, were excitedly smoking cigarettes and blaring 10-20 this and 10-4 that into their radios. Finally, the logging crew below signaled the road all clear.

Squealing their tires in a puff of smoke, the four cop cruisers bolted from the roadblock as if beckoned by the checkered flag at the Daytona 500 and roared downhill in a tight, bumper-to-bumper formation. State troopers are really quite marvelous drivers, if you enjoy a show. The Customs actually accelerated downhill to over sixty miles per hour, never deviating more than an inch or two from their tailgating formation. Thirty-two cylinders roared in unison from the tailpipes as the formation rumbled down to the truck stop.

Now, any ordinary American moron, confronting an acre-wide meringue of diesel cottage cheese, might just consider for a second or two the possibility of stepping on the brakes. Caution might be appropriate. But these were America's finest, state troopers, rigorously tested for IQ and trained in all the latest driving techniques. In perfect formation, the Daytona Four swerved right and headed straight for the sooty pool of diesel cottage cheese.

Oh, it was beautiful, a valorous, visual orgy, what happened next. As the police cruisers hydroplaned into the truck stop, a magnificent spray of diesel cottage cheese surfed across the sky. An inland lake of diesel cottage cheese doesn't halt four speeding Ford 500s right away. Instead, the cruisers began this wonderfully confusing bumper car dance, clanging off one another's fenders, rear-ending each other, and skittering off sideways as the tsunami of diesel cottage cheese arched up for the swamp. The diesel cottage cheese had splashed up and been scorched by the hot crankcases of the Fords. Then it bubbled up onto the hoods as a brown and crusted crème brûlée.

When the troopers got out of their cars together and hit the slippery goo, they somersaulted backwards onto their asses. Curds of diesel cottage cheese dripped from their visors and gun belts as they pulled themselves up by their door handles.

"Ah, shit," one of the troopers said. "What *is* this stuff?"

"Fuck if I know," another said.

"Is this a hazardous materials event? Somebody better radio Lee."

The bystanders in the truck stop parking lot laughed at the troopers and then moved on to what they had to do—every disaster scene has its comic moment. After that, I could never look at a cop again and not remember the West Stockbridge tornado.

In a lot of ways, my education as a reporter began that afternoon. At first, I was merely aware of feeling vaguely uncomfortable, pushed aside by the herd of older, more experienced reporters. They flitted en masse from one interview to the next, harrying the bewildered survivors. It's actually quite hard to gather accurate information, a complete picture of what happened, in the chaotic conditions of a major news event. Desk editors hundreds of miles away in Boston or New York, sifting through a variety of reports, are frequently the only ones with enough perspective and information to piece together a full story—one reason why the best reporters often check wire copy and other reports before they sit down to write their own piece. In the chaos of ambulances racing in and out, helicopters whamping up and down, and reporters' yelling questions, something—often a great deal of information—is lost at the event itself.

But I didn't know any of that right away. All I knew was that I was frustrated by drumming up an interview with a truck driver or helicopter pilot at the edge of the fray, then being shoved into a pile of twisted fiberboard and electrical wires while eighteen other reporters brawled in and started yelling the same questions over my shoulder. It was undignified, pointless. Everybody was stuffing into their notebooks the same anguished quotes.

Far off, on a hill to the southeast, there was an old ramshackle farm up on West Center Road that looked as though it had been smacked pretty hard after the tornado blew past the truck stop. The farm was one of these Appalachian-style dumps immortalized in the *New Yorker* cartoons of George Booth, the landscape surrounding it littered with broken-down fences, the rusted hulks of farm implements, and two acres or more of derelict cars. I could see from below that a couple of the pole barns had been overturned in the blow, and there was a large, gaping hole where the tornado had torn off the front of the house.

I decided to climb the hill. One more hike up through the slash wasn't going to kill me, and I'd let the story of that farm and the people who lived there complete my remarkable day.

·   ·   ·

The farm belonged to a family named Kie. It was a brown circle of dust jammed to the fence-lines with the rusting carcasses of old tractors and cars, baby carriages, and Lawnboys abandoned where they broke down. The afternoon twister had blown all of this from the bottom to the top of the yard. When I got there, several members of the Kie family, as well as a contingent from a local motorcycle gang, had pulled couches and stuffed chairs from the wrecked house out to the yard. They were sitting outside on this impromptu lawn furniture, enjoying beers, discussing the tornado, and staring down the valley to the beehive of activity at the truck stop. The Kies were extremely friendly and offered me a beer and a spare stuffed chair when I arrived.

The oldest son, Billy, who must have weighed 250 pounds and wore his hair in a long, greasy ponytail, perked up when he heard that I was a reporter with the *Eagle*.

"Oh boy! Oh boy! Ma, Pa, did you hear that? This guy's a reporter! Mr. Reporter, have I got the poop for you!"

When the tornado hit, Billy had been in Pittsfield with his cousin, making his rounds to the body shop and an auto parts store, picking up supplies for a Volkswagen Bug that he was restoring. When he heard a radio report about the tornado hitting the truck stop below his house, he sped off through the blackened skies of the storm in his 1967 Lincoln Continental.

Billy's father, William G. Kie, had just retired from the Penn Central Railroad, which ran through Pittsfield, his mother was terrified of storms, and he was afraid that their house had been whacked by the tornado. As he raced down Route 20 toward home, a group from his motorcycle gang, the Warlocks, sped by in the opposite direction, and Billy flashed his lights. The Warlocks executed a 180-degree turn on their Harleys and pulled up behind the Continental to assume an escort formation.

All the way home, Billy was yelling for his parents.

"I'm comin', Ma, don't worry! Hang in there, Pa! Billy's comin' home to save your ass."

The gray Continental and its escort of Harley Fat Boys encountered their first roadblock at the big hairpin turn in the furnace district of Richmond, where state troopers had set up a barricade. They weren't letting anyone through, even residents of the neighborhood. Billy politely backed up the

Continental and then floored it, sending the cops flying as he ran the roadblock with the Harleys in hot pursuit. The next roadblock was at Maple Hill Road and Route 102, and Billy waved the Harleys ahead to soften up the troopers so he could get the Continental through. Swerving the big Lincoln around the barricade and then past some fallen limbs, he lost control and skittered sideways up Maple Hill Road. When the Continental got hung up on a concrete catch-basin and lost its front end, Billy and his cousin charged out of the car and raced the rest of the way home on foot.

Ma and Pa Kie, as it turned out, were fine. A little shaken up, but fine. Mrs. Kie had not been at home and old William Kie had huddled down in the cellar with his daughter Vivian when he saw the funnel cloud approach over Canaan Mountain, a move that had probably saved his life.

The Kies were a little worried about how they were going to live now. Mounds of field hay had blown all over their property, their Great Dane had been injured by a flying hubcap, and there was a big hole in the front of the house where the kitchen had been. But they were glad to see Billy and the Warlocks. It was Pa Kie's idea to retrieve some beers from the overturned refrigerator inside and carry the furniture out to watch the show below.

The big mystery was Billy's prize possession, the VW Bug that he was nearly finished restoring. It had disappeared. When they got there, the Warlocks had looked all over for it, because they knew that the Bug was the one thing Billy would be concerned about, after Ma and Pa. When Billy asked about it, they all just stared at him sheepishly and scratched their heads. That's the thing, Billy, they said. When we all came up the road? Lots of tree limbs, old tires, and other shit in the way. But no VW Bug.

Billy was upset about it. The Bug was practically his whole life.

"It's a '64 Bug, you know? Practically a collector's item now. It was almost done. Now its ass is AWOL. Tell me something, wil'ya? Where would a tornado take a whole frickin' car?"

Once they had enough furniture out on the lawn, Billy and

his friends fanned out across the property to look for the VW, dodging the tornado-strewn detritus of dog bowls and hay. It was Billy, actually, who found the car. Crunched to about half its size, the VW was planted thirty feet up a sugar maple at the top of the ravine, wedged in between a stripped leader and the main trunk. Somehow, as the tornado picked up the car and flung it into the tree, a long section of power cable from down along Route 102 had wrapped itself around the VW's front bumper. The cable dangled down from the tree in an inelegant diagonal that stretched across to the Kies' yard.

Billy was disconsolate about losing his car, but his facial expressions progressively brightened as he told me the story. He was working himself up into a lather about all the different ways the *Eagle* could play the tale of his ballistic Bug.

The afternoon twister had blown a gaping hole in their house, but the Kie family was a wonderful hillbilly clan who helped deliver me to a great story.

"Okay, okay, I can accept it, see? Yeah, my freakin' Volkswagen is toast, but I can see it already in the paper," Billy said, spreading his arms wide as he imagined out loud what the headline should be. "I mean, all they have to say in the paper is, 'The Love Bug of Kie Hill.'"

I told Billy that I considered him a genius. I promised to fight for that headline. In the meantime, I was anxious to see the levitated car. Grabbing my camera, I followed Billy down across the debris field of his yard.

As soon as I saw the Volkswagen in the maple I knew that I had a great picture. I doubted that anyone back at the *Eagle* would appreciate what I saw in the image, but I quickly crashed through those doubts and decided to just shoot for myself. The Volkswagen in the tree was a simple, potent symbol of the power of a tornado, and I would trust my instincts and try to remember all the lessons Sheila had taught me. There was no room for screwing up. Bracket a lot for f-stops, fill the frame, peel away the layers of the image until I had stripped it down to its cleanest, most unadorned form.

When I was out of film, I walked back up through the yard and said good-bye to the wonderful Kie menage. Billy handed me another beer and offered to ride up the mountain on one of his tractors, once the road was cleared, to recover my Pinto. One of his pals would give me a ride on his Harley back to Great Barrington so I could fetch my own bike and get into the *Eagle*. That turned out to be the worst ordeal of the day, because the wind racing by scalded my bruised cheeks and hands. Still, I was jubilant. I knew that I had one great picture from the tornado.

.   .   .

When I got to the *Eagle* building in Pittsfield, the newsroom was pulsing with activity, all running bodies and editors and reporters shouting out across the floor for more details and facts. County correspondents who I didn't even know worked for the paper had rushed into the newsroom to help, and photographers were darting back and forth from the darkroom with big sheaves of contact sheets under their arms. The pressrun had been delayed so the *Eagle* could get out a big keeper of a special edition on what was already being called the Great Berkshire Tornado.

Bill Bell was astonished to see me. He couldn't understand how I'd become marooned at the tornado when I was supposed to be all the way down in Great Barrington, interviewing the Japanese potter. He'd been calling all over the county to get me back into the newsroom to compile a weather sidebar as part of the *Eagle*'s tornado coverage. I was too exhausted to battle him this time, so, as meekly as I could, I told him that I'd write the sidebar, pound out some "feeds" for the other reporters, and turn in my film.

"Film? What film? Okay, good, turn in your film then," Bell said.

Bell looked annoyed. The *Eagle*'s award-winning team of photographers had been assigned to cover the tornado, and they'd come back with dozens of rolls of exposed film. The last thing the paper needed right then was more film to process from a greenhorn like me.

On busy days like this, Gerry Dougherty, an amateur photographer who worked down in the composing room, was pressed into service helping out in the photo-developing lab. Gerry was a frenetic, jerky-limbed fellow with a pasty complexion and brown protruding teeth, invariably dressed in a stained work apron. He was one of these antic blue-collar types who insisted on having a sarcastic nickname, a "handle" he called it, for everyone in the building. Because Tom Morton's middle initial was "O," Gerry called him "Tom-o." Gerry considered Rory O'Connor's articles far too long and esoteric, so he was "Boring O'Connor." As soon as I arrived in the newsroom, Gerry found my name irresistible and came up with a handle for me too.

"Stinker Fuck!" Gerry said, the afternoon we were introduced. "That's your handle from now on, good buddy. Stinker Fuck."

"Ah c'mon, Gerry," I said. "Let's be fair to my mother here. She's not going to like that."

"Oh, please. Your mother," Gerry said. "She's the one who gave you this shithead name. Sorry. You're now Stinker Fuck."

Other than that, Gerry was exceptionally kind to me. He taught me how to "push" my film for exposing in shadows and made many useful suggestions about ways that I could improve my portraiture and nature shots, so that Tom Morton would accept them for Page One or the Local Page. He and Tom Morton had an unusually strong collaboration. They had been friends for years and when Gerry emerged from the darkroom with certain frames on a contact sheet circled in red grease pencil, Tom was confident that he'd picked the best shots.

When I got in from the tornado and knocked on the photo lab door to hand in my rolls of film, Gerry was working the vats. He seemed very harried and he wasn't pleased to see me.

"Ah Christ, Stinker, what the hell are you doing here?"

"Gerry, I've got film from the tornado."

"Yeah, you and eighteen other fucking boneheads. Look, I'm working almost a hundred rolls of film in here. Scram, Stinker."

"Gerry, please. I think I've got one really good shot, okay?"

"Yeah, maybe," Gerry said. "But just *maybe*, you hear? And you're a flaming asshole for this."

Twenty minutes later, while I was still working on my weather sidebar, Gerry burst out of the photo lab with a contact sheet in his hand, bounding across the newsroom with this queer, spasmodic gait that he had. He blew right past my desk and went straight for Tom Morton.

"Oh boy, oh boy, oh boy," Gerry said. "Hey, Tom-o, wait'll you'll see this! It's *the* picture."

Morton took out a magnifying loop and examined the contact sheet. When he looked up he had this bemused, satisfied half grin on his face.

"Jeez, Gerry," Morton said. "This shot is perfect. Perfect. A car in the tree. Who took it?"

"Little Stinker over there, Tom-o," Gerry said, jerking his arm out in my direction. "Stinker Fuck!"

"Buck, huh?" Morton said.

"Stinker Fuck!" Gerry said. "I mean, you know, the exposures are all wrong and I had to save his ass in the vats, and he didn't get down low enough under the tree. But, hey! Stinker Fuck took the shot of the day."

Morton called out across the floor.

"Kiddo, what is this thing anyway? Where'd you shoot it?"

"It's a '64 Bug, Tom," I said. "I shot it up on West Center Road. It's owned by a guy named Billy Kie."

"Oh, Billy Kie, huh?" Morton said. "What, they let him out jail just for the tornado?"

"I guess so. He's not a bad guy, actually."

Morton happily dabbed his forehead.

"Kiddo, you aced it. This baby is right out of the park. It's everything we need to know about the storm."

As soon as I saw the VW in the tree I knew that I had a great shot.

Morton skimmed the contact sheet across his desk and told Gerry to make up extra prints. He wanted to move the image on the photo wires of the Associated Press and United Press International. The Volkswagen-in-the-tree shot wasn't "newsy" enough for Page One or even the lead photograph with the story inside—an aerial shot of the tornado damage, and a wide-angle picture showing the roofless diner at the truck stop, were much better for that. But the Volkswagen-in-the-tree shot had what Morton called "attitude." It was a unique, non-newsy take, a pithy, one-glance summary on the impact of the storm. Morton ran it prominently on a back page with the *Eagle's* tornado coverage the next day.

As he left to make up the prints, Gerry stopped at my desk and clapped me on the back.

"Stinker Fuck, you are my kind of guy," he said. "Everything I taught you about taking pictures?"

"Yeah, Gerry?"

"You fucking forgot. Still, you came back with a great shot, Stinker."

"Hey, Gerry, thanks," I said. "I appreciate your support."

I didn't know enough then about the AP and UPI wires to expect much from them. A couple of days after the tornado, however, I began receiving calls from old high school friends from as far away as Richmond and Seattle. They had seen the car-in-the-tree shot, with my photo credit, in their local papers. A photo editor from AP called and asked for a copy of the negative—they wanted to keep it for their "stock" files.

All told, about 150 papers across the country used the shot that week, and the Volkswagen-in-the-tree shot would be frequently reprinted in photo history and weather books. I didn't know about any of that at the time, of course, but by October I'd received almost $700 in "use fees," a huge windfall, more money than I'd ever received at once in my life. I was elated about that and one day took the checks over and showed them to Tom Morton.

Morton was jubilant about those checks too, and it felt great, being able to make him happy that way. I had already crashed through my first instincts about that picture. Initially, I had felt guilty about it, as if I was conning the world again, because I had lied about my abilities as a photographer to get this job, and now I was being rewarded for dishonesty. But, screw that. After the Volkswagen-in-the-tree shot, Tom Morton treated me like pampered talent—I was his "photo race horse," he said, and he often sent me out just on shooting assignments. Creative deceit, I decided, could be quite useful and even thrilling when you could pull it off, and I felt liberated about something else. Some days, this job didn't feel like *work* at all. I was coasting on natural ability and enjoying it.

Looking over the checks from the wire services, Morton dabbed his bald head and smiled.

"Hey, kiddo. A bird in the hand. Cash on the barrelhead. Now you can fix your Pinto."

CHAPTER SEVEN

BY THE FALL, I had settled down into a regular Friday night routine. I generally bounded out of the newsroom by 9:30 or 10, raced south to Lenox and followed the road out past Andrew Carnegie's old estate, and then slowed to a crawl over the summit of Lenox Mountain, exulting in the chilly, anthracite vastness of the peaks towering all around and the moonlight shimmering far below on Stockbridge Bowl. Then I surrendered to the slope falling through the hollows of West Stockbridge, coasted into my familiar haunt at the Westbridge Inn, and goofed off with the biker babes while enjoying a couple of quick beers and a bourbon. From there I rumbled south for Stockbridge.

In those days there were two pretty good hangouts in Stockbridge. The first was a grotto bar in the cellar of the Red Lion Inn called the Lion's Den. The Den was an understated, tasteful place, with small wooden tables decorated with flowers and candles, exposed beams on the ceiling, and a quiet, hippie-dippie folk group strumming on banjos and guitars over in the corner. The lead singer was usually an ersatz Joni Mitchell type, therapeutically banging a tambourine on her hip while she sang about her boyfriend problems.

On Friday and Saturday nights, the Den was filled with lovely rich girls from Shaker Heights, Ohio, or Chappaqua,

New York, relaxing with a drink while they completed the final phase of their treatment for nervous breakdown or drug detoxification at the Austin Riggs Center. The Riggs Center was just down the road on Main Street, and it was a well-known psychiatric resort for the rich and famous—Judy Garland and James Taylor had recovered from their various addictions and mental meltdowns there. The Riggs Girls, as everyone called them, were an important social presence in Stockbridge, and during the summer they mixed pretty well in the Den with the glitterati of Boston and New York, who were up in the mountains to take in Tanglewood or the Berkshire Theatre Festival. This clientele changed perceptively with the first snow in December. The winter crowd was more high-rent and suburban, skiers from Fairfield and Westchester Counties spending the weekend at Butternut Basin or Catamount, and now the Riggs Girls were outnumbered by a fun-fun gang of luscious ski bunnies. There was dancing there—slow, gentle numbers while the hippies played, a fast jitterbug or retro twist when the band took a break and the bartender played records—but the wooden, elevated dance floor was quite small. If you met someone that you liked and elected for more serious boogying, you left the Den together and drove two miles through the oxbows to Glendale, the northern terminus of the Stockbridge mansion district, where there was an excellent, dance-till-you-drop place called Fred Mundy's Bar.

Mundy's was nothing more than a big parking lot built above the oxbows with a large cinder-block building in its midst, a ratshack biker bar out of the pages of Tom Wolfe's *Electric Kool-Aid Acid Test*. On weekends, Mundy's was crowded and loud, its location right next door to the Musgrave and Clark estates wildly incongruous. The Stockbridge selectmen were always threatening to shut the place down, but everyone knew that they would never have the courage to do this because there were too many votes along Mundy's spacious wooden bar. Mundy's was a legendary American bar, as good as anything you could find in Provincetown or Key West.

Mundy's contained a splendid genetic and sexual cross

section of life. Middle-aged and elderly crazy Stockbridge millionaires, in their Mahkeenac Yacht Club blazers, met their girlfriends there. Their daughters bought drugs from the bikers in the back room. In one corner there was a lesbian contingent, looking lovely together as they electric-boogied and crashed their breasts, next to them there were the gay men, then the Riggs Girls, who particularly enjoyed dancing with gays, then the interracial couples group, the marital swingers, and so forth. Ski-bunny weekenders and the wives of Tanglewood musicians would ditch their husbands at the bar to dance with single guys like me. There were a lot of Pittsfield girls too, wondrous in their variety, and they tended to converge on Mundy's in packs—the sexy, ultrabosomy daughters of GE engineers and shop stewards, in their tank tops and tight jeans, with a smattering of Berkshire Hills Country Club daughters dressed in the uniform of upper-middle-class girls then, the modified hippie look, a long flower-print or paisley skirt with a denim work shirt up top. They considered themselves very sophisticated for having "discovered" Mundy's as a place to buy drugs and to dance.

Mundy's and the Lion's Den were a kind of joint cauldron where the sexual revolution of the early 1970s was played out. In 1971 Norman Mailer had published *Prisoner of Sex*, which was followed two years later by Erica Jong's thermonuclear ode to the orgasm and emotional honesty, *Fear of Flying*. Everyone was talking about those two books then, and for a while it felt as if they were the only two contemporary titles worth reading. Because both Mailer and Jong were part-time residents of the Berkshires then, nationally celebrated for writing a twin set of great sex books, the local connection was somehow guaranteed to deliver everybody to extra helpings of sex. Mundy's was where it all came together. The place pulsed with great bodies, suggestive talk, drug buys, and crazy-ass pool tournaments in the back rooms.

At first I suffered a few problems of adjustment. I started frequenting the Lion's Den on Thursday nights because I was often assigned the night shift on Fridays and had the whole day off, so this gave me a jump start on the weekend. Over in the corner by the band there was usually a large group of guys milling around together and dancing, which at first I hardly noticed, because there were also a lot of gorgeous Riggs Girls there. It didn't occur to me to put two and two together. Everybody knows that men simply don't dance like that, guy-on-guy. I wasn't seeing what I thought that I was seeing.

Besides, the atmosphere along the bar was very friendly. Lots of nice men. It was the usual smattering of Berkshire County types, ponytailed potters from Mill River or New Marlborough, urban refugees from New York who now sold real estate, a business executive or two. They bought me drinks, engaged me in long, knowledgeable conversations about Shaker furniture or the latest books, and they all seemed very interested in *me*, qua me. A couple of times these guys asked for my phone number, or offered me their phone numbers, but by then I was so shitfaced there was no way to cognitively process what that meant.

"Hey, thanks, buddy," I would say, stepping up to leave. "I've sure enjoyed our conversation. Take it easy."

"You're very nice," the fellow would say. "Will I see you again?"

"Sure, no problem," I said. "I'm here every Thursday night."

One Thursday night, a public relations executive for the Berkshire Life Insurance Company in Pittsfield pulled me aside. His name was Howard and he knew me pretty well through Peter Scheer.

"Hey, Rinker," Howard said. "Can I ask you a personal question?"

"Sure, Howie. Shoot."

"You're into girls, right?"

"Girls? Of course I'm into girls, Howie. Everybody's into girls."

Howie sighed, took a sip from his drink, and stared at me as if I was just about the dumbest act to come along since David Eisenhower began dating Julie Nixon.

"Rinker, you're a baboon, do you know that? Hasn't anybody told you that the Den is a gay bar on Thursday nights?"

Ah, shitbag, I thought. What a numskull I could be. I was the genius who could smell out an ex-priest, but I couldn't even tell that I was in a gay bar. But I wasn't going to let the Berkshire Life flack know that I was so clueless.

"Hey, Howie, big freaking deal, okay? There are guys over there dancing and holding hands. I'm not prejudiced, okay?"

"Oh, I see," Howie said. "In other words, some of your best friends are gay?"

"Yeah, sure," I said. "You got a problem with that?"

"No, but I hope you don't have a problem with it," he said. "There's a guy up at the bar who just told me that you have the cutest ass in the Berkshires. He wants to take you home."

"Yeah, well, you know, what the hell, Howie," I said. "It's easy to get the wrong impression."

"Yeah, I'll say," Howie said. "But now you know, okay?"

"Yeah, thanks pal," I said. "I'll try to remain a virgin."

Gay bar. Hmmmm. Interesting new concept. One of my closest friends in college was gay, but, funny thing, David had never mentioned guys *avec* guys going to bars. The whole notion of "bar" subsisted powerfully in my mind as guys and gals together, exclusively. Sexually, alcoholically, I was stuck way back there with Jim Crow and segregation. But now I was excited, intrigued. I just happened to like being in the Den on Thursday nights, the friendly atmosphere and laughter, the guy-guy fun, and I wasn't going to stop going there out of a fear of being known as gay.

Howie screwed me good on this. He leaked the news of my Thursday night visits to the Lion's Den to Peter Scheer. At first, Peter just laughed about it. But then one day, while he was trying to finish a big story on deadline, I emptied my pipe into his wastebasket, igniting a fire that sent flames leaping up toward Peter's desk. So Peter got pissed off and told Tom Morton and Pat Faucett that I was hanging out at gay bars, and they in turn trashed me with Linscott and Pete Miller. I was the laughingstock of the newsroom for several weeks, the butt, so to speak, of every "light in the loafers" joke.

Still, I didn't care, and I never stopped going to the Den on

Stockbridge's Red Lion Inn was a genteel tourist mecca, but what happened in the grotto bar downstairs was another story.

Thursdays. I loved the new kind of male bonding I discovered around gay men. Until then, male companionship for me had consisted of hanging around at airports or drinking with my college friends. With the airport geezers, I discussed such pressing topics as how to clean mud ants out of a pitot tube, or the mediocre rate of climb achieved by the Aeronca Champ. With my college friends, I discoursed on how to recover after getting ditched by the babe.

But now I had a whole new crowd, gay guys. With them, I could indulge my need to book-turd for a while or palaver away about Shaker antiques. Gay guys were very interesting and steered conversations toward topics that I didn't discuss with anyone else—what my family was like, the psychology of handling a boss, how I felt about my body. They didn't mind when they figured out that I was straight, because they wanted to talk about that too. Who were my girlfriends? What was my "type"? Did I like her better in a sweater or a work shirt? I enjoyed the candor of gay men and being surrounded by a new group of caring, sensitive friends. Gay men also tended to be intellectual and very bookish—repressed, troubled childhoods often drive adolescents into obsessive reading—and much more than straight men, gays are acutely sensitive to the nuances of style, class, and character, subjects that interested me a great deal. Straight men are generally more desperate than they admit for male affection, and I found this along the fun-fun bar at the Den on Thursday nights. The swirl of emotions and support was wonderful and very real.

On Friday and Saturday nights, the Lion's Den and

Mundy's abruptly shifted sexual tense. Up and down the
Berkshire range there was a great night-emptying as all of the
cultural institutions let out, and then everyone who was restless, sexually needy, or just spiritually charged up flocked to
Mundy's in Glendale. Musicians and hangers-on from Tanglewood, actors and actresses from the Berkshire Theatre Festival, and these pert little tag teams of skinny-hipped dancers
from Jacob's Pillow all piled in together. The bands were loud
and insistent—there was this strange, plaintive new sound
coming on then, a kind of electric Irish, with bits of reggae
and country thrown in, great dancing music—and all those
lithe bodies mixed wildly and well with the music and the
psychedelic lights whirling from the ceiling. Everybody
bought drinks for everybody else and there was a spontaneous joie de vivre about the mating ritual. *Oh, wow. Do you
really work for the* Berkshire Eagle? *My Dad's a cellist. BSO.
Wanna dance?* I loved being at Mundy's and kicking over my
rudder for a pretty girl.

The Jacob's Pillow girls, really, were the main reason to be
there. They were a visual feast together, a thing of choreo-
graphic beauty. Since its founding in the 1930s, Ted Shawn's
dance barn up in Becket had drawn most of the world's great
companies and ballet stars, and the festival's mountaintop
campus was filled all summer with professional dancers and
students from all over the country. The Jacob's Pillow girls
had a look, a sorority glow, as they all came in through the
door together after the last performance let out at ten. Smart-
smart, superpert, the girls with the shiny pageboy hair and
the muscular, smart-aleck breasts. They dressed in a way that
accentuated their unpretentious style—sleek department
store jeans, dark leotard tops, and goofy canvas shoes Made
in China.

Life inside a big dance company was pressured, intense,
and this was their one night of the week to blow it all out.
They didn't really care if anyone watched them or not. They
were there for themselves, to do the Jacob's Pillow lesbo-line
together out on the crowded dance floor. Over in the corner,
as the electric flutist with the fedora started to uncork, all the

Jacob's Pillow girls would form this long line together, bump their skinny hips, and do this great formation boogie. Dip down together with the pageboy hair flying, lean in with the muscular shoulders and chests, now out with this Made in China shoe, then the other foot, all laugh at once because *she* missed it, then break out in pairs or trios for a while and do this modified aerobic-frug body ecstasy together and don't be afraid to hug and crash those breasts together and kiss on the lips because we're *it*, we're *there*, we're *dancers!* no rules exist for us, we're the Jacob's Pillow girls, Great American Chicks unwinding on Friday night, and now let's hold hands and kiss lips to pageboy hair or lips to shoulder, or lips to lips again, and then walk off together hip-hugging in a lovely herd because the electric flutist is finally spent and God do I need a drink. It was spectral, just watching them. As far as I was concerned, you could just make one big pile out of Mount Greylock, Butternut Basin, and Norman Rockwell's kitschy Main Street and take it all out with a hydrogen bomb. There was only one reason to be alive in the Berkshire mountains of western Massachusetts, circa 1973. That was Friday night at Mundy's Bar in Glendale with the dirty-dancing Jacob's Pillow girls.

.   .   .

Pete Miller was regarded nationally as a man at the top of his form, the best small-town newspaper publisher in the land, and one of the wealthiest men in western New England. He had no equal as an avatar of print or as a model of Waspy, cerebral noblesse oblige. After Roger Linscott won his Pulitzer in 1973, the line of bright, snappily dressed job applicants from Mount Holyoke and Columbia Journalism School got longer on Eagle Street in Pittsfield. They all wanted to be part of the miracle of quality that Pete had wrought in the mountains. But there was one secret that no one had bothered to tell them about. Pete Miller was absolutely bonkers over money. His life was just one long mental breakdown over cash.

I first encountered Pete's bizarre disturbance over money early one morning in October, two and a half months after I arrived at the *Eagle*. He strolled across the newsroom in that elegantly spastic gait of his, with a large bandage covering a bruise on his forehead. The bandage, which was held in place by small pieces of masking tape, looked as though it had been self-applied after being found in a drawer devoted to recycled office supplies. As soon as he disappeared into Linscott's office, the whole newsroom started buzzing about what might have happened to Pete.

The *Eagle* rumor mill was a well-oiled machine. It commenced operation early in the day, usually with Mary Jane Tichenor over on the social desk. She would dial over to huffy, overweight Madeline Winters in the *Eagle* library, who would in turn consult with Roger O'Gara, a stroke victim who edited the Sports Page. Once in a while the *Eagle*'s legendary political columnist, a brooding Buddha named A.A. Michaelson, would get involved in the act, but usually that was just to tell Madeline Winters to shut up. Once Mary Jane, Madeline, and O'Gara had agreed on a version of events that they liked, the rumor was released for consumption by judicious leaking to the city, county, and copy desks. It was a pretty reliable system, quite good, in fact, if you had a message to get out.

One Friday night in late September, after Peter Scheer had kick-started the rumor that I was gay, I was down in the Lion's Den dancing with an old high school flame, Helen Hartley Platt, when I saw Mike Meserole from the *Eagle* sports department, up by the bar. Harty was voluptuous and tall, with this great flying mane of blonde hair. I told Harty about my problem and what we had to do. Harty was quite game for things, so we pushed out to the edge of the floor and danced slow and close over by Meserole, and then we just really started demonstratively groping and kissing each other all over, with lots of groin smashing, and Mike got the point. On Monday morning, as I passed the sports department, I heard him telling Roger O'Gara all about my girlfriend with the "very impressive pair of headlights." O'Gara took that right over to Mary Jane and Madeline, and then it came back through Meserole and O'Gara for extra amps, and by the noon deadline I was back among the heterosexual ranks. I heard all about it from Rory O'Connor. *Rinker, pssst! Good news. You're not gay! Mary Jane says that you molest college girls!*

That's how it worked. The morning Pete came in with the bandage on, numerous unofficial tales were whispered—Pete's wife, Amy Bess, had finally lost patience and bopped him on the head with a skillet; Pete had walked into a door last night after too many martinis—but by 10:30 or so Mary Jane had checked in with Pat Faucett and had a version fit for circulation.

Pete had crashed his bike. There had been a collision that morning down on East Street. According to the rumor, the accident involved either a mail truck or a pedestrian—Pete's legendary inability to establish eye contact was probably the cause—but otherwise the details were obscure. Impatient about that, I decided to go straight to the most reliable source, Pat Faucett.

"Oh, Rinker," Pat said, laughing. "You'll love this one. Pete's got a real problem now."

Pete lived in a large colonial house about three miles east of town on Williams Street, an unpretentious, graceful manse that commanded expansive views west and south to the oxbows and down across Herman Melville's old lands on Holmes Road. In the summer, and as long as the warm weather lasted into the fall, Pete rode into the *Eagle* every day on a creaky old bike. On the calves of his legs, to protect his flannel pants from getting snagged on the pedal chain, Pete wore these ridiculous-looking metal clasps that a friend from Williams College had brought back from England. The bike was a three-speed Schwinn that he'd bought at a tag sale back in the 1950s, the sort of thing that you'd expect to see Katharine Hepburn, in a straw hat and looking marvelously tanned and chipper, steering around her estate on the Connecticut shore. Pete's Schwinn had balloon tires and hand brakes, a rusty metal basket up front, and one of these cheery little bells on the handlebars activated by thumb. *Ring-ring! Ring-ring!* Every cop and school-crossing guard that he passed on his morning route got the ring. City councilmen and lawyers got a polite hand salute and a cheery greeting; for the mayor, the brakes were applied and Pete stopped for a chat. Everybody in town knew and loved Pete Miller and waved as he passed.

Pete regarded his rickety Schwinn as a personal expression of his frugality.

"Hah! The Schwinn!" he would exclaim, stepping off his bike and chaining it to a light pole in the *Eagle* lot. "Twenty-eight bucks at a tag sale in Lee. 1956. No gas! These wheels have saved me a bundle!"

That October morning, as he got up past East Street near the Appleton Avenue corner, Pete encountered a sight that filled his heart with joy. A foot or two above the sidewalk, wedged into a gnarled rose trellis on a picket fence, was a $20 bill. The wind had picked it up and blown it into the thorns.

Pete didn't have it in him to pass up lucre that good. If he was walking down North Street on the way to lunch with the president of the Berkshire Hills Conference, he would stop to pick up pennies. Senator Ted Kennedy or a delegation from the National Audubon Society would be visiting the Berkshires, making their required stop with the *Eagle* major domo, and Pete would bend over to retrieve a nickel from a restaurant floor.

Pete was so excited when he saw the $20 on the sidewalk, so concerned that the bike would overhaul the cash, that he immediately clamped hard on the left brake and froze the front wheel. The bike upended tail first, and the richest man in Berkshire County went airborne over the handlebars and flew head first for the trellis.

But Pete was jubilant, immensely pleased with himself. Just prior to impact with the trellis, he nimbly reached out and snagged the $20 from the thorns. It was secured in his wallet and concealed in the rear pocket of his shabby flannels in a flash, even before Pete realized that he was injured. He was bleeding from the scrape on his forehead now. But what's a little headache when $20 falls right out of heaven like that? Righting his bike, dabbing his forehead with a handkerchief, Pete rode one-handed the rest of the way into the *Eagle* offices and found some used gauze and masking tape to repair his head.

But now he had a moral crisis on his hands. Pete's Puritan conscience was troubled. He didn't mind being known as cheap, someone who would provoke a midair collision with a rose trellis just to snatch an extra $20. But the Jeremiah of Berkshire County, a man whose rectitude was celebrated far away in Washington and New York, couldn't just accept the happy accident of finding $20 and not at least make attempts to identify the rightful owner. This wasn't polite. Twenty bucks was a lot of money, and Pete just couldn't pocket that without good-faith efforts toward establishing provenance.

Pat Faucett called me back a little while later, and we made a dandy little day out of it, nursing Pete through his moral emergency over the $20 bill.

"Oh, Rinker, I don't know what I'm going to do," Pat said. "Pete is driving me nuts. Nuts! He wants to place a classified ad. We have to find the owner of the $20. But he can't get started on the copy."

This was another attractive weakness in Pete. An absolute genius and very quick at editing someone else's prose, he was a painfully slow writer himself. Pete's monthly odes to country living, published in his *UpCountry* magazine, were right up there in the John McPhee–Hal Borland league, but he just took forever with his essays, brooding and fussing down there in his inner sanctum, endlessly rewriting, doubting himself, rewriting some more. Pat endured the burden of this—she was the one who ceaselessly retyped draft after draft from Pete's cursive. Occasionally when Pete was really stalled, Pat would suggest an opening sentence or two, just to get him started.

Because she was tall, leggy, and wry, I enjoyed goofing off and flirting with Pat. She was a completely safe office crush. And Pat liked me, mostly because she had completely fallen for this personal bullshit that I'd thrown at her about being a good Catholic boy. We worked well together.

"Oh, Rinker, I don't know what I'm going to do with this," she said over the phone. "I'm stalled myself now. But Pete needs copy for the ad."

"Pat," I said. "How brain-dead could this be? All you've got to say is 'Found on street, $20, blah blah blah.'"

"Oh, Rinker, could you? Would you? It's not for me. It's for Pete."

Putting Pat out of her misery was going to take all of five minutes. Besides, I loved the image. Pete was chortling all over down there. The one thing he could do for free at his own paper was place a classified ad. I was glad to help. And it was going to be good, too, long and juicy. The ad was free. No charge per word. We could make it as informative as we wanted.

But I was sincere about it too. We were genuinely attempting to reunite a former owner with his or her $20. That was our mission. Due diligence saturated my first draft:

"LOST CASH: Found on corner of East Street and Appleton Avenue by bicycle rider Tuesday morning at approximately 8:30 A.M. $20 in recent U.S. currency, serial No._____ (Pat: fill in serial number of bill here). If you live in Pittsfield or towns nearby and were driving or walking by this vicinity and happened to lose $20, we're sincerely trying to locate you. Please contact Eagle Reply Box No. _____ or call (413) 447-4300. Request Pat or Pete."

After I walked the copy down and dropped it off at Pat's vestibule office, she gave me regular updates for the rest of the day. I had the usual overflow of work that morning. There were multiple stiffs from Remo and Fran, the weather, and Bill Bell was driving me insane with this dumb-ass local angle on an AP story, a desperate national shortage of wire hangers. My job was to collect the kind of brilliant quotes that could only be obtained from the owners of dry cleaning establishments in North Adams, Pittsfield, and Lee.

Pat's cheery bulletins about Pete's rewriting of the classified ad broke the monotonous drill of my day. At noon, Pete decided to forgo his regular martini run out to an elegant restaurant in Stockbridge or Lenox and just dine on a grilled cheese sandwich at the Soda Chef on North Street, so that he would remain "alert" for the editing job. In the middle of the afternoon, the rewrite of the ad was slowed down when Tom Winship from *The Boston Globe* called and he and Pete talked for more than half an hour. Just before 4 P.M., however, Pat finally called and invited me down to inspect Pete's final draft.

When I got down there, Pat showed me the results of Pete's work, neatly typed on a printed form from the Classified department. It was the final, edited copy:

"Found on street. Small denomination specie. Claimant must prove legal ownership of same. Contact Eagle Reply Box 458."

It was absolutely brilliant, a small, spare, stone monument of prose. Pete had vaulted right up through the lower altitudes of mere Pulitzer-quality writing and bagged himself the Scrooge Nobel Prize. Who the hell would answer a classified like that? *Yup. Here I am, Mrs. Faucett. This is my lawyer, Mr. Burbank. We're prepared to prove legal ownership of specie.* No one, of course. Not a soul among the *Eagle*'s 30,000 readers replied to the ad and Pete was off the hook.

Pete never let go of that $20. For as long as I remained at the *Eagle*, he still had that bill in his wallet. I loved to chide him about it.

"Hey Pete," I would say, "Have you still got that $20?"

Then the *Eagle* publisher would do the Miller twirl, open his wallet to verify specie, and scratch his rump with glee.

"Twenty bucks! Hah! Found on street. Every time I ride by that corner now, I still look to see if there's any money."

.   .   .

When I arrived at the *Eagle*, in addition to obituaries, the weather, and local angles on wire hanger shortages, Bill Bell gave me the assignment of covering Hancock Shaker Village. Several *Eagle* veterans warned me to be wary of that assignment. In the early 1960s, the Hancock Shaker Village had been rescued and then lovingly restored by Pete Miller's wife, Amy Bess, a jovial and very pretty New Hampshire heiress whose exquisite taste and bubbly presence had been just the right combination of qualities required for preserving a valuable historic site. The Millers had diverted considerable amounts of *Eagle* profits to the Shaker village, and it was now a popular tourist destination, its restoration highly regarded among museum directors nationwide. At the time, Shaker design and furniture were undergoing a popular revival, and Amy Bess authored several books on the Shakers and made regular appearances on the morning talk shows in New York. But this presented a problem for *Eagle* staffers. Amy Bess might be fun and bouncy, America's Shaker Queen, but I was told that she could be a real lizard lady if you stepped one inch out of line covering Hancock. She'd appeal through Pete and get you nailed. Bill Bell, everyone said, was just trying to screw me.

Stepping up to that challenge turned out to be a real confidence builder for me. As soon as I met her, I knew that I could handle a dame like Amy Bess. All I had to do with a high-rent lady like that was to put on a clean shirt and tie, watch my language, and then just awesomely kiss butt, and that's exactly what I did. Eddie Haskell was *rude* to Mrs. Cleaver compared to the way I sucked up to Mrs. Miller. A new exhibition on Shaker seed catalogues? I was there and wrote it up big. Newly unearthed correspondence between Brother Alonzo G. Hollister and Count Leo Tolstoy? I book-turded by phone with scholars all over the country on that one, and Tom Morton liked the story so much he put it on Page One. The only trouble I ever made for Amy Bess was climbing on a ladder one day up to the roof of the Brothers' House to photograph carpenters installing a new belfry. Down in Springfield, an inspector at the regional offices of the federal Occupational Safety Health Administration saw the photograph in the *Eagle* and was concerned that none of the carpenters were wearing safety harnesses. When he drove up to Hancock for a closer look, Amy Bess was cited for sixteen safety violations.

As soon as I heard about the OSHA violations, I called out to Hancock and spoke with Amy Bess.

"Mrs. Miller, I'm sorry about those OSHA violations," I said.

Amy Bess Miller, America's Shaker Queen, was demanding, but I learned how to handle the publisher's high-rent wife.

"This is my fault. But I was just trying to do my job."

"Oh, Rinker," Amy Bess said. "It's all right. You're such a nice boy, and it wasn't really your fault. Isn't the federal government ridiculous? Nobody fell off my belfry."

So, we became pals, the Shaker Queen and I. Whenever I was lonely or depressed or Bill Bell was on my case, I'd disappear down West Street and chat up Amy Bess. Hancock—especially the collection of nineteenth-century Shaker spirit drawings—was refreshing, a supremely relaxing place. Under the guise of "covering my beat," I frequently sneaked out to Hancock and goofed off for the afternoon. In the administration building, there was an extra cubicle and phone that I used to make private calls to my girlfriends, and I took long, restful naps on a couch in the basement of the Brothers' House.

One day in the fall I was hanging upside down by my legs from the rafters up in the Round Stone Barn. Pete Miller had decided that he liked my writing and asked me to submit an article on mortise-and-tenon construction for *UpCountry* magazine. Museum director John Ott was up there with me, explaining all about hand-hewn peg joints. From upside down I saw the pretty, matronly figure of Amy Bess walk in through the wide double door.

"Rinker Buck? Is that you up there?

"It's me, Amy Bess."

"Oh, good. Well listen, Pete and I are having a little soiree out at the house tonight. Would you like to come? Interesting people will be there. That's what my Pete said to tell you. 'Tell that young man that interesting people will be there.'"

"Well sure, Amy Bess. Thanks!"

That night, after driving out to the end of Williams Street, I was delighted to see Pete's house, which was understated but beautifully appointed. The motto that he applied to the *Eagle*—that its prose and design should be as pristine as "moss on a stone wall"—had been employed here as well. The big white house was sided with cedar shingles, had an inset porch on the south wing, and elegant brick chimneys facing east and west. Inside, the place was exquisitely tasteful, a big center hall domain with Shaker and Hitchcock furniture, old family portraits and landscape paintings, and lots of fashionably threadbare orientals on polished wood floors.

When I got there, Pete was at the bar built into the north end of the spacious living room, spastically mixing up a batch of martinis in a big aluminum shaker raised over his shoulder. Amy Bess was the ideal hostess, a natural ego booster who could put anyone at ease. I had borrowed a new tweed jacket from Peter Scheer.

"Oh, just look at you, that tie and jacket together," she said as I came through the door. "I so love a boy who knows how to dress."

The guests that night included a Williams College professor, John Ott from the Shaker Village, the owner of a local silk mill, a lawyer related to the Millers, and many pretty wives. I test-piloted my first martini and, during dinner, was impressed by the view out the window of the comely oxbows turning silver under the moonlight.

One thing happened that night that affected me greatly. On an Elizabethan couch in the Millers' living room, I noticed two needlepoint pillows, quite expert I thought, unique. One was a tapestry pattern with a sort of American-primitive wild hare in the middle, the other a traditional oriental design. Pete was standing there and I asked him about the needlework.

"Hah! The needlepoint," he said. "I'm touched that you noticed, but my answer might take you aback. I am the author of those pillows."

I was surprised. Also, martini glaze on the brain was preventing my usual flow of speech. Pete jumped back in.

"Oh, let me explain, young man. Several years ago I was taken down for several weeks with an illness. I missed the newsroom terribly. Truth is, I was depressed. So, I started to do needlepoint, the only thing you can do in bed besides reading. Those pillows are mine."

The needlework on the pillows was impressive, but I was also surprised that Pete would speak to me about his depression. After a martini or two, Pete's glacial reserve seemed to melt a bit. He was relaxed, emotive, almost needy for companionship. It felt liberating, just to hear him talk about depression. Depression was a familiar companion of mine and many of my friends, but it was never dealt with, rarely discussed, and certainly not with a successful, prosperous adult. If you were Roman Catholic and got straight As in high school and college, depression simply wasn't happening to you.

Nobody had ever bothered to explain to me that for single men in their twenties, depression is practically axiomatic, the result of several anxieties—worrying about the future, about girlfriends, about submitting to the authority of a boss—all crashing in on each other.

Pete could see that I was meditating, not saying much. He decided to break the chill with a question, the Miller method.

"Depression. It's a killer. Have you ever had it?"

I knew that I had to speak now. I had to fess up. You didn't clam up and try to bullshit Pete Miller.

"Yes, Pete. I actually have. Since I was young, in fact."

"Yeah. That's when it starts. Tell me, does yours happen when you're anxious and in trouble, or when you're successful?"

Wow. Profound bells gonging in brain. I'd never thought about that before. How interesting.

"When I'm successful, Pete. You know, I graduated from college with honors. It was depressing as hell. I still can't figure out why."

"Right," Pete said. "Exactly. Well, here's the thing. You can't beat it. You just trick it. Change your schedule, go away, pick up something new. I did needlework. And anger. Anger and depression come as a pair. When I got that way, I'd just go into the paper early and write an editorial. The depression didn't disappear right away, see?"

"Yeah, but?"

"It was a good editorial," Pete said. "That's what everyone would say. Pete, that's your best editorial in several weeks. I didn't feel better right away, but I was distracted. You can't beat depression. Just trick it."

I accepted another martini from Pete and felt like a million bucks. I drove away from Williams Street that night considering myself as reformed as Saint Augustine. Pete was old and successful, renowned and rich. Not only did he experience depression, but he was willing to talk about it to a younger man with no fears of vulnerability. It was okay. I could admit it. All kinds of new thoughts flooded my brain. Maybe this explained my behavior, who I was, my antic appetite for motorcycles and planes and sex, the insatiable need I had for new views from peaks. Be successful, get depressed, run away. Pete had opened up a magic mental space for me. There were whole new things to consider.

. . .

The next morning, a Saturday, I decided to walk off my hangover by hiking up Mount Everett in south county. There's a good logging trail that winds up to the north-south escarpment and an old fire tower up top. From the summit, purple-black Appalachians fall in every direction with astounding views into five states—Massachusetts, the Catskills in New York, the Litchfield Hills in Connecticut, the Greens of Vermont, with New Hampshire's Monadnock poking through the northeastern horizon.

While I was up there, I couldn't resist one other sight. Far below, near the middle of the large bowl formed by Mount Everett and Butternut Basin, trainer planes from the short macadam strip at Great Barrington were circuiting the field, the pilots practicing their takeoffs and landings. I was broke now, a newspaper reporter, and couldn't afford to fly. My last flight was eight months ago. But flying had practically defined my life up until college and I missed it. So, why not? My logbook was in the car, my medical was still good. One modest forty-five-minute lesson wasn't going to break the bank. I scrambled back down the mountain and dead reckoned to the field by navigating against a bend in the Green River that I had seen from above.

The Great Barrington Airport turned out to be a pretty good find, a nice American place somewhere in between a public golf course and a town dump. In the pilots' shack, two old-timers on a worn Naugahyde couch were arguing with a young plumbing contractor about the relative merits of the Franklin versus the Continental engine. The most prominent art on the wall was a printed motto that read: **FARTING REQUIRED**. The owner of the place, Walt Kolodza, looked over my logs and agreed to take me up.

Walt was a pretty good airport geezer, a former test pilot of the Corsair fighter plane. He smoked cigars, pumped fuel with a bow tie on, and drove a long shiny Cadillac. He had this shitwreck old Piper Cherokee out on his line, the one with the bell-crank trim handle and a panic bar for brakes, 140-horse. I used my checklist and got up okay, and Walt told me to fly south for the practice area, which was over the Sheffield oxbows.

Walt asked me to do some tight turns and stalls, and then he pulled the power on me for an emergency landing check, and I did all right lining up and slipping down for an approach on the long fields of a sod farm. Then we flew back to Great Barrington and did a few takeoffs and landings. There was a strong crosswind blowing and we landed to the west. I was young and rusty but I'd been educated by the best there is, barnstorming-era pilots, and it was fun for me showing Walt how I liked to do it, holding my crab into the wind right down past the ground effect and then touching down first on the windward wheel. Bounce-bounce, skitter all over the runway. But that's okay. In a bad crosswind like that, landings are never pretty. The point is maintaining directional authority with the plane.

After the last landing, we taxied up to the fuel ramp and Walt opened the door to get out.

"Kid, there ain't much I can tell you about flying. Take her up for an hour and have some fun. It's on me, and welcome to our airport."

God, I thought, these mountains are perfect. So many good people.

I back-taxied down the strip and then got off briskly and curled tightly around into the wind, flying north for Greylock to familiarize myself with the area from the air. It was a beautiful evening with low cumulus hugging the summits, an orange disc for sun, and gentle turbulence on the lee side of the terrain. I circled Greylock a couple of times, shot a touch-and-go at North Adams, and then flew through the pastel dream-space along the Massachusetts-Vermont line, where the Berkshires and the Greens meet. The church spires of Williamstown and Bennington are lovely from the air, especially on an autumn evening, when the sun setting over the peaks colors them as glowing, pink tetrahedrons. Then I screamed back south quite low, through the Taconics on the New York side. Near Hillsdale, there's a good stretch of farms with dairy herds and lots of silos to buzz.

I drove home feeling triumphant about the day. One tall mountain, two hours of flight in good skies. It was a pip, a keeper. I was happy now, excited about the challenges I was facing every day, as good as old Joshua charging down his hill. New concepts were arriving almost daily. It was possible to be out in the world, working a job, and loving every last miserable inch of who I was.

II

—

Rossiter Road

—

CHAPTER EIGHT

Now that I could drink martinis with Pete Miller and survive Bill Bell, it was time to take on the next big challenge of personal growth, housing. But there wasn't any housing to take on. You could drive all day from Sheffield to North Adams and not find a single place to live. Peter Scheer and I were typical young renters, miserably so. Peter had rented space at a rundown old farm in Lanesboro, a fake hippie colony that reeked of hashish, carrot juice, and old motorcycle parts. Meanwhile, I had traded in my furnished room in Great Barrington for a bungalow on Laurel Lake in Lenox, which I rented from a gay anthropology professor whom I had met during one of my Thursday night prowls at the Lion's Den. The bungalow was hideously decorated with faux-Michelangelo busts, Acropolis curtains, and turquoise formica in the kitchen, and after a while I realized that I'd made a big mistake moving in there. The anthropology professor visited occasionally on weekends, waltzing through the rooms in hot blue Jockey briefs, a silk scarf, and cowboy boots with silver spurs.

It was Pat Faucett, with an assist from Amy Bess Miller, who came to our rescue. The year before, Pete Miller's brother Don had died of cancer, a loss that was still painfully felt at the *Eagle* because Don had been a very merry publisher whose partnership running the newspaper with Pete had inspired a great deal of confidence. Don's widow, Rhoda, had made matters worse by going right out and remarrying the first available man, a retired Canadian Army brigadier general whom she met during a recuperative swing through Europe. Nobody at the *Eagle* liked Rhoda very much and the newsroom rumor mill was vicious about her. Still, the House of Miller had an obligation to watch after her. Now, for the winter, late October through May, Rhoda and her brigadier general were going off for an extended honeymoon in Spain. The Millers needed someone to house-sit the place.

House-sitting a Miller property required flawless credentials. Don's manse was a grand old colonial with graceful and large additions thrown out at either side, and sat at the top of Rossiter Road, an attractive, hidden dirt lane out in the estate country of Richmond. Amy Bess had scoured the country for her brother-in-law, filling the rooms with expensive, museum-quality Shaker antiques. Pat Faucett, who handled this kind of chore for the Millers, wouldn't put just anyone in there. The Millers would be worried about parties, the potential damage to their antiques. They wouldn't want to put someone in there who smoked a lot, drank, or, God forbid, engaged in a lot of sex. Essentially, Pat was looking for two vestal virgins.

One afternoon in early October, Pat called to solicit my help in finding the right winter occupants for Don's house. She seemed to have made up her mind that a pair of women would be best. Pat was particularly curious about two single reporters in the newsroom at the time, Joy and Elaine, who were fairly typical of the *Eagle* style then. They were both graduates of good colleges, Bryn Mawr and the University of Virginia, and came from successful, middle-class families in suburban New York. I didn't know a blessed thing about Joy or Elaine, except that I'd seen Joy with her boyfriend once, down at Mundy's Bar. I considered them rather standoffish and prissy, and they weren't a part of my social set at all. But at this point, I'd realized that Don's place would be perfect for Peter and me, and I felt that I had a sincere obligation to help Pat make the right decision.

"Pat, I don't think you have to worry much about Joy and Elaine," I said. "They're totally normal."

"Oh," Pat said. "What's normal? I mean, Elaine smokes."

"Yeah, Pat, but let's be fair to Elaine, okay? She's cut back to one pack a day now, and I heard her say the other day that she's enrolling in a Stop Smoking course. She's really trying. It's her second time in the course."

"Oh," Pat said. "What about boyfriends? Rhoda doesn't want a lot of strangers in the house. Do you think they have a lot of boyfriends?"

"Nah," I said. "They seem to be totally normal that way."

"Oh," Pat said. "What's normal?"

"Pat, c'mon," I said. "They're totally normal. They both have two guys, you know, the regular alternating weekend kind of deal, but I'm not really part of their social set. I don't see them all the time. You know, probably, there's a third guy in there too. They're attractive, popular. Three guys apiece would be pretty normal for those two."

Don Miller had died the year before I arrived at the Eagle; *he had been a very merry publisher whose absence was still missed.*

"Oh," Pat said. "What about drinking? Rhoda wants me to be careful about that."

"Oh, you don't have to worry about Joy and Elaine," I said. "I've only seen Joy drunk once, and Elaine twice. Drinking's not a factor at all with those two. They're almost boring, you know? Totally normal."

"Oh," Pat said. "Okay. I'm going to think about this."

As soon as Pat got off the line, I dialed out to the Shaker Village and spoke with Amy Bess. I sweet-talked with her for a while about a story on Shaker rockers that I was promising to write, and then gently nudged the conversation over toward Don Miller's house.

"Oh, you mean that *you* might be interested in Don's place?" Amy Bess said. "Well, I can't intervene. This is Pat and Rhoda's decision. But do you want me to put in a word for you?"

"No, you don't have to do that, Amy Bess," I said. "Only if you felt like it."

"Oh but I *do* feel like it, Rinker. I *do!*"

By this time, I knew that Peter Scheer was regarded as an exceptionally wholesome young man, an ideal house-sitting candidate for the Millers. Peter was Tom Morton's newsroom darling, but not simply because he was a gifted writer and reporter. Peter was the second cousin of a legendary Berkshire County entrepreneur, Mervin Weinberg, the founder of the Adams Supermarket chain and one of the *Eagle*'s largest advertisers, who had originally set up an interview for him with Pete Miller. Mervin drove himself around New England searching for supermarket sites in a car equipped with a mobile phone, which was considered quite new and exotic then. From the car, Mervin was always calling Peter and inviting him over for the Rosh Hashanah or Yom Kippur holidays, and Tom Morton went wild every time it happened, inordinately impressed by Peter's relationship with a prominent New England retail tycoon. With Pat, Morton could be relied upon to vouch for Peter's outstanding moral character.

Peter had another major advantage, a superlatively talented and attractive girlfriend, Judy Lesser. Judy was a

Smith College Goddess who had instantly impressed everyone in the newsroom. While she was waiting around for a year to enter Harvard Law School, Judy was turning over one cylinder of her brain working as a special assistant to Massachusetts Governor Frank Sargent. She was spunky bright and fun-fun all the time, extremely driven, but with a very caring and cynical New York Jewish sensibility, and she brought a lot of glow to a room. Judy had a lovely oval face, a pageboy bob of black hair with natural brown highlights, and a petite, sleek body accentuated by strong but unpretentious dressing—lots of bosom-clinging leotards, short skirts, and sexy knickers. She and Peter were adorable together, a Jewish Ken and Barbie, and Judy had this one other quality that I noticed and admired in New York City Jewish girls that I'd known in college. She loved-loved-loved her man, and in almost any environment or setting, she wasn't afraid to snuggle up to him and show it. From the moment I laid eyes on Judy, I knew that we were all going to have a whale of a time being friends, and of course Peter seemed even more appealing for having a steady lover as good as this.

Of course, this was all a hideous crock, but that was part of Peter Scheer's enormous charm. In the two years that we were up there together, Peter Scheer banged more Berkshire beauties than any guy I know, certainly a lot more than the nearest competition, which was me. He smoked, Kents, drank like a sailor, and had a driving record worse than Evil Knievel's. But because of the Mervin Weinberg connection, and his drop-dead beauty of a girlfriend, Peter's character was considered flawless.

So, that narrowed the investigation down to me. Pat was pretty sure that I was being truthful about being a good Catholic. But she also knew that Catholics can be sneaky, especially at my age. Some of them, just a few young Catholics, had secret lives of drinking and sex. So, when Pat queried me about my social habits, I considered it my job to reassure her. I didn't want her to be disillusioned about the guy from the large Catholic family that she had encouraged Pete Miller to hire.

"Rinker, I'm not quite as naïve as you might think," Pat said. "I mean Peter has that wonderful, steady girlfriend, Judy, you know? What about you? Aren't there any girls in your life?"

"Pat, there's one thing about me that you really need to understand, okay?" I said. "I work so hard at the *Eagle* all week that all I want to do on a weekend is light a fire, curl up onto the couch, and read a book. That's my social life. Books."

"Oh, see, I knew, *I just knew!*" Pat said. "That's what Amy Bess said. 'That Rinker Buck knows so much about the Shakers already I'll bet you the only thing he does is read books.'"

It didn't take long for the deal to come together after that. A few days later, Peter and I were dispatched out to Don's old place in Richmond for inspection by Rhoda Miller and her general, and we drove out there one afternoon, gorging on breath mints and mouthwash, so that Rhoda wouldn't suspect that we smoked. They showed us the house, which was quite definitely top out-of-sight, with extraordinary flow between the large rooms. From the exquisitely furnished dining room on the east end, you could look straight through for fifty feet or more to the elegant, Pall Mall Club cherry wainscoting of the den. There was a separate guest suite with a full bathroom built into the den wing on the south end of the house. Upstairs, where Don Miller had lived, there was a long warren of comfortable, cozy rooms decorated out of *Town and Country* magazine.

The house tour over, Rhoda sat us down on the leather couch in the den and explained that the property was being offered to us only under certain, strict terms. Although we would pay no rent, Rhoda's regular maid would continue to let herself in a couple days a week to sweep and clean up, and the caretaker of the property would keep us stocked in firewood and drive over twice a day to feed and look after the dogs, a pair of spotted English setters. In return for that, Rhoda explained, all she wanted was a "quiet pair of boys" who didn't smoke, drink, or throw a lot of parties with their girlfriends. Peter earnestly heaved her a huge bag of Eddie Haskell bullshit on this subject, but all I could do was look

The Rossiter Road manse. Inside, on the couch where we promised Don Miller's widow that we would neither smoke, nor drink, nor feel up girls, we smoked and drank and felt up girls.

down through the big rooms and imagine the fun we were going to accomplish in here with a couple of ski bunnies.

Partnering up with Scheer performed wonders on my ego. He was very effective at creating a favorable first impression, the glow of which passed onto me, I felt. After our inquisition by Rhoda Miller, Pat seemed very enthusiastic.

"Oh, Rinker!" Pat said when she called me the next day. "Rhoda was very impressed. Peter was very talkative, she said, and you were very quiet and polite."

We moved into the Rossiter Road house over the long Columbus Day weekend in October. Peter selected the guest suite behind the den, and I got Don Miller's old haunt up in the east wing, room after room of Shaker four-posters and oriental rugs. Strolling through the broad, open rooms of the house, Peter and I were jubilant and couldn't believe our good fortune. The place was ours until the Memorial Day weekend the following year. That evening, we lit a fire in the den and mixed ourselves some drinks from the full wet bar, conveniently located in between the den and the main living room. Peter found a box of cigars in there and we lit up a couple of those too.

"Hey," Peter said. "You want to hit Alice's Restaurant tonight?"

"Nah," I said. "Let's start at the Westbridge. Then we'll hit Mundy's and see if there's any Riggs Girls around."

"Yeah, sure," Peter said. "Sounds like a program."

There was one aspect of moving into Don's place that was particularly enjoyable. I had worked my way through college in Maine performing gofer work for my professors, splitting firewood, painting rooms, and rescuing Volvos from snowbanks. All of my tools—axes and mauls, chains and come-along gears, my Homelite chain saw—were crated in a box that I had stored with friends back in Maine. As soon as I got out to Richmond, I called up to Maine and had my crate of tools shipped down on a Greyhound bus.

It was nirvana, being reunited with my come-alongs and Homelite saw. Right away, I drove down to Baldwin Hardware in West Stockbridge and did a big shop—new filters and chains for the saw, my first five-gallon gas can, a chain file, lumber and bolts to build a sawbuck. The Miller place had a good woodshed behind the house, with acres of forest all around, and the caretaker preferred to deliver just logs, not finished, split firewood. It was great getting all that exercise again, feeling my upper arms and chest firm up from the work. The woodpile grew, and when I got ahead of the caretaker, I ranged out into the woods for fallen limbs, or thinned out the small shaggy-bark cherry and maple.

I was excited now. The snow came early that year and I loved the new, felicitous mixture of life and work. Every day I rose at five, made coffee and a quick breakfast, and chopped wood for an hour before waking Peter up and then bounding over the hills for the *Eagle*.

.   .   .

Judy Lesser drove out from Boston every Friday night in a yellow Ford Maverick that was a miracle of transportation. Judy was an astonishingly reliable driver and crashed the Maverick at least once a month, taking out one fender or door at a time. Her appointments at her auto-body shop in Boston were as regular as her appointments at her hairdresser's, but this was good, Judy thought, because her Maverick was perpetually being rebuilt and repainted and always looked brand new. The proprietors at her auto-body shop, Vinny and Rico, were infatuated with Judy and would do anything for her, so they just kept a permanent stock of Maverick hoods and grilles for her, twelve months of the year. On Friday evening, at 7:30 or 8, we'd see her headlights poking through the trees and hear the straight-six engine lugging in third gear—she always forgot to downshift for the last hill. Sometimes, Judy made the turn off the dirt lane and missed the big maple at the edge of the gravel driveway, but usually she timed it just right and hit it. But it was comforting, hearing her pull up outside. Through the frosted panes of the den windows, we'd hear the sound of a bumper and fender scraping against tree bark, and then one last wheeze as the Maverick landed on the snowbank.

"Hey!" Peter would exclaim, putting down his drink before the fire that I'd made in the den. "Jude's here! It's JUUUUDY!"

Being around Peter and Judy was enormously relaxing for me. They weren't simply beautiful and hilariously witty together. I had grown up exclusively around Christians and never been close to a couple who were as warm and openly affectionate as them. At night, sitting by the fire in the room where we'd promised Rhoda Miller that we'd never smoke or drink or feel up girls, we smoked and drank while Peter and Judy felt each other up, and then we'd get into these long, tangled arguments about the new David Halberstam book or Erica Jong's *Fear of Flying*. I liked being around women who were smarter than I was, and Judy's mind was both capacious and very quick. When she weighed in, explaining to us how we should really feel about Watergate or the Cuban Missile Crisis, Peter and I had to face the truth about ourselves. We had Ken-L Ration for brains.

Judy had another compelling trait. Her love for humanity in general and guys in particular didn't have bounds—she had to express feelings for everyone who was around. When we all sat on the couch together, Judy would grab me by the neck or the shirt collar and pull me down toward them, hugging me and inviting me to return the warmth, so that we were all group-groping together after a while.

After Peter dozed off on her lap, Judy and I could talk alone. Sharing intimate conversation with a close friend's girlfriend, I decided, was almost better than having a babe of my own. Because I wasn't trying to impress or make Judy, I could just be myself. And Judy was refreshingly direct. There were things about me that were fun but Peter couldn't provide, and vice versa, and she enjoyed bombing out to the mountains for the weekend, having both of us to pal around with. Jewish boyfriends, for example, didn't chop a lot of wood, and she'd never been around someone who so enjoyed scrambling around his woodpile all weekend. On Saturday evening, during our group grope on the couch, she'd squeeze my biceps.

"Hey, chopper-boy, how many cords of wood did you split this week?"

"Ah, not much, Judy. One or two."

"Yeah, well, it's really attractive the way you're outdoors all the time, doing things. Peter's very different that way, you know? These fires you make us are so nice. Oh, and you know there's one other thing I want to thank you for."

"What?"

"For making the worst part of my week the best part of my week. When I drive back to Boston now? I feel so happy. Peter's not lonely now. You're taking care of him. Thanks."

Good moments like that were spaced throughout the day. On Saturday and Sunday mornings, we invariably followed the same routine. Peter slept way late for my taste, until 8:30 or 9, but Judy was sleep-gaited like me and rose early. I'd work out in the woods for a couple of hours and then come in at 7 in the morning, finding her bustling around the kitchen in one of her knockout outfits—a tight, spandex turtleneck that profiled her perky, calisthenic breasts, and sexy black knickers. In the kitchen, while Judy baked challah bread and made me a breakfast of bacon and eggs, we flirted and laughed, discussing my latest girlfriend problems or the books we were reading. Then I'd round up my saw and come-along chains and head back out for the woods with the English setters.

When he woke up, Peter had a problem, the same damn problem every Saturday morning, which was Judy's car. It was stuck in the snowbank and blocking the drive, tying up three cars at once. This was a problem because at noon they needed to drive. The burden of being Judy was awesome. She generally rose at dawn to hit the kitchen, baking up an oven-load of challah and planning dinner that night, and then she read all of her reports from the governor's office, flirted with me for an hour, and then broke for a phone chat with her mother or sister down in New York, or just a needy friend who she knew that she should call. By the middle of the day the poor little rich girl was exhausted by all this work and emotive devotion. To clear her head, she just needed the good commercial air of a shopping district in Lenox or Stock-bridge. Peter was very good for her that way; he didn't mind taking his woman shopping, even though it was boring as hell. And Judy had this witty, intelligent sense of humor about herself.

"Hey, does anyone mind if I shut down and stop being brilliant for the rest of the day?" she said. "I'm reverting to JAP, okay? I shop, therefore I am."

God, it was awesome how Judy and Peter could do the marathon JAP shop. They'd come in at the end of the day laden down with all this *stuff*, tchotchkes-in-a-bag—glass vases with dead flowers and cattails sticking out, Lilliputian Japanese tea sets, a new corduroy shirt for Peter, a ski-bunny down vest for Judy,

Judy Lesser, spunky-bright and fun-fun all the time, was a Smith College Goddess who instantly impressed everyone who met her.

new table napkins and wax candles, baskets, pantyhose and cosmetics, exotic coffees and deserts for dinner, just an amazing amount of shit. It was all worthless, but they enjoyed buying it together.

Eventually, all this loot ended up in the Maverick trunk, and then, after Judy had backed into a UPS truck, Vinny and Rico would have to take it all out before they rebuilt the rear end. Vinny and Rico were too horny and dumb to know what was happening to them. But Judy knew. She considered it historic justice. At last the Jews were getting back at the Romans.

Peter accepted his fate. After breakfast, he headed out to the snowbank in the drive to free up the Maverick. I'd be out in the woods, wailing away with the Homelite, but I could always tell what Peter was up to. The smell of burnt clutch rubber and refried transmission fluid wafted down to me in the forest. He was really spinning the tires up there, rocking the Maverick back and forth. Ah, shitbag. Here we go. It's Saturday morning and Peter has hung up the Maverick again. Gathering up my come-along and chains, bringing the maul along in case I needed it, I walked up to the drive.

When I got there, Peter was sitting in the stalled Maverick and pounding the steering wheel. He'd ripped the filter off a Kent and was violently smoking it, to bring that nicotine in raw.

"Fuck! Fuck, Fuck, Fuck, Fuck! I am so F-U-C-K-I-N-G pissed! Goddammit, Judy."

When he saw me, Peter got out and kicked the door of the car. Instead of merely being wedged in by the bumper, the way Judy had "parked" it last night, the Maverick was now on top of the snowbank, thoroughly dug in.

"Fuck!" Peter said.

"Peter?" I said.

"Okay, okay, okay. I know. I'm pissed off at her because I'm angry at myself. I made it worse."

"Peter," I said. "Go in the house."

"No! C'mon Rinker, I want to help. It's not fair to you. I should help this time."

"Peter?"

"What!"

"In the house."

"Okay, okay. I'll just finish my cigarette."

"Fuck your cigarette. In the goddamn house. *Now!*"

"Okay, okay, okay. See? I'm going in the house."

It was enjoyable out there, once I got rid of Scheer. I liked the solitary work. Extracting the Maverick from a snowbank after Peter and Judy were done with it was a bit like root canal work, chip a little here with the shovel underneath the rear axle, whack there with the maul, but don't hit the tranny, ease her downslope. When I was almost down to level terrain, it wasn't hard from there to get finished by running the come-along and chains between the rear chassis and the trunk of the big maple. Afterward, I always opened up the hood and checked all the connections and fluids, then ran the Maverick down past Roger Linscott's place at the end of Rossiter Road, to make sure that the brakes were okay and that Peter had not burned out the clutch. The vehicle was now signed off for its next demolition-derby run into Boston.

An hour or two later, as they departed for Judy's therapeutic shop, I stood in the drive waving them off, filled with the best feelings for them. They were so lovely together, caring and funny, just the right amount of fucked up, two new people in my life so willing to express affection and how they felt about themselves, and me. I could enjoy the rest of the day alone, chopping wood or hiking up on the peaks. Late in the afternoon, as the sun fell behind the Taconics and the woods turned bluish, Peter and Judy would roll back in and unload their bags from the car. We all enjoyed one of Judy's dinners together and then group-groped on the couch before the fire. When I turned in for bed, my muscles and joints ached from chopping wood. But with Peter and Judy in the house, I always felt emotionally safe.

·   ·   ·

One Thursday night in November, Judy called from Boston to say that she was coming out for the weekend, but she was feeling deprived of female companionship and missed her old Smith College friends. The atmosphere with just Peter and me around was too masculine sometimes. So, Judy had invited her friend Betty Sudarsky to come along. Betty was goofing off that year, commuting between her parents' house in West Hartford and her boyfriend's in Northampton, while she figured out her life. Betty was tall and willowy, with attractive, thin legs, a deadly sense of humor, and she was a very able Book Turd as well. Often, after Judy left for Boston on Sunday night, Betty would elect to stay behind with us for several days, and she even worked part-time at the *Eagle* for a while, and Peter and I loved having her around.

One Saturday afternoon just before Thanksgiving, I came in from the woods while Judy and Betty were sitting on the couch together, chatting and gossiping, working away on these dorky little plant-holder and dried-flower kits that Judy would bring back from her marathon shops. Judy and Betty were supremely attractive as a pair, two Smith College Goddesses with excellent smirky-smiles. They followed me with their eyes as I crossed the room with a load of firewood in my arms and then stoked the fire.

"Hey, Rinker, guess what?" Betty said. "I am going to fix you up with the brainiest, most beautiful girl in the world. Her name is Comfort Halsey."

"Oh my God. Comfort Halsey," Judy said. "Comfort is the most godawesome beautiful shiksa I've ever seen. She's perfect for Rinker."

I couldn't believe what I was hearing here, because I already knew Comfort Halsey. Comfort was the daughter of the headmaster at the all-girls school in New Jersey that most of my teenage girlfriends attended. The place was called the Kent Place School, which inevitably got translated by all the local boys into "Cunt Place." The school was a big, fenced-in compound with Tudor-style classroom buildings and broad green athletic fields, and whenever I drove in there to pick up one of my girlfriends, there would be all these tanned and blonde rich girls with exquisite thin legs, chasing around in short tartan skirts and shin-guards, whacking away at each other with field hockey sticks. I had seen Comfort Halsey there, but only from a distance—she was tall and irrepressibly cheerful, with the sweetest personality and high chirpy voice, an ultima rich girl. But Comfort was too top out-of-sight for me to ever ask out.

Betty went over the moon when I told her that I already knew Comfort, her matchmaking impulse on a rampage.

"Oh my God, Rinker, please don't tell me this," Betty said. "You're such an idiot. You mean you *know* Comfort and you never asked her out? Judy, we're doing this. End of story. Case closed. Next weekend? Comfort gets handcuffed and is coming up here, for Rinker."

"Oh my God, Betty, this is so, so cute," Judy said. "Rinker's blushing. He's afraid to date Comfort. There is actually a girl too beautiful for Rinker. We're doing this, Betty."

"Look, you two girls can just stick your heads in a bucket of manure, all right?" I said. "Comfort Halsey is way too nice for me, and she's not coming up here. If it will make you feel any better, I'll go to Mundy's tonight and find a ski bunny, okay?"

"Oh, Judy, this is just so *perfect*," Betty said. "Comf and Rinker. We're doing it."

"Yeah, this is going to be so much fun," Judy said. "Grade A Wasp meets our little logger-boy, you know? I can't freaking wait."

As I headed across the house to take a shower before dinner, I could hear Judy and Betty behind me on the couch together, laughing hysterically, goosing each other, making plans.

"Rinker! We're doing it. Comfort Halsey is *you!*"

Well, I have to admit that it was absolutely great to see Comfort Halsey again. Betty arranged for Comfort to come up just after Thanksgiving, so we all had a long, chummy weekend in the big house together.

Four years of college had perfected Comfort out. She was a bit taller now with a minute but appropriate weight gain, thoroughbred shoulders and lithe swinging arms, and a face with exquisite aquiline features. Her pout was straight out of

John Singer Sargent. Restrained but awesome natural beauty. Comfort had this one other exceedingly rare trait for a Wasp, a recessive Latin gene left over from the Roman occupation, and she would tan up beautifully after just a few minutes on snowshoes on a sunny day. I would look at Comfort and just laugh at myself, at all men, for preferring huge bosoms. Her figure was modest but beautifully proportioned, up there in the Greek Goddess League.

I didn't waste a minute with Comfort. As soon as she arrived, I wanted that incomparable beauty of hers out where it belonged, in the Marsden Hartley scenery and air, ice-skating or snowshoeing. The skating pond was just below the house, very private and pastoral, surrounded by a lovely birch forest. It was wonderful the way Comfort walked down the hill with me, thrusting her arm into mine, chattering away about Edward Hopper's lighthouses or Emily Dickinson's poetry, and making all these wonderfully old-fashioned requests, such as would I tighten the laces on her skates or make a outdoor fire to warm us when we rested.

Meanwhile, Judy and Betty were excited. When Comfort and I were alone together, just sitting quietly on the couch and talking, Judy and Betty were smirky-smiling from across the room, poking each other in the ribs if I touched Comfort's hand. Rinker had his Porcelain Protestant Beauty now and they were determined that this would work. While Comfort and I were down on the pond skating, matchmakers Judy and Betty were watching from the window of the den.

Oh my God, oh my God, Betty check this out. He's holding her hand now, look at the way they do it, this hands-on-hips skating thing. God they're so corny, Christians are so weird, the Currier and Ives trip. Dammit, Rinker do it, c'mon, do it, you wimp. God, he's so retarded, you know? He takes so long. Betty, look! Holy shit! He kissed her! Oh this is great. This is so freaking great, Betty. They're making out.

Comfort was interesting in a number of other ways. She was touchingly close to her friend Betty and also devoted to her family, which was unusual in the wake of the countercultural influences that had roiled through families in the late

1960s. I also intuitively sensed that she had another boyfriend back in Princeton, New Jersey, where she taught at a day school, asked her about it, and she was honest and forthcoming about that. There was another guy. I discovered that I enjoyed the emotional ambiguity of that, of never knowing for sure, and living with jealousy. It seemed to free me just to enjoy her as she was, when she was there, without trying to force the relationship further.

Besides, it wasn't a secret to any of the Smith College Goddesses that Peter and I were hardly sexual angels. During the week, as soon as Judy and her Yellow Maverick disappeared over the horizon for the Mass Pike, Peter and I ranged out. Our ex-girlfriends from college visited and frequently stayed for several days, and we both enjoyed flings with ski bunnies and *Eagle* staffers. We were very reasonable and mature about this, I thought. Fidelity is a very advanced level of the game, and Peter and I didn't want to push it until we were ready for that big step.

Comfort gave me one other gift that winter. She preferred to be chaste. We were very affectionate and loving together, and I enjoyed nothing more than clasping up to her in the four-poster bed in my room, talking softly and joking about things, sharing thoughts about Betty and our other friends, cupping my hand up to her comely neck and enjoying her flannel night-gown warmth as I fell asleep, soothed by her personality and goodness. Her body was regal and thin, as attractive as any that I had ever been near. But no fucking. Her chastity desire

Comfort Halsey cut a portrait straight out of John Singer Sargent, and her personal restraint made romance mysterious and complex.

broke me through to a new place. I enjoyed the challenge of learning new behavior, of satisfying her expectations, which seemed to lock me in a new embrace with femininity. I was fascinated by how various women were, how unique each of their demands, and how protean I could be in responding to their wishes. When my ex-girlfriend from college visited, we often logged in the woods for several hours together, which turned us both on, and then we returned to this same four-poster and made love all afternoon—she wanted more, more, more, and stamina in a man was her big demand. Merrill, a ski instructor at Catamount whom I occasionally dated over the winter, worshiped oral sex, so I got into that, big time. But with Comfort I was chaste. The choices that women made for me were a lot more thrilling than the choices I might make on my own. Serve her. Keep her happy. You never know what she might ask next. Comfort's restraint made sex even more mysterious and complex.

Besides, there was a pleasing emotional swirl to the Rossiter Road house now. In the morning I rose early and chastely, logged for an hour or two in the woods, and then, out on the skating pond, cleared the snow that had fallen overnight. When I got back into the house, Judy was alone in the kitchen, bustling around in her sexy knickers and an apron.

"Rinker, is Comfort still asleep up there? Oh, she's such a beautiful sleepyhead, you know? Let's make her breakfast in bed."

"Yeah, what the hell," I said. "She'll probably like that."

So, goofing off and flirting together, Judy and I whipped up some bacon and eggs, and Judy was very adept at stashing all these parsley garnishes, cut-up pieces of fruit and other doodads on the tray, so that the finished product looked like it had just come out of the kitchen of the Plaza Hotel.

Judy handed the breakfast tray over with a gentle smile and squeezed my arm.

"Okay, okay," she said. "Now Rinker, don't go up there and pull your macho-boy shit on her, all right? *Be nice.* Treat her gently. Comfort's really special and you have to treat her right."

"Yeah, yeah, yeah, Judy. I think I can handle that. Christ."

When I got up to the bedroom, Comfort rolled over sleepily, lovely and tan in her flannel nightgown, smiling and grateful for the room service. She was just the most gorgeous girl in the world, and I loved pleasing her that way. While she ate, I sat on the corner of the bed and stroked her leg underneath the blanket.

"Oh, Rinker, look! The pond is clear. After breakfast, can we go skating?"

.   .   .

One last pair brightened our weekends at the Richmond house, and they were quite an education. Judy and Betty both had younger sisters, sixteen and seventeen years old, two tight-body filly JAPs, one having followed older sister Judy to Fieldston, the other following Betty to Loomis Chaffee. They were the ultimate Lolita dream. Black-on-black pageboy hair, sexy, spandex-body-action dressing, and great—and I do mean *great*—automatic facial smirks. Judy and Betty adored having their younger sisters around, and Peter and I were content because entertaining the little sisters made the Smith College Goddesses so happy. All weekend, a warm sisterly embrace filled the house. It was fun, too, for the younger sisters. *Oh yeah, like, you know like it will be our college-weekend warm-ups, you know? Judy's Peter is picking us up at the bus station.* Peter named them. They were "the nymphets."

The little sisters were quite mature, top out-of-sight beyond their years. In the evenings, the little sisters would join Judy, Betty, and Comfort in the kitchen, helping their older sisters fix up a dinner of beef Stroganoff and noodles, gabbing away about their college plans, their boyfriends, or some art history essay that Comfort was helping them with. Peter and I knew that we weren't welcome in there. But it was great JAP shoptalk, with a bit of the Porcelain Protestant Beauty thrown in, and we couldn't resist being with them, sneaking in there to listen. Peter and I would make up some dogmeat excuse to wander into the kitchen—more ice for our drinks, a cheese and crackers refill—and we'd hear the most amazing things.

"Oh yeah, well, like, you know? I was going to wait on it with him, I was really into like waiting and everything, like our relationship wasn't ready for this yet. But then he popped the tickets to the concert on me. Like, you know, then I was ready. We went right upstairs and did it."

Peter and I were shocked. The girls we dated before college weren't this advanced. We had waited, like, forever.

"You *what?*" Peter asked. "What? What did you do upstairs with your boyfriend? Judy, we really need to talk about this."

"Peter, shut up," Judy said. "Get your ice and leave."

The little sisters ganged up on him too.

"Oh, Peter, like, don't be so naïve. I mean I know this is like real weird for you and you're like getting your rocks off and everything, but, like, it's not what you think. I *love* my boyfriend. I do it for *love.*"

"Okay, Judy, now this is *serious*," Peter said. "Do you realize what your younger sister is talking about? Your *younger* sister, Jude."

"Peter, shut up and get out of here," Judy said. "I'm talking with my younger sister and I don't need some horny jerk like you around, okay? Out of the kitchen. *Now!*"

"And that includes you too, Rinker Buck," Betty said. "Did I invite Fred MacMurray in here? No. I'm talking with my younger sister. Now get out. *Immediately.*"

Peter and I went back into the den, threw some logs on the fire, and got smashed. We were morose about it. Women just had so much more fun than men, and their level of candor with each other was alluring. If our younger brothers had visited, we would never sit around the kitchen all night and talk about their future college careers or their sex lives. We would talk about the new Shelby Mustang or hydraulic log-splitters. Being a man was just a total letdown, a prescription for boredom, and Peter and I had to face the truth about ourselves. We had Ken-L Ration for emotions too.

After dinner, Peter and I were tired and lazy from consuming several helpings of beef Stroganoff, wine, and challah, and we just wanted to collapse on the couch, do the group-grope with the Smith College Goddesses, and doze off in front of the fire. But no. The little sisters insisted. They had worked hard all weekend, writing art history essays with Comfort, skating in circles around the pond, yapping their heads off while they helped their older sisters cook dinner. Now they just wanted to blow it all out and do a real college-weekend warm-up.

"Okay, like, I mean, you know? You guys are taking us to Mundy's Bar. Period, end of conversation. The bitch feels like dancing."

The little sisters were ideal for Mundy's, junior Jacob's Pillow girls. Their bodies were gorgeous because they were so young and limber, with all this great ultra-action spandex movement from the hips. They enjoyed being sexy and showing us how well they could dance. *Wow! What a weekend! No boyfriends to worry about! Peter, like, buy us drinks, okay?* The band was the same one from the summer, and the little sisters dancing together really made the night at Mundy's. Bump those hips and lean down together, do the spastic nylon-body-limber together, God we're good together, we're *hot*, we're cool, we're sexy, we're showing the older sisters how outrageous we are and just loving our weekend with them. By the second or third dance they had thrown off their sweaters and all they had on underneath were skimpy T-shirts. Perspiration glistened on their necks and moisture rings showed off their perky, smart-aleck breasts. The band refused to stop and just played on and on for them. Everyone watched, and the lesbians over in the corner just loved the way those spandex-body teens went at it. *Hey, check out these two little chicks. They're great together.* The whole place stared in awe as the little sisters dirty-danced.

At home, the younger sisters were finally spent and wanted to go to bed. They ran off together to change upstairs in my wing. In the den, Peter and Judy were snuggled up together on one end of the leather couch, Comfort and Betty were leaning shoulder to shoulder at the other end, looking at the cartoons in *The New Yorker*, and I was bustling about, bringing in wood for the fireplace and filling the ice bucket for nightcaps.

The little sisters came back down to say good night in their Lolita pajamas, turquoise and all-black cotton long johns that showed off their slinky bodies. I loved the way they all said good night, the affection and open physical warmth of thoroughbred JAPs out of West Hartford and New York. *Oh, good night Judy, good night Comfort, good night Betty, you guys were so cool to take us dancing.* With their slinky bodies in the long johns, they leaned down and kissed lips to pageboy hair, lips to lips, and lips to forehead, stroking each other's shoulders and hugging. The Smith College Goddesses and their pretty younger sisters weren't afraid to touch each other and to embrace, crashing their breasts together as they said good night. The little sisters especially loved Comfort, smooching up to Comfort's baby-skin cheeks, which they prolonged, because she was so beautiful to be near. When they disappeared through the living room, holding hands and giggling together, Judy, Betty, and Comfort sighed and smiled, looking at each other.

Oh, God, the little sisters. They're smart, they're hip, they're so beautiful and cool together. What great lives they're going to have.

When they got to the top of the stairs the little sisters called back down, almost in unison.

"Hey, Comfort! Comfort Halsey!"

"What? What dear?"

"Thanks for the help on the essays! We're going to get As!"

"Go to sleep, girls. We love you!"

The end of the year, November and December, was difficult for me now. I'd spent a few Christmases away from my family recently and found that I enjoyed the escape from family obligations. My father wasn't well and sounded desperate on the phone, and my mother made me feel guilty for not coming home—the younger children, she insisted, missed me so much. But there would be great parties up here, if I stayed in the Berkshires for Christmas. The holiday season was hell, because I was perpetually torn between pro forma family obligations and a selfish need to start leading my own life.

But it would work out this year, I felt, either way. I was up in the mountains in the Miller manse, cushioned by the bosom of assimilated America. Peter and Judy, Betty, Comfort, and I were enjoying a good weekend. In the morning I would wake chastely, and the scent of fresh challah would fill the house. I'd chop wood and join Judy in the kitchen for an hour, and then go for a snowshoe with Comfort. Peter and Judy would make the big grocery shop, enough to last us a week. A good, new friend for me, two awesome JAPs, and the Porcelain Protestant Beauty. The spandex body-action teens. They were the Everything Girls and Peter and I were lords, so to speak, of our own manor.

CHAPTER NINE

IN EARLY December, while crossing the newsroom one morning, I heard something that made my heart stop. John Wayne was coming to town. Something called the Cowboy Hall of Fame in Oklahoma City had commissioned a portrait of the Duke, replete with cowboy hat, leather vest, and six guns, to be painted by the American King of Corn, Stockbridge's Norman Rockwell. I couldn't resist this merging of primal American motif. Wayne, the embodiment of Hollywood's exaggerated Old West, would be meeting with the eternal old fart of New England, Norman Rockwell, who'd made his fame epitomizing adorable babysitters and lovable runaway boys on the cover of *The Saturday Evening Post*. The story was mine and I had to do it.

It wasn't merely Wayne the man and the actor, the hero of *The Alamo, True Grit,* or *Green Berets,* that I wanted, although that would have been rich enough. Wayne was up to his ears in Watergate right now and had become that coveted interview code-named "FOP," or "friend of the prez." President Richard Nixon had other celebrity defenders—the evangelist Billy Graham, the morally upright performer Sammy Davis Jr.—but none were as famous as the Duke. Wayne had enthusiastically supported Nixon's election in 1968 and his re-election in 1972, and stood by the president and Henry Kissinger's Vietnam policies all through the bombing of North Vietnam and the comic-opera Paris peace talks, the student strikes, and the marches on Washington. Wayne had been notably embarrassed, that October, when his vice presidential pal, Spiro Agnew, got caught with the milk lobby cash in a brown paper bag and was forced to resign. But he was the Duke, the hero who slaughtered Indians, chased the Mexicans back across the Rio Grande, and aw-shucksed up to women, and he wasn't going to back down now that his president was in trouble. The national press was hounding him, scrambling for quotes every time Wayne stepped out in L.A. It was undignified for the Duke, being chased by all these rat terriers from the press. So, he had clammed up. No more interviews, no grab-quotes on the street, the publicists said. The Duke had gone underground and the first reporter to get to him would enjoy fifteen minutes of fame.

Step aside Woodward and Bernstein. The Book Turd from *The Berkshire Eagle* is coming to the rescue, heading off the Duke at the West Stockbridge Pass. I was instantly obsessed about it. I *had* to get the Duke and make him spill his guts.

Incredibly, the south county reporter already assigned the story didn't want to do it. He was typical of many of the "town news" reporters assigned to the outlying villages, a capable ambulance chaser but intellectually lazy, and he didn't see the possibilities of doing Wayne up big. Besides, he was annoyed that the Wayne story would require him to work on a weekend. So, I cooked up a story—one of my girlfriends, I told him, was "making me" take her to lunch at the Red Lion on Saturday anyway—and the gullible flunky cheerfully gave up one of the best stories of the year.

Meanwhile, out in Hollywood, John Wayne's publicists didn't want to have anything to do with my plan. The *Eagle* wasn't even supposed to know that Wayne was planning on being in town, and the large talent agency that managed the star's press had already decreed: no interviews, no press. But I was persistent and went over the head of the first two flacks I spoke with, and the agency finally turned me over to Wayne's personal publicist.

The publicist was a total crabcake, a male bitch. Well, since *I* represent *Mr. Wayne*, and you merely represent *The Berkshire Bird* or whatever it is, *we're* not doing an interview! Screw you, buddy, I've got a plan going in the back of my head here. Just give me fifteen minutes with the Duke.

"Oh, so *you* want fifteen minutes with *Mr. Wayne*? I'll see if he's interested."

I detested kissing this guy's ass, but I knew that I had to do it.

"Sir, I really thank you so much."

"And look here. *No* Watergate, *no* Richard Nixon, *no* politics *what-so-ever!* Those are the terms. You can't *mug him* on Watergate."

"Sir, I am not interested in that subject. Mr. Wayne is coming to Stockbridge to pose for a portrait. I merely want to ask him if he's planning any more films."

An hour later the crabcake called me back and told me that Wayne would do it, just fifteen minutes, out of courtesy to the great Norman Rockwell. The artist's people had been bugging the talent agency all week, hoping to get some mileage out of the visit by Wayne. The publicist gave me the name of the agency's associate vice president to the senior vice president of all publicity for talent, who would be traveling to Stockbridge to be with the Duke. I was to be at the Red Lion at eleven sharp tomorrow morning.

"And remember," the crabcake said, "you have exactly fifteen minutes with Mr. Wayne. That's *it*, you hear?"

Yeah, buddy, I thought, and go perform on yourself an impossible physical act.

"Sir," I said, "I thank you so much."

So, a little bit of victory so far, but not much. Fifteen minutes with the Duke hardly fit the extravagant literary demands of the Book Turd. I would need more time. But I did have one big ace in my pocket, I thought. She was an old girlfriend, my personal Desdemona, the inimitable Helen Hartley Platt.

Harty's family was old, old money, and their summer home was an attractive white farmhouse down the road in "The Little Berkshires" of northwest Connecticut, in Norfolk. At the moment, Harty was pursuing higher education at a small hippie colony over in New York State, Bard College. But she kept her horse, a magnificent bay hunter, in Norfolk. On the occasional weekend when Comfort Halsey or my old college girlfriend wasn't around, I'd go down to Norfolk to see Harty. Harty was usually at her parents' place in Connecticut by early Friday afternoon.

As soon as I got off the phone with Wayne's publicist I dialed Harty in Norfolk. I knew the number by heart and I started mentally channeling through to her right away. Harty, you've got to *be* there for me this time. *Be* there, woman. Do *not* be going out with that worthless hippie art professor this weekend.

Pay dirt. Harty picked up on the third ring.

"Rinky! Rinky! Rinky! Oh its so good to hear your voice. How *are* you, Rinky?"

"Harty, I'm fine. But look. I've got this plan going here, okay?"

"Rinky. Stop. You haven't even asked me how *I* am, and you've got some plan going. You're a jerk."

"Harty, look. C'mon. Let me just say it, okay? If I say it, you'll understand right away."

"Rinky, you are a total pill. No 'hello, how are you, I still love you, how's your boyfriend' or anything, just oh, heah babe, hello, I've got a plan. I mean sometimes Rinky the way you treat me—"

"Harty. John Wayne is coming to town and we're going to meet him."

"Oh my God. *The* John Wayne? The Duke?"

"The Duke, Harty. It's the Duke. But look, I need your help."

"Rinky, I'm there for you, you know that. Especially if it's really John Wayne. But, number one, if you're lying, I am going to murder you. Number two, why didn't you tell me in the first place?"

I gave Harty the scoop—the Norman Rockwell visit, my appointment with the Duke, the measly fifteen minutes, how I needed her to stall for time while I maneuvered the Duke toward the big Watergate quote. Harty couldn't have cared less about Watergate. She was in a league of her own and didn't have to waste time like other rich girls, furtively studying *The New York Times* up in their bedroom so they could sound politically adroit at grandma's dinner party. But while we talked, I could tell that Harty knew everything, *everything*, about the Duke and all the early films, how director John Ford had built him into a star with varied roles in *Stagecoach*, *She Wore a Yellow Ribbon*, and *The Searchers*. And it was just bingo, another big bingo with my Desdemona, how Harty and I could always do it together.

And Harty was excited. Nothing and nobody fazed Harty Platt. Her friends and dates were millionaire Italian spaghetti tycoons, Brazilian playboys, shipping magnates from Crete. Later, she would marry a pedigreed Du Pont. Men did back flips for her off the Spanish Steps in Rome, waited for hours, flowers in hand, near the entrance to the Louvre, just dying for a chance to be insulted by a great-looking American Aristocratic Babe straight out of the pages of Henry James. Men were her metier, her expertise, and she was immensely self-confident about them. But Harty was impressed about the chance to meet the Duke. She couldn't wait.

"Oh, Rinky, this will be so much fun. The Duke! John Wayne. Don't worry. I get the picture. I'm your jailbait. Whatever you need, I can do it."

"Okay, great, Harty. Now, here's the thing. Clothes. I mean, you know—"

"Rinky, shut up. Like, you know, I'm doing *you* the favor of meeting John Wayne, and you're giving *me* a lecture on what to wear? Give me a break."

"Okay, Harty. Okay. C'mon. I'm just saying—"

"Rinky, what did I just say? I said: *Shut up*. You're so serious. God, it's really offensive. So, you know, like don't hit on me about clothes. I think I know what to wear for John Wayne."

"Harty, okay. Okay, okay. I'm sorry."

"What time am I supposed to be there?"

"Eleven o'clock. I'll meet you on the porch of the Red Lion."

.   .   .

Harty Platt was what you would call my femme fatale. I fell into her arms on the back of a hay wagon during my personal Summer of Love, 1967, when I was sixteen. It was natural that we should meet. My father was the local headcase Democrat of Morris County, New Jersey, and Harty's father, a gentleman farmer and veterinarian named Adrian T. Platt, was the local headcase Republican. But they were good friends and it was arranged that I would work as a stable hand and all-around farm boy that summer on the Platts' vast estate. Harty was descended on her mother's side from a munitions magnate, the late Marcellus Hartley Dodge of Remington Arms, whose Hartley Farms the Platts now controlled, and there was quite a bit of step-and-fetchit work to be done during the summer months keeping up Mr. Dodge's elegant old place.

The haying season was the big event of the summer on Hartley Farms. Dr. Platt rode ahead on the big John Deere tractor, pulling the New Holland baler, while sons Michael, Nicholas, and Alexander expertly swept up the cut hay with Farmall row-spinners. Then they jumped into Chevy pickups to transport the finished, stacked bales down to the big brick barn near the Platt house. Harty and I brought up the rear of this efficient operation on the hay wagon behind the doctor, stacking the bales as they were kicked off the rear of the New Holland.

As the work began in the morning, Harty looked as sensibly dressed as any other rich girl playing Anne of Green Gables for the day—work shirt opened down to the third button, blue jeans, and Made in China flip-flop sandals. Still, her physique was hard to ignore. On Mrs. Platt's side Harty derived from impeccable aristocratic stock, the Meads, the Hartleys, and the Dodges, and Dr. Platt had added to this the solid genetic contribution of Dutch milkmaid. It was spectacular breeding. Thick, natural blonde hair that turned blindingly bright in the summer, battery-operated teeth, high cheekbones and creamy complexion, and the best hourglass waistline and bust in America since Evelyn Nesbitt. Harty stopped traffic. I saw her do it once while we were visiting together at the Mead family compound at St. Croix in the Virgin Islands. Harty rode down into Christiansted in a bikini on a bike and the whole damn island had to be shut down for an hour. That summer, as we threw the bales together, I had to keep disciplining myself. Rinker, relax. She's a whole year younger than you. Just fifteen.

As the day grew hotter, Harty would progressively disrobe. First she ditched the work shirt, revealing underneath a very inadequately tailored, sky blue bikini top. Then she ditched the blue jeans to tan up the Barbarella legs. Even flip-flops were too much clothing for her. She could really scramble around a hay wagon in bare feet and a bikini.

One July day a great storm blew up while we were haying. The doctor called out to his troops to work faster, so we could get the last hay in before it started to pour. Jubilant after we had accomplished that, he unhitched the hay wagon with Harty and me on it and happily bounced off with the tractor and baler for the barn a mile away. Michael and Nicholas had already sped off in the pickups. I gradually realized that I had a crisis on my hands. The Platts had forgotten about us. Harty and I were stranded in a remote meadow, in an approaching storm, all alone together on a unprotected hay wagon. It was a lovely sloped field, quite romantic actually, right up against the fences of the neighboring Kirby estate. The clouds were dropping quite low now.

Now, if you happen to find yourself on the back of a hay wagon on a charming old American estate, and a monster rain cloud has just decided to unload directly on top of Harty Platt in a bikini, believe me, this moment will not be spent agonizing over whether you're going to grow up and run for president or write the Great American Novel. What happened from there was just not my fault. It was an act of God.

Mr. Dodge had built a lovely little hunting cottage nearby. Harty and I ran over there in the rain, laughing and sloshing across the polo fields. Harty knew where the key was hidden. Inside, there were attractive prints on the walls depicting rustic Wasps shooting ducks with Remington rifles, a worn but comfortable leather couch, wool blankets, and a brick hearth with cured wood stacked beside it. Harty suggested that I build a fire so that she could dry off her bikini. If you require additional help from here, forget it, just go out and buy another book—I don't need you for a reader. However, I do recall that Harty was quite reassuring.

"Rinky, please, don't worry, okay?" she said, as libidinous puffs of vapor rose from her bikini. "Nobody back at the house is going to miss me until dinner."

So, now we were teen lovers. There were midnight bareback rides up through the woods to the polo fields, midnight assignations at the Shinn mailbox, midnight visits to the hay mow of the barn. We considered our relationship special, unique, even astrologically fated, because we both shared the same birthday in late December. When the weather got colder in the fall, we dirty-danced in the second floor room of the new addition on the Platt house. These were the years of the Beatles, the Doors, the Association, and James Taylor. Harty's favorite, her "personal theme song," she called it, was *Lucy in the Sky with Diamonds*.

Harty ditched me the first time right after Christmas that year. She did love me, she said, but there was a problem with boys, which was that they tended to get boring if you only had one at a time. A member of the opposite sex just wasn't interesting to her until she had watched him suffer. I got thrown aside for a taller guy named Dan. It was painful for a while, but then I learned a pretty good lesson, which was that the competition had a very reliable habit of neglecting the babe. Every time Dan went away with friends on a sailing yacht or vacationed with his family, Harty was back.

"Rinky, how *are* you?"

That was the pattern. We were the Serial Breakup Ken and Barbie. But there were great times too, especially after we both left for college, reunions in London and Paris, sleigh rides with the ponies in the winter, moody, dreamy liaisons down at Campbell Falls in Norfolk during the summer. She would just be back from Portugal or Greece and the boyfriend had decided to push on for Morocco alone, and I was just back after eighteen months in England with a very bad case of Australian Beach Babe withdrawal. So, Harty and

I hooked back up. Really, sometimes people just devote way too much thought to the steady date they happen to be with right now. It's your long-term commitment to the serial breakup partner, the Desdemona ghost of your past, that defines who you are and what the tone of life will be.

Harty and I knew each other well. We'd been through a lot together and considered ourselves professionals at the game of life. I slept chastely and quite well in Don Miller's four-poster the night before the interview. I was ready, with Helen Hartley Platt at my side, to take on the Duke.

. . .

The next morning, at the Red Lion, as soon as Harty got out of her Fiat sports car, I knew that we were going to be fine.

"Rinky!" she said, pecking me on the cheek. "Oh God, look at you, so trim! Are you hiking? Chopping wood? Oh God, Rinky, I love you so much when you're taking care of yourself again. It's *so* important."

Harty was dressed perfectly, tastefully voluptuous. She wore a long black wool skirt, vented to midthigh, and above that a black leotard tightly adhered to her buxom contour. A wide leather bangle-belt was fastened on her hourglass waist, and her black go-go boots lifted her close to six feet. That was the look among girls at the better hippie schools then—she never took off the leotard, she never stopped driving men wild. Harty's fundamentals were so strong that she didn't need jewelry or makeup. With her moist lips, high cheekbones, and Arabian mane of flying blonde hair, she didn't need anything more.

Stockbridge and the Red Lion were lovely in the winter, a natural and inevitable tourist trap. Norman Rockwell had blown the town over the top. His *The Marriage License*, *Becky Sharp*, or *After the Prom*, which you could see just down the street at the little Rockwell museum, drew travelers all year, a viewing clientele heavily skewed to the American South and Midwest. They were mostly old ladies from rural Virginia or Illinois, the kind of folks who every December brought down from the attic a framed reproduction of Rockwell's classic *Home for Christmas*, a snowy townscape of Stockbridge's Main Street with the dark rim of mountain behind, a Desoto passing by with a Christmas tree on its roof rack, and the well-porched Red Lion Inn on the right, just above Rockwell's signature block-type name. During the winter, they all came to see the quaint town in the Berkshires where Rockwell found models for his paintings among the village residents, and several groups of tourists were sitting on the couches and chairs in the Red Lion lobby when Harty and I arrived.

The lady behind the reception counter was a stiff board dressed in the style of a librarian, no-nonsense print skirt and white blouse, very sniffy. That was the Red Lion style, the marketing genius of its owners, State Senator John Fitzpatrick and wife, Jane. The help was to act as if they were better than the guests. Harty could tell right away that I would blow it with this dame so she stepped right up to the desk.

"Helen Hartley Platt and friend to see Mr. John Wayne. And please, dial right away. We prefer not to wait."

"Well, ah, oh yes! Miss Platt, we'll do that right away."

On the way upstairs I was nervous and concerned. Harty, I thought, had not been sufficiently briefed.

"All right now, Harty, here's the scoop," I said.

"Rinky, shut up. Like, you know, I think the girl can handle this? All you have to do is write things down in your little reporter's notebook and watch me do this. It will be fine."

"Harty, okay. But, you know, just one word? One word."

"Rinky, *one* word. But, number one, it better be just one word or I will murder you, and, number two, that word better not be Watergate."

"All right, Harty. Ah, the word is Nixon. That's my one word. Nixon."

"Rinky, shut up."

When we knocked on the door of the Wayne suite at the end of the long hall, it was opened by a mouse in tasseled loafers and a blue blazer, the associate vice president to the senior vice president of all publicity for talent, whose eyes popped out when he saw Harty in the leotard.

But from within the room I could hear the rustle of two big legs in perfectly pressed flannel, a great brisket of chest pushing air. When he got there and looked over the shoulder of the associate vice president for publicity, he placed two large hands on the blue blazer shoulders and physically moved them three feet off to the side.

John Wayne was framed in the doorway, with soft sunlight from the large windows behind highlighting his massive shoulders. He gave Harty the visual once-over, smiled broadly, and rubbed his hands.

"Well, hellllooo darlin'! What do we have *here?*"

It was the Duke. A little more corpulent in the midriff than I expected, a bit more jowly than I'd seen in photos, but definitely, quintessentially, the Duke. The baritone voice, cured by the mixed elixir of whiskey and honey, was unmistakable.

Harty played him just right. She wasn't going to twitter and slobber all over him like a recent, star-struck graduate of a film school in L.A. Coy, but unconcerned, she flicked her blonde mane back over her ear with the long fingers of her left hand and then smiled, but just a little. That was her seduction style, her subgenre: Aristocratic American Babe. Hard to get, very few words at first, flawless manners.

"Oh, Mr. Wayne," she said, extending her hand. "It's such a pleasure to meet you."

"A pleasure. Hah!" said the Duke. "Well, I'm just kinda like thinkin' here that the pleasure is goin' to be *allllll mine*. C'mon right in here, young lady, and let's get intra-duced."

When called upon, Harty had touches of greatness. When the Duke finally let go of her hand—he had held it for several seconds in both of his—Harty let it fall discreetly across the love handles on his waist and gave them an affectionate pat or two. Her hand said: Pardon me, Mr. Wayne, but I just can't resist doing that. All men let me do this to them.

Then she glided across the room, considered the furniture and the possible seating arrangements, and gracefully sat down on the corner of the bed that faced the room. The Duke, speechless, but with this great smirky-smile on his face, followed her in and sat down opposite Harty, dwarfing a stuffed wing chair.

I was just a doormat at this point, the associate vice president to the Belle of the United States, Her Majesty Helen Hartley, and I found another stuffed chair in the corner. Wayne had been polite to me though. He crushed my hand with a vise grip as I came through the door and told me that he "really liked my friend."

From his chair, his elegant gray flannels crossed knee over knee, cowboy boots shining, the Duke got down to bidness.

"All right now here, young lady. How 'bout that name? I'd be willin' to bet yours is a real winner."

"Helen Hartley Platt."

That's all she said. That's all she needed to say.

"Goldang," Wayne said, smiling. "See? Helen Hartley Platt. You know, a fella like me looks at a gal like you and then hears the name, and you know what he thinks?"

"No, Mr. Wayne," Harty said, flicking her hair again and offering him a laugh, but a small one. "What does he think?"

"She ain't lyin' to me, that's what he thinks! I mean, you just plum have a name that fits you to a T!"

Harty gave him a twitter, but just a little, flashed her battery-operated teeth and fluttered her eyebrows a few times. Just enough. Don't be afraid to hold your horses back a little at the beginning.

"Well now, look here, Helen Hartley," the Duke said. "You can call me either John or the Duke. Which do you pre-fur?"

"John," Harty said. "I really like John, as a name."

"Hmmm. Good," said the Duke. "Now, tell me, what is a gorgeous gal like you possibly plannin' on doin' with her life?"

That's where we won the Super Bowl, right there. Harty kicked a luscious field goal right back to the Duke, not with words, but with body action.

Leaning over and smiling at Wayne so that her bust settled in the leotard, but just a little, Harty insouciantly rested her chin on her hand and gave the Duke an uninterested gaze. It was the stare, the Harty stare. Her cameo was indifferent, but it was saying something: *Oh, what do I do? Do you mean in between riding with the Spring Valley Hounds all fall, squeezing in a visit with Barbara and Marco Butoni in Rome, seeing my boyfriend in Paris, and then visiting grandmother in St. Croix for Christmas—in between that, what do I do?*

The Duke was entranced by her. He couldn't remove his eyes from her leotard. He was waiting for her reply. Yeah, little mustang, what could you possibly be plannin' on doin' with your life?

"I'm an *artist*," Harty said. "I study painting and fine art."

The Duke beamed and spread his arms wide. He was just so pleased.

"Goldangit anyway, that's what I thought. An *ard-ist*! Every time I ask a pretty young woman these days what she could possibly be plannin' on doin' with her life, that's what she says! An ard-ist. Po-etree. Arky-tek-tur. You meet a girl, get to talkin', and dangit, she's studyin' *arky-tek-tur*. Young ladies these days? You better watch it, John, I say to myself. They've got *brains!*"

While all this was going on, I was furiously taking notes. I wanted color, what the man was like. Two things about the Duke immediately impressed me.

First, he was a gorgeous specimen of human flesh. Yes, there were love handles on his waistline and liver spots on his hands, and he wore the copper geriatric bracelet favored by senior men in those days. But at sixty-six, having just "licked the Big C," cancer, as he put it later, he was in top shape. The face was tanned and firm, the chest as broad as the Lincoln Memorial, the expressions and hand movement graceful but lively. Aw-shucksing Harty, he reached over several times with his massive right hand to pat her knee when he hit a punch line. Wayne was dressed in an expensive cashmere polo shirt and a western-cut herringbone jacket. Around his neck he was wearing a maroon and yellow patterned kerchief, the Bert Bachrach fag-rag look favored by swank men then, but the Duke was pulling this off, I thought.

The other thing about the Duke that I liked was that there seemed to be almost no discrepancy between his formula-western screen image and the John Wayne being revealed to me now. He was larger than life, as he was supposed to be. In the past, I'd been disappointed by film stars in person. My father always had a few actors or actresses hanging around for a political fund-raiser, or else we met them driving our horses and carriages as extras when the Hollywood film studios came east to shoot pictures. But I was usually let down. Patty Duke, whom I met during the filming of *The Miracle Worker,* didn't quite have the lycra-tight body that I expected. Lorne Greene of *Bonanza* was fat. But the Duke lived up to his image. It seemed to me that he hadn't been *in* movies, he *was* the movie.

The problem I had, though, was that I *liked* him. Harty was supposed to be mugging him soon over Watergate, which I was anxious for her to get to, and Wayne could be depended upon to say something stupid, which would force me to trash him, or so I thought. But, I liked this great specimen of flesh and his aw-shucks style. It was going to be a problem when I sat down to write the piece.

Harty had her big tuna on the line now but she was too good to reel him in quickly. She asked Wayne a series of questions about his films, running him through a sort of curriculum vitae from *She Wore a Yellow Ribbon* to *Rio Bravo* and *The Sands of Iwo Jima.* Wayne told her all about making *Chisum* and *Sons of Katie Elder.* It was great, an education for me, material for my article, and something else started happening too. There was more to Wayne than I thought, and when he got to a serious subject and momentarily took his eyes off Harty, he stopped dropping the end of his syllables and aw-shucksin' us to death. If he had to, he could speak the eastern Wasp dialect. He could be au courant. But mostly, he liked being who he was, unhip and a throwback, which was almost hip.

When we got to Watergate, it was all just one fluid body action and finessed word on the part of Harty. She really brought Wayne onto the deck smoothly.

Harty's gift with men derived from her artistic sensibility, her innate appreciation of light and color and what they did to human form in a room. In this instance the painting technique was ultratorso chiaroscuro. She leaned forward slightly so that her leotard and its contents were carved like black marble by the sunlight streaming through the large pane window facing out to Icy Glen. She touched the Duke on his knee.

"Now, John," she said, "My friend Rinker here wants to know about Watergate."

Wayne didn't bristle and he didn't run either. He seemed to have expected us to try to set him up, but Harty's acting was just so damn good he couldn't bring himself to get annoyed.

"Well, you see now, Helen Hartley, that's just the problem with the bidness Rinker here is in. He's gonna take my quote out of context, put it in his own words, and then everybody's all riled at the Duke for poppin' off again."

At this point the mouse in the corner, the publicity agent, stepped over and attempted to end the interview. It was an enormous pleasure watching a star get annoyed at one of those.

"Hey, feller," the Duke said, holding up a tanned hand. "Thanks a whole bunch, but I don't need your help just now, okay? I'm talkin' here with Helen Hartley."

Harty leaned forward again and touched the Duke's knee.

"John," she said, "Rinker would *never* take a quote out of context. Number one, if he did, I would murder him, and number two, how can he take anything out of context if you haven't said it yet? You're not *afraid* of Rinker, are you?"

Great Desdemona body action right there, by the way. Down with the irresistible leotard, dig gently with the nails into the star-quality knee, out with the go-go boot, skirt vent fully exposing alabaster thigh, then way high up with the come-get-me-feller hair as she leaned back on the bed to laugh. The leotard voluptuously giggled: *Imagine, the Duke afraid of Rinker Buck!*

"Well now Helen Hartley, I know just what you're doin' here. You're wrappin' ole John Wayne right around your little finger. And you know what?"

"What?" Harty said, as if she didn't know.

"I like it! I like it. Helen Hartley, you're just somethin' else."

You could hear the Winchester mentally coming out of the saddle holster when the Duke swiveled in his chair to face me. He placed two feet firmly on the carpet and stared me down.

Son, he seemed to be saying with his broad face and wide chest, you're the one with the sense to have brought Helen Hartley along today. Fair's fair. You win.

Then, with a theatrical sigh and a cock of his head, the Duke locked and loaded and opened up with both barrels at once.

And it was great stuff, just what I needed for the piece. The Duke wasn't going to let me down.

"Watergate, my sweet buns," the Duke said. "There ain't nothin' happenin' down there in Washington except a media conspiracy."

The Duke had an epithet for Woodward and Bernstein down at *The Washington Post*. They were "Woodchuck and Burnboy," and they weren't fit to "lick Richard Nixon's boots." The "articulate liberal press, which has never done me any favors either," had deliberately connived and ganged up on the Nixon White House because they hated a Republican being in power. Dick Nixon was too busy figuring out what to do with "Chiner," "Cuber," and "Nam" to have any time to run his own re-election campaign, which was the only mistake he had made. Other men, weenies like John Dean, Jeb Magruder, and E. Howard Hunt, had blown it for Nixon, and now they were proving what weasels they were by testifyin' before the Watergate Committee. And so forth. Watergate's importance, the Duke insisted, had been exaggerated by that "kid Dan Rather at CBS News," and *The New York Times*, which had proven its bias by publishing the Pentagon Papers. It was all the fault of the press.

For me, the Eagle had landed. Houston, we have contact. I couldn't wait to get home and write this piece.

Harty was bored at this point. She knew that I now had enough in my notebook. Leaning back on the bed with her arms, she kicked out a go-go boot and stifled a yawn.

"You see?" the Duke said. "We're borin' her to death. Helen Hartley couldn't care less about Watergate."

It was time to go—Wayne had his appointment with Norman Rockwell.

Harty stood up, faced Wayne, and stretched her arms high, cracking a few joints. She was one of the few women I knew who could pull that move off in company. The calisthenic body stretch made to look aristocratic. Her Desdemona breasts

Helen Hartley Platt and John Wayne.

perked upward in good Berkshire light, her hourglass was muscular, and then she performed this brief, sexy pony-shiver all over as she came back to the at-ease position and smiled at the Duke. Awesome, awesome lines. You couldn't be in a room with Harty Platt and ignore her presence, she knew that about herself, and she had doled out her sexuality and her charm in a disciplined sequence to nail the Duke. It was like viewing art, just watching her do it, and I owed Harty big time now.

When we left the room and walked down the long hall of the Red Lion, the Duke did a nice thing. He chose to walk with me, not Harty. She walked down the hall behind us with the publicity flack. The Duke wrapped his beary right arm around my shoulder and gave it a vise-grip squeeze.

"That is some gal you got there, fella," he said. "I like a woman who comes all the way up to my shoulder."

Outside, on the porch of the Red Lion, Harty said that she had to go. Friends were coming over for the weekend from Bard, and she needed to get back to Norfolk and get ready. With a last flick of her hair and a peck on the cheek for me and the Duke, she stepped into her maroon Fiat and squealed off around the corner, and I felt sentimental watching her drive off, with the ring of white peaks rising above her. Harty Platt was a great American beauty, and nobody had done the Duke better than her.

.   .   .

Stockbridge went wild that day for John Wayne, which was unusual. The town was accustomed to celebrities and didn't pay that much attention when Paul Newman and Joanne Woodward came up to goof off for the weekend, or when James Taylor or Carole King came up to visit Arlo Guthrie. But the Duke was different. Tourists flocked around him as we walked down South Street together toward Rockwell's studio in a converted carriage house a few doors away, and Wayne loved it. He stopped for autographs and let all the husbands from Milwaukee and Lynchburg take snapshots of him with their wives, buoyant about all the attention.

"Goldang it anyway, Mr. Buck," he said to me. "This is one heck of a town, ain't it? You get old and they still love you."

The session at Rockwell's studio was not a formal portrait sitting. Rockwell had already begun his portrait of the Duke on the basis of pictures sent east by the Cowboy Hall of Fame. This was just a session for Rockwell's regular photographer, Louie Lamone, to get some close-up facials of Wayne, and for Rockwell himself to check skin tones, bone structure, and the like. The artist was legendary for his fastidious attention to detail. He could work all morning just sketching and resketching an ear or a policeman's cap visor until he got it right and the concept could be moved over to the canvas. When we got there, Rockwell wanted Wayne in full western regalia, and the Duke changed in a small anteroom into his Stetson and blue jeans.

After Wayne changed into his cowboy gear and began the photo shoot with Lamone, Rockwell walked over and talked with me.

At first glance Rockwell seemed like the most ordinary man in the world, a white-haired, hound-faced grandpop noodling with his birdhouse projects back in the garage. But after a few minutes I felt as if I were in the presence of an enormously disciplined man who was shrewd about the business he was in, said very little, but knew exactly what he needed to do to get the most out of a situation. When he did speak, it was with flat vowels and crisp diction, and no discernible accent. It was hard to place his voice because he never took the gnarled English briar out of his mouth. He stared directly at my face as we spoke, which was unnerving, and sized me up from head to foot impassively, as if withholding judgment. We chatted for a while and I found him charmingly knowledgeable about the sort of bric-a-brac stuffed into my head. He was also an extremely adroit newshound. He wanted publicity. That's what reporters were for.

"You're Mr. Buck from the *Eagle*," Rockwell said, extending a pallid handshake. "The Hall of Fame told me you were coming. Very good. How's Pete?"

"Pete's fine. I saw him this week. I'm doing an article for *UpCountry*."

"Subject?"

"Sleighs."

"Sleighs," Rockwell laughed. "That's Pete. He's probably the only newspaper publisher left interested in sleighs. You had better be up on your subject Mr. Buck—cutters, two-bobs, the vis-à-vis, and the like."

John Wayne and Norman Rockwell.

Rockwell chatted amiably for a while longer, telling me how much he enjoyed Pete Miller's *"Evening Eagle"* and describing the commissions he was working on at the time.

There was one other thing about Rockwell that was extremely pleasing, which was the space he worked in. His studio was well organized but casually unkempt, with ceramic jars and old coffee cans everywhere, stuffed with brushes, piles of newspapers, still-life models, and worn Hitchcock chairs. There was an openness and simplicity of purpose that reminded me of a one-room Mennonite school-house in Pennsylvania.

Meanwhile, the Duke was getting impatient. The white sheetrock walls of the studio had been flashing for more than fifteen minutes from photographer Lamone's strobes.

"Goldang it anyway," the Duke said, standing tall in his western outfit. "Photographers. Just one more, Mr. Wayne, just one more. Fire that thing, boy, would you, fire!"

Rockwell twittered a little so that the pipe vibrated in his mouth. Oh, these subjects of mine, he seemed to be saying, they're always so delightful.

But Lamone wasn't done. The schedule for the day included photographing the historic encounter between Rockwell and Wayne, and he asked the artist to step over. When Rockwell got over by the lights, he fussed for a bit about his positioning, and Wayne comfortably sidled up and placed his arm on the artist's shoulder. Rockwell's wavy nimbus of white hair came up to the brim of Wayne's Stetson. Their physiques formed a wonderful juxtaposition—the bearish, hulking American cowboy looming over the frail, natty New Englander.

But there was a problem. Rockwell didn't want Louie to start shooting yet, and he was very fussy about it.

"Louie, I need a prop," Rockwell said. "The papers won't use this unless I'm holding a prop."

The Duke understood immediately. His sense of the camera was good.

"Well, here you go, Norman," Wayne said, pulling a six gun from his holster. "Use this."

Rockwell cradled the gun in both hands and held it up, a natural ham, and stared straight into Louie's lens.

"The prints will be up at *Eagle* first thing Monday morning," Lamone told me. "They know they're coming."

It was the first that I had heard about it. Rockwell's publicity machine was a very efficient operation.

I left Wayne and Rockwell there. I was in a hurry to get home to get started on my story. Wayne was now sitting on a tall stool near the far window so that Rockwell could record notes for his portrait. The sitting was conducted in both natural and artificial light, with a shaded lamp focused on Wayne's face. It was best, I thought, just to leave quietly so that Rockwell and the Duke could finish their work alone.

"Hey, hold your horses there, buddy!" the Duke called out as I neared the door. "You're going to leave without saying good-bye? No way. Norman, let's just hang on here a moment."

I walked back across the studio and Wayne strolled over to meet me halfway, the percussive ring of his spurs jangling smartly as he walked.

Wayne pumped my hand and then squeezed my shoulder hard.

"Hey," he laughed. "This has really been a good day for me. You and Helen Hartley made my trip to Stockbridge. I mean it. And one other thing, son."

"Okay, John," I said. "What?"

"Just put in that damn article whatever the hell you want. And I'm not sayin' that because I'll never see your paper. I'm sayin' it because you listened to me and you were polite. You do your thing. Got it?"

"John, I got it. Thanks, and I mean that too."

"Yeah, well, good-bye then, son. Take good care of that Helen Hartley. She's a special gal."

I turned to leave and had one last vision of the Duke as I reached the door. When he returned to the stool where he would sit again for Norman Rockwell, Wayne swung his leg wide and waist-high and sat down all at once, the graceful saddle mount. He was the Zeus of Hollywood, one of the great carryover talents of his generation, and he liked who he was and wasn't afraid to project it. I had set out that morning to mug John Wayne on Watergate, but I ended my time with him liking John Wayne and his grand style very much. Walking toward my car on Stockbridge's snowy Main Street, I decided that I could accept both sides of the man, and that this would be the challenge of the article I had to write. I was learning to inhabit contradiction.

.   .   .

It was midafternoon when I got back home, and Peter, Judy, and Betty were out shopping. Good. Three hours of reliable quiet until they got back. Upstairs in my room, I pulled my old Smith Corona portable up from its storage underneath the bed, set it up on the Shaker table, and went to work, rereading my notes, highlighting them with colored pencils, contemplatively dragging on my pipe before I began to type.

Then a nice little miracle happened. Effortlessly, in forty-five minutes, I batted out a first draft that was pretty adequate and even good. Still, I had a problem. Writing wasn't just the thing I did for a living now. A story about John Wayne and Watergate, which would be carefully picked apart by Tom Morton and Bill Bell, was a personal reflection of me. Every sentence, every comma even, would be a barometer of my self-worth. The piece had to be perfect.

So, I went to work tearing apart my own story. My first draft was too mushy about John Wayne here, and it didn't have enough about Watergate over there. Tom Morton was always faulting me for being too "high rent," too literary and intellectual for his tastes. So, I cut back on a lot of analytical material about Wayne's movies. Over the next twenty-four hours I rewrote my story on John Wayne at least a dozen times.

My biggest difficulty was resolving my personal feelings about Wayne. I couldn't accept that I *liked* the Duke. This was anathema for the times, especially for an eastern liberal college graduate like me. My mission, I thought, was to trash

John Wayne, to make him look like a Hollywood buffoon. But that wasn't the man I met with Harty at the Red Lion. I'd discovered someone a bit different and more subtle than I'd expected. Being honest about that meant rejecting the prevailing atmosphere of Nixon-hating and gloomy prophecies of doom. My peers in the newsroom would accuse me of being soft on the Duke.

I was rescued that afternoon, however, by the memory of something that had been said to me by a new friend in the newsroom, a man who would become one of my favorite colleagues at the *Eagle*.

Richard V. Happel wrote the "Notes and Footnotes" column on the editorial page of the *Eagle*, which was one of the most popular and well written items in the paper every day. Dick was an incredibly old, emaciated William Burroughs type who waddled through the newsroom at odd hours, invariably dressed in a heavy wool or gabardine suit, so threadbare that it was worn right down to the lining along the lapels and the ends of the sleeve. In an old Whitman's candy box in his desk, Dick maintained a special collection of felt-tip pens for touching up his suits—black for the black suit, brown for the brown plaid suit, and so forth. He sat right next to me, separating my space from Rory O'Connor's. His column required only an hour or two of work each day, so he had plenty of time to converse softly and offer me his friendship while he worked on his suits. Dick had one great thing going for him, an identity that I cherished and from which I learned a lot. He was a solid, no-nonsense, salt-of-the-earth 1950s-era homosexual. He lived with his boyfriend in Lenox and drove around the Berkshires gathering material for his "Talk of the Town"–style column in a long, brown Cadillac Fleetwood.

Dick regularly dispensed advice to me and treated me like a young god. He always knew what I was up to and would volunteer thoughts about the things being said about me in the *Eagle* rumor mill. Comfort Halsey, he had heard, was "smashingly pretty," and the ski instructor I was also dating, "very athletic." He noticed the smallest things about me and he wasn't afraid to raise them in conversation. My physique, he thought, had become leaner that fall, and when I finally went out and splurged on some new clothes, he perked up and smiled, and couldn't resist paying me a compliment.

"Oh, sonny," Dick said. "That is a very nice jacket and tie combination. Regimental ties go so well with Harris tweeds. When something works for you like that? Please. Wear it every day."

I enjoyed Happel's avuncular presence and the calming effect that he had on me. I also considered Dick clairvoyant about me and even had a theory about it. Forty years in the sack practicing serial monogamy with guys had made him intuitively brilliant about just that—*guys*. Because he was so quiet and old, nobody in the newsroom paid much attention to him, so he was extremely grateful to me, just for the rare pleasure of conversation. I bought him coffee—he insisted on Dunkin' Donuts, never Friendly's—and ran him back and forth to Lenox when the snow was too heavy for his longboat Caddie. He was an important part of my coming into the mountains and learning to write at *Eagle*, and helped form my view that gay men, particularly older, wiser models like Dick, were a national treasure. I loved the Hap.

Dick's "Notes and Footnotes" column was chatty and informative, an *Eagle* gem. If the organizers of the Swamp Road Garden Tour in Richmond were pestering him for coverage, Dick would give them their line or two, but this was merely a launching pad for him to write an entertaining discourse on the history of the day lily. A new Longfellow letter found in a Pittsfield attic became an essay on "Hiawatha."

However, Dick disliked many of the people that he wrote about. For instance, he was annoyed by the fact that many of his Garden Club sources, mostly women, had fat legs. For some reason, Dick loathed the sight of a woman with fat legs. But here's what he'd say about her: "Our gardening friend in West Stockbridge, who has lovely knees . . ." The First Church minister in Pittsfield, who had a Ph.D., annoyed everyone in the newsroom by insisting that he be referred to as "Dr." instead of "The Rev." In his column, Dick called him "our well-educated preacher."

For years, Happel had conducted a vendetta against his Cadillac dealer. Every time he brought the Fleetwood in for an oil change, the dealer would discover the need for expensive repairs such as new transmission gaskets or a muffler job. The dealer was servicing him into the poorhouse, Dick thought. So, he introduced both his Cadillac and his Cadillac

Columnist Richard V. Happel was one of the Eagle's *most elegant wordsmiths and often saved me with his sage advice about the subliminal use of language. "If she's a bitch," he would say, "Call her delightful."*

dealer as regular characters in his column. He fit them in slyly, briefly, just as he was going by. The McKinley monument in Adams, for example, was "just around the corner from my surprisingly inexpensive Cadillac dealer." He referred often to "bargain basement Cadillac parts." He once described his Caddie as "a very large vehicle with a very small gas tank."

Curious about all this, I asked Dick about it one day. I wanted to know why "Notes and Footnotes" featured so many women with "lovely knees" and crazy Stockbridge millionaires who were invariably described as "eminently sensible."

As I began to query him on the subject, Dick pulled out a felt-tip pen, draped his suit jacket on his knees, and comfortably adjusted himself for a long conversation while he retouched his lapels.

"Hey, Dick, how come you're always so polite to these people?" I asked. "It's your column, and you can say what you want. Since you obviously don't like these folks, why not just shit on them?"

"Oh, no. Never do that, sonny," Happel said. "Never, never, never-ever be mean in print. It doesn't work. If she's a bitch, don't say so. Call her delightful."

Dick's theory was that if you were bitchy in person, people would just conclude that you were having a bad day. But be bitchy in print and it lasted forever, a matter of public record. It would stick to you for life, define you as a writer. Bitchy did not translate from the spoken to the written word.

"My readers know," Dick said. "They are very loyal to me. I've trained them over the years to read between the lines. If I call a college professor brilliant, my readers *know*. He's a frightful bore. If I happen to learn that a minister is having an affair, the next time I mention him in print, I call him very moral. The minister cannot complain about this, but my readers know. So, don't be bitchy, Rinker. Be nice. It kills them every time."

Don't be bitchy, be nice. This made no sense to me. I was training to be a journalist, a writer. My job was to scour the world for evil, for Phoney Mahoneys, and then rid them from the field with a steel plow. Arrogance, mendacity, and corruption were to be discovered and removed with strong, harsh language. Woodward and Bernstein down in Washington, I was pretty sure, were not very nice.

But I was in a pickle now with the Wayne piece and decided to try the Happel technique. I didn't understand the principle yet—good material, a good tale, didn't have to be *written* so much as just laid out in order—but, damn, Happel's rapier was working for me. Every time I rewrote and applied Happel's rule—"Don't be bitchy, be nice"—the Wayne piece got better. I couldn't tell why, but it was better.

"Bulging midriff," for example. I didn't feel that such words applied to the Duke. "Corpulent dignity" fit him better. Or, even smarter, just quote the Duke himself. "I'm carrying thirty extra pounds in the saddle now." The geriatric copper bracelet got tossed out. I replaced it with a better, fresher image of age: "tiny deltas of blood vessels near the surface of his nose." When I rewrote the Watergate section, I found this in my first draft: "Wayne truculently defended his stance on President Nixon, which has been roundly criticized in the national press." That became simply Wayne's "pistol-gripping confidence." And so forth. I compulsively whittled away all Saturday afternoon and most of Sunday.

In the evening, Peter returned with the Smith College Goddesses. He built a fire in the den, put his feet up, and relaxed with a copy of *The New York Review of Books*. Meanwhile, Judy and Betty skipped around the kitchen in their sexy knickers, making daiquiris in a blender from a recipe in a cookbook. They had bought new leotards at the Arcadia Shop in Lenox— deep purple for Judy, hot aquamarine for Betty. They looked just spectacular tonight, especially supple and bosomy, and I loved being in the kitchen with those two. But then I'd get halfway through a daiquiri, reconsider things, and run back upstairs to fix a line. "Rotten, fetid Stetson" needed to be changed to the simpler, more universally appealing "ten-gallon hat." Peter, Judy, and Betty were annoyed at me. I was preoccupied, obsessed. I refused to join our usual group-grope flirt down in the den.

"Rinker, you're freaking on this thing," Peter said. "It's just one article. Can't you ever relax? God, you're so *serious*."

At ten o'clock that night I was so frustrated and angry at myself, so exhausted and high from rewriting, all I could do was go down to the yard, switch on the outside lights, and chop wood. On Sunday, I took a brief hike, but I spent most of the day whittling away some more on the Wayne piece.

On Monday morning, I was too anxious to get into the *Eagle* to bother much with the woodpile. I knew that Tom Morton would be there—he was an even earlier riser than I was and was always the first into the newsroom, alone at his green metal desk along the east wall.

"Top of the morning to you, pal, how ya doing?" Morton said. "What brings you in so early?"

"Well, you know, Tom, nothing really. I did my interview with John Wayne."

"What? John Wayne? The Duke? I'm supposed to be running this damn place, but nobody ever tells me anything. *You* interviewed John Wayne?"

Incredible. Morton didn't even know about it. But it made sense. I'd told Bell, who was working the day shift Friday, but Morton had worked the Friday evening shift. Obviously, they hadn't talked.

"Tom, yeah. I got the Duke."

"Creepers. Watergate? Did he talk about Watergate? How about Nixon? Did you think to ask him about that?"

"Tom. I'm not *that* stupid. The Duke spilled his guts. About everything."

"Jesus, Mary, and Joseph," Morton sighed. "All right. Sit down and bat me out a first draft. This is going to take a lot of rewrites. If your obits get backed up, we'll make Scheer write them. That Little Lord Fauntleroy hasn't written a damn obit since he got here. I'll get him back for you, okay?"

"Tom," I said. "It's already done. I wrote the story over the weekend."

"Jeepers creepers. Rinker, you're the pip. The eager beaver. Let me see it."

These were the days before computer graphics and digital

type. Stories were written on manual typewriters with separate sheets of cheap copy paper. To hand in a finished piece, each "take," or sheet of paper, was pasted to the bottom of the previous take with the glue-pot brush on every reporter's desk. The "final take" was then rolled up into a cylinder and affixed with a paper clip before being turned in, so that as it was processed through the editing desks, parts of the story wouldn't get lost. Turning in a story felt like handing over one of the Dead Sea Scrolls.

"Here you go, Tom," I said. "I hope you like it."

I stood there and hovered, waiting for him to read it. The early signs were good. When he was happy Morton had a placid half-smile, and he dabbed his porcine bald pate with his stubby fingers.

Then he looked up, frowned, and reached into the back pocket of his brown trousers for his wallet. He held up a $5 bill.

"Would you please get the hell out of here? How am I supposed to read this when you're breathing down my neck? Here, get some breakfast for yourself and bring me a coffee. God, why did I ever hire you anyway?"

"Tom, I'm sorry. I'm sorry. I'll go for breakfast."

When I got back twenty minutes later, Morton was more effusive than I'd ever seen him. As he told me how much he liked my story on John Wayne, my faced turned red and the little stubbles of hair on the back of my neck stood straight on their ends.

"Kiddo, this thing is the pip," Morton said. "Over the top. I mean, you didn't just get Wayne to talk about Watergate. There's all this extra grillwork in here—tiny deltas of blood vessels on his nose, pistol-packing confidence, and everything. You blew the gaskets and hit one out of the park, pal. I'm just so grateful. This is a huge improvement over your earlier writing."

I was mortified. It was just awful having to stand there and receive this praise.

"Yeah, well, you know, Tom. I worked hard on it."

Morton wanted to change just two things. My description of Wayne's voice as a "mellifluous baritone" was redundant, he thought. Readers would have to look up the word "mel-lifluous." I agreed, so we took out the extra word. Morton liked the material about Wayne's movie career, but thought that I'd stretched that section too far. He wanted it trimmed.

"Tom, you're right," I said. "I'll fix this stuff. But look. Is the piece, ah, you know, all right otherwise? Do you like it?"

"Oh, Jesus. I just said that, didn't I? It's *great*. You not only bagged the Duke, but you've got all this stuff in there about Stockbridge going wild for him and everything. You got a problem, son, with me calling you an ace?"

"Tom, no. Of course not. I don't have any problems. I just wanted to know if you like it, that's all."

"Christ, I like it, okay? Now. Let's just figure out our success here, Rinker. Let's go to school for a minute. How many times did you rewrite this? And don't bullshit me either."

I knew that I couldn't be honest about that. It wasn't enough for reporters to get good material, to synthesize well. They also had to be lightning fast. If I told Morton the truth, that I'd spent two whole days rewriting the story, he'd never give me a promotion.

"Oh, you know, Tom," I said. "Just the usual number of rewrites. Once or twice."

"Bullshit. And for that I'm assigning a value of three rewrites. Every time you lie to me, you get three more. Now, how many times did you rewrite this?"

"Three, Tom. You just said it. Three."

"Okay, that was bullshit again. We're now up to six. Would you like to keep going?"

"Tom. There were no top-to-bottom rewrites or anything like that. I just noodled with paragraphs."

"Nine, we're up to nine, Rinker."

"Tom, that's way too many. Nobody rewrites something nine times."

"Twelve, kiddo. An even dozen. Would you like to stop there?"

"Okay, Tom. I rewrote this piece a lot, okay? A lot. I admit it, I'm sorry, but I was just trying to make it good. I'll try and get faster, okay?"

Morton dabbed his bald head with his hand and sighed. "Jeez. Trying to bring you along is like trying to teach an elephant to dance. The story is good, damn good, Rinker, *because* you rewrote it so many times. Do you know how many reporters I've got here who think they're too good to rewrite? Who won't work weekends? Your story is excellent. You rewrote to perfection. Rewriting is key, and you seem to understand that. Do you have a problem with me saying that to you?"

"Tom, I don't have any problems. Who says I've got problems? You're saying it's okay to rewrite. So, that's what I'll do. Rewrite my ass off."

"Yeah, that's the lesson," Morton said. "Bingo. We've hit the trifecta here. Christ. I should have been a shrink down at Riggs."

Morton wanted me to do one other thing. In the middle of Watergate, with the Senate hearings broadcast on the radio every day, what John Wayne had said would be interesting to the wire services. Most newspapers and radio stations wouldn't run my story out of Stockbridge as a big piece, but they'd use it as a feed to their main stories that day. Tom wanted me to write a stripped-down version of the Wayne story for the Associated Press and United Press International wire services. I should change the lede, cut out all the extra color, and add all the Watergate quotes I had in my notes. It would be a just-the-facts-Ma'am "takeout" for UPI and AP.

As I turned for my desk, Morton asked another question.

"Hey, by the way, how did you get the Duke to talk? Why did he give you all this stuff?"

"Well, you know, Tom, just basic interview technique, I guess. And you know, sort of, actually not sort of but really, I brought along a friend."

"Oh, Christ. A friend, huh? Do I want to know about this?"

"Nope. You don't want to know about this."

Morton sighed and dabbed his head.

"All right. Get your butt over to the typewriter. I'd like to send this story to the wire services by 10:30. That's your deadline, kiddo. If we move it by then, John Wayne will make the afternoon news."

CHAPTER TEN

RACHEL CAME TO work for the *Eagle* on the Miller Economic
Plan. Pete Miller was a coveted dinner guest at all the right
mansion parties in Stockbridge and sat on the boards of
Williams College and the Austin Riggs Center, and nearly
everywhere he went, the *Eagle* publisher was pressed to hire
the bright, idle sons and daughters of the people he would
meet. After a martini or two, Pete would agree to take on these
kids as summer interns or winter editorial assistants. So, young
Jay, Simon, or Melissa would camp out at the family ski chalet
in Otis for several months or even an entire year, pursuing the
semblance of a career by writing *UpCountry* stories or design-
ing layouts for *Berkshires Week*. Pete's informal intern program
was one of the secrets of his success, the *Eagle*'s stealth weapon
for quality. Most of these interns were quite talented, they kept
the paper young and continuously freshened by new ideas
coming off the college campuses, and, best of all, the price was
right. Pete paid them practically nothing.

Rachel was a very springy, attractive smart-talker out of the
golden Jewish suburbs of northern New Jersey. Her father was
a wealthy business executive in New York, a friend of a friend
of Pete's, but I never learned much about him or Rachel's family
because it was understood that you didn't pry too deeply about
a certain class of Berkshire County girl. Rachel was up in the

mountains for a while getting her head straightened out. She had a "doc" down in Stockbridge, "double sessions" every Tuesday and Thursday afternoon, and then the awful penance of group therapy after that. Monday, Wednesday, and Friday from eleven to four, but really just whenever she wanted, she did layouts and design at the *Eagle*. There were intimations about her, things that would pop out, or that I just surmised. The doc, she'd say, was working with her on her "father issues," and they were into the "jackhammer and dynamite phase" of that now. There might have been big problems with boys, or millionaire pals of Dad hitting on her too much. Maybe there were eating disorders back there, too, and a big breakdown at one point, but Rachel preferred to be vague about that. The mystery about who she really was, and her aura of vulnerability, was quite alluring.

Everybody at the *Eagle* loved her. Rachel was fun-fun all the time, super-brainy, a wild-ass Jewish girl out of New York, waltzing through the newsroom in a tight mohair sweater, dirty-dancing jeans, and mannish but sexy hiking boots. She was dark-skinned and exotic looking, almost Asiatic in appearance, with dancing brown eyes, high cheekbones, and a delightful bob of frizzy black hair with unique beige and auburn highlights. Her breasts were beautiful and full and her figure dropped sharply to an hourglass tightwaist. Just gorgeous. A Jewish Margaret Trudeau with chipmunky cheeks. Tel Aviv on a sunny day. Prime, first-class beauty.

Rachel had learned layout and design at the New School in New York and from working summers at a Manhattan advertising agency. She got away with murder at the *Eagle* because she was very good and Pete Miller adored her. She could do anything with an exacto knife and a pile of cold type, and Pete called her "my layout princess." If everything was being held up because Pete was agonizing over a page, she burst right into the inner sanctum whether or not Pat Faucett said that was all right, expertly teased Pete with a sexy-babe flirt, and dynamited the logjam free.

"Hah! It's Rachel! What can I do today for the layout princess?"

Rachel was warm and physically demonstrative, and she used her body as an asset to get what she wanted and to express how she felt about someone. I met her the first time when she came over to my desk to explain that a story that I'd written for *UpCountry* needed to be cut to preserve more white space in the layout. Bending low in her mohair sweater, she nonchalantly perched her arm on my shoulder, letting her other hand come to rest against one of mine, and coaxed me out of the extra words.

I instantly loved her, instantly understood that she had secret issues, instantly dreamed her agenda. I was intoxicated by her prankster-JAP style, her rich-girl dressing, and the fact that she was so obviously needy. She was lovely, a radiant burst of energy, a natural empathy magnet. She was up in the mountains getting her head back together and would require a lot of maintenance, this gal, but my mind involuntarily leapt ahead several steps every time I was around her. God, do I love this girl and her issues, and I want to be there some-day to see this. One of these days this brave chick with the head problems is going to pack up the BMW and head south on the Taconic Parkway for the last time, finally busting free.

Rachel, Peter, and I became friends because of the social sit-uation in the newsroom. We often ate lunch with Pat Faucett and Mary Jane Tichenor at the Soda Chef on North Street. Most of the other reporters in the newsroom were either married or deadly serious about their careers, and they didn't want to goof off for an extra hour at lunch and get into long arguments about Watergate or books. Rachel always made a point of arriving at the Soda Chef by noon, wiggling her cute tush into the booth beside us and lighting up our lunch with her wisecracks and her hilarious imitations of Pete Miller.

Peter and I were doctrinaire about not watching television. We considered television a low-watt medium for cultural morons and found it hard to take anyone seriously if they watched a lot of TV. But Rachel watched TV almost every night, and we liked her too much to blame her for it. After a while we decided that Rachel's television addiction was a good education for us. Five minutes with her at the Soda Chef three days a week and we were back on track with popular culture. On *All in the Family*, Edith Bunker was going through menopause. Rachel kept us up to date.

Rachel assigned everyone TV or movie names. That was her mentality. You didn't really exist, you weren't fixed as a person, until you had been confirmed with a TV or movie name. Ted Baxter on *Mary Tyler Moore* was a double for Bill Bell, according to Rachel. Tom Morton was Kojack, and so forth.

Rachel's name for Pat Faucett was, obviously, "Mary," because Pat was painfully earnest, pretty, and tall, just like Mary Tyler Moore. Peter Scheer was "Eliott," for Eliott Gould, the Jewish studmuffin from *Bob & Carol & Ted & Alice* and *The Long Goodbye*.

Rachel called me "John Boy," after the Richard Thomas character on *The Waltons*. John Boy was always coming into the kitchen on Walton Mountain with an anguished but determined look on his face. *The American Mercury* had just rejected another one of his short stories. But he was going to be a great writer someday, the next Sherwood Anderson or John Dos Passos. He was the one who would make it; he would never give up.

"Hey, John Boy, did *Harper's* Magazine reject your essay on Thomas Pynchon yet?" Rachel would say to me, across a full Soda Chef table. "Don't be depressed. I'm sure that *The Atlantic Monthly* will be happy to reject it next."

"God fucking dammit, Rachel. That was supposed to be a secret."

Rachel smirky-smiled and threw back her head to laugh, so that her ringlets bounced. She loved annoying me.

"Oh, excuse me, everybody," she said. "I always forget that Rinker's in denial about wanting to be a famous writer."

When everybody started to laugh, Rachel wiggled over to me in the booth, ran her long nails through my hair, and kissed me on the cheek.

"Sorry, sorry," she said. "I just couldn't resist. Oh, look everybody! He's blushing. God, John Boy, you're perfect. You make it so much fun to be a bitch."

.   .   .

Rachel and I had a pact that I was quite proud of, and I was determined to make it last a good while, even forever, if need be. No sex. She was up in the mountains working on the jackhammer and dynamite phase of therapy, dealing with men issues and other things. She wasn't ready yet for the "physical thing." She and the doc were still working on that. Yes, she was sexually very powerful and attractive, a JAP beauty whom I just instantly wanted to cry for and to touch, and by this time I was entranced by the circle of effusive, sexy-brainy women gravitating around Peter Scheer, convinced that I absolutely *had* to find a Jewish girlfriend. But Rachel wouldn't be the one, I decided. I loved her too much as a soul mate. Her mental baggage made me feel very comfortable and built my confidence, because sharing conversations about her problems and hang-ups licensed me to reveal all of my own. I could be as troubled as I wanted around her, because she was never going to push me away for that.

So, that's how we were together, John Boy and Rachel, talking, laughing, exchanging our mental baggage, but not sex. On Tuesday and Thursday nights we did the bars and the pool halls together or danced at Mundy's, and that fall I just fell into a good, abstinent groove with her. Rachel was my chastity training for the weekends when Comfort came up.

Thursday nights could be awful for Rachel. After she finished working at the *Eagle* on Friday, it was a long three-day haul over the weekend until her therapy resumed on Tuesday morning, and she was anxious about being lonely all weekend. But this fit well with my schedule. I often worked late on Thursday nights, turning out some extra piece for Morton or Bell so that I could make the Friday deadline for the all-important Saturday *Eagle*.

Usually, I was coming in over Lenox Mountain for the Westbridge Inn in West Stockbridge at around 8:30 or 9 o'clock. Rachel's rental house was just up the hill, above Card Lake, so she just started waiting for me there on Thursday nights, goofing off with the hippies and the motorcycle gang members who hung out at the Westbridge. I enjoyed the familiarity of coming over the mountain on Thursday night and knowing that she would be there, with her sexy smirky-smile when I pushed through the door. As soon as she saw me, Rachel ordered what I liked, a Jack Daniels bourbon with a chaser of Rolling Rock beer.

Rachel had one habit that I found both lovable and annoying. She'd been in therapy for so long she just couldn't resist applying her doc's various techniques and analyses to me. I came to think of this as an unavoidable by-product of therapy, a halo effect—the patient starting to practice on all of her friends what she'd learned from the doc. It was evident that Rachel spent a lot of time discussing me with her therapist. Without exactly meaning to, Rachel seemed to be carrying back messages from him, behavior cues for me. I grew comfortable with this and after a while developed the sense that Rachel's doc wasn't simply treating her. He was treating us as a pair, a relationship to be explored. I'd never been in therapy myself and had a bias about it, mostly because the sort of community that I'd been raised in, the kinds of families I knew, reflexively equated therapy with mental instability, conceding weaknesses, failure. But now I was surrounded by this bumptious group of Jewish girls, brainy and physically warm, willing to discuss intimate subjects that I never got into with Christian girls, and they were all addicted to their relationship with a shrink. Being around someone in therapy was a tonic, but it could also be a pain in the ass.

"Okay, like, this is kind of neat, you know?" Rachel said one night at the Westbridge. "The doc *really* seems to like you. He likes the fact that you're needy. I've found someone needy who will listen to me."

"Rachel, that's bullshit," I said. "*I'm* not needy. *You're* needy. Jesus. What bullshit."

"Oh, my God, I can't wait to tell the doc this. Rinker Buck, not needy? John Boy, you're so pathetic sometimes it isn't even funny."

"Ah, c'mon Rachel. This is horseshit. Needy. Christ."

"God, you're so clueless. John Boy, needy is good. Needy is

attractive. But you're such a freaking little macho-boy that you can't even admit that to yourself. You're in denial about being needy."

I began to call this process "shrink-wrap," shorthand for the Shrink Wraparound Protection Program. The doc thought that he was treating just you. But then *you* go out and informally treat all your friends. You get accused by the doc of being in denial, which you deny, and then you go out and accuse all of your friends of being in denial, which they deny, but you're not going to let them get away with denying that they're in denial. There were only two states of being permitted in America. It was an infinite regress of denial. Either you were stuck in Denial Resistance Syndrome, or you were recovering from Denial Resistance Syndrome. Shrink-wrap. With Rachel, it became a big element of my life.

One Thursday night I got down to the Westbridge and I was ravenous. Very hungry. It was the beginning of Chanukah and Peter Scheer was off for a couple of days. Peter had told Tom Morton that his grandmother, who had recently been widowed, would get despondent if all the beautiful Scheer grandboys weren't back for the holidays. This was a crock, of course. Grandma was on a cruise ship down in the Bahamas, falling in love with her dance instructors, and Peter had merely used her as cover to sneak off to Boston and have a good time with Judy. But I didn't mind, because as soon as Peter left I got a chance to cover his beats and something was always happening. The mayor's urban renewal plan had collapsed again, and General Electric was hosing the Housatonic with PCBs. So, Chanukah was good for me. Peter had absconded to Boston and I got to prove to Morton that I could cover something more than the stiffs.

But I was hungry. I'd worked right through the lunch and dinner hours covering the stiffs and GE.

When I got to the Westbridge, in addition to bourbon and beer, I wolfed down a bowl of bar nuts.

"Oh my God, you're *starving*," Rachel said, calling out to the bartender. "Can you get John Boy a menu? Thanks. He's really hungry and I'm buying him dinner."

"Rachel, you don't have to buy me dinner. C'mon. I'm not even hungry."

As soon as Rachel said that she was going to buy me dinner, I could feel my face turning red. I had a complex about women buying me dinner. I was poor. I worked for *The Berkshire Eagle*. But every time I turned around, there was a high-rent lady in my life who expected dinner. Of course I had to pay, because that is how I was raised, and I didn't want them to think I was going to be poor forever. But if I got into a subject like this with Rachel, she would accuse me of having hang-ups.

"Oh, like I'm not noticing or anything," Rachel said. "It's so brain-dead, Rinker. You're in denial about being hungry because you're in denial about being embarrassed because I'm buying you dinner. And that's the worst. Double-denial."

"Oh, God, Rachel. I ate a bowl of peanuts. Do we have to drag Freud and Jung into this whole thing? I ate a bowl of peanuts. Big deal."

"No, Rinker. No. Do you *mind* if I say something to you?"

"I probably will, but go ahead."

"Okay, like, do you know how much of a difference you and Peter treating me nicely has made? Nobody else my age in the newsroom could care less, okay? And, you know, it's no secret that I usually have money and that you work for the *Eagle* and are broke. So, we're together tonight. I buy you dinner. Big deal. But, no, big Rinker guy, chop wood and fly airplanes Rinker, he's not going to let the babe pay. God, it's so retarded, Rinker. All of the advantage of knowing you? All the fun? You just bummed it all out."

When she was done saying that, Rachel turned her head and stared off to the corner of the room, with this vacant but lovely pout, and I was afraid that she was going to cry.

While she pouted, nervously rubbing her fingers underneath her eyes, I instantly and intensely loved her, and I was overwhelmed by a desire to back off and to try and please her. If she went away, life would be boring and I would miss her. The exchange of vulnerabilities between us—her need for company, to buy me dinner, my embarrassment over my poverty—was touching, and I was filled with both excitement and sadness for us.

"Rachel, I'm sorry. All right? You can buy me dinner, okay? I *want* you to buy me dinner. I just got past it."

"Okay, but don't fake me out. Do you mean it?"

"Rachel, does it matter if I mean it? I'm uncomfortable when the babe buys me dinner, all right? But, I'm willing to suspend my hang-up, for you."

Rachel reached over and squeezed my hand.

"Okay," she said. "I can dig that. And you know, Rinker, when you say really nice things like that, when you drop your macho stuff? It's beautiful and I love you."

"Good," I said. "I feel the same way."

So, the woman bought my meal, and I got over my dandy little head-fuck about that. I always remembered that dinner at the Westbridge—braised calf's liver in Merlot, garlic-mashed potatoes, and string beans—because Rachel was so happy watching me eat it, smirky-smiling every time I took another bite, reaching under the table to squeeze my knees and telling me how much fun I was. I was on a roll now and I wasn't going to stop.

"Hey, after dinner?" I said. "We're doing the Den and then Mundy's."

"Yeah, great idea," she said. "It's Stonewall Night. Maybe I'll run into some friends."

"Good, because you're paying. You're buying all my drinks. I'm going to get out of denial about this one so fast your head's going to spin."

When she laughed, Rachel's hair bounced, and she reached over the table to squeeze my hand.

"Oh my God, I can't believe this. I'm going to have to get my hearing checked. See? See? The doc is right. John Boy. Johnny Angel."

I always liked making the winter run from West Stockbridge to Stockbridge with Rachel. When it snowed it made no sense to take two cars, so we drove together in Rachel's BMW, and I loved handling that car. All the way over the mountain Rachel sat curled up on the passenger seat in her sleek ski-bunny jacket, chattering away about her head issues or the sitcoms or movies she was watching. And it was always fun at the Den on Thursdays, gay night, where Rachel was the fag-hag Queen of the Bop. The gay guys all loved her and wanted to talk about why she was wearing the gray mohair tonight, or the hot fuchsia V neck, and they all called her "Honey" or "Babe."

One of her closest friends was a fellow named Randy, a schoolteacher from North Carolina who'd moved north to the Berkshires to get away from the awful environment for gays down in Tarheel country. Randy had all kinds of mother issues and other crap that he liked to debrief with Rachel, but he was also one hell of a dancer. He did this *Grease* retro thing with a lot of jitterbug and Chubby Checker in it, and Rachel was just great too and could pick up on all his moves. They were wonderful together, a solid straight-gay dancing pair. After they'd jitterbugged for a while, Rachel would go aerobic all alone, dancing all that denial out of herself, hair flying and laughing while all the gay guys watched her, a bosomy, sexy, gorgeous fucked-in-the-head girl who had a perfect ass for dancing and could really move her hips. I loved her and dreamed for her future. Go, Rachel, go. Do the Bop. One of these days, babe, you're going to pack that car for the last time and bust free.

.　　.　　.

A week or two after that, I got down to the Westbridge on a Thursday night and Rachel was there. It was just before Christmas and my annual holiday crisis had been resolved. My sister McNamara, who was closest to me in age and whom I enjoyed very much, lived over in Northampton and needed a ride home. I was going home to see my family after all. I would enjoy the trip over the Catskills with Macky, cruise a few bars with my brothers Andrew and Nicholas, and go sledding on the graveyard hill with my younger brothers and sisters. My father would pester me about my career. When he was my age, he already had a job at *The New York Times*. My mother would want to know if I had dated any Catholic girls lately. Home for Christmas.

Rachel looked beautiful that night, very relaxed. She had exquisite taste in clothes, which always made me feel proud to be around her and sexually charged me up. Tonight she was wearing a new teal-colored mohair sweater that fit her body perfectly, and she had this way of wearing these very natural and clingy bras that made her breasts look spongy and welcome, almost irresistible to touch. I realized by now that the long sexual tease with her was having an interesting effect on me. The energy that I couldn't pour into a physical relationship was coming out as thoughts instead, a willingness to venture and express things about myself that I'd never considered. Every conversation with her was arousing, a prolonged and enjoyable mind-fuck. But my whole gestalt with her now was stretching things out forever, proving to myself and to her that I wouldn't press her sexually. Love her, love her forever, love this troubled girl. But I'd never try to get her into bed, because she needed to know that someone cared for her beyond that.

Rachel was excited that month. Her family was coming up during Christmas week to ski at Butternut, her first long visit with them since she began therapy, and she and the doc had worked on this, rehearsing scenarios and working out behavioral techniques that would get her through being with her family again. She was ecstatic about that, and I sat at a Westbridge booth with her, listening to her chatter away about her family issues and how excited she was about their Christmas week visit.

"Okay, so, like, you can never really get rid of all this family shit, you know? But you can learn to cope and just get along with them. And, John Boy, I'm going to do it. I'm just going to do it, you know?"

Bingo. She looked so beautiful and buoyant when she said that. Her olive skin glowed. The miniscule crow's-feet around her eyes, the little creases beside her mouth, were gone.

Rachel perched her elbows on the table and her chin in her hands as she stared at me across the table.

"Okay, so that's me," she said. "Now, what about you? What's happening with your family?"

I told Rachel about my plans for driving home with my sister, how my father would meddle and my mother would interrogate me about my dating life, but, screw it, there was a good steep hill in the graveyard, and I could always escape out there with my younger brothers and sisters and race through the drifts on a sled.

"Okay, okay, but how do you feel about that, Rinker?" Rachel said. "How do you *feel?*"

"Oh, Rachel, you know, I could just cry about it," I said. "I feel like crying about it. But what the hell. It's my family and I'm just going to go home and make the best of it."

"Oh, wow. I need to get my hearing checked again. Did you just say what I think you said?"

"Rachel. It's not a big deal, okay? I don't mean boo-hoo crying, that I need your shoulder to bawl on. I just mean, I could cry about it. What families come down to. I'm a failure, you know? That's why I go home for Christmas, to be reminded that I'm a failure. I don't work at *The New York Times* yet, and I haven't had a date with a Catholic girl in five years."

"So," Rachel said, "you hate them. Is that what you're saying? You hate your family?"

"No, Rachel. I happen to love my family, and you can stop your shrink-wrap right there. I love my family, but sometimes at Christmas they make me feel like crying. Do I have your permission for that?

"Okay, okay. I'm sorry. I didn't mean to give you the Third Degree."

"Yeah, well, there's something even better that you can do," I said. "I've only got $75 to spend for Christmas, so I'm just going to buy presents for my youngest sister and brother. Next week, we'll go over to the mall in Albany together and you can help me pick stuff out."

"Oh my God. John Boy, are you sure you're all right? Should I be taking your temperature or something? I can't believe that you just asked for my help like that."

"Yeah, well, you know, Rachel. I don't know dickshit about what to buy for my little sister, and you're going to help me."

Rachel was red-cheeked and perky when I said that, pensively smiling.

"Ooooooooooo, boy. I can't wait to tell the doc about this. John Boy is finally opening up."

When we got over to Mundy's that night, Rachel didn't want to dance with her gay pals. She felt "lazy and dreamy," she said, and asked me to buy her a wine at the bar. We sat and talked and held hands for a while and then, when the band started up again and played a couple of slow numbers, Rachel asked me to dance. We'd slow-danced before, but never very close. I usually tried to keep her at a distance, with a very light touch on the waist. She wasn't ready for physical contact and probably never would be, and at this point I just loved mind-fucking her so much I told myself that I didn't care.

But we just fell into a very different groove that night. When we started to dance I couldn't get a grip on this slippery, lycra-mohair kind of deal that she was wearing, and I wanted to feel her skin anyway, so I just reached up underneath and held her tightly by the small of her back. Rachel responded by giving me a hard torso pull, docking up against my corduroy pants, and then cupping my hand up into hers and between her breasts. She kept massaging my hand and hers on her breasts, enjoying that sensation, so that together we were hands to breasts, seductively felt through slinky mohair, but all of this just very relaxed and mellow. I liked the way that her breasts and her torso slightly rode up on my body when she stood on her toes to speak into my ear, and the sheen of her springy hair tickling my cheek.

"Oh, John Boy. I'm sorry I made you wait for this. I don't know how you can stand me. But, look, I'm getting past the physical thing, okay? Come back and see my place tonight. You can touch me all over like this."

That was the wonderful thing about Rachel, something powerful to love. Everything was overt and had to be discussed and carefully spelled out beforehand. But that only made me more forthcoming and honest about my feelings. I still didn't want to take Rachel—the long tease was just too good. We were laughing and joking all the time, sharing all kinds of mental baggage, and maybe if we got physically involved, this would end or get all bollixed up in the emotional entanglements of love. I was enjoying the ambivalence and tension of a prolonged relationship too much, and she wasn't getting me yet.

"Yeah, well, you know, Rachel. Let's just go back to your place and have some coffee. We don't have to plan everything out."

It was snowing very hard when we got outside, a real Berkshire blizzard, my first. As I fishtailed the BMW home, Rachel leaned over from the bucket seat in her slinky mohair sweater and down vest, with these fuzzy mittens and a scarf on, touching my knee and telling me funny stories about her little brother. She'd pulled back a little more and seemed relaxed. We pushed on for Card Lake and the views ahead were narrow but whirling, with twisting vortices of snow, very beautiful, one of Edith Wharton's wild white scenes.

.   .   .

When we pulled up to the house above Card Lake, Rachel wanted to talk, so we sat in the car for a while with the engine running and the heater on. She and the doc had shared a number of conversations about us, and they had agreed that she was now ready to enter the "physical phase" of a relationship. There were a lot of things about her that I hadn't heard yet, and she still wasn't comfortable discussing them. I had never had such a frank discussion with someone. I wasn't sure that we should break our vows. Rachel and I were close now, a good support system for each other, and there were just a dozen reasons, I thought, that we shouldn't jump the harness and go over to the carnal side. I told her that if I drove away right now and we just completely forgot that we ever had this temptation, I wouldn't have any hard feelings at all. And she wasn't to be confused. She was a great soul mate to be around, always, extremely sexual and attractive to me. But this would be changing our friendship now.

Rachel sat in the car seat listening to this, pony-shivering all over and stroking the palm of my hand with her nails, moody and contemplative. By this time my intuition for the shrink-wrap was pretty good, and I could tell that she'd rehearsed all this with her doc.

"Okay, like, you're being very considerate and sweet, but, no, it's all right, I want to be with you. I mean there's just this one thing that's so embarrassing, I just have to blurt it out. Christ, I've had to say it like a hundred times in group therapy, but it's hard doing it here, with you."

"Okay, so blurt it out. How bad could it be? I think you know by now that I'm not going to blame you for anything."

"Okay, okay," she said. "I'm climax-blocked, all right? God, it's so embarrassing. I mean, obviously, you know by now that I have a history, that I've had problems. I'm not up here because I enjoy the scenery. But I've worked through most of my issues and I'm almost done up here, and now I'm terrified that I'm still climax-blocked, and I just want you to know. Maybe there's nothing we can do about it, but at least I'm telling an available man, okay? That's new. Brand new for me."

I didn't have the foggiest notion about what to say, but I had learned something important with Rachel. If it was in my head, I could just say it.

"Rachel, I don't know what you expect me to do with the information you just gave me, but it's not embarrassing, okay? My take on you is that you're just too much fun to avoid. You're fun, you're a smart-ass, and you're beautiful. Can't we just have fun?"

"Yeah, yeah, thanks," she said. "But now you know. Just go slow with me and don't expect much. I've told you and now you know."

At this point I just wanted to get inside the pretty farmhouse and be romantic. This sexual tease had lasted long enough, I decided. It was time to light the candle and get Alan Shepard off the pad.

We walked arm in arm to the house. It was a beautiful night, with the wind kiting the snow around, the rumble of trucks with their plows down on the road below, and splashes of light on Card Lake from the Shaker Mill Tavern. Snow had already drifted on the porch. Inside, I was delighted with Rachel's place. She had the whole second floor of a capacious, immaculately restored Federal-style farm-house, with tall ceilings, a large fireplace, and windows over-looking Card Lake and the hollows climbing to Lenox Mountain. Rachel had tastefully decorated her floor with lots of braided rugs, halfway decent art, and reproduction Shaker rockers.

When we got inside we got down to business, which was playing Ma and Pa Kettle for a little while and getting used to each other in the environment. It was a pretty big deal for Rachel because she hadn't had a lot of men around. While she went into the kitchen to mix me up some special drink she wanted me to try, I went out in the swirling snow to the woodshed, found an axe and the woodpile, split up some kindling, and came back up with an armload to build a fire. The smell of maple burning mixed well in the air with the per-fumed fragrance of the tall candles on the mantle that Rachel had lit. When she came back out with my drink, which was mulled cider with brandy, Rachel looked slinky in her teal mohair and did this great couch-kitten default beside me, plunging down on the couch with her legs draped across mine.

Everything moved slowly and comfortably after that. We'd already spent so much time talking and holding each other that we felt very relaxed. It was all just one fluid motion of love. In the middle of telling me about a new movie that she'd just seen, Rachel leaned toward me with her lovely sponge of breast, just as I was leaning out to place my drink on the cof-fee table and we met hand-to-breast, accepted each other, and gently kissed. No teenage stuff, hot and fast. Very slow and chill, mellow, let it find itself, and just talk and laugh and touch and be relaxed. Hey, Rinker, this could be an education for you. Slow. Very slow. Slow-flight. Pull the power back and drop some flaps. Kiss her that way, in slow flight. It's amazing how calm a plane can feel, slow flying in still air.

After a while I went into the kitchen to find some wine, got back and put another log on the fire, and sat down beside her. I felt completely relaxed around her, uninhibited. Sorry, I can't resist this, your breasts are so beautiful, breasts felt through mohair. She leaned her head back on the couch and closed her eyes. That feels so nice. This is so much easier than I thought. That feels so nice. You're not trying to rip my bra off, you know, having fixations or anything, just touching me through my sweater. What did you fantasize about? What did you want to do when you dreamed about me? And don't BS me, okay? You had fantasies, obviously, so tell me what they were. Oh, you know, this. Kissing your breasts through a sweater. Hmmm-mmm. All night. We could just spend all night doing that. What else? Nothing, just, you know, chaste, seductive stuff. This. I always wanted to unzip your jeans but then do nothing about it. It's: Hey Rachel, you're really great and sexy. We're such good friends. Just let me unzip your jeans and see what your underwear looks like. If I came over here in the middle of the day because your oil burner broke? Yeah? Just, oh well, she's in her underwear and I like being with her. It's cool, but I don't have to touch her. Sexy underwear.

Oh yeah, well, wow, it's a channel or something, I was going to ask you the same thing. Let me take off your belt because it scratches my waist. The great thing about knowing each other for so long and being gentle and trusting, I mean just enjoying everything, is that I'm not afraid to tell you, like, I've had this fantasy and now I can just do it. We didn't start out with all the girlfriend-boyfriend stuff, you know? So we didn't wreck it. I've always wanted to just unzip your jeans and put my hand between your legs. Crazy, because that's practically identical to what you just said to me. Oh yeah, I could just like, clutch, just clutch you on the leg like that all night. God, talking is great isn't it? Talking through it. And this is a great fantasy, too. That day you took me for the motorcycle ride and we walked up Icy Glen and I just said, God lady, get on with your life, your problems are such a bore, why would you hold back with him but then you never touched me, and I just said, oh man, it's going to be wonderful when I do oral sex with him. When you drove me home I kept pushing my breasts up hard on your back but you didn't pick up on it and I thought something was wrong. That was my fantasy that day. What will it be like to get him home and just say, sorry if you get the wrong impression, but I would just like to be close to you this way. It's how we should end our day after Icy Glen. But then the guy was here to fix the house. You drove away and I was so sad but I said to myself well it's a signal. A signal that I shouldn't do it yet. But then I kept thinking about it.

The fire, now viewed across her lovely flat back of teal mohair. Yeah, that's right. Squeeze me with your knees, okay? I love it when you squeeze me with your knees like that. Can we take forever? We should do it long and slow, okay? The moist enclosure of her lips, full and olive-tan, lips and tongue to penis, lips and tongue and tingling nails to thigh, her oral vulva hypnotically relaxing as I place the tips of my middle fingers lightly in her ears and hold her soft feline hair, unison and flowing motion together, from the palazzo the wheat undulating in the breeze, his ocean now, he said, Greylock on porphyry horizon his humpback whale, that distant summer afternoon of hazy pastel light on forest evoked here by fire glow on teal, rhythmic baleen swell her sweet oral vulva cheeks and fine hair gently lifting and falling in my hands. The gams. How long they lasted if sailors were patient and trusted slow converse. Slowly. I lifted her up so we could go even more slowly, slowly Rachel, slowly lean into me your teal lycra slinky feline beauty. And then she wanted to kiss me hard for a while and kneel tall astride with her knees on the soft couch on either side of me and with a thespian flourish calisthenically off with the teal mohair and yes just like that, it feels so sexy being kissed through a bra. Lips to aureole and nipple through nylon-cotton, nice astringent taste, and her perfume, something she got at a good store, chalky jade fragrance, so sweet but also like smelling salts to the nose as she clasps my hair and kisses lips to lips hard, lips to forehead lips to ears. I broke from her lips to kiss her breasts. The muscles of her flat torso taunt and then she forces hard with her hand on the back of my neck, the hard, hard lips to nipple-aureole suckling. Yes that's good motorcycle man. I really like it when you kiss me hard there. With the bra on, so sexy. Thank you thank you thank you guy. And you know oh just thanks this is great, I love talking too, and it's so good we've done this. It's been so long. Yeah, I like kissing you there. It feels like the first time, practically.

It was slow. We had all night, till dawn if need be, and I wasn't into rapid penetration or rough ritualistic scouring of breasts, just slow, slow, the feel of my fingertips on her soft sponge of breast just barely touching, a sensation almost through air. And, motorcycle man, listen, why do the bedroom, let's just pull the coffee table away and lie and watch the fire for a while and, yeah, I've got these blankets. I can get a sleeping bag for underneath us if you want. The fire is so nice. No. I'm not laughing for that reason. I'm just laughing at myself. Just satisfaction. I was afraid to be with you and now it's so easy and natural. Ummmm. Yeah. If you suck me with my underwear on, yeah right on my vagina, it's just so nice. Through clothes. I just love the feeling. Clothes. I love the feeling of clothes.

And then she reached down with long nails and took that off too but kept her bra on. We both liked that. The calisthenic push-up feel of beautiful breasts with the bra still on. We would make love like that all night, I thought. Rachel-Rachel so lovely with her dark aureole and nipples, all night with her bra on. And then she tasted so wonderful, all perfumey sweet vagina, and she put her index fingers in my ears and enjoyed massaging my temples while I found her clitoris and enjoyed the purchase so much, just good suction and miniscule sensation, and enjoying the way *she* enjoyed it so much and loving her and the push-up feel of her bra-breast when I reached up for that, and loving her and knowing we could do it all night just like this. No stupid guy-guy thing, oh damn what's she going to think now, none of that, just gentle relaxation and pleasure when I ejaculated on her ankles and shin. Oh, see? she said. That feels so good. Animals breeding. It feels better on the outside. Skin. Hey, goofy me, all right? I never want to go to sleep tonight. The big sleepover when we talk till 4 A.M. I'll make another mulled cider for you. Logs, what are we going to do for more logs?

Rachel, I said, I left some on the stair landing.

Oh, good. I'll do mulled cider and you do logs.

When she came back with the hot cider and hot chocolate she had on men's Brooks Brothers pajamas, just the bottoms, men's pajama bottoms with a bra on. We just talked, talked and watched the fire, and drank mulled cider, occasionally touching each other and leaning shoulder to shoulder, watching the pastel flames with a blanket shared between us, contented and feeling romantically close and warm.

Rachel wanted to tell me all about her favorite movies—*Klute* and *The Thomas Crown Affair*, *On the Waterfront,* and *Women in Love*. In the spring, when Bernardo Bertolucci's *Last Tango in Paris* had come out, she'd been visiting her aunt in New York—it was her first official visit "home" that the doc had allowed. They went to see *Last Tango* together. God, Marlon Brando and Maria Schneider together. That was sexual tension, beauty.

But she really liked the early Bertolucci work the most, especially anything with Dominique Sanda. Rachel was obsessed with Dominique Sanda. One day, when I was with her down at Nejaimes Market in Stockbridge, there was this cheap, tabloid movie magazine with Dominique Sanda on the cover and Rachel bought it just to read that story. It was something that I really liked about this new crowd of Jewish women that I was meeting, their candor about female beauty. If a Christian woman thinks for a moment that you're considering another woman's beauty, she clamps right up. Ooop, he's thinking about cheating on me. Jewish girls just come right out with how they feel.

"Okay, Dominique Sanda in *The Conformist* or *The Garden of the Finzi-Continis*? That's just an amazing face and body. You know, she can pull anything off with small breasts. I would kill for her body and hair."

"Oh, Rachel, that's kind of ridiculous. With your looks."

"No. Dominique Sanda. Tragic, romantic. I mean it's like us here tonight, so beautiful. The seduction scene in *The Conformist*. Dominique Sanda is the ultimate Bertolucci heroine. By the way, what's yours? What's your favorite movie?"

"Oh, that's easy," I said. "*Hellcats of the Navy*."

"Oh my God. I've just had oral sex with a total moron. That's the movie you like?"

"Rachel, c'mon. *Hellcats of the Navy*. You're the one saying be honest and everything. It's a great movie."

"Wow. Am I really hearing this? Everything I just said back there, forget it, okay? Oh, motorcycle man. Motorcycle man, touch me there again. God, how retarded can I get?"

"Rachel, look. I really like epics. Military epics, history epics, romantic epics. David Lean's *Lawrence of Arabia*, you know, is a great, great movie. Peter O'Toole and Omar Sharif blowing up trains and slaughtering the Turks with a great soundtrack playing. John Huston's *Treasure of the Sierra Madre*, the Russian *War and Peace*, *Dr. Zhivago*, *Ben Hur*, whatever. *Spartacus*. I could have tried to impress you with, you know, my filmic erudition. I could have said *Cool Hand Luke*, *Easy Rider,* or *Hud* to psyche you out and make you love me. But I'm not. I'm being honest, okay? *Hellcats of the Navy* is the best."

"Oooooooo boy. Are you sure you're not the Boston Strangler? I'm revising my opinion of you now."

"Rachel, chill," I said. "John Boy wants to change the subject. Say something romantic."

"Yeah, okay," she said. "I'm feeling so mellow tonight I can say anything."

"So, say it."

"Okay, so I went into my bedroom and put on these pajama bottoms because I was cold. And as I was coming back with the hot cider I said to myself, wow, they have a fly. Rinker could make love to me right through them, with them on. Isn't it interesting that I had to go through all this stuff to reach a new point? A new point. Talking, being sexy and romantic. I feel so sexy with some clothes on. Sex through clothes."

"Yeah, it is sexy. I never realized it before."

"Yeah and when you were doing me before, I had this strange flash."

"What?"

"Well, it's strange but it's the truth. I mean someday I'm going to be done and get out of here. I really want to get out, find the right man, and just marry and have babies. God how many babies I'm going to pump out. And all I want is like some little Tudor house somewhere, babies and a husband who will make love to me through clothes. Pajamas. Sexy. Through pajamas, every night. It's strange. But if you've been through what I've been through, that's all you want. Pretty Tudor house like my parents had at first, good husband, sex through clothes. That was my flash."

"Right, exactly. Me? Settling down and being in a Tudor house somewhere? That's strange. But you saying it, that's not strange."

"Exactly. Motorcycle man soul mate. He loves me. He only asks certain questions. He takes me to the Den so I can be with my gay friends. Then, I get out of here finally? Never look back and keep it as a perfect memory. It's gone. It's done. The bitch has flown the coop."

"You really do need to get out, don't you?"

"Totally. Get done, get out, never look back. I hate my fucking doc. I want out."

"Yeah, but it's such a different reality for me," I said. "I love these mountains, already. Sometimes I never want to leave."

"Totally. I'm totally into that reality for you," Rachel said. "Rinker is really into Pete Miller's mountains."

I kissed her breast through nylon. The fire was so warm now there were sexy beads of perspiration between her breasts, tasting salty and marine. Just slow, very slow, no rubric of time exists for us, her mound of hair reached through cotton orifice, the taste salty and addictive, a swim under amber sunset in the Marquesas, the clitoris an infantile but divinely pleasurable fixation, the pony-shiver of her belly as my tongue finds her magic oracle there, the breast I reach for now because it is so comforting, oracle to aureole joined by me, teal the forest that day and love her, love her, love her all for her, the satisfaction of her moaning now, it's all for her. She is moaning now, very loudly, calling out with joy, a place of sexual beauty. Slow, just very slow. Liberate yourself from speed. From guilt. She talks to you now. It's okay, it's okay, God you're good to me. I feel so creamed, she says, and repeats it, just so beautifully creamed.

Oh, and something else to consider, because of how she said it. Her beautiful orgasmic cream, her spongy breasts felt then by your hand. Lips and tongue to clitoris, lips to thigh, lips to lovely tightwaist, and lips and mouth all over her, no climax-block here really, just a head-trip played on self from some past trauma or hurt. Maybe it's not a block at all. Just frigidity about missionary position sex. Female head-trip played on self. Mention it? No. Good, that's smarter Rinker. All these creamy little breakthroughs for you tonight. You don't have to say everything. Just feel, commune, love her, love her, the way she squeezed your temples and shivered, and then what she said.

And then, through cotton, the final clasp, the slippery baleen mount, through cotton the dark, slender legs seductively felt. Wonderful undulating union. I want to make love to you forever in my pajamas. Minimarriage simulation. Marriage fantasy now, also okay. Rinker, I'll never come this way but it feels so good. Just your body on me. So skinny. It'll take forever, she says, you can laugh at me because I am laughing at myself, let's stop and rest if you want, more cider and talk of little brothers. Nice fire now. Mound of orange coals. Once a new log was thrown on, the flames tickled up around the edge and burst out of smoke.

I was moody and reflective now, staring into the fire. But Rachel said that was okay. She just wanted to sit and relax and hold me.

Good, because I needed to ponder something that had happened. Our lovemaking had taken me to a new place tonight. The experience was so intense, the sensation so welcome but strange, that I just wanted to think about it for a while.

While I was suckling Rachel's vagina, a Greek chorus had

appeared to me. The voices and the faces were all familiar. They were all women that I had known and cared for deeply, some of them lovers, some not. The older sister of a girlfriend, the one who had introduced me to sex, was there, and so was that girlfriend. There were two college flames and some of their close friends, and a bevy of girls that I had dated in high school. Judy Lesser was also there, mostly, I guess, because Judy was often in my thoughts and had had such an influence on me this year. They all seemed to be speaking to me, appearing beside me as a communal vision while I enjoyed my hard clasp on Rachel and she pulled my hand harder to her breast. They were a sorority of women, all these wonderful people from my past, reaching over the mountains and extending a sisterly embrace for Rachel.

Do it Rinker, do it, slow, slow, slow. Remember how it was with me? Well, try that—it's our sisterly embrace for Rachel. It's from all of us. Rinker, she's beautiful. She needs a life. Get her out of there. Breast to breast, the sisterly embrace of love, no jealousy exists for us on this one, lips to lips and hearts to all women, the sorority of women was there beside me as I loved Rachel. Rinker you've been shameless with your life and always been crazy and you drive too fast, but you're a romantic and a lot of fun, remember what we've taught you but at all costs get her out of there, please. She's trapped. It was the most beautiful part about being with Rachel, the sorority of women who mind-wandered in for me there, right beside her. I could feel their sisterly embrace over the mountains, for Rachel, and for me. Rinker, fuck her, fuck her good and love her. Fuck her slow and fuck her one more time for us. Forever tonight. Cream and fuck her gloriously. Feel her up, cream her through cotton, fuck her brains out if that's what it takes, but fuck her hard and fuck her well and fuck her out of those mountains for good. For us. Get her out of there. Please. She's lovely and we'd like to see her free.

I didn't really know what the Greek chorus meant, or why the sorority of women had appeared to me. Years of book-turd smarts were of no use to me here. Maybe it was just my own conscience speaking, working on a moral dilemma, justifying my promiscuous past and liberating me from all the hypocrisy of Catholic sexual doctrine. Certainly the residual anxiety about pushing the sexual envelope with a vulnerable girl created a need for me to seek the permission of other women, and thus the sorority might have appeared out of my own subconscious desire for consensus. But I didn't really care about figuring it out either. Oral sex is immensely satisfying to deliver, I loved doing it for Rachel, and sharing that prolonged suckling with the sorority of women from my past greatly enhanced my pleasure. I considered it a spiritual experience, and I felt free, wonderfully free. The old equation of sex and guilt had been lifted. I'd held off forever with Rachel, just listening, talking, enjoying, and would have held off even longer, until she invited me in. And then my suckling of her vagina had been sacramental, and the sorority of women had appeared. I loved the universal communion of women who appeared while I was alone with Rachel, and their sisterly embrace over the mountains. The sorority had freed me, too.

I was exhausted now, but spiritually charged up, and I broke for a moment to step into the kitchen for more wine. When I got back and Rachel placed her hand on my leg, I felt that we could last forever. We'd done it slowly all night and talked, taken breaks to watch the fire, enjoyed glasses of wine together, and kissed some more. That's the embrace we fell into now. They were kisses of joy, joy of just knowing her, joy of her beautiful place. Joy of her beauty and the sorority of women.

Lips to lips, lips to nylon bra, lips to salty crevice, lips to purple rim, and here we go again. Slow. Forever tonight. Yeah it's nice. On top me like that. I'll never come but it's just so nice being with you. It's just so nice. I love dreaming. I love it through clothes.

Then all of a sudden that ship of hers just came barreling down the centerline, hit V1 just past the mile marker, rotated and lifted off. She got her wheels up smartly and cleaned off the wings, engaged autopilot, and captain, we've got positive rate of climax here. Wow, I thought, this is something unexpected. We're climbing out here at the missionary angle of attack. It was very prolonged and expressive, ahhhhhhh just a beautiful emancipation to experience with Rachel. She's ballistic now, Friendship 7 back with Houston after passing the radio veil. *Godspeed Rachel, you're cleared for three orbits.* Oh God, Rinker, isn't it great, I can talk right through it, Wow I can't believe this. She was there now, this was it, she was the bingo climax-girl, flawless on the middle marker, she was getting out of the mountains someday for sure and I felt like crying about it.

It was spectral. Rachel was there. I just felt so happy.

It was warm and couch-kitteny afterward. More wood on the fire, a nightcap of mulled cider and brandy, the nubby afghan thrown over our shoulders, and the salty perspiration on her bra resting against my chest. We talked and goofed around and stared romantically into the fire, held hands, and shared whatever crazy-ass old thing came into our heads.

"Oh, I feel so fulfilled now," Rachel said. "I can't wait to tell the doc. It's like, well, yeah, I had this little strange thing you know, pajamas? But I told him all about it, doc, and that's how Rinker and I did it."

I was touched by what Rachel said and, afterward, could never figure out what changed me the most, Rachel herself, or Rachel and all of her shrink-wrap. Before I met her, I would have been humiliated by the idea that every detail of my love life with someone, right down to the fact that we enjoyed it through pajamas and not nude, was being shared with someone else, even a professional therapist. But I was past that now because I was so jubilant for her. She was there, she was beginning to break through, she'd fucked her boyfriend and had fun that night. Someday soon she'd be packing that BMW for the last time and speeding down the Taconic Parkway. Whatever it takes, Rachel. My privacy belongs to you and the doc now. It was a thrill, just being a part of her life.

Our lovemaking and long chats together by the fire, looking out through the window and its prism of gutter icicles to snowy Card Lake, continued all through the winter. Many nights I went home first, had dinner with Peter, and then wandered over to Rachel's after he started reading or looked like he wanted to turn in for bed. And it was wonderful being at Rachel's, doing the Ma and Pa Kettle routine together before we sat down by the fire. Some nights we passionately made love, other nights we just sat and held each other and talked. I loved the familiarity of being in her place, the ways our bodies fit together, and I grew as addicted to her sarcasm as to the sex.

There was one other thing that I never minded and didn't try to change her mind about. No matter how late I was there, no matter how prolonged our lovemaking, she preferred if I went home afterward. It was still a thing she was working on. The all-night sleepover with a man would imply commitment, something longer lasting. She conceded that she didn't understand this little phobia herself. And she was afraid to tell the doc. He would make her work on it and that would slow down her escape from therapy. It made sense to me somehow. But it didn't matter, anyway. The Richmond manse was just down the road.

The ride home from Rachel's was wintry and quiet, a route fixed in memory to signify a time of life. Sometimes Rachel gave me a hot mulled cider in a mug to drink while driving home. Kiss her good-bye at the door, frisson of postcoital regret, the lovely feel of the elastic waist of her pajamas as we embrace. Out the snowy driveway, down the road to the bridge over the Card Lake sluice, up the hill past the old gas station, and then into darkness with the anthracite rim of peak all around.

I loved the feel of approaching home, the rutted Rossiter Road dipping up and down as my headlights probed the canopy of trees. Pulling in, I felt tired and cold, enjoying the knowledge that I wasn't getting enough rest. The last smoky residue of the fire that Peter had abandoned an hour earlier hung in the air. Read in bed, five hours of sleep, get up and chop wood in the morning, over the mountain and hit those obits. I enjoyed it, burning on empty all the time.

Rachel, Rachel. The sorority of women. That winter, especially on nights when I had been with Rachel, I slept quite soundly. The blackness of the Berkshire night and the delicate, purple aura up along the peaks were very soothing.

CHAPTER ELEVEN

MOTHER SNOW dropped her narcotic white blanket on the
Berkshires shortly after Thanksgiving that year, turning the
peaks into a glittering horizon of silver and cobalt. I had
entered the Hawthorne country of western New England
brooding and antic, prone to inexplicable mood swings, but
the winter changed that. Snow was my great protector, and
the pristine dunes of powder laid down over the hills had a
calming effect. I rose happily every day with the still, quiet
Berkshire dawns, brushed the white dusting from the night
before off of my woodpile and then split logs for an hour,
soothed by the exercise and the low lavender light. Then I
drove north toward work, meditating on the beauty of the
forests and the pink disc of the Shaker round barn.

My first winter in the Berkshires was a tonic for me, a season of mental health, for another important reason. It all
began with a phone call on a Saturday morning, shortly after
Peter Scheer and I had moved into the Miller manse.

"Say, it's an outrageously beautiful day out and I have in
mind a modestly ambitious circuit of the tornado district. I
have not yet properly surveyed the full extent of the damage
left behind by this improbable meteorological event. Are you
up for a junket, a hike, a felicitous spell in the woods?"

Roger Linscott was our closest neighbor now, living just

down the hill at the end of Rossiter Road. He was perpetually "shy" a weekend hiking companion, and I was anxious to learn the local terrain, and I soon found that I enjoyed this gruff but endearing man immensely, and over the next two years Roger Linscott bosomed me in his mountains. We hiked almost every Saturday or Sunday together—some weekends, both days—covering every inch of high ground from Mount Riga in Connecticut to the Dome and Equinox in Vermont, nearly all of the far New England parapet, with frequent "asides" as he called them, "western forays," into the blue Catskills and the black Adirondacks. Linscott was an ideal mentor and companion for many reasons. Physically inexhaustible and intellectually restless, he loved to range out across the peaks, discoursing all day about Winston Churchill or the crazy Stockbridge millionaires, a grand festival of talk as hungry for companionship and local adventure as I was. At night, after descending from the icy peaks thirty or forty miles from home, we worked our way back down the range by stopping at bars. We never tired of hiking, we never grew bored with each other, we never ran out of subjects to discuss. Linscott and those mountains together were the best benediction of all.

Linscott was a tough man to get used to, and I was initially intimidated by him the first few times I arrived at his pretty Cape Cod house at the bottom of the road. He was, after all, the "Great Linscott," fresh off his Pulitzer, abrupt and scaldingly sarcastic most of the time, the sort of fellow who would tire quickly if you couldn't keep up with him, verbal riposte to riposte. To him, the earth was populated by only two classes of people. There were, first of all, "good eggs," individuals of genuine merit and good conversational skills, who were worthy of his company. Eccentricity and a healthy dose of mental baggage were important attributes for him. Pete Miller, of course, was eminently a "good egg," and Roger also admired Dick Happel, whom he considered one of the better writers on the paper and "a refreshingly open queer." There were a few others. Linscott's friend in Lenox, the legendary journalist and foreign correspondent William L. Shirer, wasn't simply brilliant and self-deprecating. At cocktail parties, Shirer shamelessly chased young women, which Linscott considered "charmingly obnoxious."

But that, pretty much, was it. Everyone else in the world was an "egregious boob." Linscott was forever railing against the "hideously self-important jackasses" who served on the Pittsfield City Council, the "philandering, mountebank ministers" who ran the local churches, the "preposterously ignorant" editorial assistants that Pete Miller assigned to his department. The normal emotional and intellectual inadequacies of people drove him insane.

"Gad, that fellow is atrociously *stoooooo-pid*, 'tisn't he? I fantasize that one day he'll do us all a favor and leap off the Holmes Road bridge."

Linscott invested even the simplest walk out the back door with a sense of adventure by poring for a half an hour or more over his U.S. Geologic Survey topographic maps, amiably discoursing on his planned route and the local natural features while he sat in front of the fire in his cluttered, book-lined library. While this was going on, the house filled with the smell of fried bacon and scorched butter. Lucy Linscott was preparing us a pre-expedition lunch of grilled cheese and bacon sandwiches cooked just the way that Roger liked, which was burnt to a crisp.

One afternoon in mid-November, my second or third time down there, Linscott and I were munching blackened sandwiches as we examined his maps when a magnificent, angry clatter suddenly erupted from the barnyard above the house. Some kind of awful brawl was beginning, and it sounded like the Battle of Chancellorsville up there. The pounding of limbs against flesh resounded down through the yard.

"Oh Jeeeeeez-us motherless fucking Christ to hell," Linscott growled. "That egregious donkey of mine. Fucking abomination."

From the kitchen, Lucy called in, very agitated.

"Roger! Roger! You forgot again! They're fighting! Get up there!"

Then, faster than I thought a big man like him could move,

Linscott shot up out of his chair, bolted across the center hall, and pushed through his back door. He had bounded across the yard and jumped into a small enclosed animal pen beside the barn before I could get up there behind him.

When I got up to the barn, Linscott was scrambling around the animal corral, cursing and flailing out with his arms, desperately attempting to separate two of his pets, a Peruvian llama and an Abyssinian donkey. Apparently, llamas and jackasses don't get along very well. It seemed to me, watching the two beasts in the Linscott corral biting, whining, and wheeling around backwards to line up kick-boxing moves at each other, that the conflict between llamas and donkeys was primordial, a genetic incompatibility going way back, some sort of old evolutionary conflict between the mountain and desert species.

These animals really hated each other. The surest sign of that was neck and nostril biting, and they were savagely going at that now. I happened to have considerable experience with this. My father's farm in New Jersey had been just one long brawl between squabbling children and sociopathic Belgian shepherds and billy goats, a huge embarrassment that I was still recovering from. I was almost gleeful, watching Linscott attempting to referee his beasts. If the Great Linscott could have a headcase existence like this, what had been so wrong with mine?

The problem, Linscott explained to me later, had cropped up early in the relationship between the family pets, namely, the day Linscott brought the llama home because he thought that his donkey was "lonely." They fought, instantly and viciously. Since then, Linscott had been careful to keep them apart in separate stalls. But once in a while when he let the llama out into its walking pen, he forgot that he had not locked the donkey back in the barn. Ergo, Chancellorsville in the backyard.

The donkey and the llama were really going at it now. They pivoted and wheeled while Linscott tried to get in between them, the llama occasionally spitting out these immense globs of mucous, aimed at the donkey but generally hitting Linscott in the back of the head. Meanwhile Roger himself had finally gotten hold of the halter of the donkey and was being wheeled around by the jerks of the donkey's head while trying to establish footing in the manure-strewn pen.

No amount of yanking and cursing at a donkey works, of course. An Abyssinian jackass doesn't even notice this. Centuries of careful breeding by sadistic Bedouin goatherds have made donkeys impervious to all human control.

Then the Linscott mayhem got even better. The family dog was a fully grown Standard French Poodle named Mattie. It is a mistake to consider poodles cuddly and nice. Poodles are, in fact, a hunting dog, and quite malevolent when aroused, as good as a Rottweiler, I would say. In the middle of Linscott's yanking on the donkey and the llama's squealing and spitting and kicking up a dust storm, Mattie came bounding across the lawn, leapt into the animal pen, and started savagely attacking the donkey too.

Mattie was a very dirty fighter, but an effective donkey-herd. After landing a couple of pretty good snaps on the nostril and foreleg of the donkey, just to show the beast that it had arrived, Mattie yelped up between the donkey's legs and snapped at its balls.

Via a combination of that, a sort of ongoing castration by the poodle and Linscott's hanging on the halter, the donkey was subdued and convinced to return to its stall in the barn. Linscott threw home the dead-bolt lock on the Dutch door and leaned against it with his shoulders, heaving a sigh of relief.

"Fucking egregious donkey. Gad, do I rue the day I brought that maniacal beast home."

Linscott stepped over to sooth the llama, talking to it quietly and stroking the long, luxuriant hair on its neck.

"Now there, Dolley, it's okay," Linscott said, affectionately cooing to his pet. "I'm sorry, Dolley. I did it again."

That was the llama's name. Dolley. As in Dolley llama.

His llama pacified, Linscott scrambled back over the fence, leaned on a post, and lit a cigarette to calm himself down. Mattie the poodle came over for affection and Linscott leaned down and stroked her face, thanking her for her help with the donkey.

"Gad, my lunacy in pets is indisputable, wouldn't you say?" Linscott sighed. "Why would anyone own such an infernal jackass? I'm quite sorry. Animal fights are woefully disagreeable."

"Roger, no problem," I said. "I enjoyed watching you do that."

"Bravo. I can see that you're going to be slavishly tolerant as a friend. But shall we conclude our lunch? I should like to get on with our hike."

.   .   .

Roger Linscott regarded the proper mastery of snowshoes a prime virtue, an important expression of character. Snowshoes were simple and refreshingly therapeutic to operate, the ideal means of pushing up through Mother Snow to reach the high, noble purple-black rim, where there were few distractions from the outside world. Slosh-slosh up through the hemlocks and the silvery groves of gray birch, turn perpendicular to the grade and crosshatch up over the steep granite cobbles, bush-whack a little to the first false summit of Perry's Peak or Mount Everett. Here, we paused for a rest and the proper merging of talk was essential. Linscott would lean against a birch, light up a Kent, and amiably discourse on the novels of John Dos Passos, what a "mean drunk" William Faulkner was, or the extramarital adventures of the crazy Stockbridge millionaire whose mansion he would be dining at tonight.

On the summits, if it was a sunny day, Linscott and I liked to remove our snowshoes and then lounge on the snow for an hour or so, eating the packed lunch I had carried up in my backpack and discussing the books we were reading, or what-ever was on our minds that week. At first I didn't feel comfort-able with him or entitled to share so much of his time. But these feelings of inadequacy gradually broke down, mostly because, for all his bristling intellectuality, Linscott was also a deeply humble and honest man. He told me several times how "hideously lonely" he became on weekends and how difficult it was finding companions willing to cover vast miles of woods in a single day, with no assurance that they'd reach recognizable landmarks by nightfall. Over time I just came to accept that I was a natural companion for him. I was capaciously well read for someone my age, in need of what he had to offer, and the idea of having to navigate all day by creek beds or the sun seemed normal to me. I enjoyed being lost in the woods at night.

The Great Linscott atop Perry's Peak.

When we finally emerged on dry road, Linscott loved to prowl the shitkicker bars down along the New York state line, or swing by and take in Mundy's in Stockbridge. They were mostly blue-collar and biker bars, and a pool-playing ethos prevailed there. Losers bought a round for winners. We had a lot of fun in the boozy warmth of those places and became addicted to playing pool together, challenging teams from the Warlocks or the Raiders motorcycle gangs. I could usually sink at least one ball on the break and then maybe a ball or two on each visit to the table after that, protecting us until it was Linscott's turn and the table was cleaned. We rarely lost and Linscott was so good at pool that over the next several winters we drank for free, and the bikers *loved* Linscott. They called him the "Professor."

"Look at this old fucking fart, would you? The Professor just whipped our asses again."

When we returned to Linscott's house, if he and Lucy didn't have a mansion party to go to, we usually lit a fire in his den, drank bourbon, and played backgammon. Lucy Linscott served us a dinner of chicken livers and bacon burnt to a crisp, pan-fried potatoes, and a salad. I felt welcome and comfortable at the Linscotts, and Lucy, Roger, and I drank and laughed until quite late.

Moonlight glittered on the brook ice and a purple aura glowed on the peaks as I stumbled up the hill toward home. I was exhausted, my face was scratched and raw from the snapping limbs as I had bushwhacked over the hills behind Linscott, and Judy and Peter always laughed at my wasted state when I returned after a hike with Linscott. But I was high, revived. Linscott seemed to be curing me of a number of things at once. My wanderlust and dreams of escaping out west seemed to be receding, mostly because I was learning that there were plenty of distractions right where I was.

.   .   .

Up there on the summits, while we lounged and talked before resuming our snowshoes or hikes, Linscott seemed to understand another important thing about me. I was the twenty-two-year-old with the maxed-out brain. Most people are more fucked up at the age of twenty-two than they'll be at any other time of their life, a bundle of neuroses and phobias dense-packed in as a result of adolescence, bad relationships, failed love affairs, schooling, and family. Debris removal is now required, and that takes time, a good listener or two. Linscott could see, for example, that I was tormented by ambition and harbored unrealistic expectations of early success. He listened patiently while I bitched about my problems with Bill Bell and described my father's extravagant dreams for me, making light of it with his sardonic barbs and introducing the idea that I might adopt a sense of humor about myself. I was, Linscott thought, "egregiously self-promoting," the "prototypical young man in a hurry." He shared with me details from his own life. Luck and personality, Linscott

thought, largely determined success, and I needed to appreciate that people in positions of authority could simply be
wrong about me. In 1948, when Linscott had interviewed at
the *Eagle*, the news editor hadn't wanted to hire him, because
he didn't consider Linscott the sort of talent who could
"report on a dog fight on the end of North Street." But Pete
Miller had insisted on taking Linscott anyway, assigning him
to cover politics. That was fortuitous, because the uninspired
mayoralty of James Fallon was about to be swept aside by the
two-term regime of Robert Capeless, a progressive and
enlightened lawyer who ushered in an epic period of urban
rebuilding and city planning and went on to become the state
treasurer of Massachusetts. Linscott, merely by covering
Capeless and becoming his friend, shared in his glow, and so
distinguished himself writing about urban reform that his
elevation to editorial writer was inevitable. The news editor
had been wrong, and the timing of Linscott's hire had been
perfect—a classic Pulitzer trajectory. But it was largely an
accident of fate.

"Self-importance is odiously boring," Linscott said to me
once, as we paused to catch our breath up on Perry's Peak.
"You shouldn't lust too much for success. All I did was work
hard for Pete and sit around and wait for good things to happen to me."

"Yeah. But, Roger, at my age you didn't have to write obituaries."

"Oh nonsense, you egregious boob. At *your* age I happened
to be sitting on the deck of a Navy destroyer, watching while
kamikazes dive-bombed my head. And do you know what's
important about that?"

"No, what?"

"Nobody gives a flying fuck. And nobody will ever give a
flying fuck that you wrote obituaries once."

There were other bonus benedictions from being up there
with Linscott. I may have faked my way onto the *Eagle* by
lying about my photographic credentials, but by the winter I
had acquired a decent sense of composition and I realized
that, high up on the peaks all weekend, I was in great black

and white country. Joel Librizzi, the *Eagle*'s award-winning photographer, never minded when I came back from a hike with Linscott with four or five rolls of film to throw into the chemicals with his stuff, and he was a total peach of a man who didn't mind editing my proofs and telling me if I had anything worthwhile.

Mostly, all I did was shoot ersatz Ansel Adams pictures, but it was important to me and I never stopped trying. One day, up on Perry's Peak in Richmond, I took a picture of Linscott standing on his snowshoes in hard black profile against the cirrus sky. It epitomized everything about him up there, and Joel Librizzi suggested that I show the picture to Tom Morton. Morton loved the photo, and even though there was a policy against using pictures of *Eagle* employees, he ran it a few days later as a "nature scenic" to anchor the Local Page.

A week or two later I came down from Perry's Peak with a photo that I just loved. It was a view looking west off the low, forested false summit. The image captured the moody, black Taconics through the narrow aperture of two frosted Norway spruce with a small wafer of sun poking through low cloud. I showed this one to Morton too.

"Hey kiddo, send this one down to the Museum of Modern Art, will you? They're going to love it."

"Hey Tom, c'mon," I said. "That's a good shot. The classic Berkshire winter scene."

"Yeah, well, fine, Rinker, but there's no people in it. What are we supposed to say in the caption? Mr. and Mrs. Pine Tree enjoying their view out the front lawn? Sorry, kiddo."

Screw you, Morton, I thought, returning to my desk. What did he know about photography anyway?

Two days later Morton was back at my desk, begging for the "Mr. and Mrs. Pine Tree" shot to anchor the Local Page.

"Sorry, Tom, I don't have it," I said. "I already sent it down to the Museum of Modern Art."

"Hand it over, kiddo," Morton said. "Joel Librizzi is out sick today and I'm up shit's creek for a picture."

Morton and I agreed that, to make the use of the photo look deliberate, we needed a story to go with it. So, only because there was a lovely, silvery fringe of ice on the trees in the photo, I called around to all my meteorologist sources and cooked up a story about how occluding fronts and clashing temperature gradients produced freezing rain. It was good book-turd filler, and I happily banged away on my Royal typewriter, pleased to be doing it up just right for Morton.

I was enjoying the haphazard exigencies of the real world. It seemed to fit my personality and lifestyle. Whatever happened, I made a story out of it. It was a refreshing change from the lockstep academic regime of college, a liberation from term papers and exams, where you had only one chance, one moment, to shine. Out here, yesterday's reject had a way of becoming today's brilliant move, if the boss happened to be up shit's creek, and none of this would have been happening if I wasn't up on the peaks with Linscott.

In early December, Linscott and I snow-shoed Berlin Mountain in Williamstown, sloshing up the long, curving logging road that ascends the east face of the peak from the parking lot of the Williams College ski slope. After a long climb, the trail dips and bobbles along a graceful ridge facing the Taconics to the west. It was a beautiful, sunny day and we lounged on the summit and enjoyed the views for a while, eating the sandwiches that I had carried in my

I had initially lied about my abilities as a photographer, but by imitating an ersatz Ansel Adams style I managed to place many "scenics" like this in the pages of the Eagle.

231

backpack. Then we snowshoed south along the Appalachian Trail until we came to the cleared entrance for the Williams ski slope.

Linscott stood in the bright sunlight, cupping his hands against the wind as he lit a cigarette.

"We face an amusing choice here" he said. "We can either continue on south down the trail and then pick up the spur to the AT, bushwhacking down from there to an available road. Or should you elect, we can take on the ski slope."

The steep ski slope glittered brightly in the sun, a sheet of ice. Snowmobiles had packed it hard with tracks, and then several warm sunny days followed by cold nights had turned the surface into a slick hardpan that wasn't going to be easy to negotiate.

"Roger," I said. "The ski slope? I don't think we can get down that very nicely right now."

"Oh, the words of a rank amateur," Linscott said. "I can see that you haven't been sufficiently educated in all the snow-shoeing arts."

With that, Linscott pulled off one of the most graceful mountain-man maneuvers that I've ever seen. Bending his long legs and crouching down almost to a sitting position, he grabbed the upturned tips of his snowshoes with his insulated mittens and flexed his body nimbly once or twice. Then he shimmied forward several feet and launched off the ski slope, racing downhill.

It was very elegant, that Ethan Frome toboggan slide of Linscott's, an act of wintry abandon and foolhardy beauty. Crouched in a seated position on his snowshoes, bouncing in and out of the snowmobile ruts, Linscott scissored out with his legs to descend the slope, telemarking around in a series of graceful S-turns down the steep incline. It just didn't seem possible that anyone could do this on snowshoes. Before he disappeared around the big jug-handle turn, Linscott howled with joy a couple of times and cut a wonderful profile against the white snow, his logger's cap and Rushmore profile a portrait of determination and sporting grace. He was doing a good fifteen knots and really smoking now, throwing off a rooster tail of frozen snow behind the tails of his snowshoes. Then he skittered around the corner and disappeared down the big straightaway downhill.

Now, I was alone atop Berlin Mountain.

Ah, balls. Why did I like this man so much? He was going to kill me someday. But, what the hell. I may as well follow the headcase Linscott down Suicide Hill.

So, I did that dumb-ass thing. Crouching down low and flexing my body a few times, I reached forward with my gloves and gripped my snowshoe tips, shimmied forward and launched. I built up speed very fast. Within thirty yards I knew that this was a big mistake.

My problem was that I couldn't do those elegant telemark turns that Linscott accomplished, controlling my speed by escaping the snowmobile ruts. The first time I tried it I flipped into the hardpack snow and was tossed head over heels. I tried again and somersaulted out of the snowmobile track once more, grinding my face in the hard crust of snow. By this time I knew Linscott was down below waiting for me, smoking a Kent, and cursing about what an egregious wimp I was for being so slow. So, screw it. I snowshoed back over to the best snowmobile track I could find, crouched and launched, and just held on for dear life, allowing the snowmobile rut to hold me in.

By the time I hit the big turn I was doing a good twenty knots in that snowmobile rut, way too fast, but I didn't have a choice now. I swung wide off the jug-handle turn and almost lost it, fishtailed into another snowmobile track at the edge of the slope, and just stayed with it, racing downhill. For a brief moment I could see Linscott's profile down below, watching me, and the blur of a birch grove going past.

Then I completely lost all sensation except the one of speed. The racing wind howled through the ear flaps of my cap and frothed up tears in my eyes. My face was bitterly cold from the exposure. But I was really flying now, seeing nothing, with just the sound beneath me of the ash snowshoes screaming down the icy snowmobile track. I thought that I might be all right, if I just relaxed a little and let myself flow with the bumps and the little moguls along the steepest part. At the bottom I went sailing past Linscott, still moving so fast I could barely see him. When the snowmobile track jagged hard left, I flipped out of it and somersaulted over a couple of times, the hard impact of crusted snow on my knees, and the crunch of the snowshoe harness against my ankles, making me ache all over. I came to rest with my face smashed hard into an icy crust of snow.

"Bravo!" Linscott was yelling behind me. "Bravo!"

Yeah, Linscott. Bravo. My face will be roadkill tomorrow and both of my shoulders need to be replaced, but Bravo.

I rolled over and stretched out my legs, brushed my cheeks off with a gloved hand, and stared up to the sky. I always liked lying on snow after a big sled downhill, aching all over but enjoying the cold. Berlin and Greylock rose all around, big mounded brows of gray and brown, and the sun was an opaque yellow fire pushing through a long cirrus cloud.

I was up high in country that I loved with a good headcase of a man who was caring for me well. He and that landscape were a piece together, the abundant recompense that I needed. On a summit with Roger Linscott I did see and feel and pulse with color in new ways, I was merged with the purple-blacks and cobalt silver of winter. With him up there I felt fully suffused with pure sky.

CHAPTER TWELVE

IN DECEMBER, a couple of weeks before Christmas, the Everything Girls came up for a long stay, and we all had a nice, lazy, preholiday bash. In the mornings, while Peter and I reported for work at the *Eagle*, the younger sisters slept in late, and Comfort, Judy, and Betty drove into Lenox to Christmas shop and buy groceries. As soon as the noon deadline passed, Peter and I provided Morton and Bell with apocryphal accounts about all the articles we were working on, and then we raced back over the hills to be with our harem. It was peaceful in the house. At night, while the wind moaned through the gutters and the fire crackled in the hearth, we all drank wine together and catnapped on the couch. Nothing pleased me more than nodding off to sleep with two or three Everything Girls draped across my body.

The little sisters had a big problem that week, and by Friday night, they were frantic about it. Their college applications were due and they were still stalled on their personal essays. They were a lot like their older sisters this way, little Smith College Goddesses in training. Outwardly, they were fun-fun and cynical all the time, smarty-pants teenagers trashing everybody and everything, but deep down, they were perfectionist and manic, insecure about their writing. Those essays had to be just right, but they were writing and rewriting themselves into a stupor.

Judy's younger sister was particularly antsy about her essay. Her first-choice school was Bowdoin College, and she'd heard that the admission office there placed a lot of emphasis on an applicant's personal essay.

"Oh, I mean, like, writing is such a bitch, you know? I'm never getting into Bowdoin with the crap I've done so far."

Judy cupped her sister's face in her hands, kissed her forehead, and then massaged her shoulders, trying to calm her down.

"Oh, c'mon sweetie," Judy said. "Chill. Rinker went to Bowdoin and he knows their brand of bull, okay? In the morning, *he'll* help you."

This was the first I'd heard of the plan, but it sounded okay. Everybody knew that college essays were a farce. The Bowdoin admissions officer was going to take one look at Judy's younger sister and instantly mark her up for acceptance, so that part was already a done deal. All we had to do with the personal essay was prove that the little rich girl could write in English. So, it would be fun, more or less just a matter of moving the group-grope into another room.

"Okay, cool, cool," Judy's younger sister said. "But I want Comfort's help too. I gotta have Comf."

"Dear, relax," Comfort said. "I promise. We'll do the essays in the morning."

The next day was blustery and cold, with a low, gray overcast spitting off a blurry mixture of snow and freezing rain that pelted the bedroom windows. It was too nasty outside for me to obsess on my woodpile, so I went down to the kitchen and made coffee, and then Comfort and I dawdled in bed for an hour, leaning against the headboard with pillows propped against our backs.

Early, while Comfort and I were still sitting up and talking in bed, the little sisters poked their heads around the corner of the bedroom door, all smirky-smiles and noses crinkled with earnest expectation, anxious to get started. In their slinky long johns, crushing their notebooks and sheaves of paper containing their essays against their chests, they skipped across the floor, plunked down on the end of the bed, and began reading their essays to Comfort. Slipping out from underneath the covers and pulling on a bathrobe, I stepped over to my desk in the corner, set up my typewriter, and began rustling around for some typing paper.

A little while later Judy and Betty showed up, bearing plates of challah and scrambled eggs, and we quickly settled down into a sensible division of labor. Up at the headboard, huddled shoulder-to-shoulder against an embankment of pillows, Comfort and Betty goaded the little sisters through their first rewrites, passing the versions down over the end of the four-poster as a continuous river of copy. Judy and I spelled each other on the typewriter, clattering away on the Smith-Corona and rewriting some more, occasionally squabbling over a word.

"Hey, Rinker, you changed her adjective from 'absurd' to 'surreal.' I'm not sure she's using that word yet."

"Ah, bullshit, Judy. Get with the program here. Every other high school brat is going to use the word 'absurd,' but then your little sister comes along and uses 'surreal.' Bingo. They let her into Bowdoin College."

"Yeah, maybe you're right," Judy said. "She *is* brilliant."

Nobody had bothered to change out of their pajamas yet, and I liked the sorority glow in the room. When Judy bent low over my shoulder to argue about another verb, the gossamer tips of her hair tickled the side of my face. When we were done arguing, Judy massaged my shoulders and neck, just to reassure me that our differences were purely academic. Then, when she spelled me on the typewriter, I couldn't resist leaning on Judy's shoulder, or running my finger down the thin crevice of her spine beneath her pajama top. She was small-boned and light, almost angelic to touch.

But I disciplined myself to ignore the vaguely sexual aura hanging over the room. Our bustling writers' camp was alive with the percussive clatter of the typewriter and the pensive murmurings from over on the four-poster, which seemed to create a purposeful zone of warmth against the chill outside. Once more I was reminded of how lonely the winter would have been without the Everything Girls.

So, content in my role as a capon typist for the little sisters, amiably sparring with Judy over the verbs, I whiled away the rest of the morning. It was the perfect book-turd day.

I probably should have known that the maid would show up to spoil all this. The maid spoiled everything in that house. By now it was abundantly clear that Rhoda Miller had left her behind just to spy on us. The maid was a tall, haggard Zeena Frome type who, beneath an air of irrepressible good cheer, was maniacally on the prowl for signs of deviant behavior. Once or twice a week, while Peter and I were working at the *Eagle*, she let herself in with her own key and fussed around for an hour or two with a vacuum cleaner and a dust mop, and then she spent the rest of the day devouring *Reader's Digest* and smoking cigarettes at the kitchen table. Small things, meticulously documented in a weekly phone report to Pat Faucett at the *Eagle*, mattered a lot to the maid. She noticed every time that Peter and I raided a frozen TV dinner from the big freezer in the cellar, or when a wine glass was missing. The maid was especially protective of Rhoda Miller's bedroom, which she considered sacred space. Occasionally, Comfort and Betty would duck in there, to change their clothes or iron a skirt. The next day, when Peter and I came in from work, a note from Zeena Frome was waiting for us on the kitchen table.

"Mr. Buck: One of your friends used Mrs. Miller's hairbrush in the bedroom. The one on the bureau. I found hairs in it. Could we please avoid this in the future?"

On that Saturday morning, while we were finishing up the college essays, Zeena just "happened" to be passing by the Rossiter Road manse, detouring several miles out of her way as she drove toward the Congregational Church to drop off some Christmas decorations. When she noticed all the cars in the drive, as she later told Pat Faucett, she decided that perhaps Mr. Buck and his "guests" would appreciate it if she stopped by for a quickie weekend cleanup. But the driveway was blocked, so Zeena parked way down at the gravel pullout by the pond, tramped up through the snow on the far side of the house, and then quietly slipped in through the kitchen door. Grabbing her upright Hoover vacuum and the little plastic buckets filled with brushes and spray cans of furniture polish that she always carried around, she stole upstairs, quiet as a cat. According to Zeena, it was just a coincidence, a "fluke of nature," that we never heard her coming.

Meanwhile, our happy Brook Farm up in the bedroom had kicked back into a sweet, languorous mood. The essays were done and we were all lounging together on the four-poster, giving our collaborative work one last read. Judy remembered that we still had a bottle of champagne left over from dinner last night, went down for that, then climbed back up the stairs with the bottle and an armful of glasses clinking in her arms. We popped the cork and poured ourselves champagne while we read the essays, comfortably arranged in the little piles we'd formed when we'd regrouped on the bed. I was lying diagonally across Comfort's chest, reading Betty's sister's essay for Dartmouth and Connecticut College, occasionally taking sips from the champagne glass in her hand. Betty was reading Judy's sister's essay for Bowdoin and Brown and had her legs sprawled across Comfort and me. The pyramid formed by the intersection of all these legs supported Judy. The little sisters were lying hip to hip at end of the bed with their legs kicked up.

The slinky, bosomy, pajama-party laziness of them all, surrounding me on the bed, was wonderfully intimate and refreshing. But it was all quite chaste and noble, of course, and I had only the healthiest of intentions. When the weather cleared and we were finished with the essays, Comfort and I were going to snowshoe up West Stockbridge Mountain.

Comfort could be quite fastidious about word choices, the ultimate Smith College Goddess. In one of the essays, the word "seminal" bothered her a lot. She didn't think that a little sister would use a word like that without our help.

"Hey everyone," Comfort said. "'Seminal'? She wouldn't use that word. An admissions officer is going to read that and figure out that someone like Rinker wrote this."

"Comf, chill," Judy said. "She'd definitely pick 'seminal.' *You're* the one whose got a problem with 'seminal.'"

Everybody started laughing about that, the absurdly affected "seminal," which epitomized the absurdly affected form of the college essay itself.

Judy howled and spilled some of her champagne and then arched back with her shoulders so that her small, calisthenic breasts rose muscular and high in lovely profile, and her glossy splash of hair fell across my knees. Judy was too much not to touch at that moment so I squeezed her shoulders and cupped her sheen of hair in my hands while taking a sip from the nearest champagne glass, Betty's, who leaned down, laughed, and whispered into my ear, "Hey, the babe is seminal." Then Comfort reached over to kiss me, just to show everybody that she didn't mind the way I had grabbed Judy, or that everyone was laughing about her objections to "seminal." Comfort's kiss, her thin perfect lips, tasted softly of champagne.

That's when Zeena Frome arrived. The optical richness of great New York JAP hair flying and then chaste Wasp kiss was suddenly interrupted by the maid framed in the doorway. Zeena was hideously erect and openmouthed, the Hoover vacuum and the plastic buckets quivering in her hands. The only thing that she could think to do was scream so loud we were all lifted off the bed.

Later, I would think of that scene as a fascinating question of perception, the appearance-versus-reality motif. In fact, there was nothing going on in the bedroom that morning. On an old Shaker four-poster, five women in their pajamas and one cub reporter for *The Berkshire Eagle* were drinking champagne and laughing, spoofing an adjective, "seminal."

But the maid had never imagined herself taking in such a remarkable scene. She couldn't impute to that bed an ounce of restraint. On her way to drop off poinsettias at the Congregational Church, Zeena Frome had been ambushed by sin.

"Mr. Buck! *Mr. Buck!* This is an *orgy! An orgy!* Oh my Lord! An orgy in Mr. Miller's bed!"

With that, the maid quickly disappeared, frantically clattering back down the stairs with the buckets and the vacuum cleaner dragged behind her. All the way down, the Hoover banged off the steps and the banister rails. We heard a few closet doors slamming downstairs and then the maid was gone, as quietly and quickly as she had arrived.

"Orgy? She calls this an orgy?" Judy's younger sister said, staring with serene indifference back over her shoulder to the doorway where the maid had been. "If my boyfriend was here, *that* would be an orgy."

"Yeah. What's her problem?" Betty's younger sister said. "Can't anybody just write their college essays in peace anymore?"

Judy was howling again, fumbling backward with her hands to clutch me by the knees.

"Mr. Buck! Mr. Buck! An orgy! An orgy! In Mr. Miller's bed. Oh, Rinker, thanks. Thanks. I've finally had one of those."

"Yeah, yeah, yeah, Judy," I said. "An orgy. Monday morning in the newsroom, I'm toast."

Our mood was broken now, and we all drifted off. While Peter took everyone else down to Stockbridge for a shopping junket, Comfort and I went snowshoeing. Later, after dinner, we peeled off in two cars for Mundy's Bar. The little sisters wowed the crowd once more with their rubber-body dancing, and while Peter goofed off with Betty and Comfort, Judy and I hung out at the bar. Judy could tell that I was boozing it too hard because I was worried about the maid.

"Rinker, would please chill? You're wrecking everything with your stupid Catholic guilt. I mean, you were so sweet with those girls today. Relax. You can't get arrested for helping my little sister get into college."

.   .   .

I could see what kind of trouble I was in as soon as I got into the *Eagle* Monday morning. The long stairway leading up past Pete Miller's office emptied into the newsroom directly in front of the clip morgue, where librarian Madeline Winters sat. Madeline considered this positioning ideal because it gave her the opportunity, as everyone arrived for work, to dispense the first rumor mill headlines of the day. Madeline was opinionated but quite pleasant, a big harumphy gal with extra bulges of flesh on her waist and arms and a generous, expressive bosom.

"Well, here he is," Madeline said as I pushed through the newsroom door. "Hugh Hefner himself."

"Oh c'mon, Madeline," I said. "Is that what they're saying already? It wasn't like that at all."

"No? Well, you better avoid Pat Faucett today. She's very upset. Of course, *I* say that she's just being naïve."

"Naïve? About what?"

"Well, when *she* said, 'I just can't believe that the fourth of eleven children would do something like this,' *I* said, 'Pat, how do you think you get to be the fourth of eleven children? Orgies. Lots of orgies.'"

"Madeline. It was *not* an orgy. The only thing going on—"

"Oh, this had better be good, Hef. I can't wait to hear this one. And don't tell me that five women in their nightgowns corralled you into Don Miller's bed to lead them in morning prayer."

"Madeline. I was helping them with their college essays."

Madeline considered this the funniest thing she had ever heard. As she laughed, she threw back all five of her chins and her battleship bosom heaved with delight. This information was so rich that she had to broadcast it live over to Roger O'Gara in sports.

"*Hey Roger! Get a load of this! He was helping them with their college essays!*"

"Yeah!" O'Gara called back across the floor, "That's what I always tell them. 'Honey, I'll do your homework.'"

I decided to ditch Madeline for someone more reasonable, Mary Jane Tichenor, over on the social desk. Mary Jane was one of Pat's closest friends, but she wasn't a prude. She'd already been divorced a couple of times, and one night, shortly after I arrived at the *Eagle*, when she was returning from a cocktail party in Lenox, she was apprehended by the police for taking a nap in her VW Bug in the middle of Park Square. This was not considered a detriment for a Social Page writer at the *Eagle*. The regulars on the social circuit she covered did a lot of drinking themselves, and they liked a party girl who got into the same kind of trouble that they did. I knew that Mary Jane would be sympathetic and help smooth things over with Pat.

But Mary Jane wasn't listening. She held up her hand as I approached her desk.

"Rinker, never complain, never explain," she said. "Don't even start by denying the facts. The maid saw what she saw."

"Mary Jane, that's the point. What the maid *thinks* she saw is not what she saw."

"That's what I told the police officer when I ended up in Park Square," Mary Jane said. "'Officer, this is not what it looks like.' That never works, okay? Now, let's stick to the facts. There were five of them in the bed with you, right? Partially naked, from what I hear."

"Mary Jane, no," I said. "Everybody had their pajamas on. It was early, all right? We hadn't changed into our clothes yet."

"Oh, okay. That'll help. But what about the liquor? The maid saw liquor."

"You see?" I said. "That's a total lie. This really shoots the credibility of the maid."

"Oh. So there was no liquor?"

"No liquor," I said. "All we had was one bottle of champagne."

"Oh, great," Mary Jane said. "We'll have to put a correction out on that. Liquor, no. Champagne, yes. I'm sure Pete will want to include that in his telegram to Rhoda."

"Telegram? Oh, Christ. What telegram?"

Mary Jane was the one who told me what happened. After the maid had stormed out of the house and dropped her decorations off at the church, she had rushed right home to call Pat Faucett. Pat was noncommittal. She didn't want to believe what the maid was saying about me or get caught in the middle of an ugly situation. But Zeena was determined to be a good spy. So, that very afternoon, she had driven into Pittsfield to send a telegram to Rhoda in Spain, and by Sunday morning Rhoda had already wired one back to Pete Miller, care of Pat at the *Eagle*.

Rhoda's bulletin across the Atlantic had specifically used

the words "orgy," "Mr. Buck," and "five teenage girls in my deceased husband's bed." Over the weekend these details had caromed back and forth on the telephone lines between Richmond and Pittsfield—Pat to Mary Jane to Madeline to Roger—and become embedded as rumor mill "fact."

The week progressively got better for me after that, but I was too inexperienced about being mired in scandal to enjoy myself at first. I was uncomfortable, for example, around Tom Morton, who by Tuesday that week had begun calling me "the whoremaster." To Tom, calling one of his reporters a "whoremaster" was meant to be a high compliment, but I didn't understand that yet.

"Hey, top of the morning to you, whoremaster. That was a great shot yesterday of those kids sledding in Onota Park. Good show. We needed it."

"Tom, thanks," I said. "But look. Bag this 'whoremaster' stuff, okay? The maid got it all wrong."

"Oh, I see. You weren't really doing it with five teenage girls?"

"Tom, only two of them were teenagers, all right? And I wasn't 'doing it' with anybody. I was helping them with their college essays."

Tom dabbed his forehead and laughed.

"Oh. Sorry, kiddo. Just two teens, huh? Helping them get into college. Well, excuse me. I've maligned you. You're really quite a gentleman and a scholar, my friend."

"Yeah. Thanks, Tom."

"No problem. Now, get back to work, whoremaster."

Dick Happel was the only one who tried to be helpful. Over coffee and doughnuts one afternoon, he congratulated me about the "smashing news" that I'd been caught in bed with five "ladies." This was going to perform wonders for my career, Happel thought.

"Hey, Dick, c'mon, don't rub it in," I said. "I just bought you coffee. You know perfectly well that my name is dirt around here now."

"Oh, sonny, no. No, no, no," Happel said. "Never, ever say that. Dirt is good. A scoundrel's reputation is never going to hurt you. People always need an excuse to consider you interesting. And you are, my dear boy, very, very interesting."

Happel always had a soothing effect on me, and once more his gay clairvoyance seemed to be working. But, still, I wasn't sure.

"Oh, I don't know, Dick," I said. "I'm supposed to be up here earning a reputation as a writer. But now my boss is calling me a whoremaster."

Happel dipped his cruller into his coffee, took a bite with the rotten points of his front teeth, and gave me a look of profound disappointment.

"Sonny, you're boring me now. There's nothing more tedious than a sinner who repents. If you did it, fess up. That way, when you go right out and do it again, you're living up to people's expectations. Look at me. For the past thirty years, I have cohabited with a succession of male housemates, in Lenox, Massachusetts, no less. But I still have the best sources in the county. Everyone returns my calls. It's deliciously sinful for people to share their secrets with an old fag."

"Yeah, okay, Dick," I said. "I'll try and remember that. I guess I'm the whoremaster now."

"That's the spirit, sonny! By the way, the jacket and tie combination today is very dashing. You *look* like a whoremaster."

After that things became a lot easier, and I was even able to finesse Pat Faucett. Pat and I had been dodging each other all week, practicing the Catholic Doctrine of Silence. But Pat taught me something important about the Doctrine of Silence, which was that it actually worked quite well for me. A good Catholic woman sits around all week mulling over the latest news of sin, and then just decides that its too complicated and edgy living that way. It's a lot easier just to pull the blinders back on and pretend that nothing ever happened. When I finally steeled up the courage to call her, Pat sounded relaxed, very realistic about events.

"Oh, Rinker. Five in one bed. I don't believe this thing for a second, but I'm going to be telling this story about you for years. It's so good."

"Yeah, well, you know, Pat," I said. "Just stop and think

about this for a minute, all right? Do you think that I could go home and face my mother at Christmas if I'd slept with five women?"

"Exactly! That's what I told Mary Jane," Pat said. "Rinker might be able to talk one girl into doing that with him, but he wouldn't be able to find five of them at once. It's got to be bunk."

"Okay, good," I said. "So we're clean then. But look, what about Pete? What's Pete going to do?"

"I don't know, Rinker. He hasn't said anything yet."

Pete Miller, as it happened, turned out to be an absolute peach. On Saturday morning that week Peter and I were sitting around the den, trying to figure out what we'd do with the weekend. Comfort, Betty, and Judy weren't around, because it was the weekend before Christmas and everyone had headed home to be with their families. Roger Linscott couldn't go hiking, because his wife had made him go Christmas shopping, a once-a-year event that he considered "odiously loathsome." I was feeling unaccountably listless and depressed about wasting time on a Saturday morning when out of the corner of the den window I saw Pete Miller's familiar, dented Volkswagen bump over the hill, S-turning around the frozen ruts of Rossiter Road.

"Oh, Christ, here we go," I said to Peter. "The big inspection visit."

"Yeah," Peter said. "We're going to get our asses thrown out of here."

But it wasn't like that at all. Pete's visit was a marvelous farce. After dawdling outside to inspect my woodpile for a while, Pete strolled in through the door, mixed himself a drink at the bar between the den and the dining room, and sat down on the faded leather chair in the corner, absentmindedly scratching the elbows of his tweed jacket and thumbing the note cards in his shirt pocket. By now Peter and I had grown accustomed to the long, pregnant silences in a conversation with Pete. He would steer the talk in the direction he wanted.

"So, here we are," Pete said. "Hah! Well, fellas, I'm disappointed."

"Ah, Pete," I said. "I think I can explain. You see—"

Pete held up his hand.

"How can you explain when you haven't even heard what I'm disappointed about?"

"Oh, okay, Pete," I said. "You're disappointed."

"Yeah! Where are the girls?" Pete said. "I'm disappointed. This place looks like the most boring whorehouse in the world."

Pete disliked people who beat around the bush, so I thought I may as well acknowledge the existence of our girl-friends.

"Ah, Pete, everybody's home for Christmas," I said. "They went to see their families."

"Ah, yes. The birth of Jesus," Pete said, his possum cheeks creased in a cryptic smile. "After several weeks of strenuous orgies, the girls celebrate Christmas."

"Ah, Pete, maybe I should just explain," I said. "The prob-lem with this maid that Rhoda has—"

"Whoa, young man, you can stop right there," Pete inter-rupted, forming his fingers into a steeple and propping it underneath his chin. "I don't give a rat's ass about this alleged maid and her, her, *reports*. But Pat Faucett seems to feel that you're terribly concerned about this, so I drove out here this morning just to tell you that. You know what the problem is? You know what we've got out here?"

"No, what?"

Pete leaned into his subject now, pointing with his steeple of fingers across the room and fixing us with his stare.

"I'll tell you what we've got here young man. What we've got is a heinous violation of Fourth Amendment rights out on Rossiter Road."

I was too stupefied to make much of a reply to that. But Pete spoke up.

"You *do* know, of course, the Fourth Amendment?"

Shit. It was just a problem I had with the Bill of Rights. Why did they have to number them, anyway? I had the same problem with the Ten Commandments. I could always get through the first two articles—free speech and the right to bear arms—but after that it was just all a jumble of jury trials, due process, and the right against self-incrimination. Now I was stumped, and Peter Scheer, Henry Steele Commager's favorite little Book Turd, had to make it even worse.

"Privacy," Peter Scheer said. "Protection against unlawful search and seizure."

Shit again. This was happening to me. In front of Pete Miller.

"See!" Pete said, wagging his steeple of fingers in my direction. "*He* knew that and *you* didn't, Rinker Buck. I'm going to make certain that Tom Morton is aware of this when he doles out the next promotions in the newsroom."

"Okay, Pete, sorry," I said. "I'll study up. But look, what are you going to tell Rhoda?"

"Oh don't worry about *Rhoda*," Pete said. "I've had years of experience handling her. I'll just wire her some folderol, some comforting fiction."

"All quiet on the western front," I suggested.

"Hah!" Pete said. "Yeah, I like that. All quiet on the western front. That'll take care of the old gal."

Pete stared around the room for a while, stroking the arms of his chair. I could see that he was wistful about Don's old place. When he and his brother were building up the *Eagle*, they'd spent many happy nights here together, partying and drinking. Don's place had been his weekend refuge away from the paper, a place to escape his responsibilities at home. This was one of many times over the next year when I would intuitively sense in Pete a terrible loneliness and maybe even a fear of encroaching old age, a need to evade the present by embracing the high purpose and fun of his past.

"Yup, the high point of the year around here was always the New Year's Eve party we had out here at Don's place," Pete said, staring nostalgically around the room. "Of course, that kind of went away when Rhoda showed up. I've always thought we should try another one of those someday."

Pete lapsed into another one of his long silences then, which was fortunate, because I needed a few minutes to gather his drift. I had to remind myself that I was dealing with Pete Miller here, what his logic would be. A heinous violation of Fourth Amendment rights had occurred out here on Rossiter Road. One of Pete's reporters had been caught in bed with five girls. The constitutional remedy for this was obvious. Yeah, I thought, I had it now. I was channeling right through to Pete.

"Hey, Pete," I said. "Let's have a New Year's party! We'll throw a bash. Thanks for the idea."

"Me? Who said anything about me, young man? This isn't *my* idea! But if it's your idea to throw a New Year's Eve party, I'll sure plan on being here."

"Done," I said. "We're going to have a New Year's party."

"Hah! Great! A party out at Don's house."

Pete was positively chortling now, rubbing his hands with satisfaction against his flannels and then scratching his rump. He was delighted about the idea of a party.

Pete dawdled outside again inspecting my woodpile, asking me long, involved questions about how I split this wood, where I found birch and cherry, and so forth, and gazing fondly down to the woods that I'd cleared of fallen limbs and brush. By the time he'd left, he had assigned me an *UpCountry* article on selecting fuel for woodstoves.

Then he was off, as unobtrusively as he'd arrived, a curious, detached man, looking forward to a party now, bumping in his Volkswagen over the glistening ruts on the road, and then disappearing over the hill.

·   ·   ·

The House of Miller had a furtive, but efficient, method for throwing parties. Officially, the *Eagle* didn't expend valuable funds entertaining the editorial help. However, everyone knew that Peter Scheer and I had nowhere near the money required to sustain a New Year's Eve party for the kind of serious alcoholics who worked for the paper. So, unofficially, Pat Faucett advised me that a tab for me had been opened at a liquor store on West Street. When the final liquor bill for our party was tallied, the store would "trade out" the costs with a free *Eagle* ad or two. I spent several hours that week happily ferrying crates of booze back to Richmond in my car, amazed at the buying power I'd achieved with the imprimatur of the *Eagle*.

The food wasn't going to be a problem either. As soon as the Everything Girls heard about our New Year's party, they made plans to ditch their families a day or two after Christmas and race back up the Berkshires. They were excited about it, determined to prove that they could entertain with a vengeance.

Judy, Betty, and Comfort arrived on the same afternoon that week, piling into the snowbank outside in the driveway in Judy's shitwreck Maverick and this swank but mechanically hopeless Austin Marina that Betty owned. The next morning they disappeared into Stockbridge and Great Barrington for a huge shop and then they established various command posts around the house, ordering Peter and me around and generally pussywhipping us into shape. While Judy cooked, filling the house with the fragrances of hams, basted turkeys, and pies, Comfort and Betty decorated the rooms with cut flowers, pine boughs that I carried in from the woods, and all these dead cattails in vases that Judy had stashed all over the place. In a matter of hours, the place looked better than the Red Lion Inn.

Judy was particularly ferocious in the kitchen, focused like a gnome on getting ready for the party. By now, we were both very comfortable with our kitchen-flirt routine. While she moved between the stove and the counter in her leotard and sexy knickers, I nailed cloves into the ham and basted the turkey. I just couldn't get over her devotion to cooking.

"Hey Judy," I said. "Mind if I ask a question? Why? I mean, you know, cooking? Why? You're a rich girl. You're headed for law school. You don't need to cook."

"Oh my God, Rinker. You're such an idiot sometimes. Cooking is basic, elemental. I can control the results. At the governor's office, I don't control the results."

"Judy, that's bullshit. I'm sure they consider you brilliant there."

"Oh, they do, they do! But I don't really *know* that. I'm just winging it at my job, you know? Being brilliant but not knowing why. But I can control cooking. Also, it's really, really gratifying doing this for you and Peter."

"Oh Christ. Here we go. The guilt trip."

"No, no. See? You're clueless. You and Peter are total fuck-ups, totally irresponsible, totally hopeless around the house. And I'm going to slave away in this kitchen for the next forty-eight hours just so you two guys can get all the credit for throwing a good party. And I love that, I love you and Peter. Getting ready for the party is something I can control and I *know* I can do. So, shut up and don't complain. Everybody loves you, you know?"

"Christ. Women. I'll never understand women."

"Oh, you're such a liar, Rinker Buck. You totally understand women, you have us completely wrapped around your little finger, but you just don't want to admit it. Now. Get out of here. I want to do my piecrusts alone."

·   ·   ·

It was a good old-fashioned drunk, a '40s-era binge, that we staged for our elders at *The Berkshire Eagle* that night. Pete Miller was so excited about the nostalgic reprise out at his brother's house that he arrived early and took over the bar, happily and spastically tossing the martini shaker above his shoulder while he dispensed advice to Peter Scheer on how to keep the mixture dry. I sat on the couch in front of the fire and chatted up Amy Bess. Then Pete circulated the room with his first pitcher of martinis, doing this goofy, faux-elegant jig while he poured everyone's glasses, an old white possum effusively pleased to be competently running a bar. By the time all the editors and reporters from the newsroom started piling into the house with their boyfriends and wives, we were already looped. The place got very merry and loud after that.

Everyone was astounded by the Everything Girls. They couldn't get over the contrast between what they saw that night and all the nonsense transmitted by the maid through the rumor mill. The house was beautifully decorated and the big Shaker table in the dining room attractively arrayed from end to end with all the sides of meat and dishes that they'd slaved over for the last two days, and Comfort, Betty, and Judy, with their shiny bobs of hair and party dresses, were circulating around and chirping up all of our friends from the newsroom, goofing around with Tom Morton and Rory O'Connor. Judy was particularly effective at performing this brainy, flirt-flirt routine with Pete Miller, who was an absolute sucker for a bright, pretty girl with a good job in the governor's office. When she touched him on the sleeve or patted his waist to make a point, Pete didn't flinch. He was so sloshed on martinis at that point that she could have done anything to him.

Comfort also aced the night. All week, I had been worried about Dick Happel, who had been uncharacteristically squeamish about the party. One afternoon in the newsroom, Happel had told me that he was nervous about attending the big *Eagle* party with his companion, whose name also happened to be Dick. I was surprised that Dick felt this way, but he explained that he'd had trouble before. At formal events, Happel said, Berkshire County homosexuals were still expected to be "incognito," sexless. It was okay to be gay, even to have a companion discreetly stashed back at the house, but you just didn't show up together at a big mansion party. Confronting male lovers made people feel uncomfortable, and they didn't know what to say. Outraged by this, I browbeat Happel into coming to our party, plying him with coffee and doughnuts all week and buttering him up by wearing all the jacket and tie combinations that he liked. I'd told Comfort that we'd have to make a special effort to make old Happel feel welcome, and as soon as Dick and Dick arrived, she bounded right over to the door and started chirping them up in her high-Wasp diction. Comfort was stunning that night, tall and perky in her burgundy velour dress, and I could tell that Happel was infatuated with her. When I stepped over to say hello, he was practically speechless.

"Oh, sonny, where did you ever, ever locate such genes?" he said. "Ordinarily, I am quite disappointed by women. They almost never live up to their billing. But Comfort Halsey is a pure thoroughbred."

Meanwhile, there was trouble brewing down in the cellar. A couple of sportswriters had started a lively tournament at the Ping-Pong table down there, and as per his usual, Roger Linscott had ambled downstairs and trounced everyone, slashing violently with his backhand and generally slicing the ball so hard that nobody could return his backspin. After Comfort had established Dick and Dick over on the couch in a prized position near Amy Bess Miller and Pat Faucett, she and I wandered down there. We stood against the wall for a while, nuzzling each other and enjoying the show. Linscott was plastered from martinis, but still, he trashed player after player.

When the last player had been dispatched, Comfort gently kissed me on the cheek and then walked over to the Ping-Pong table. She picked up a paddle, coyly tossed it back and forth between her hands a few times, and flashed down to Linscott this great prep school grin that she had.

"Hey, Roger! I'll play you!"

Linscott stared out through his glasses with a look of benign annoyance.

"Aha. A *female* contestant. I should warn you that I show no quarter for gender."

Comfort had had her fill of Linscott by now. She didn't like his gruff manner, the way he called everyone an egregious boob, or the fact that I always returned from a hike with him stone-ass drunk. But she was too reserved to engage him verbally. So, she just waited there at the end of the table, crouched and ready for his serve, smiling again.

"Sure, Roger. I won't go easy on you either."

"Preposterous," Linscott said, scowling. "I won't go easy on you either. This is another prime example of the fraudulently named Rinker Buck presenting a hoax to us all. A girlfriend who challenges *meeeee* in table tennis."

Linscott slashed sideways with his backhand and slammed

the ball over the net. Effortlessly, it seemed, her arm graceful and weightless, Comfort returned the ball to Linscott's side, and it bounced once and went sailing by his ear.

Linscott shook his big head, perplexed, and stared incredulously down the table.

"Preposterous. Mere beginner's luck. Let me just have another sip of my martini here and straighten this out."

"Oh, sure, Roger," Comfort said, politely. "Take your time."

But there was no straightening it out for Linscott. Comfort had a lightning hand for the paddle. Naturally, I thought to myself. Comfort Halsey would be great in the racquet sports. In a matter of minutes, Comfort was up on Linscott by ten points, and there really wasn't much of a contest after that. When word got around upstairs that Linscott was losing at Ping-Pong, everyone piled down into the cellar to watch.

It was spectral, watching Comfort destroy the Great Linscott, the high point of the party. She was tall and limber-limbed in her burgundy velour, posture-perfect and all smirky-smiles every time she smashed out a serve. As she played, her silver necklace bounced delicately on her clavicle. God, Comfort was just so gorgeous that night, the best Porcelain Protestant Beauty in the land, smashing left and right with her backhand, but making it look so easy. As the points piled up against him, Linscott was boiling over with fury, morose and red-faced, muttering curses as he tossed his big, leonine head left and right. He paused several times to refresh himself from his martini. But he couldn't return Comfort's backspin.

At the end of the room, I was contorting my body in every imaginable way, begging Comfort with my face to go easy on Linscott, just let him score a point or two and have some dignity in defeat. But, no, Comfort wasn't going to give Roger Linscott an inch. But she was infinitely gracious about it, blushing with excitement every time she scored a point, gently smiling as she stood with her long, thin arm perched on her tightwaist, waiting for Linscott to take another sip from his martini. After she had soundly thrashed him at the first two games of a three-game series, Linscott peevishly dropped his paddle on the table, annoyed to have lost in front of a crowd.

"I do not even remotely regard this as my comeuppance," Linscott growled, staring down the table at Comfort. "We have merely established a reasonable handicap here. Namely, *I* drink martinis, and *yooouuuu* do not! We shall resume this tournament at a more suitable time."

Comfort flashed him her best Smith College Goddess smile.

"That would be nice, Roger. I'd be delighted to play you again."

"Oh, tarnation! She'd be delighted to play me again. Rinker Buck, this was a conspiracy maniacally organized by *yoouuu* to humiliate *meeeeee*, your alleged friend. This is all your fault, and I shall not forget your atrocious manners."

With that, Linscott disappeared back up the stairs to find another martini. For months afterward, he pretended to forget that he'd played Ping-Pong that night, and Linscott snarled and cursed at me every time I mentioned Comfort Halsey.

Dick Happel was one of those who had come downstairs to watch the Linscott-Halsey contest, and I'd never seen him so happy. He was standing quietly in the corner now, gazing with admiration at Comfort with a sly grin on his face.

"Oh, sonny, that was positively delicious," Happel said. "That Roger Linscott gets too big for his little britches sometimes. He is not a modest man. But your Comfort handled him well. She is divine, simply divine."

The party got very rowdy after that. I'd purchased way too much liquor for the bash, but since it was all free, on the House of Miller no less, everyone from the *Eagle* felt obligated to drink the bottles right down to the last drop. By midnight, we were all howling drunk. Outside, two inches of new snow had fallen on a layer of freezing rain, and the driveway was treacherous. It was mayhem, getting everyone and their cars out of the drive and headed toward home.

Mary Jane Tichenor, in her VW Bug, was the first to launch. Mary Jane was unbelievably skilled at driving while intoxicated, an absolute pro. She got past the big maple all right, but then she panicked in the turn, hit her brakes, and did a beautiful flying-saucer spin into the ditch across the way on West Road. Rory O'Connor and I ran out there to push Mary Jane out of the ditch, but then Happel came careening around the corner in his big Fleetwood and hit the same spot. Rory and I were too drunk to be upset about it and we had a good time rocking the big Caddie out. But now Happel was spooked. He slid over in his seat next to companion Dick, insisting that I drive him out to the dry road on Route 41. As I was walking back from that, Pete and Amy Bess Miller, wedged into Pete's VW, slid down the hill and skidded sideways to a stop. Pete rolled down his window.

"Hah! Very respectable party, young man. I've never had a better time at Don's."

"Yes, Rinker, very good job," Amy Bess piped in from across the car. "And your lady friends are exquisite. Those girls are so, so—"

"Prepared!" Pete said. "That's the word for them, Amy Bess. They are very prepared young ladies. No wonder Rinker wanted all five of them in bed!"

"Peter Miller! Now you stop that," Amy Bess said. "That was *not* appropriate."

I realized at that moment how touched I was by the Millers. They were such an odd but gracious pair. Pete, the redoubtable publisher of the *Eagle*, Amy Bess, the Shaker Queen, the very tippety-top of the Berkshire peerage, perfectly content to drive home in the snow together in Pete's shitwreck VW. They were a picture of elegance and simple taste.

From the hill, I waved good-bye and then watched as they drove off, bouncing down the ruts in the snowstorm.

When I got back to the house, Roger Linscott had made a total hash of his departure in the red Duster. Linscott would later tell two versions of the story. In the first version, he claimed to have been blinded by the lights of Tom Morton's car, and thus forced to accelerate into the field across Rossiter Road. In the second version, he claimed that his gas pedal got stuck. Either way, it was a disaster. Roger, Lucy, and the Duster were now stranded fifty feet away from the road, on a hill way up in the hayfield.

Rory O'Connor had trudged out there in the snow to help, but it wasn't any use. Linscott wasn't very equipped for driving that night, and he wasn't in a festive mood. They rocked the car for a while but just dug it in deeper, embedding the rear axle in a trench of mud.

"Jesus tarnation to hell anyway, Rory," Linscott growled out through the window. "This is all your goddamn fault. You got my car stuck."

Rory shrugged his shoulders and just gave up on the deal, leaving the Linscotts out in the middle of the field. When he got back to the road and looked back, Lucy Linscott had abandoned ship and was walking down the hill toward home, gingerly stepping through the snowdrifts in her stocking feet while she held her shoes in her hand.

Rory said good night, piled into his own car with his wife, and drove off. The driveway was now pretty much deserted and I stood alone on the hill. The snow had matted my hair, and my feet were wet from pushing all the cars out. But I was happy and high. We'd had such a good party.

I could tell that Linscott and his Duster were still stranded up there in the field. His cursing and moaning echoed down the slope, and through the falling snow, I could just make out the roof of the car and the orange glow of Linscott's cigarette.

Christ. Freaking Linscott. Why did I love this man so? I yelled across the field.

"Hey, Roger! Are you fucking all right out there?"

"Oh, indisputably!" Linscott bellowed down the hill. "Of course I'm fucking all right! Why would you ask if I'm fucking all right? Don't I *LOOOOOK* fucking all right?"

"You look fucking fine, Roger! Real fine. Happy New Year!"

"Oh, fuck your abominable New Year! Go home! Go to sleep! Kiss your adorable girlfriend! And by the way, I wish to record for posterity an incontestable fact."

"What's that?"

"Rory O'Connor is an egregious boob!"

III

———

Communications Arts

———

CHAPTER THIRTEEN

DURING ALL this time a deep foreboding hung over the country, particularly the hill towns of New England. Back in August, the *Eagle* had run a story about a meeting of the Berkshire Association of Business and Commerce, which was recommending that rudimentary steps be taken to avoid an energy shortage over the winter. The Berkshires, isolated at the end of the delivery chain in western New England, far from the refineries and ports of Boston and New York, had experienced energy difficulties before. The interior Northeast was the first to feel the annual "midwinter spike" in home-heating-oil prices and spot shortages of gasoline, and the last to see it recede in the spring. Now, with America more dependent than ever on foreign crude and another Mideast war in the offing, everyone was expecting a hellish winter.

This prophecy was realized in early October, when Egypt-ian and Syrian troops poured across the Sinai Peninsula and the Golan Heights, precipitating the Yom Kippur War. The fierce Israeli counterattack propelled the Arabs back across their borders in a matter of days. A humiliated King Faisal of Saudi Arabia, who had largely financed the Arab attack, quickly exacted his only possible revenge. By the end of the month the Saudi-controlled Organization of Petroleum Exporting Countries had announced an immediate halt in crude oil shipments to the West. The first energy crisis had begun.

The Arab oil embargo of 1973–1974 wasn't simply about long lines at gas stations and desperate shortages of home-heating fuel, the West's wake-up call about its new threat zone in the Arab world. It was also about guilt, classic American guilt, our notable and unsettling ambivalence about the nation's stunning postwar success. As soon as the crisis broke, the country's newspaper columnists and network news anchors put on their hair shirts, bemoaning America's myopia and arrogance, our inefficient, gas-guzzling cars and ludicrously over-heated homes. The country had brought this all down on itself.

Some of this was true enough, but to twenty-two-year-olds with maxed-out brains like Peter Scheer and me, this was breathtaking news. We were secretly jubilant about this turn of events. At last we had a national catharsis that we could wrap our arms around and use to escape the peculiar mental burden of our upbringing. We had all grown up listening to our parents' tales of the Great Depression and World War II, a legacy of patriotism and sacrifice that we were expected to revere but never imitate in our own lives. My father had been particularly gifted at dispensing this dandy little guilt complex. As a boy, I had sat patiently by the fire night after night, struggling to remain awake while he shared his Horatio Alger tales of growing up during the Great Depression in Scranton, Pennsylvania. In the Pennsylvania coal country, of course, it snowed or rained every day, twelve months of the year. But this did not deter my hard-working father from bolting out of bed every morning at four to deliver newspapers and then report for his job as a short-order cook. As a teenager, inspired by his example, I hungered for my own newspaper route. But my father adamantly refused to let me have one, on the grounds that the neighbors might think that we really needed the money.

The administration of President Richard Nixon had splendidly reinforced this message while we were in high school and college. Such inspirational speakers as Vice President Spiro

Agnew and Attorney General John Mitchell never missed an opportunity to deride our generation—the ones, anyway, who didn't serve in Vietnam—as "soft" and "effete." Our elders had flown in the Battle of Midway and stormed the Normandy beaches. We were hippies and conscientious objectors. One of the reasons that you could never pull Peter Scheer's face out of a new book about the Cuban Missile Crisis, or mine out of a book about the Battle of Britain, was that we truly lusted after a scary gestalt like that, a bona fide crisis that put the country on a wartime footing and forced us to prove ourselves. We were depressed about it. Basically, the only thing that we'd done with our lives so far was to excel upward through college and bang rich girls. We knew that we needed something more. What we really wanted was our own private Iwo.

Now, King Faisal had handed us just that. Peter and I scrummed into that winter with enormous romance and elan.

Peter could type like the blazes and was innately skilled at synthesizing complicated subjects, and he soon distinguished himself in the *Eagle* newsroom with a long series of articles on oil stocks, natural gas prices, and the big New England wood-stove boom. By January, the price of gasoline had almost doubled, from about thirty-five cents to over seventy cents, and the federal and state governments had imposed "odd-even" days of gas rationing, based on license plate numbers, and a ten-gallon limit on all purchases. As long lines began to appear at the gas stations, Peter imaginatively roamed the county, interviewing motorists and fuel company executives, effortlessly spinning off colorful, insightful articles on the emerging national crisis. One of Judy Lesser's responsibilities at the governor's office in Boston was energy policy, and when she traveled out to the Berkshires every weekend, she loved to regale us with stories about how all the governor's aides and policy makers were avidly reading Peter's stories in the *Eagle*. This symbolized to me everything that Peter had going for him and I did not, and it was hard to contain my envy. Peter had been catapulted onto the best beat at the paper, and he was vastly more talented as a writer and reporter than I was at this point. Now, on weekend nights, I also had to sit there on the couch at home and listen to this great sexy-brainy girlfriend that he had ramp up his ego by telling him how brilliant he was.

It was maddening, sometimes, just how good he could be. Peter didn't need "hard news" events to craft a story. One of his strongest stories that year was a nostalgia piece about gas rationing during World War II, based on interviews with the geezers who had administered the program during the 1940s. Tom Morton, a World War II vet, loved it. Another time, Peter discovered that all the toy stores in town were selling out of board games. With all the economizing and driving restrictions during the energy crisis, families were curtailing their trips to the bowling alleys and movie theaters and instead remaining home to play Parcheesi and Scrabble. It was a great trend story, a new American "nesting instinct" induced by the energy crunch, and Peter wrote it up well.

My biggest problem was that Peter and I sat just opposite each other in the newsroom. Day after day, while I chipped through my rock pile of obituaries, I'd have to sit there and listen to Morton strut over and ladle out the praise for Peter.

"Okay, Scheer, we're really cooking now. Board games. Showing us something new about the energy crunch. Great. I'm putting this baby on Page One and sending it right out to the wires."

Nobody was going to send out to the wires the maladroit crap that I was writing. However, when a story was this big, there were no rules about poaching someone else's beat. So, every day, as soon as my slag heap of obits was out of the way at noon, I'd work the phones or range out across the county, trying to dig up a story that could compete with Scheer's latest Page One opus. One day I came up with what I considered to be a compelling piece. Basic but nonessential industries were being squeezed by high fuel costs and depressed demand and were drastically reducing production, forcing what was called "tertiary shortages" on other sectors of the economy. Take brown paper bags. Signs were going up in all the A&Ps and Adams Super Markets around the county, asking customers to save their bags and return with them when they shopped the following week, as an "energy-saving measure." I got busy on the phone, called paper company and supermarket executives all over the country, and wrote the story up in a kind of ersatz *Wall Street Journal* Page-One style that I figured Morton would like.

When I turned in the story, Morton and Bell huddled over at Tom's desk at the head of the newsroom, scratching their heads and looking bored. They didn't say anything to me about it. The next day the piece appeared in the *Eagle* without my byline, hacked down to three inches and buried on a back page, right beside a story about the new overhead doors at the Hinsdale Volunteer Fire Department. The headline was deliberately written, it seemed, to humiliate the writer: "Energy Crisis Raps Brown Paper Bags."

Other brilliant thoughts would arrive, and I would take them straight over to Morton.

"Hey Tom, how about this one? I'll go down to the GE gates and interview some union-hall types who own muscle cars. You know, greasers from the Ordnance Division or Power Transformers who own Corvette Stingrays, Camaro Z28s, or Pontiac GTOs. They're stuck with these big V-8s now. What does the American worker think about gas-guzzlers now?"

Morton dabbed his forehead, which I now knew to be counterindicative body language. It meant that he was either happy or tentative and very sad.

"Aaah, I don't know, whoremaster. Maybe if you could document that these guys are actually trading in their GTOs for Toyotas, well, that might be a piece."

"Tom, nobody's buying anything right now. Not even Toyotas."

"Yeah, well, just keep trying, kiddo. Don't get discouraged. You might just come up with a decent idea one of these days."

"Jeez, Tom, what gives here? I mean, Peter comes up with board games or vets, and you love the idea."

"Yeah, and you come at me with brown paper bags and greasers with GTOs," Morton said. "Sorry, pal. That's the way the cookie crumbles. Those are the breaks. Not everybody around here can be a star. Just keep chipping away, and maybe something will change, you know?"

There was a great deal of satisfaction, however, working outdoors that winter.

With the prices of home-heating fuel skyrocketing and supplies dwindling, everyone was suddenly desperate to load up on firewood, and I made a lot of useful contacts during my rounds at the Westbridge or Mundy's Bar on Thursday and Friday nights. A variety of people that I met at the bars, or friends that Rachel introduced me to—idle Berkshire peers, therapists at Riggs, schoolteachers from Stockbridge and Lenox—brightened up as soon as they heard that I owned a chain saw. On Saturday mornings I'd drive over to their places with my Homelite saw and mow down all the blighted elms and ash in their yards, then split and stack the logs for their woodstoves and fires. At first, I grossly undercharged for my services, just $25 a tree, but after a while I got smarter about that and demanded whatever the market would bear, $75 or more for a cord. There was more work around than I could possibly handle, and it wasn't that difficult to rake in $150 or even $200 in a single day. The joy of that—working outdoors as a sawyer and making extra money—defined the energy crisis for me. I still snowshoed with Linscott every Sunday. But on Fridays and Saturdays I chopped wood, earning on a single day more than I made all week at the *Eagle*.

There was a nice social by-product to all this. A lot of the people I split wood for were lesbians and gays that I met while dancing with Rachel at Mundy's, and I became particularly close with one pair of lesbians, two Berkshire beauties named Bonnie and Helen. They had a little farm and a pickup truck down on Intermountain Road in Sheffield. Bonnie worked as a telephone company executive and Helen was a freelance graphic designer, but they shared this dream of turning their goat herd and farm into a profit-making enterprise, and they were making extra money that winter delivering split cordwood to their friends. But they needed someone with a chain saw to help take out their bigger trees. After a weekend or two down there, I found that I enjoyed them quite a bit, and we spent the rest of the winter sharing tree-clearing projects and splitting our proceeds from selling the wood.

Helen was the younger of the two, but Bonnie, who was in her mid-30s, was the real looker. Bonnie was fit and trim, loads of fun, my introduction to the sensation that a well-preserved older gal could be sexier than one half her age. Bonnie had long blonde ringlets and an exquisite oval face that resembled Dominique Sanda's. She had this awesome and sinewy older-woman tightwaist and the prettiest ski-slope ass I'd ever seen. When we got into splitting with the mauls and the axes and she stripped down to her V-neck Hanes undershirt, her breasts athletically perspired and heaved. I did have this one, itsy-bitsy, teeny-weeny, tiny little polka-dot bikini of a perversion, which was that it was powerfully arousing to engage in hard labor beside a woman, and Bonnie often gave me a hard time for staring at her breasts, even when I'd disciplined myself not to do that for a full hour. But we liked each other a great deal, and we made a good team in the woods, joking and laughing together as we mowed through a big pile of maple. Bonnie started calling me "Brother Boy," so I called her "Sister Girl." Wail, wail with the Homelite, Sister Girl, watch out, the shaggy-bark cherry is coming down first, the dead sugar maple is next, then chop-chop, race to fill the pickup so that Helen can do the delivery. As soon as Helen disappeared out past the oxbows, Bonnie and I made a fire out by the woodpile, grabbed some bourbon from the house, and sat there and bullshat for a while, pausing between our assaults on the logs. I loved being out there with her, taking in the fine winter air and the spray of wood chips, the blue haze on the mountains all around, and the smell of two-stroke fuel on my logger's chaps.

Bonnie was amused and curious about what it had been like being raised in a family of eleven children and why I'd become such a Book Turd. I found it very easy to talk with a smart, sensitive older woman who was romantically unavailable, because I wasn't competing for her or acting out to try to impress her. I learned something important about reciprocation from her as well, which was that someone generally didn't ask you to open up about yourself unless they hungered to reveal the same sort of information about themselves. Bonnie told me all about her journey toward lesbianism, which had involved an early, thoughtless marriage, then a torrid extramarital lesbian affair, a long relationship with another woman, and then she'd found Helen. Bonnie knew that she was loved, she appreciated that she inspired confidence in others, and she had recently received a number of promotions at her job. Still, she was insecure about a lot of her friendships and tortured herself with self-doubt every time she made a decision at work. Happiness was just different for women, I concluded, listening to Bonnie talk. No matter how attractive, brainy, and successful they were, they would always question their self-image. And you couldn't change their minds either. All you could do was just sit there and listen, letting them work the thing out, conversation to conversation. So, that's what we did. Bonnie and I were prodigious together, mowing through the logs, but we also plowed through a great deal of talk.

Often, after we'd finished logging for the day, Bonnie, Helen, and I would chase off and go dancing together, up at Mundy's Bar or over at this country-western dance hall that they liked in Pine Plains, New York. They had a nice byplay together. Helen was always coming down with these crushes on other girls and running off to join the lesbo-line, which Bonnie enjoyed no end. She and I would tank up at the bar and then dance close together or make out, just to stick it to Helen, and then we'd all go howling home in the pickup together, laughing at how ridiculous we were. Other times, we ate dinner down at their place, and I often stopped down in the middle of the week too. I loved our little triad at their Sheffield farm.

When we parted at night, those crisp, high-pressure, black-on-black Berkshire nights, Bonnie and Helen gave me these long, lovely, lesbian good-bye smooches. Smooch-smooch on the cheek from prim Helen, then the big, bosomy, muscular, all-body hug from motherwoman Bonnie. The swell of her affection rode with me all the way home.

"Oh good night, baby. I love you. You're so much fun.

There's enough wood for us to deliver all week. Thank-you, thank-you, Brother Boy. I love you."

.   .   .

Babysitting Dick Happel and his Cadillac was another adventure that winter. Happel was one of the energy crunch's genuine victims—old, jittery, and the driver of a classic American road galleon with a monstrously wasteful V-8. He was an emotional wreck all winter. Early in the crisis he'd read an article in *The Christian Science Monitor* that advised the owners of V-8 vehicles to never depress their gas pedals very hard, and to drive at speeds below thirty miles per hour on local roads. Managed this way, a Cadillac might achieve fuel consumption of eleven miles per gallon. So, that's what Happel did, inching along Route 7 every morning as a snake of metal backed up behind him, the angry drivers of UPS trucks and station wagons loaded with skiers flashing their lights and honking their horns for him to get out of the way. At traffic lights, he let the longboat Caddie creep forward at idle, so that the light always turned red by the time he got there. More cars stacked up behind him. Even people driving other Cadillacs routinely gave him the finger.

"Oh, sonny," Happel said to me one day. "I am now a pariah among my own readership. The mood of the country has turned ugly. Cadillac owners are detested."

After the noon deadline, the *Eagle* newsroom quickly emptied as everyone scrambled out to their cars in the parking lot to search for a gas station with short lines, but this new American pastime was too much for Happel. In a Cadillac, a quarter of a tank could be wasted just sitting in the average, forty-five-minute line, and the ten-gallon limit barely got the needle back above the quarter-tank mark. It was a net wash, just owning a Cadillac. Besides, the gas station attendants were getting surly. Cadillac owners were the butt of every new joke.

I felt sorry for the emaciated old guy. So, a couple of times a week, I'd take a break during the midafternoon lull, when the lines at the gas stations had thinned out.

"Hey Hap," I said. "Give me your car keys. I'll find some fuel for the Caddie and then swing around to Dunkin Donuts. You're buying."

"Oh, sonny, you're wonderful," Happel said, handing over his jeweled key chain. "You are a gorgeous boy."

I liked it, peeling out of the *Eagle* lot and then squealing down First Street in the long, brown Fleetwood with the leather seats, which made me feel sexy and powerful, a teenager again, bombing around in Daddy's big set of wheels. I usually brought along my two-gallon gas can, so that I'd have enough for my chain saw over the weekend. When I finally reached the pumps somewhere, I could see right away what Happel was talking about. Cadillacs were now a national disgrace, and gas station attendants truly loathed their drivers.

"I'll take the ten-gallon limit," I said, handing the gas can out through the window. "Nine gallons of Hi-Test in the tank, then a gallon of regular in the can. Thanks."

"Oh, shit," the gas attendant said. "Fags and old ladies, you know? They're the only people who drive Caddies anymore. Always fussy. Always want something different."

"It's not my car," I said. "I'm buying gas for a friend."

"Like I said, old ladies and fags. They all say the same thing."

The gas jockey stood back from the car a couple of steps, dangled his wrist and swayed his hips.

A gas line in Pittsfield over the winter of 1973-1974. The Arab oil embargo wasn't simply about the shortages of fuel and home-heating oil; it was also about classic American guilt.

"Oh, thissssss thing? It'ssss *not* my car!"

"Hey, that's a pretty good imitation," I said. "Did you

pick it up all by yourself or learn it from your boyfriend?"

"Ha, ha, ha, swishboy. How 'bout if I pump the gallon of regular up your ass?"

"No thanks," I said. "It's easier to carry in the can."

It was worth it though, just to see old Hap brighten up. When I got back to the *Eagle* newsroom, Dick was pensively lost in thought at his desk, touching up the faded lapels of his suit with a felt-tip pen. I couldn't tell which thing pleased him the most, a two-day supply of fuel for the Caddie or Dunkin Donuts hazelnut coffee.

"Oh, was it terribly awful, sonny?" he said. "A long line?"

"Nah, nah, Dick," I said. "I like driving the Caddie."

"Yes, and I am very touched by your generosity, sonny," Happel said. "If you like, you may borrow my Cadillac some night for a date. I rather think that you and one of your pretty girls would look smashing in it."

"Dick, that's not a bad idea," I said. "As soon as the energy crisis is over, I'm taking the Caddie out some night."

.   .   .

Nobody in America, however, came up with a better tactic for subverting the energy crisis than Judy Lesser. Here again, her instincts were flawless, her sexy-brainy execution utterly peerless. On Friday nights, desperate to get out to her Peter in the Berkshires, she'd tool around Boston in the yellow Maverick for half an hour or so, but all the gas stations had lines backed up for more than a mile. Her tank was low, but this didn't bother Judy. She worked in the Governor's Office and knew the ropes. Judy was aware that during the energy crisis state troopers had been staged along the Massachusetts Turnpike so that one passed by every fifteen minutes, and that they were all required to carry an emergency can of gas.

"Those guys are all horny for girls," Judy told me one night on the phone. "Don't worry, I'll get there."

To this, Judy added another irresistible touch. She was convinced that running a car without the heater on improved fuel consumption. So, before she left Boston, to ward off the frigid interior temperatures of the Maverick, she slipped into this striking ski-bunny outfit that she had, a body-clinging nylon of hot turquoise, which she had accessorized with an Arcadia Shop scarf, matching mittens, and hat, all in black mohair. She looked stunning, as good as Goldie Hawn in her Porsche.

So, off she went. Sometimes she got out past Worcester, other times as far as Ludlow or Springfield. When the engine on the Maverick sputtered, she pulled off onto the shoulder and turned on her hazard lights. Waving a few times to passing truckers guaranteed that her position would be radioed in on the Citizen Band channels to the patrolling troopers.

Judy never waited more than fifteen minutes for Trooper Bianco or Janko to show up. While the trooper was momentarily busy in his cruiser—engaging multiple flashing lights, radioing his position, gathering up his flashlight and gear—Judy primped herself in the rearview mirror and pretended to be fumbling around in her purse for her driver's license. But she already knew which document she would be handing to the trooper.

"Driver's license and registration please, ma'am."

Judy flashed her best couch-kitten smile and handed the trooper her laminated photo ID from the Governor's Office.

"Hey! You work *there*? For Guv'nor Sargent? What seems to be the problem, honey?"

"Oh! I'm supposed to be driving out to the Berkshires to do this survey on the energy crisis. And what I do? *Run out of gas!* Silly me! Officer, I'm sorry. I'm sorry. It's just that—officer, I'm sorry but I might cry."

By this time, Trooper Bianco had thoroughly surveyed her with his flashlight beam.

"Whoa! Whoa there, Judith. Now don't be saying that, okay? I just happen to have in my trunk my own private supply of fuel for this kind of emergency. It's enough to get you to the Berkshires. Judith, we'll have you out of here in a jiffy."

The trooper raced back to his patrol car, retrieved his five-gallon can and a funnel from his trunk, and joyfully emptied his supply into her tank.

"Okay there, Judith," the officer said, handing back her ID. "You take care now, dear. And say hello to the Sarge for me, okay?"

"Oh, I will, I will! I promise. Oh, officer, you are *so, so* sweet. Our tax dollars at work, you know? Bye! Thank-you, thank-you!"

The Judy Lesser Pit Stop was ruthlessly efficient. If she had pulled off the Mass Pike and waited in the gas line at a busy Shell station like everyone else, the delay would have taken at least forty-five minutes, even an hour. But her free refueling, courtesy of the Massachusetts State Police, had taken less than twenty minutes. Now she was winging west on the Pike again, out past Chicopee, singing along with her scratchy radio as she coasted down the long, sloping Otis ridge toward Exit 2 at Lee.

If we worked together on Friday nights, Peter and I were always careful to make sure that one of us was home before Judy arrived, building a fire in the den, turning on the thermostats, uncorking the bottle so that she could enjoy her "wine fix" just the way she liked it—Chardonnay with a single cube of ice in the glass. It was a pleasure, very manly feeling, doting in advance on an Everything Girl as affectionate as her. Then we'd hear the telltale lug of the Maverick coming up the hill, the scrape of her fender against the maple tree, the crunch of Ford undercarriage hanging up on the snowbank. Judy disembarked and skipped up the icy flagstone walk, a turquoise-tightwaist beauty. Her lip gloss made Friday night smooches a delight. Once more she'd made it across the Pike.

.　　.　　.

By midwinter, to me anyway, the energy crisis seemed inseparable from the sexual revolution, but that was mostly due to a mental connection with Erica Jong and the phenomenal success of her novel *Fear of Flying*. Jong's lusty but poetic ode to therapeutic sex, her "zipless fuck"—"zipless because when you came together zippers flew away like rose petals, underwear blew off in one breath like dandelion fluff"—had completely infected the American vernacular by now. Jong was a literary enabler, granting license in print for behavior people were longing to engage in anyway. But now they had a phrase for it. I'd hear it myself, at the parties Rachel took me to down in Stockbridge, or over at Alice's Restaurant. There was a new ski-bunny argot now, even among the swank Westchester County set. "Oh, honey, I'm so bushed. I've had enough wine. Take me home and do me zipless, okay?" Or, if she was single: "Yeah. I know. He's really zipless. I watched him do the moguls." It was everywhere. Jong's zipless fuck had become a household word.

One Sunday afternoon Linscott and I blew into Mundy's after snowshoeing Monument Mountain. By now I considered Mundy's a second home, my favorite bar, a particularly welcome place on Sunday afternoons. After a strenuous, enjoyable weekend chopping wood and snowshoeing, I just couldn't face reporting to the *Eagle* Monday morning and writing up the stiffs. Toward nightfall on Sunday I always felt vacant and let down, with a big depression coming on. Mundy's and its raucous crowd had become a vital antide-pressant.

After we got to Mundy's that night, Linscott got wrapped up in some pool games with the bikers in the back, so I wandered over to the lesbian end of the bar and was delighted to find Bonnie.

There was a whole new thing going on then, or at least I considered it new, throbbing as I was with excitement that everything I observed was completely original and significant. Women from down south in the suburbs or the city, single women, bored married women, ex-nuns or schoolteachers, whoever, a lot of them, they'd make a run up to the Berkshires for the weekend, ski Catamount or Butternut all day, then check out the lesbian scene at Mundy's. Nothing serious, you know. Just looking things over. Making new friends. "Bi-curious." Mundy's was the first place where I heard the phrase. Mundy's had an active clientele of bi-curious ladies sampling along the lesbian end of its huge bar.

Bonnie and I had a couple of drinks and chatted. She was thinking of buying a chain saw and couldn't decide between an expensive, branded line like Homelite or David Bradley, or just a cheap Craftsman from Sears. Then a roar of laughter broke out way down at the end of the bar and Bonnie went down there to investigate. When she came back she was carrying a gift set of bourbons and ice.

"Okay, here's the deal," Bonnie said. "This lady down there owns a Jaguar, but it only runs on premium fuel. She's got to get back to New York."

"All right," I said.

"She's willing to trade one zipless fuck for five gallons of Hi-Test."

When we looked down there, everyone was roaring again. A couple of gay guys and one of the lesbian chicks were pointing their fingers over the head of the lady, who meekly waved. I was underwhelmed by the proposition. The lady making the offer looked kind of flabby, with extra bulges popping out of her ski-bunny nylon, and even in the dark light of the bar I could tell that she had too much makeup on. But, what the hell. I could get into the fun of it.

"Bonnie. I'll bet you a new air filter for my Homelite that we can find her five gallons of Hi-Test in half an hour."

"You're on. I'll tell her to wait."

I finished my bourbon. Bonnie bought a couple of longneck beers for road snorts and we piled into her pickup and hauled down to Great Barrington. I told Bonnie to head for the Mobil north of town. All the guys who worked there were horny for Rachel, I said, and we could probably work out a deal. This got Bonnie all revved up.

"Oh yeah? They like Rachel, huh?"

It only took us twenty minutes in line to get to the pumps, because the ski traffic had already thinned out. As we rolled into the station Bonnie stripped off her sweater and tightly tucked in her denim work shirt.

Bonnie's flirt with the gas attendant was artful, fun to watch. She cocked her head sideways and flashed her pert-pert Dominique Sanda smile, rested full-torso onto the steering wheel, toying it with one hand while absentmindedly playing with her ringlets and earrings with the fingers of her other hand. When the gas jockey rested his hand on the window well, she touched it. Both of us were rolling in cash now from our weekend wood chopping, and she offered him $5 to violate the ten-gallon limit.

"Lady, the going rate is $10."

"Oooooo. What else can I do for you?"

"You buy gas here often?"

"I will now."

The horny bastard filled us right up with Hi-Test, including the big jerry can in the back of the pickup, and refused Bonnie's bribe. We roared back up to Stockbridge.

"Jesus," I said. "Good work, Sister Girl."

"Yeah. You can tell Rachel that *I* get fill-ups for free."

At Mundy's, there was always a small crowd that had spilled out through the doors to drink or smoke dope in the parking lot, and by now word about our zipless mission had traveled through the bar. They all started to cheer and yell when we rolled in.

"Yo! Got the Hi-Test?"

"Way to go, Bonnie!"

"The five-gallon fuck!"

Bonnie and I found the lady's Jag in the parking lot and splashed in the gas. We were both pretty drunk by then.

"Okay, Rinker. You have to go through with it now. I talked to the lady. She wants it."

"Ah c'mon Bonnie. Let's not be greedy about this. Friendsies, okay? You take her. I'm not fucking some strange lady in a cold Jaguar."

"Chicken."

When the lady came out, she was very brazen about it.

"Okay, who do I owe for this?" the lady said. "Which one of you do I get?"

"Nah, nah, that's okay, perfectly okay," I said. "We both have places we have to go. But you can pay us for the gas."

"Oh, Good Samaritans, huh?" she said, handing over a $20. "Well thanks! You're *Berkshire Eagle*, right?"

"Yeah. As a matter of fact, I am."

"Good. I'll look you up. I owe you one zipless fuck."

She drove off in a spray of snow dust and gravel, and, thank God, I never saw her again, because it sounded like she meant what she said.

Inside the bar, everyone booed me. All these weird-ass hippie potters with ponytails, gay guys, and lesbians with big bangle earrings called me a "pussy" and a "wimp" because I wouldn't take the lady in the back of her Jag, but it was all pretty good-natured and I made a few more friends that night. Bonnie and I enjoyed a few more drinks and planned our wood chopping for the following Saturday. After that, Bonnie started calling me "Zipless Buck," so I called her "Hi-Test."

. . .

One Saturday morning in February I drove out across the state line to a small, family sawmill operation in Austerlitz, New York. The owner, whom everyone called "Big Danny," had a used hydraulic wood-splitter for sale that I thought I might be able to pick up cheap for my weekend wood-chopping business. Big Danny's establishment was a ratshack, hillbilly affair, tucked way back up a dirt road off Route 22. He had rustled up several large contracts to clear away the damage left behind by the West Stockbridge tornado the previous summer. Now he was making a killing selling off the cordwood from the several acres of "tops" left over in his yards. His hardwood was uncured, and he wasn't making deliveries either, but it was selling for $100 a cord, an unthinkable price before the energy crisis.

I couldn't believe what I saw when I approached his place. Pickup trucks and station wagons towing single-axle trailers were parked all the way up the hollow and out along Route 22, on both sides of the road. The line of cars waiting for cordwood was as long as anything I'd seen at a gas station so far, and most of Big Danny's customers were GE workers from Pittsfield and Berkshire County residents from the other hill towns.

This is a great story, a solid angle, I thought. Morton might blow me out of the sky again, but at least I could try. I spent the rest of the morning interviewing Big Danny and his sons, and then I walked down the hollow to interview customers waiting in line, obtaining several good quotes from people about how desperate they were for cordwood now, how everyone was installing woodstoves in their cellars and dens. Then I took some pictures and headed off for one of my wood-chopping jobs in Stockbridge.

I didn't write up the story until Sunday night, and then I couldn't find a way to get started with it, so I just winged it with a narrative, faux–*New Yorker* style. By this time I'd steeled myself never to expect much from any one story, so in the morning I dropped my copy and cans of film on Morton's desk and then dove into my obits.

Morton was busy getting the Monday paper out and didn't come over until just before the noon deadline. But I could tell from his roosterish walk that he was pleased.

"Okay, whoremaster, we're cracking now. We're cooking. I like this angle—lines for firewood as long as the ones for gas. The pictures are good too. I'm holding this baby until we've got room for a big spread."

Morton had only one criticism. In my zeal to get the story done, I'd neglected to include some "nut grafs," substantiating material from other firewood suppliers or sawmills that pinned the story on a few more sources than just Big Danny. But I could easily get that done in the afternoon.

"Hey Tom, thanks," I said. "But listen, am I allowed to ask you a question?"

"Of course."

"All right," I said. "How come you liked this one, but you didn't like greasers and their GTOs? I just don't get it sometimes. How do you know?"

Morton placed his hand on his chin, thought for a second, and gave me this impish, contemplative grin.

"Rinker, that is just this problem that you still have, the thing that we haven't drilled yet through your thick skull."

"Oh. Okay."

"Kiddo, there are days around here when I'm so desperate

for copy that any old piece of dogmeat you want to send down the pike looks to me like the best thing since sliced cheese. The next day? You're back in obit hell. I don't especially know why this is true. Sometimes nobody knows anything. But do you know why I can get away with that and you can't?"

"No. Why?"

"Because I'm the boss. Sorry, pal. I'm not perfect. Life isn't fair."

"Okay, Tom," I said. "Nobody knows anything."

"Nobody knows, pal. The sooner you get past that, the better."

. . .

By mid-March, when the spring thaw had begun in earnest, Rachel and I were mellow together, too. I was physically exhausted from the long winter of wood chopping and hiking the peaks with Linscott, but I also felt fit and mentally alert, exhilarated by the constant pressure of fighting long gas lines and supplying customers clamoring for wood. I associated the times I spent with Rachel with physical and spiritual relaxation. We were both still going through a lot of changes, but we felt gentle and carefree together, seamlessly joined.

After our marathon lovemaking sessions in the fall and the romantic early winter, we had cooled off a bit, even if you couldn't always tell that by taking our pulses in bed. She was spending longer and longer weekends down in New York and New Jersey, I was pretty sure hooking up with a new guy, and of course I was either with an Everything Girl or cruising Mundy's and the Red Lion on Saturday nights, which neither of us was complaining to the other about. Still, we loved each other, in our sexy-brainy way. On Monday or Tuesday nights, when she rolled back into town, I was always hungry for her and her West Stockbridge place. She loved our long talks.

I was still very emotionally attached to Rachel's agenda. I could feel it now, more each week. She was getting there, she would make it, Rachel would break free, escaping the mountains and finding that new life down in New York.

Still, she retained this one, residual hang-up, her fear of the boy "sleeping over" for the whole night. In the biblical sense, of course we were doing that. But in terms of actual elapsed time I was still expected to depart once we had sexually depleted each other, toward midnight or a little bit later. The big, official sleepover with the guy still represented an invasion of her space.

One night in March, I just got lazy about it. It was late and we were lounging together in bed after making love and Rachel was softly talking to me and making sarcastic remarks, running her fingernails down the swale of my back. Her breasts gently touching my shoulders were wonderfully relaxing and soporific.

I loved her whisper. Voice itself, sometimes, is really body language. It is expressing meaning other than the words. You can translate it.

By the end of winter I was lean and sinewy from chopping wood all weekend, jubilant about how America had weathered the Energy Crisis.

"*John Boy. You have to go. You need your sleep.*"

I didn't have to pretend to be asleep. I practically was. Borderline slumber. I was too lazy to go and too emotionally needy for her that night.

"*Rachel. There's an energy crisis on, remember? I don't have enough gas to get home.*"

This was a lie, but that's what I said.

The next thing I knew it was dawn and I was waking up in her bed. Rachel was turned against me and fully clad in pajamas, her full black hair splayed out against a printed pillowcase from Conran's.

I panicked hard about it,

harder than I'd panicked about something in a while. Shit. I had blown it. Maybe she'd revert. I wouldn't see her for a long while and she'd report back to me from her Stockbridge doc, how I'd disappointed him, and her, and not been the guy who respected her space.

As quietly as I could I slipped out from the sheets, grabbed my clothes in the corner, and sneaked downstairs and out the door. I let my car coast downhill to Card Lake before I turned the key.

But it was fine, or at least I suspected that. Rachel never said anything and she didn't push me away. After that it happened intermittently once or twice, then a few times in a row. I was finally "sleeping" with Rachel, but I was always careful in the morning to slip out quietly before she was awake. If we didn't say anything about it, maybe the cause of the hang-up in the first place wouldn't all come rushing back too fast. Don't force the issue. Let the minibreakthrough happen by itself.

One morning in late March I woke up at her place just as a big, wet front was howling through from the west. It was gusty outside, and the sky couldn't decide whether it was presenting sleet or half snow. The house was frigid—even Rachel had her thermostat turned down all night—so I decided to go downstairs, start the coffee myself, and build a fire. After I left, the house would be warm for her.

But the smell of caffeine, or the crackle of the fire, woke her, and she came down wrapped in a velour bathrobe, all lovely cleavage and drowsy smirks.

"Hey. You made a fire. That's nice."

She poured herself some coffee and then came over and plunged down beside me with a lazy, couch-kitten default. God, she was so lovely. All that black hair and the flawless, dark complexion. The fire illuminated delicate maiden hair between her breasts that I hadn't noticed before.

We were soft-spoken and gentle with each other that morning and didn't seem to need our usual sarcastic tone.

"Hey. You never mentioned it," Rachel said.

"Yeah. I know."

"Thanks. It made it easier. Interesting. I mean my life has been so—calm, yeah, calm, figuring it out. It made the break-through easier."

"It's not that big a deal, you know. Not really a break-through."

"Well, it was a big deal, to me. But somehow I was able to be calm about it. Thanks. You were sensitive.

"Oh, I don't know," I said. "All I did was nothing."

"Sensitive. You just did it and snuck out every morning. Never said a word or reminded me. Sorry, John Boy. That's my definition of sensitive."

"Okay. I accept that. So be happy, would you?"

"Ditto. Ahhhhhh. That fire feels warm. Rain. Are you look-ing at the rain?"

Rachel smiled drowsily, stretching like a cat.

"Hey, it's really romantic waking up with you here like this. I'm having this fantasy that we're married, but we can't stand the idea of saying good-bye to each other on a rainy day. Let's go back to bed. Morning back-to-bed sex with John Boy, you know?"

"Yeah, sure," I said. "To hell with Morton and Bell. The obits aren't going anywhere. All the people are already dead."

And it was nice, everything about it, including the pre-lude. We stepped over to the kitchen together, refilled our coffees, and then she led me up the stairs pulling me by the hand.

We were relaxed about it. We sat on the bed together watching the sleet pour down to meet the gray, thawing pools on Card Lake. We goofed around with our coffees for a while, sharing some between our mouths, drinking it from ponds on our chests and stomachs, then experimenting with positions. Familiarity. The better and more penetrating intimacy of familiar, diverse acts with a known lover. I noticed the way her moaning merged with the sound of the wind outside, the pinging of the sleet on the windows. Her breasts seemed even more sensual and exquisitely proportioned than before, her brown legs browner, her creamy vagina as moist as the day. I could last forever because I was expended from the night before, the reason, I supposed, for back-to-bed sex. She's enjoying me too, nice feeling, knowing that, providing that, her happiness, servicing her. And explicitness. Explicit talk. Intimacy is conversation. Ahhh, the rain. I'm so close. Jesus. Rain and screwing. Isn't it nice? Love her, love her, love her, gorgeous and ripe, don't obsess on orgasm now, relax and enjoy, love her, her lovely manumission soon, pure abstraction now, love her and, final orgasmic flash, when you break up with her someday it will not be a loss. She and you and it will love each other ten times more. The love-pain-beauty matrix. Watch her break free. The great year. Love her and yourself and the time, selfishness and learning, the year. Oh. Your passion for her and for rain.

We lay there afterward just talking and holding each other. I loved her bedroom, the way she'd designed it, all the throw rugs, the flea market quilt folded on the back of the Hitchcock chair, the neat pile of sweaters on the windowsill.

"Ooooh. Morning sex with John Boy. So nice."

I didn't want to go and she didn't want me to either. But my pile of obits waited and they weren't going to push back the deadlines for me. I took a shower and threw on my clothes from the day before. When I stepped downstairs, Rachel was sitting on the couch drinking coffee, and she had thrown more logs on the fire. She was dressed casually in a black woolen sweater, bra-less, and khaki pants.

"Hey. Come back soon? We'll just play lazy hubby and wife for the rest of the day. Our rain date."

"Yeah. Three or four hours, max. I'll just cook up some bullshit for Morton and Bell about a story I'm doing in West Stockbridge."

There was another thing about that year that amused Rachel. She couldn't stop asking me about it. She spoke as I crossed the floor.

"Hey, chopper-boy, how much money do you have in the bank now?"

"Oh Rachel. It's disgusting. Almost two thousand bucks."

"Ooooh. You can make investments now."

"Yeah. Hey, let's splurge tonight. Pick out a nice restaurant. Make a reservation and wear a dress. Then we'll do a late movie."

"Great. I'll go down to Great Barrington while you're gone and get gas. Hurry back. I miss you already."

As I drove north along Route 41, there was lovely spitting rain, and yearling deer plunged through deep, waterlogged snow in the fields, breaking up from their winter herds.

Rachel and I played Ma and Pa Kettle like that a few more times, through rainy March and April. If by midafternoon I was lonely for her and still had an article to finish, I grabbed my typewriter from the house in Richmond and worked before the fire at Rachel's, while she nuzzled up against my back. I was at peace with her and with the landscape, and I also appreciated during that wet spring what the energy crisis had yielded. The sequence had been ideal, moving from vulnerability to resilience. First the Egyptians had poured across the Sinai, the Israelis had pushed them back, and then the sheikhs had pulled their oil. Gas lines formed and we ran out of heating oil, so that guys like me could scramble and get lean chopping wood. Judy always made it across the Pike and Rachel started to break free. Faisal, I hope you enjoyed your palaces that year. Over in America, we had a dandy winter, and there were things that we now knew about ourselves that we hadn't known before.

CHAPTER FOURTEEN

EVERYONE BUSTED out that spring with gusto and relief.
People lusted for warmth, natural warmth from the sun,
warmth that you didn't have to purchase from an Arab.
Down along Main Street in Great Barrington or on the campus of Berkshire Community College in Pittsfield, all the girls
were bra-less again and the hippies came back out of the
woodwork, smoking dope and reciting bad Richard Brauti-
gan poems in the public parks. It was a year of sampling and
of change. People grew their sideburns long, chucked off
their old polyester double-knit suits for khaki hiking shorts,
or traded in their Chevy Impalas for Mazdas.

I was undergoing change too, religious change. That old
rust bucket of a religion that I had, Roman Catholicism, didn't
suit me anymore, and I knew that it was time to trade in the
clunker. A number of events that spring and summer would
reinforce this growing realization. This was the beginning of
what I would call my Year of Living Jewishly.

Peter Scheer and I had to move out of the big Miller manse
in Richmond in May, when Rhoda got back from Spain. We
were both disappointed about leaving that big, comfortable
house behind, which seemed to symbolize a new moment for
us. Betty Sudarsky had wandered off and didn't come out and
visit as much now, and the strain of long-distance commuting

during the energy crisis had pretty much doomed my relationship with Comfort Halsey. The winter and its good bosomy times with the Everything Girls were melting away with the snow.

Peter and I did have a knack, however, for decent living. We quickly located new digs almost as palatial, a big faux-Alps ski lodge tucked into the mountains in the village of Hancock, up by Williamstown. The village occupied the center of a long valley of dairy farms that ran east and west, before the terrain climbed sharply for Greylock. The sun didn't reach the sheltered valley until late in the morning and left early in the evening, but at midday the light poured down softly, suffusing the lawns and the rooftops with liquid, pastel hues. The landlady up there promptly developed a ferocious crush on Peter and would drop by at odd hours in a skimpy T-shirt and go-go shorts, just to make sure that there weren't any dust balls under his bed, but Peter manfully resisted her. Shortly after we moved to Hancock, I discovered a nudist colony nearby. I spent several contented weekends

My story on the nudist colony only required a single visit, but I returned often, just to make sure I got her middle initial right.

roaming the place with a photographer and wrote a story for the *Eagle*.

Before we moved out of the Richmond house, however, there was one nice event. In late March, all the college admission letters had gone out and Judy's younger sister had been admitted to Bowdoin, and Betty's younger sister got into Connecticut College.

Judy was ecstatic about this, yapping on the phone to all her relatives about it, wiggling all over with excitement and pride about her younger sister. As soon as she got out to the Berkshires that weekend, Judy raced across the house and yelled to me up the stairs.

"Rinker! She got into Bowdoin! And *you* helped her. Get down here and give me a hug!"

So, I stepped down to the center hall and Judy gave me the big smooch-smooch on the oriental carpet, stroking my back and pulling me to her hard. I didn't mind that part, of course, but some of the things she said were embarrassing.

"Oh! She got in, and *you* helped her Rinker. Okay, okay. We did it together. But she's in now and she's so, so happy. She's brilliant and she's going to have a great life."

Christ. It wasn't as if the little sister was sailing off to England to marry the Prince of Wales. I wasn't used to this kind of effusiveness. In my family, getting into college was the biggest nonevent of the year. ("Bowdoin, huh?" my father had said when I was admitted. "Is that a college, or a state park?") Still, I was touched, because Judy was so happy. She just loved-loved-loved that little sister, and it was refreshing to be around someone who could pour that much hope and support toward a sibling.

Judy regularly spent time on the phone with her mother, a New York psychiatrist. One night, shortly after her sister got into college, Judy motioned me over to the phone and handed me the receiver.

"Is this *the* Rinker Buck?" Judy's mother said. "The one who wrote my daughter's essay for Bowdoin? We can't wait to meet you."

"Nah, nah, c'mon, Dr. Lesser. Judy wrote that essay. Besides, your daughter deserved to get into a good college. She's brilliant."

"Of course she deserves it, Rinker, but that's not the point. You and Judy did a beautiful job helping her. We're so grateful. And Judy's told us all about your life up there. We consider you and Peter to be tops."

Jewish parents, I decided, were the absolute best. By this time, I had spent a couple of weekends with Peter's family in Poughkeepsie, and his parents were very fun-loving and young at heart, and it was clear that he spoke with them about things that I would never consider raising with my parents. Meanwhile, of course, I'd already developed my infatuation with Jewish girls and decided that they were the best too. As it happened, Peter was my first close Jewish friend, and he'd been more fun and loyal to me than anybody I'd ever met. I just got to be overwhelmed by this. Being born into the Catholics had to be just about the biggest screw-job of all time.

One night, sitting around and talking with Peter and Judy, I got plastered on bourbon and suddenly blurted out my feelings on the subject.

"God, things just would have been a hell of a lot easier if I'd been born into the Jews, you know? You guys really have it made."

"Oh my God, Rinker. There you go again," Peter said. "You always get it backwards. Jews are supposed to have Christian-envy, you idiot. Christians don't get Jew-envy."

Judy had a good way of handling her man. She'd kiss him first and stroke her fingers through his hair, just to make sure that it was clear how much she loved him, and then she put him down.

"Peter, no, no, no. *You're* the one being the idiot here. It's Rinker's life, Rinker's phase, okay? He wants to be an honorary Jew. So, let's make him an honorary Jew!"

.   .   .

One morning in early June I arrived at the *Eagle* newsroom and found a press release on my desk, with a note from Bill

Bell to find a "local angle." It was from an organization that I didn't know anything about but I vaguely recognized to be Jewish, Hadassah. The press release, three pages long, contained elaborate lists of everyone who had won a Hadassah "Woman of the Year" award that spring, and there were just tons and tons of names. Hadassah really seemed to be into honorees.

Peter was banging away on a story at his Royal.

"Hey, Peter," I said. "What's Hadassah?"

"It's a society of bored Jewish women," he said. "You know, doctors' wives. They build hospitals and stuff. It's legit."

I liked Hadassah, right away. The Hadassah ethos seemed to be a refreshing break from the sin-and-confess, sin-and-confess guilt rubric of Catholicism. Achieve! Be a joiner! Adopt a cause! *Everybody is a winner!* There were more Hadassah Woman of the Year recipients than there could possibly have been Hadassah women. Osteoporosis and diabetes, apparently, were official Hadassah diseases, because there were big Woman of the Year awards for volunteer work in those fields. Hadassah recognized a Mother of the Year, a Teacher of the Year, a Nurse of the Year, and there were separate awards for helping out with the Young Judaea Club, fund-raising at the local hospital, and running campaigns for State of Israel bonds. There were Hadassah Woman of the Year awards for musical education, health education, and citizenship. It was impressive. Somebody at Hadassah had to keep track of all these awards, and I liked what these gals were projecting about themselves. Hadassah members were doers, go-getters, dedicated to causes. As far as I was concerned, anybody associated with a group like that had to be a winner.

There was an easy local angle right up on top of the press release. A woman named Marcia Weiss from Lenox had been named Hadassah Social Action Woman of the Year for Western Massachusetts. She was a student over in Amherst at the University of Massachusetts, studying "Communications Arts," whatever the hell that was, and she had cofounded a remedial reading program for underprivileged kids in the

Springfield schools. All I had to do was pick up the phone, schedule an interview, and take a photo, and then I'd have Bill Bell off my back for a couple of hours. I called a couple of times in between obits and finally she picked up.

"Oh my God. I can't believe this," Marcia Weiss said. "*The Berkshire Eagle*. I'm studying Communications Arts, you know? Journalism. Everybody in my course can't believe that something as good as the *Eagle* is my hometown paper. They'll consider this a gas."

"Yeah, but relax," I said. "We're not talking a Page One story here. I'm only doing a short, local-angle write-up of you as the Hadassah Social Action Woman of the Year."

"Oh, exactly," she said. "I'm surprised you're even doing that much."

We made an appointment for that afternoon, and I drove down to Lenox after lunch.

Marcia Weiss lived in a small, attractive faux-Tudor house on a residential cul-de-sac just north of town. Everything about that Tudor was perfect—perfect little hosta plants and tulips budding, perfect little clump of birches midlawn, perfect little slate-roofed dormer over the stone steps and front door. I walked up the perfect little flagstone walk, rang the bell, and Marcia Weiss came to the door.

Whoa. The Phone Vibes had not quite prepared me for this. Weiss stood there in the doorway, with the dark foyer of the house behind her and the light from outside splashing across her shoulders and face.

She was Miss Clairol, 1957, updated for the 1970s. Pert-pert, super-cute, the gal with the gorgeous and bashful smirky-smile. She had an exquisite, hourglass figure, chipmunky cheeks, and a forest of black ringlets that other women would kill for. I had a sense that she'd dressed up for my visit and then suddenly changed her mind. She had on a dressy, sleeveless yellow sweater, the sort of thing that belonged with a skirt, but then at the last minute she'd changed her mind and shimmied into a pair of tight jeans. She'd missed a loop or two while throwing on her belt.

She was a little hyper though, nervous about my visit, saying things that she didn't have to volunteer. But I always liked that, anxiety in a woman. She was vulnerable, self-conscious about herself, which made it easier for me to relax.

"Oh gosh," she said. "*The Berkshire Eagle*. And I'm getting written up, for *Hadassah*. My husband will never let me forget it. I always dreamed I'd be famous for something else. Not Social Action Woman of the Year."

When Marcia mentioned her husband, I was annoyed at myself. Of course, she would be married, I thought. Hadassah wasn't an organization for single women. But I was experiencing difficulties with impulse control, having another one of my instant crushes on a beautiful woman. This wasn't supposed to happen if she was married.

Inside, the house was pleasant enough, but unfinished. In the living room the Weisses had an elegant tapestry-print couch and decent flea market chairs and Persian rugs, but the coffee table was cheap and out of place, a pine Adirondack-style piece from a catalogue. The art on the walls was reproduction French impressionist and Currier and Ives village scenes.

Weiss's story was actually kind of interesting, I thought. She was twenty-eight and had grown up in the iron district of northern Michigan, where her father was the comptroller of a large mining company. The place was so far away from cities that her family had to commute on the Interstate for more than an hour to reach their synagogue. She was bright enough to get into Northwestern University and had met her husband, a law student, in her sophomore year. She dropped out of college in her junior year after they got married, a good thing, she realized now, because she needed to "find her head" and hold down a job while her husband was finishing school. She ended up working as an assistant copywriter at a Chicago advertising agency, loved the job, and received rapid promotions. The details of coordinating copy and art and researching a company's brands fascinated her, convincing her that she really wanted to be a writer or a journalist of some kind. She was very ambitious, a Midwestern go-getter, but obviously still finding herself.

After completing his bar exams, Marcia's husband had found a job at a Chicago law firm, but after two years he was disenchanted with corporate law and had accepted a management position offered by one of his clients, a General Electric division. They'd lived in Ohio for a year before being transferred to Pittsfield. Marcia's husband traveled a lot, managing the details of complicated commercial and military contracts. Marcia was lonely sometimes, but she enjoyed the freedom of her new life. She'd enrolled at U/Mass, commuting over to Amherst several days a week and finishing her bachelor's in eight months. She was now finishing up a year of graduate work because she wanted to take more courses in creative writing.

"I'm considered exotic, you know?" she said. "All the other girls in my course are twenty-one and have boyfriends. I'm the weirdo who's married, practically thirty, you know?"

"Yeah, well, you know," I said. "Thirty's not *that* old."

"Thanks. But we're *never* leaving New England. That's what I tell my husband. *Never*. I love it here."

Except for her honeymoon, Marcia had never left the Midwest. Moving to the Berkshires had liberated her from her family and her past. She loved all the hill towns and their white steeples and her drive out to U/Mass, along the shadowy ravines of the Mill River in Cummington and Leeds. None of her friends back home believed her stories, so she had just stopped telling them. At the bookstore in Lenox, she frequently bumped into the writer William L. Shirer, who flirted with her, and at Nejaimes Market in Stockbridge one day, Norman Rockwell had helped her pick out a bug repellant.

I was intrigued by Marcia, not simply because she was attractive. She reminded me of two slightly older women from my hometown in New Jersey, both about Marcia's age. One of them was a devout Catholic and mother of three, separated from her husband now and enjoying an affair, who had visited me at the Richmond manse during a skiing vacation that winter, and we'd talked a lot about her situation. The other was the divorced older sister of a past girlfriend. I found their situation interesting. They were older baby boomers, born just after

World War II, and they had entered college by the early and mid-1960s. The rage of the young against the Vietnam War had not yet peaked and the term "counterculture" had not yet arrived. So they'd gone off to school and performed as expected, marrying early and having babies. Now they were waking up to a society drastically changed—younger sisters, and the younger sisters of friends, coming home from college talking about all the boys they were sleeping with, drugs, and the new dream of having careers. This was unsettling for the older boomer women. They were bogged down with marriage now, pursuing the model of their mothers' generation, just as all the rules had changed and everyone else was having all the fun. I'd met a few more of these older boomers at Mundy's Bar, and they always fascinated me. They were caught in the undertow between two generations, profoundly challenged by the early '70s environment of change.

I didn't want to go overboard and typecast Marcia too rigidly, but she seemed to fit that mold.

But I had to move on now. Bill Bell wasn't going to appreciate that I was goofing off down in Lenox, flirting with a married source. He just wanted twelve inches of copy on the Hadassah Social Action Woman of the Year.

So, I asked Marcia to step outside for a photo, and positioned her near the clump of birches. I used my eighty-five-millimeter portrait lens to get up tight on her face, marveling at her complexion and long eyelashes as I focused and peered through the viewfinder.

"Hey, thanks for the interview," I said. "This will probably make the paper tomorrow. Nothing big, you know."

"Oh, you're leaving? But I didn't learn anything about you! I mean, how did you find your job at the *Eagle*? What's it like?"

"Oh, not much," I said. "I write obituaries and articles on commemorative stamps."

"Yeah!" she laughed. "And Hadassah. I'm so embarrassed about this."

"Relax," I said. "You can send a copy of the article home to grandma, you know?"

"Okay, okay, but if I call you, is that all right? I want to know how you found your job."

"Sure. I'll be there. I'll save a few copies of the article."

"Cool," she said.

So, I left her there by the edge of her lawn and the birches, taking one last peek through my rearview mirror. In the liquid, afternoon light, her yellow sweater and blue jeans were splashed with Berkshire pastel.

Such a lovely person, I thought, with such an earnest, attractive disposition. Maybe she'd call as she said, but it wouldn't amount to much. I'd never see her again. Besides, I was depressed about myself now. That happened whenever I met someone reasonably close to my own age and saw how well they were living. I was working for *The Berkshire Eagle*, being paid all I was worth, $130 a week to write obits. No future like this existed for me. She was the pretty married gal in her pretty faux-Tudor house in pretty Lenox, features of a settled life that I would never obtain for myself.

.   .   .

I went a little crazy that spring on a nature story, almost literally a wild goose chase.

One morning in late April, shortly after a big storm front had thundered up from Long Island Sound, an amateur naturalist and bird artist in Sheffield had made an important sighting. Along the big sandy oxbows of the Housatonic River, he saw a rare and exotic wading species, a demoiselle crane. Two days later, just south of there, the warden at the Bartholomew's Cobble nature preserve in Ashley Falls also saw a demoiselle. Within a matter of days, a curator at the Berkshire Museum and the director of a bird sanctuary in Lenox had confirmed the sightings. A demoiselle—maybe even more than one—had inexplicably found its way into the Berkshires.

Within the fanatically devout birding community, this was electric news, and the Housatonic was quickly overrun with Audubon Society birders and ornithologists from as far away as Washington and New York. The demoiselle, which was somewhat similar in appearance to the great blue heron, with distinct, ashy blue-gray plumage and elegant, elongated breast feathers, had never been sighted in North America before. The species was Eurasian, migrating along the river valleys between Turkey and as far north as Sweden and Denmark, or between Southeast Asia and northern India and China. To reach Sheffield, the bird would have had to have made an epic ocean crossing over the Atlantic or Pacific, and then survive among new estuarial feeding grounds in North America. It just didn't seem possible.

As the reporter assigned to The Berkshire Museum, it was my job to track this story down, and I was already aware that this had been an extraordinary year for bird sightings. Earlier in the spring, a Ross's Gull from Alaska had wandered down to the coast of Massachusetts, causing a stampede of ornithologists and bird-geeks along the beaches. *The New York Times* and *The Boston Globe* had extensively covered the sightings. That winter had also been declared an "eruption year" for the Canadian snowy owl, which had wandered into New England in record numbers. I had managed to photograph one while snowshoeing up on Perry's Peak with Roger Linscott. Now we had the improbable arrival of the demoiselle crane.

Birding was an important constituency for the *Eagle*, one that Pete Miller understood a lot better than most of his editors. After World War II, southern Berkshire County and northwest Connecticut had emerged as one of America's first "enviro-tourist" sites, a mecca for bird-watchers drawn to the teeming bird life along the region's network of oxbows and swamps. The low country rimmed by purple-black peaks running between Stockbridge and New Milford was an ideal habitat for large wading birds, and almost a dozen species of ducks and mergansers, of which many were making strong comebacks after the banning of the pesticide DDT and the introduction of tougher wildlife protection laws. The Berkshires had also become a popular sighting area for the big raptor birds—the red-tailed hawk, ospreys, and bald eagles. Pete prized birding as well because it appealed to the highbrow caste of Berkshire Peers and weekend intellectuals from New York who largely determined the *Eagle*'s reputation. Birding got aggressive coverage.

This was fine with me. I was always looking for an excuse to escape the newsroom and get out into the swamps or the high raptor country that I loved. When the demoiselle story came in, I went down to Pete's office to book-turd up on wading birds, and Pat ushered me in while Pete was agonizing over some *UpCountry* copy. I pulled down from his shelves Roger Tory Peterson's *A Field Guide to the Birds* and some Audubon titles.

Pete rested back on his swivel chair and cupped his hands behind his head, so that his bony elbows stuck out through the holes in his shirt.

"What are you up to, young man?"

"Oh, just that demoiselle story, Pete. I'm going to find that bird and figure out where it came from. You know, probably it just escaped from a zoo, but it would be interesting to prove which one, and explain how it was able to survive in the wild."

"Hah! That's the spirit. Ambition. Moxie. Let's find that bird, huh?"

"Yeah. I'm going to find it."

Pete obsessed very well himself. It was one of his more touching features, the quality that made him such a strong journalist. He was inspired when one of his reporters got fired up by a story and could be quite useful at such moments because he had such good sources and ideas.

"All right now, young man, get ahold of Roger Peterson down in Old Lyme, Alvah Sanborn in Lenox, and you should probably also talk to Hal Borland. Pat can give you their numbers. But your real man on this will be Dillon Ripley. Just dial him up down there and tell him that I said to call."

Damn. Who the hell was Dillon Ripley?

"Pete," I said. "Sorry. Dillon Ripley?"

Pete looked at me somewhat aghast, but tried to be polite about it.

"S. Dillon Ripley. He is the secretary of the Smithsonian

Institution in Washington, DC. Dillon is the world's foremost authority on Asian birds, and a distinguished American. I'm surprised you've never heard of him, young man. During World War II, he worked as an agent for the OSS in India, posing as a bird-watcher. He tells wonderful stories about Lord Mountbatten and the Burma Road. Call him. He will know the demoiselle."

"Pete, I'm on the case. I'll call him."

I was intimidated, dialing Washington and asking to speak with the secretary of the Smithsonian, but Pete had said that I could use his name. Dillon Ripley's assistant said that he was in a meeting but that he would call me back, which Ripley did an hour or two later.

"Mr. Buck, Dillon Ripley here," he said. "How's Pete?"

Pete was right about Dillon Ripley. Despite his high profile as a master builder in Washington—at the time, Ripley was supervising a massive expansion of the Smithsonian, including building the Hirshhorn Museum and the National Air and Space Museum—he was very down-to-earth and enthusiastic about my search for the demoiselle. Aside from being the coauthor of the monumental, ten-volume *Handbook of the Birds of India and Pakistan*, Ripley was an excellent source for another reason. He was an old New England Brahmin himself and owned a large estate just south of Berkshire County, in Litchfield, Connecticut, which included a private aviary with over 100 species of birds. He was legendary down there. Ripley's flamingos and hawks were always getting loose and flying out to Cornwall or Sharon, and then he and his caretakers had to spend the weekend in pickup trucks, chasing all over Rattlesnake Hill to retrieve his expensive pets. Ripley was sui generis, America's aristocratic headcase for birds. But Ripley knew the Housatonic River valley quite well and had bird-watched extensively in the Berkshires.

Ripley's knowledge was encyclopedic, and I soon had three notebooks filled with information about the demoiselle. In the 1950s, Ripley had made several studies of the migratory habits of the big Asian wading birds, chasing them up the rivers and streams of India and Vietnam. The demoiselle, he said, would fly north this time of year, never straying far from feeding grounds along the Housatonic and its extensive network of trapped wetlands, but it might get "stalled" once it reached the river's headwaters at Pontoosuc Lake. Then, Ripley said, the bird would fly south to repeat its course up the river, getting trapped again by the high country up by Greylock. He was convinced that the demoiselle sighted in the Berkshires had either escaped from a zoo or a private aviary like his. This would be relatively easy to confirm because the demoiselle would be banded on one of its legs—it was too valuable a bird for an owner to neglect an identifying tag.

Ripley considered it vital to find the bird. The speculation that a demoiselle had crossed the oceans was "poppycock," but needed to be publicly debunked. He sounded as excited about my search as Pete.

"Son, we need to get that demoiselle," Ripley said. "This is important for science."

Ripley suggested several promising search areas—the Sheffield and Canaan oxbows, of course, and the vast wetlands out past Lenox Dale retained by the western slopes of October Mountain. He predicted that I would locate the demoiselle somewhere between Pontoosuc Lake in Lanesboro and the high country near Williamstown. I was impressed with Ripley, and it was exciting just working with him on the phone. Here was a man who had camped with Lord Mountbatten on specimen expeditions in India and Ceylon, but he also knew every back road and swamp in the Berkshires where a wading bird might be found.

Ripley was adamant about one other thing.

"Son, don't hold your copy. Don't write one big story. Publish a short one every day."

"Well, all right Mr. Ripley," I said. "I'll try. But why's that?"

"Birders all talk to each other," Ripley said. "They'll be following your pieces, and sooner or later the stories will flush out whoever lost this bird."

Before he hung up, Ripley asked me to keep him informed and gave me his home phone number. The resources of the

Smithsonian, he told me, were at my "disposal," and he gave me the name of several ornithologists on his staff.

I spent the next couple of hours at my desk, poring over maps of the county and planning my search for the demoiselle. Then the phone rang and it was Pete Miller, which was unusual because he generally communicated only through Pat Faucett. He was getting very revved up about this bird search.

"Young man, I have just gotten off the phone with Dillon Ripley. He's very keen on your finding this crane. Now. Dillon and I have decided to share responsibilities for locating this demoiselle. We will be calling this the Joint Expedition of *The Berkshire Eagle* and the Smithsonian Institution. You may tell our readers that."

"Well, all right, Pete," I said. "But, you know, it's pretty much going to be an expedition of one. Me."

"Jeez! Don't tell the readers that! They'll never know the difference. Just say 'A Joint Expedition of *The Berkshire Eagle* and the Smithsonian Institution.' And keep me informed. Understand?"

"Pete, I got it. I guess I really have to find this bird now, huh?"

"Young man," Pete said. "You have now been deputized by the Smithsonian Institution of Washington, DC. Spare no horses on this."

Ah, fuck me. The Joint Expedition of *The Berkshire Eagle* and the Smithsonian. What bullshit. But I loved obsessing on something like this, and it would be for Pete. No problem. For as long as it took, I was going to ceaselessly freak on finding that bird.

Every day after that I followed the same schedule. I woke early and arrived in the newsroom at 6 A.M. to motor through the pile of obits that had accumulated from the night before. At 9 A.M., I told Bill Bell that I was leaving to commence my hunt for the demoiselle, put up with the incredible shit that he gave me for that, and then departed the newsroom to begin my wanders of the Sheffield oxbows or the swamps of Interlaken.

A few weeks earlier, Peter Scheer had decided to buy a new car, and I had finally ditched my humiliating baby blue Pinto and taken over Peter's boxy and dented Subaru. The white Sube, as we called it, was a lot more suitable for my image and needs—it was indestructible and fashionably rusted out, with a sturdy, front-wheel-drive transmission that made it ideal for the back roads and boggy logging trails I would be encountering on my bird hunt. The white Sube became the mobile command unit for the Joint Expedition, its back seat stacked with topographic maps, yellow legal pads filled with field notes and "search grid" plans, a pair of binoculars borrowed from Roger Linscott, my camera, dry socks, and canteens.

Rumbling over the hills in the white Sube, I covered miles and miles of terrain every day. I was exultant about discovering new, remote country and living out of a day pack until sunset forced me back to my car. It was spring, and the wetlands in the dark shadows below the peaks were exploding with wildlife. I saw everything out there—herons and egrets, red-tailed hawks and ospreys, muskrats, beaver colonies, even a bear with twin cubs. But no demoiselle. Still, I loved the wetlands adventuring, the challenge of finding my way through so many unfamiliar swamps and then getting back to my car in the dark, eliminating more terrain each day. It was vital therapy for me, spring wanderlust that came packaged with an excuse. The Housatonic oxbows and the backcountry wetlands connected to them are geographically unique, a hidden and rich environmental paradise, and in a little over a week I covered the whole stretch, from the Connecticut line clear up to Vermont.

Every morning, in between finishing my obits and departing for that day's segment of *The Berkshire Eagle*-Smithsonian expedition, I wrote up a short piece from the day before, consulted with my new network of birders, and left behind a progress report for Pete. Dillon Ripley checked in a couple of times and I learned just how fanatical bird-watchers were—ten or fifteen calls from them would accumulate every day, with fresh suggestions on where I should search. It was exciting, what life should be, a manic junket in the woods that everyone was following.

Still, Bill Bell was not pleased with me. My insistence that each article contain a reference to the joint *Berkshire Eagle*–Smithsonian expedition annoyed him, reviving his fears that I was spending too much time cozying up to Pete Miller. I was "going overboard on this bird thing," he said, and neglecting my beat. While I was gone all day wandering the oxbows and the swamps, the post office was issuing new commemorative stamps, and local dry cleaners were experiencing desperate shortages of benzene spot remover, stories that Bell considered more worthy.

But, abetted by a ferocious case of spring fever, my attitude toward work was improving. The $130 a week that the *Eagle* was paying me, I thought, just about covered the two hours a day I was spending writing obituaries. The rest of the time I was supposed to be having fun. Bill Bell could just stuff it. I wasn't returning to the newsroom full-time until the work of the "joint expedition" was done.

The most enjoyable leg of my demoiselle hunt was a late-afternoon airplane flight. Toward the end of the joint expedition I was finishing up at a large swamp out beyond the Bousquet Ski Area when I looked up and saw the threshold of the north-south runway at the Pittsfield Airport. Why had I neglected this possibility? I had never heard of anyone bird-watching from a plane, but I was willing to give it a try. At this point, I was frustrated by the relatively meager amount of estuary I could cover in a single day on foot. But there was enough light left for me to make it all the way down the Housatonic to New Milford and back.

So, I punched the White Sube over the dirt lanes to Barker Road, pulled in at the airport, and rented the high-wing Cessna Skylane that I'd been checked out in over the winter. The Skylane was not the best plane for the job, but lightly loaded with just me in the plane, the Cessna, I was confident, could be maneuvered well enough for low-level spotting.

It was a beautiful evening with unlimited visibility, dry, still air, and just a few murky cirrus high overhead. At the end of the runway I fire-walled the throttle and then turned east at the wind sock for Lake Pontoosuc, throttling down and pulling back the prop once I got to 600 feet. Over the lake I turned hard to the south and then leveled the wings, easing back on the yoke until the stall horn wailed. Two notches of flap and trim for slow flight. That's how I flew the river and all the swamps that evening, low and trimmed for slow flight at sixty-five miles per hour indicated, peering out for the demoiselle through my binoculars and steering the plane with my knees.

The Housatonic is a majestic river from the air, a pastel ribbon falling 150 miles to Bridgeport. From the headwaters in Lanesboro, the river snakes around and loops back on itself through gently sloping meadows and villages with white steeples. On a summer evening, as the sun drops below the Catskills to the west, the oxbows glow like lanterns and along the banks the dairy pastures and sod farms are extensive and awesomely green.

The birding was good as soon as I got down past South Mountain and the swamp country east of Lenox. There were considerable numbers of herons and white egrets down there and large flocks of mallards and canvasback ducks. Farther south, behind the Green River in Great Barrington, and then the Sheffield and Canaan oxbows, I identified several new estuarial areas that I hadn't known about before, and marked them on my maps for searches by foot. Then I swung south for New Milford and hopscotched over the peaks to the massive Blue Swamp estuary, just behind Dillon Ripley's estate in Litchfield.

No demoiselle yet, but it was such a lovely night to fly that I didn't care. The Continental engine throbbed on its mounts, the wind whistled through the air vents over my head, and I enjoyed the sensation of flying low and close to the earth, letting my curiosity and what I saw through the binoculars draw me along. When I got up through the Sheffield oxbows again, I saw Bonnie and Helen up ahead, turning over the garden at their goat farm. Yeah, what the hell. I'll give them a buzz job. So, I punched the Skylane down hard to the trees, and pushed the throttle and prop controls all the way forward. Yeah, great. Here we go, gals. I was blowing right past 150 knots when I went by their heads. Then I honked back hard on the yoke, put my left wing over, and circled tightly above them, staring down to the garden as the oxbows and the peaks swirled through my windshield. Bonnie was shaking her spade at me now, wiggling all over with annoyance, and I could see her ringlets bobbing in the twilight. Oh, you beautiful, tough-ass chick, you are a total winner, Bonnie. I loved communing with her that way, circling hard in a plane just above the stall, laughing my ass off while she shook her spade. Buzz jobs are just the best, I thought, almost as good as sex. I pulled hard out of the turn, wiggled my wings at them, and flew on north.

Dillon Ripley had been correct about everything. My articles in the *Eagle* whipped up a frenzy of interest among birdwatchers, and by the end of the week, when I came in each morning, there were phone messages stacked up from as far away as Long Island and Vermont. One of them was from an elderly bird fancier from Monroe, Connecticut, just north of Bridgeport along the Housatonic. Louis Rinkovinski owned the Sundial Bird and Animal Farm down there, and he had been breeding demoiselles in captivity for years, selling them to zoos and private collectors. He'd lost two demoiselles in the big windstorm that had blown through a couple of nights before the sightings in Litchfield and Berkshire counties, and he was convinced that they were his birds. They were both banded on the legs, he said, and he gave me the numbers embossed on the plastic identification tags.

That weekend, I was determined to search some of the swamps that I'd seen from the air, particularly the ones bordering Great Barrington and Alford along the New York state line, within the Green River drainage. By this time the joint expedition was the laughingstock of the newsroom because everyone was convinced that I'd never find the bird. Roger Linscott, however, was amused by the whole junket and insisted on joining my search. So, we spent the weekend together in the swamps out below the Taconic range, swatting mosquitoes and peering through the cattails with our binoculars. When we stopped to eat the sandwiches that I carried along in my backpack, Linscott groused because the pack of cigarettes in his pocket had gotten soaked.

"You are an infernal jackass and this is a preposterous undertaking," he growled. "However, I am quite enjoying myself. No one has ever invited me on a crane hunt before."

Early the next week, I received a phone call from a homeowner in Stephentown, New York, just over the state line from our new place in Hancock. The man reported that he had observed a large wading bird along a small, swampy creek behind his house over the weekend. The bird seemed almost tame and he could approach almost close enough to touch it. On Monday morning, when he went out to look again, the crane had fallen over and died. Its leg was banded.

"Say, did you happen to read the number off that band?" I asked.

"Yeah. I've got it right here."

It was one of Rinkovinski's demoiselles, and the bird had become "stalled" in between Pontoosuc and Williamstown, at exactly the northern terminus that Dillon Ripley had predicted. We never did find the other bird, but there wasn't much point now. The mystery was solved. That afternoon I drove up to Stephentown and retrieved the slightly moldering remains of the demoiselle, stashed it in a plastic garbage bag in the trunk of my car, and met Rinkovinski at the halfway point for both of us along the river, the Collins Diner in Canaan. Rinkovinski was a bit of a coot, but he was extremely grateful to receive that demoiselle carcass and bought me dinner.

Dillon Ripley was pleased, too.

"Congratulations, young fellow," he said when I called the Smithsonian to deliver the news. "We found that bird."

"Well, I don't know Mr. Ripley," I said. "It was dead when I got to it. I don't feel successful."

"Nonsense," Ripley said. "This was a captive bird, zoologically insignificant. Do you know how many specimens I've shot in India for the sake of science? Hundreds. It was important to debunk all this foolishness about a demoiselle jumping the oceans, and that's what you've done. I have quite enjoyed your tenacity here."

Ripley asked that I send him copies of all my articles on the joint expedition and a short report of my doings. They would be retained in two places at the Smithsonian, he said, the Department of Ornithology and something called the Bureau of Phenomenal Events. At least I had learned that there was something called that.

Pete Miller was jubilant. All week, he'd been pestering me with hand-written notes, or sending Pat Faucett to the news-room for updates on the crane hunt. Now Dillon Ripley had called to formally thank the *Eagle* for its work, and after that Pat called me and told me that I'd been invited out to the Millers' again for dinner. They hoped I could come on Friday night.

Out at Pete's house on Williams Street a few nights later, we celebrated in the usual way, over martinis. When I got there, Pete was rubbing his hands with satisfaction and scratching his rump, gleeful all over, and he bored Amy Bess to death telling her all about the bird hunt. I was anxious to change the subject.

"Hey, Pete, c'mon," I said. "It's not that big a deal. I found a carcass, you know?"

"Nonsense, young man! Our mission was to find that bird, dead or alive. And we did that. The joint *Eagle*-Smithsonian expedition was a success!"

CHAPTER FIFTEEN

OVER THE LONG July Fourth weekend, Rachel dragged me to a mansion party in Stockbridge. The event was the annual charity fund-raiser held on the grounds of a Prospect Hill estate called Naumkeag, a many-gabled Stanford White design, built in 1885 for Ambassador Joseph Hodges Choate. From the sloped expanse of the south lawn there were breathtaking views to Monument Mountain, and elaborate stone steps descended gracefully through a birch grove. The raised perennial beds bloomed with purple loosestrife, blue and white platycodon, and several shades of rare iris. The crazy Stockbridge millionaires were all there in their Mahkeenac Yacht Club blazers, and their daughters were attractive in their print dresses, blonde and freckled and effortlessly conversational, as sunny as Cybill Shepherd in the movie *Daisy Miller*. While Rachel chased off to find some friends, I enjoyed a long book-turd chat with Mrs. Reinhold Niebuhr. Then Rachel came up from behind and tugged at my jacket sleeve.

"John Boy, come with me," she said. "There's someone who wants to meet you."

Rachel pulled me by the hand across the sloping lawn and then presented me to a short, portly older man with a drink in his hand. The fellow wore a black beret with a nimbus of white hair poking out underneath and was contentedly drawing on an old briar pipe through his white beard. He was framed from behind by a pod of Japanese maple and dogwood trees.

Rachel pushed me toward him with her hand splayed on my back.

"Bill Shirer," she said. "Here's Rinker Buck."

Damn it all now, Rachel. You could have at least warned me about this. Christ. It was the great William L. Shirer.

But Rachel wasn't going to allow me to be flustered. She wrapped her arm around my waist and clutched my belt with her hand, docking hard up against me with her left breast and hip, the big party-snuggle from the lovely girl that would give me courage.

"Well, thank you, sweet thing," Shirer said to Rachel, taking her in with a detached but hungry glance before he turned to me. "Well, young fellow, it certainly is a pleasure to meet you. I've enjoyed your book reviews quite a bit. How do you find the time for that when you have a regular beat to cover?"

"Bill, it's what I told you," Rachel said. "Rinker never sleeps. All he does is work and read."

"Rachel. Now look," I started, but Shirer took a quick draw on his pipe and wouldn't let me finish.

"Oh, now listen here, young fellow," he said. "Never resist the blandishments of a young lady. It doesn't matter if she means it or not. She's lovely! That's all that counts."

Rachel threw her head back and laughed, and then reached over with her free hand and gave the sleeve of Shirer's herringbone jacket a playful tug.

"Bill! Stop it," she said. "You're embarrassing me again."

Jesus, I thought. What the hell is going on here? William L. Shirer is putting the make onto Rachel, and she's giving him a big flirt back.

"My dear," Shirer said. "It would be impossible to embarrass you enough. You're too lovely."

"Rinker," Rachel said. "It's okay. Bill's a reader too. Big time."

"Yes, always have been," Shirer said. "When I got to the Paris *Herald-Tribune* in the '20s, James Thurber used to goad me about that all the time. 'Shirer, get your face out of that book and do some work.'"

"And what did you say to him, Bill?" Rachel said.

Shirer drew on his pipe and tittered a little before he replied.

"I told that half-blind jacksnape where to go," Shirer said. "'Jimmy,' I said, 'I *am* working. Reading is work for me.'"

Rachel laughed again and performed from her hips this wonderful body-wiggle that she had, which seemed to drive Shirer wild with distraction, but she wasn't neglecting me either. She docked hard against me again with her party-snuggle and then reached under my jacket to stroke my spine with her nails.

"Oh, like, this is heaven, you know?" she said. "John Boy, I just knew that you *had* to meet Bill."

It was heaven, in a way. Book-turd heaven. Thus began a relationship with another older man, one that would help shape the rest of my time at the *Eagle*. I was both intimidated and excited to meet William L. Shirer.

William Shirer wasn't simply a legendary war correspondent and now a spectacularly successful author, which itself would have been enough of a draw for me. His best-known book, *The Rise and Fall of the Third Reich*, had been the first serious work of history or nonfiction that my friends and I read, the book that we graduated to after growing out of the Hardy Boy adventures. As teenage boys, we were fascinated by the Nazis. The consummate evil and political sadism of Hitler and his Nazi goons was irresistible, and Shirer's immense book had allowed us to gorge on the Nazis for what seemed forever—the *Rise and Fall* could take could take six weeks or more to finish. Our perception of the events leading up to the Cold War years we were living through was formed, in large part, by Shirer's epic.

Shirer had a great deal of personal mystique as well. The story behind his book was also epic. After being fired by CBS for refusing to curb his liberalism on the air, Shirer had retreated to a remote farmhouse in Torrington, Connecticut, and had endured a decade of poverty, obscurity, and a disastrous extramarital affair, plodding away every day to complete his masterwork on the Nazis. Few acts of writing in the century could match what Shirer had achieved with his monumental *Rise and Fall*, and he was now famous for it.

So, now I was meeting the great man. But I was disarmed at first by the obvious familiarity between Shirer and Rachel. She had mentioned him to me offhandedly before, how she had met him at a Lenox dinner party and then become friendly with him over the winter, running errands to buy him tobacco or books, helping him organize his files, and so forth. I knew that they went out to dinner together a lot. Still, I didn't expect my literary hero to be such a horny old man.

Shirer's lady-killing ways, however, complemented an otherwise delightful character. He projected perennial youth and spontaneity. He enjoyed nothing more than to sit around Alice's Restaurant at night with Rachel and a couple of her friends, or an adoring young journalist like me, regaling the table with the remarkable stories of his romp through the century. Shirer had covered and known almost every world leader there was, from Hitler to Churchill to Gandhi, and told marvelous stories about them. Shirer's other specialty was famous, beautiful women. During his Paris years, Shirer had known Isadora Duncan, Zelda Fitzgerald, Sara Murphy, Anais Nin, Marlene Dietrich, the Hemingway wives, and the Picasso mistresses, and he didn't mind intimating, if you were willing to believe him, that he'd bedded many of them. He was extremely grateful to have a young audience for these tales and seemed revived by the attention this brought him. The year I met him, Shirer was seventy-one, and it was enjoyable spending time with someone that age who still enjoyed pretty girls and nighttime boozing. We offered him the companionship of the young that he craved, and he offered us great stories and the thrill of knowing an older, famous man.

That same afternoon, Shirer invited Rachel and me to dinner at the Curtiss Hotel in Lenox. I was entranced by his tales of Paris in the '20s, his friendships with Ernest Hemingway, F. Scott Fitzgerald, Thomas Mann, and James Joyce. But Shirer was also refreshingly open about his personal life, the many mistakes he had made, how his career had been successful

The legendary William L. Shirer was a font of erudition, told great stories about Paris, and never met a pretty girl that he didn't like.

mostly because it was so intuitive and unplanned. He talked about himself with amazing candor and seemed to view his life as confessional fodder, something he was offering up so that we could learn from it. At the time, Shirer's second marriage, to a crazy Lenox millionairess named Martha, was a train wreck. Whenever Martha traveled alone, which Shirer encouraged her to do as often as possible, he'd pick up the phone and call some lovely young thing that he'd just met on the Lenox or Stockbridge party circuit, which this year happened to be Rachel. It all got to be an awful tangle and a big tabloid story the next summer, when Shirer celebrated the completion of his first book of memoirs by going off on a European junket with another one of his girlfriends and Martha finally got fed up and locked Shirer out of the house. I got drawn into the mess because Martha's lawyers were convinced that Shirer and I were swapping too many girlfriends between us, and I was called as a witness at their divorce trial.

But I never minded that, because the man was too much fun. By the middle of the summer that year he'd become a regular part of my weekly routine. Shirer was lonely after his days of writing and fascinated by Watergate, and he would invite Rachel and me over to his house in Lenox a couple of nights a week to drink bourbon and watch Dan Rather and Daniel Schorr assault Richard Nixon on the *CBS Evening News*. Peter Scheer and Judy Lesser came along a lot of times, and the Linscotts were often there too. A lot of our girlfriends were put off by Shirer's voyeurism and suggestive remarks, disillusioned by his behavior. But Shirer was essentially harmless, and I ended up immensely appreciating a few things that he taught me.

As soon as Rachel introduced me to Shirer, I was very curious about the nature of their relationship, but I wasn't going to give Rachel the satisfaction of knowing that. I refused to discuss it whenever she broached the subject, an important breakthrough for me in understanding the management of the guy-gal relationship. Don't be afraid to drive her insane with disinterest. I could tell that she was frustrated by this, but I quickly changed the subject every time she wanted to talk about her relationship with Shirer.

One night that summer, Rachel and I met Shirer for drinks at the Red Lion in Stockbridge and then he went off alone for a mansion party over on the oxbows. Rachel and I decided to enjoy some wine together up on the Red Lion porch. It was a lovely, crisp night out, with crickets screeching from Icy Glen behind us, the whoosh of big Oldsmobiles going by on Main Street, and pretty couples from New York oohing and ahing at the beauty of the Rockwell facades.

"Okay, Rinker. You win. I totally concede defeat," Rachel said, reaching over from the rocker she was sitting in and digging her nails into my arm. "You're driving me *nuts* on this! You know perfectly well what my thing for Bill Shirer is, and don't try and bull me either."

"Hey, Rachel, relax. I haven't lied to you about seeing other women. I know that you're meeting a new crowd in New York. What's the big deal here? I don't particularly like sharing you with Bill Shirer, but, hey, it's your life. I'm sure he's a great date."

"Oh, Rinker, don't pull this sophisticated crap on me. I mean you couldn't possibly think that I'm sleeping with him."

"Rachel, if you're sleeping with Bill Shirer, what I'm going to do is stuff you into the trunk of the BMW, drive over to Stockbridge Bowl, and throw you in. Then I hope you sink to the bottom like a rock."

"*Exactly!* It's not that. But, c'mon, let me explain this! It's important. I mean, you know, it's really more about you and Peter. God, I care about what you think. Okay, no offense?"

"Yeah, yeah. No offense."

"Okay. Now look. You and Peter? You've saved my life. I *love* you guys. I mean, making me a part of your group and everything. You and me together. I'll still be crying about you guys when I'm an old lady. But, you know, *ahhhhhh*—"

"Rachel," I said. "It's okay to say it. If I was a babe and it was up to me? No way. I wouldn't want a date with me either."

"*Exactly*. Thanks for being honest. It's just, you know, you guys. 'When am I going to be famous? Do I have writer's block this week? Bill Bell is shitting on me again. Who am I more in love with this minute? Comfort, Betty, Judy, Jamie, Betsey, Susan, Becky, or Barbara Van Nice?' Christ, it's like being a character in a baby-naming book with you guys. Sorry, John Boy. No offense. But guys your age are just too high maintenance sometimes."

"Yeah, and Bill Shirer makes a pretty good Daddy, doesn't he?"

"Ouch. That's too close. But yeah. It's not just the way he takes me out to dinner and tells me all his stories about Zelda Fitzgerald. I just feel so secure and happy with him. He's not worrying about money all the time. He's not a lot of work. He's gracious and he's always making these goofy little moves at the table that show how proud he is just to be seen with me. And, you know, when he drops me off and I peck him on the cheek, he's just totally, totally grateful that I've spent time with him. I mean he's, what—"

"Fun," I said. "He's fun. A real date."

"Yeah! He's easy. Bill Shirer is easy. And he's so totally obligated to me that I have *no* obligation to him."

"Yeah, well, whatever," I said. "Rachel, it's fine. You know it's really fine. I'm almost relieved to hear all this."

And I was relieved, too. Rachel and Shirer helped deliver me to a nice place. When I was in college, almost all of my girlfriends had an extra, older man on the side. Generally I didn't learn about them until a relationship was about six or eight weeks old, after sexual intimacy had broken down prior barriers to honest conversation. *Oh, yeah. About this weekend. Ah, see, I've got this other guy I go with once in a while. He's, like, older, you know? I met him at my uncle's house.* Most of these fellows were from Boston and New York, prosperous and successful, sometimes married at the time, sometimes not. They were law firm partners, foundation presidents, and museum curators, hip, fortyish guys who wore expensive Italian sports jackets and drove Mercedes SLs. I wasn't to feel threatened by this. *Don't worry. I knew him way before you. Way before.* And here was the weird part about it, this dandy little head-fuck that all girlfriends seemed to have in store for me. She wanted me to meet him. *I can't* wait *for you to meet him!* Showing me off to him and him off to me was a vital act of our mating ritual. I ate a lot of pretty good meals in Boston and New York off this deal.

Gradually, I got the hang of that thing. Harty Platt was always there to save me and I was chasing around during those years with a pretty fast gang from Bennington College, where it was practically expected that a girl sleep with at least two or three of her professors. *Rinky, it's not just about sex, you know, but you do learn a lot of things. He takes you out to French restaurants and buys tickets for off-Broadway shows. This battle I'm having with my father now? Gerald knows what to do.* Every time, she said. Gerald knew what to do.

After a while, I wasn't particularly naïve about what happened back at the pied-à-terre. Some of the girls I went out with considered talking about their relationship with the older man sexy, and others were mentally gaited to tell you the truth later, after we'd broken up and I now enjoyed ex-officio status as a confessor. The accounts varied, but there were consistent themes. With the older guys, nightcaps of oral sex seemed to be heavily preferred, but of course they did all kinds of sex. I found this fascinating, because it helped solve a mystery. I'd always wondered why women even performed oral sex in the first place, and why they were so aggressive about providing it in certain situations. Now I was beginning to understand. She'd been squired around all night, listened to as a mature woman, an adult, taken care of by an established man. She felt appreciated and loved. He was there for her, as comforting as a good psychiatrist, whereas at the end of a date with a young wacko like me, *she* had to be the shrink. So, sex with the older guy was often great, because she didn't really care about the sex, qua sex, the physical act. She cared about acknowledging feelings of love, the caring and warmth of that night. Wacko college boys might profess love, but mostly they were doing that just to get the physical sensation of sex, quite a different thing.

That Indian summer night on the porch of the Red Lion, with the crickets screeching from Icy Glen and the tourists browsing by, I suddenly felt liberated and buoyant about all this. I cared too much for Rachel to deny her this fun. She liked being with Shirer, and this was good for me, because it took a big load off my back. I couldn't possibly provide all that she needed. Jealousy, I suddenly realized, is a useless drag on relationships. It gets in the way of love. The whole concept of fidelity, premarital fidelity anyway, is a hideous crock. If she's at all worth being with, she needed a whole lot more than just me.

That was my attitude now. However, sometimes things with old Bill could get just a little bit too kinky for my tastes. I would be over at Rachel's at night just goofing off and talking, or maybe making love with her on the bed, when the phone would ring. It was Shirer, checking in for one of his regular, good-night chats with Rachel. She would speak with him for fifteen or twenty minutes while I twiddled my thumbs under the sheets, and then finally I'd lose my patience with this charade and grab the phone.

"Hey Bill," I said. "Do you mind? I'm trying to wrap up a few things with Rachel here."

"Oh, my dear boy!" Shirer said. "Let's not be puritanical about this. We can share her!"

Jesus. It took me a while to get the old billy goat off the line because now he wanted to talk with *me* about my latest book review. Once we were done with that, Rachel would take over again and do this whole kissy-poo conversational routine to get him off the line, and then we could be alone again.

"Christ, Rachel," I said. "I wish he wouldn't call late at night like that."

"Who asked you, Rinker? This is *my* house, you know? Shirer's old, he's lonely, and he's needy. I *like* helping to watch over him."

"Yeah, yeah, yeah. But look. You forgot to remind him to take his Geritol pills."

"Ha, ha, ha. But you can't deny me this. It's my choice. He's my grandpops and I like knowing him."

Grandpops. What the hell. It was my job now to get used to just about anything.

We enjoyed ourselves together that summer. Shirer had an old sailboat out on Stockbridge Bowl, a faded blue Day Sailor with a wobbly mast and tattered sails, moored just north of the Mahkeenac Yacht Club. He loved taking us out there and sailing up and down the lake, sipping from a jug of French table wine, palavering on about Hemingway and Fitzgerald, how he considered Erica Jong to be the "voice of the '70s," and, oh God, youngins, the lake is so pretty today and reminds me of the times I spent with my bride up by Lucerne, getting away from the Nazis for a long weekend. Shirer was devoted to his two daughters and excited about being a grandfather now.

Often, complaining about his failing eyesight and his arthritis, Shirer would turn the tiller and jib over to me, and then crouch down in the cockpit, fixing his gaze on Rachel, who was sunbathing up on the bow in her Speedo bathing suit. Rachel would fall asleep during her sunbath, and I would enjoy long talks with Shirer as we sailed up and down the lake. He encouraged me to talk about myself and seemed hungry to be of some use. Steering the boat, I felt lazy under the sun. When I ran low on wine, Shirer would reach for the jug between his legs and refill my glass.

"*In vino veritas,* young man," he would say, stroking his beard with his hand. "You seem quiet today. Anything troubling you?"

"Oh, I don't know, Bill. I get depressed sometimes, you know? I'm twenty-three years old and I haven't done anything with my life yet. I'm writing obits at *The Berkshire Eagle.*"

"Oh my dear young lad. Please. Depression is merely stored energy. It is your dreams overtaking your talent at the moment. You'll be fine. I know it. Besides, look at someone like me."

"Bill," I said. "You? What do you mean by that?"

"Oh my Lord, son. I'm seventy-one years old and I'm still trying to figure out my life."

There were other interesting things about the sort of triangular relationship that we had. I found that when I was around another man who obviously lusted after my girlfriend, I was more aroused than usual, and Rachel was revved up too, flattered by Shirer's attentions. It was pleasurable, getting back to her place in West Stockbridge and lounging around in our bathing suits for a couple of hours before we drove over into New York State for dinner. We both felt lazy and fulfilled from too much wine and sun on the lake, but sexy together. Our bodies glided effortlessly together from the lanolin sheen of perspiration and suntan oil. Both of us liked the nylon glean of the Speedo too much to even consider removing it, so we enjoyed prolonged sessions of oral sex, or invented new ways of making love through a Speedo. In between, we sat on the bed and goofed off, sharing wine and telling stories, making up skits about Shirer. When we made love for the second or third time, the mosaic of our shared perspiration on her Speedo felt silky and cool.

I wasn't competing with Shirer for Rachel, I decided. He had merely created a new and different emotional zone for us, prompting new reasons for loving her.

One afternoon in July, Tom Morton walked over to my desk in the *Eagle* newsroom and asked to see me alone in the conference room. He seemed subdued, a bit nervous. I was acutely sensitive to his moods and instantly concluded that I was in trouble again. A few days earlier, I'd gotten into an argument with Bill Bell and called one of the ministers I had to cover a "horse's ass." Bell didn't mind if I called a politician a horse's ass, but he didn't like me saying that about an ordained minister, and he must have reported me to Morton. But Morton could also be hard to read. Once we reached the conference room, he settled down a bit, dabbing his bald pate a few times and looking at a manila folder with some personnel files in it.

"Say, Rinker," he said. "Now that Nick King is leaving for the *Globe*, we're thinking of shifting beats around a little. How would you feel about doing a few other things around here and being taken off obits?"

The relief was instantaneous and enormous, a physical sensation. My heart raced and I could feel the back of my neck warming and turning red. I didn't realize until that moment just how humiliated I really was being an obituary writer. I was beginning to feel very comfortable in the Berkshires and meeting new people, even famous writers, enjoying the summer mansion parties, but it was always degrading to me to explain to strangers that I wrote obits. No amount of encouragement by Peter Scheer, Rachel, or Roger Linscott could change my mind. I was stuck in obit hell, a beat that my predecessors had held for years.

Now I was elated by what Morton had said, but speechless for a moment.

"Tom," I finally said. "How would I feel about a date with Julie Christie? Of course I'd like to be taken off obits. Do you mean it?"

"Yes. I do. We'd like you to take over Nick's old beat of the environment, land conservation, and the great outdoors, which you are obviously quite suited for, and we also need someone to relieve the city staff by covering the county commissioners. That's politics. You've already done well at that when you filled in for other reporters. So, what do you say?"

"What do you mean, what do I say, Tom? This sounds great."

"Yeah, but there's one hitch," Morton said.

"Okay. What's that?"

"Well," Morton said, "Charlie Bonenti really appreciates how you hump it for him on Friday nights. We'll still need someone on the late shift Fridays to do all the dumb stuff—obits, weather, church news, car wrecks, and so forth. You'll be free all week to pursue these new beats. But Friday nights? I'm afraid you'll just have to keep your oar in the water shoveling the shit."

I *loved* Tom Morton at that moment. I loved him for all time. There wasn't a boss in all of America who could hand out a promotion with such verbal richness.

"Tom," I said. "I'm in on this deal. From now on, Friday nights? My oar is in the water, shoveling the shit."

"Yeah. Okay, you little creep. Now. Let me just say one other thing here and get it off my chest. Nobody around here can remember when a reporter got off obits this fast, less than a year. I'm real proud of you. You and Scheer are the first hires I made around this place, and look at how well you've both done. Thanks, kiddo. And I mean that."

I felt very emotional about what Tom said and started to well up inside. But I also felt sheepish and meek, unsophisticated. It had never occurred to me that I'd react this way. Women made me emotional. Buzz jobs and snowshoeing up Perry's Peak with Roger Linscott made me emotional. But you weren't supposed to get emotional about a job promotion. Christ.

"Yeah, well, you know, Tom," I said. "I don't know what to say. But I'm grateful. Thanks."

"All right, pal. Good. Now, there's just one more thing. Bill Bell mentioned this."

Ah, balls. Here we go. I could probably head this one off.

"Tom, I'm sorry, okay? I'll even tell Bill that. I shouldn't have called Rev. Gray a 'horse's ass.'"

"No, no. That's okay, kiddo. Rev. Gray *is* a horse's ass. But, we're concerned about the hours that you keep. Bill seems to feel that you're acting out sometimes because you're overworked. You push yourself too hard."

Overworked? Good Lord. I considered myself the biggest dick-off in *Berkshire Eagle* history.

"Tom," I said, "*over-worked?* Is this a joke or something? You're the boss. You're supposed to tell me to work *harder.*"

"No, and you can stop right there, kiddo. That's where you're wrong. Dead wrong. My job is to get you to pace yourself a little. You know, throttle back, rein in the ponies, rest your feet. I mean, on Fridays around here, you regularly work from seven in the morning until eleven at night. That's crazy. We can't continue to let you do that."

After my commentaries and reviews began appearing on the editorial page, the Eagle *asked me to pose for this "columnist mug."*

I couldn't believe what I was hearing. It was so easy to con the world. Yes, I loved double-shifts on Fridays, but I didn't work from seven to eleven. In the middle of the day I always goofed off, driving over to West Stockbridge for a snuggle with Rachel before she shoved off for New York, or wandering down to Lenox to browse around the bookstore. Linscott and I played pool together just about every Thursday or Friday afternoon. Now Morton was accusing me of working too hard. I'd run into this before in life. Fuck up, be a hero.

"Tom. I don't work nearly as hard as you think I work, okay? Last Friday, after lunch, I took Happel's Cadillac down to Sears for an oil change."

"Oh, I see," Morton said, dabbing his forehead. "And that's not *work*, huh? You're *here*, Rinker, all the time. Everybody loves you for the way you nursed Happel and that ridiculous car through the energy crunch. It made a big difference in how people felt about themselves around here. You think that isn't *work?*"

Sorensen say... will not finish...

By Rinker Buck

Theodore C. Sorensen, special ...unsel, speech writer and poli... ...al strategist for President ...n F. Kennedy predicted here ... President ...

that cares litt... vasion of its n... erties," to avo... of impeachme... added that a c... speaking up i... massive natio...

Books

Can marriage save ...

NAKED NOMADS. By. George F. Gilder. Qua... rangle/The Ne... 'Times B... ...

...kshire birdwatchers spot ...emoiselle from Europe

By Rinker Buck

...EY FALLS — A demoi... ...ane was sighted here ...y near a pond at ...Wilhelm's farm on the ...ide of Route 7A. The ...selle is an exclusively Eu... ...bird and the sighting is ...mely rare for North Amer...

...e sigh... ...Bartlett... ...tor of ...m, an ...mer of ...ley S... ...dely ...Hen... ...Ash... ...on ...he ...She... ...nat... ...R... ...B... ...F...

...confirmed ...nce

form a zoo somewhere in North America.

George Watson. ornithologist with the Smithsonian in Washington, D.C., said last night that the chances are almost a hundred to one against "a bird of this species blowing across the Atlantic."

More likely. Watson said, is that the bird has escaped from a zoo south of the Berkshires and migrated northward by instinct.

"Even if the crane had been in captivity for a long time." ...son said. "the inner clock-... ...cies has would tell ...the same ...its

Alonzo G. Hollister
Admiration from Russia

Elder Frederic Evans
An American nationalist

Count Leo Tolstoy
Chastity's strange proponent

R... fo...

h...

Russia's Tolstoy wrote Shakers praising chastity, scholar finds

By Rinker Buck

...hen the Russian writer Leo Tolstoy ...brooding over the last pages of his ...l on marital jealousy ...

was part firebrand, at the other. part religious mystic; so his brief inter... Shakers ...

Rich...

Stock Averages

(Noon) Dow Jones (Shearson, Hammill & Co.)

30 Industrials	881.73	— 6.10
20 Transp.	193.90	— 1.51
15 Utilities	92.92	— .41
Sales 5,700,000		

Nixon
s term

Second Section

The Be

the in—
opinion, as a law
al lib—
zen, he (Nixon) is
ation
Sorensen com
ensen
million that
tizen,
raised for his
of a
campaign and
sys—
Nixon raised ir
uence
that "clearly,
money is raise

Frost's 100th anniversary
to be noted by new

The 100
birth of

<u>Name in the news</u>

Energy is her delight

erican society?

society at all: his violence just
shows up in a different set of
statistics. Unfortunately, for
many of the men Gilder's statis—
tics represent, marriage is just
this kind of tradeoff.

All societies have a given
quotient of violence determined
by their political system, their
marketplace and their morals,
and America's quotient of vio—
lence has always been high.
Marrying off our violent men —
like the failed attempt of the
Spanish conquerors in South
America to promote assimila—
tion and preserve political unity
by allowing European sailors to
marry Indians — will only pro—
duce another crop of psy—
chologically damaged child—
who will be the next
of violent me
Marri

n Blake said. "is eternal

leather McHugh must have
xim at birth, in the way in—
of strength travel several
he poet to another.

d "transient and taster of all
thinks of the Berkshires as
nent home," she was the
k of a $5,000 grant from the
ent for the Arts. The grant
to write a second book of
free her from the teaching
eral hustling," as she calls it.
alive for the past few years.
or the past year a member of
artment at Berkshire Commu—
McHugh has published in The
arper's, Atlantic and several
es. Her first book of poems
livered by Female I
blished

Poet Heather McHugh: A taste of life

psychiatrist' dismissed
g a check of credentials

er Buck
wn man, hired
go by the Berk—
ation Center as a
rist, has been dis—
he holds neither a
medicine nor psy—

oney, 35, a Carmelite
director of the Thor—
n Carmelite Fathers
n Williamstown start—
,000-a-year position at
iilitation center Nov. 26
d not be reached for the
t today.

ec. 8 The Eagle pub—
a story based on a press
from the center which
that Mahoney "attended
Hopkins University in
nore where he received an
and a Ph.D. in behavioral
nce from the department o
chiatry." The credentia
ck was initiated by
gle after a reporter i
wed Mahoney at the reh
tion center last Thursday
A letter from the
ecords office at John

confirmed that Mahoney attend—
ed courses at the university
from October 1969 to August
1970 as a fellow in psychiatry.
But a spokesman at the regis—
trar's office at the Johns Hop—
kins Medical School said that
the course Mahoney took in sui—
cide prevention
was "non-
matriculating tov
a medical
degree" and w
nara—
therapist cours
rect clinical
medical exp

Dr. Vin
Pittsfield
the reh
this m
staff
cen
hon
su

interviewed for the job. Barn—
aba said.
Dr. Barnaba said he dis—
missed Mahoney yesterday and
he reported that fact to the cen—
ter's board of directors last
night.
"And this is the irony of the
entire situation," he added.
"Everyone was very pleased
with Mahoney's work, I would
say, in fact, that his contribu—
in the last three weeks has
e most significant of
e hired in a num—

nter. was

The mysterious case
of the missing hangers

By Rinker Buck

Wire hangers, very literally
mainstays of the dry-cleaning
business, have joined an in—
creasingly long list of manufac—
tured items — paper clips, plas—
tic bags and manila file folders
to cite a few — that are in odd—
ly short supply.
Raymond S. Frenkel, owner
of Pane's Cleaners on South
Street, said that, because of the
shortage the price he must pay
for hangers has crept up from
$14 per thousand two years ago
to a recent order when he paid:
$22.50 per thousand, or about 2
cents a hanger. Li
Berkshire Cou
suppli

tempting to account for it is a
lesson in obfuscatory econom—
ics. Those who feel the pinch of
the shortage — dry-cleaners and
their suppliers — cannot explain
how and why the hanger short—
gan. Hanger manufacturers can
and do give possible ex—
planations for a hanger shortage
— but then turn around and
deny there is one in the first

While the hanger shortage is
only an indirect result of the
energy crisis, it is no
the rule it

a hanger manufacturer i
mington, Del.. also denie
there is a hanger shortage.
Demand is up

McClain said demand for-v
hangers have increased si
the Arab oil embargo bega
principally because the plast
hangers once favored by gar
ment makers — made from
derivative plastic
longer

tation from Radcliffe in 1970 seem, in
t, to have been purposely kaleidosco
njoyed a considerable poetic output,
lot of pool while holding down
floors, teaching retarded children
rving drinks and dancing nude i
recent past has the kind of elan,
d with serious artistic work, that
with a near-reputation would like
s or her collected "experience."
ears of art-colony fell
Hampshire, in Pr

Rinker B

"No, of course not. Work is work, you know? Changing the oil in Happel's Cadillac isn't work."

"Okay, here we go. I've got to be your shrink again now. Rinker, babysitting Hap's Caddie is *work*, all right? W-O-R-K. Got it?"

"Yeah, okay, Tom," I said. "I'm not sure I agree with you, but I'm nodding my head yes. All right?"

"Good," Morton said. "And do you mind if I say one other thing?"

"Oh boy. What'd I do now?"

"Here's what you did, pal. All through the energy crisis last winter, whenever I came into this newsroom at nine or ten o'clock at night, there were always two people still working. You and Scheer. Now, what do you call that?"

"That was work, Tom. I'm not taking that away from myself. The energy crisis? Peter and I humped."

"You're damn tooting you did. And I'm just saying, pace yourself. You're talking to an expert here. I'm the classic workaholic myself. But you've got to throttle back a little, call in the dogs, you know? I mean, learn fly-fishing. Find a babe. You can't live, sleep, and eat the *Eagle*."

"Tom, okay, okay! I'll increase my dick-off time by at least 15 percent a week. All right?"

"Yeah, good," Morton said. "Now. Any questions for me?"

"Yeah," I said. "Tom, how did you make this decision? I mean, what did I do to earn this?"

"Oh Jesus. I should have been a shrink at Riggs. I just told you that. You worked your butt off, okay? I mean, look at the way you chased after that damn bird story. I was very impressed with that."

"Oh c'mon, Tom. The bird was dead by the time I found it."

"Oh hell, that damn bird was dead-on-arrival in Berkshire County. Everybody knew that. But you humped butt on the thing. You wouldn't give up. Christ. The *Eagle*-Smithsonian expedition. What crap. But I'd like to see you apply some of that energy of yours to the environmental beat."

"Okay, Tom, thanks," I said. "Do you mind if I ask how much of a raise is associated with this promotion?"

"Nope, I don't mind at all," Morton said. "There is no raise whatsoever associated with this promotion. At your one-year review next month, we'll award you the princely sum of five more dollars a week, okay? You're still working for the House of Miller."

"Yeah. Thanks, Tom," I said. "But look, can I keep something on my old beat?"

"Sure, I guess. Shoot. What do you want to keep?"

"The weather," I said.

"Oh Jesus, Mary, and Joseph. *The weather*? You just amaze me sometimes, Rinker. Nobody keeps the weather. It goes with obits. It's shoveling the shit. If we let you keep the weather, everybody will think we demoted you."

But I was passionate about this. I loved doing the weather reports for the *Eagle*, waking up every day and knowing which fronts were rumbling in over the Taconics, calling around to all the meteorologists and learning new things about occluded fronts, dew points, and the jet stream effect. By the weekend, I always knew whether the conditions would be right for snowshoeing or flying.

But maybe I was learning something here. I could exploit Morton's absurd guilt about how hard I worked.

"Tom, how about this? Let me keep the weather just because I like it. I love doing the weather reports. Isn't that a good reason?"

"Okay. Now we're talking here, kiddo. You like the weather? You can keep it. But look. Why don't you go out tonight and celebrate? You've worked hard, and I want you to enjoy this moment."

"Good idea, Tom. It's gay night down at the Red Lion. All the guys will buy me martinis."

"Oh Christ. Here we go. Get out of here, would you? Get out of my sight. The day I hired you?"

"Yeah?"

"I really screwed the pooch."

CHAPTER SIXTEEN

WHEN MARCIA WEISS called after my short piece about her appeared in the *Eagle*, I thought that I knew how to handle the situation correctly. Catholic boys are raised to follow a strict protocol as regards married women. During childhood and early adolescence, we were instructed to kiss ass and always remember our "pleases" and "thank-yous," buttering them up just the way Eddie Haskell did Mrs. Cleaver. After that, no further guidance was required, because puberty had arrived and we were beginning to imitate our fathers. In our town, all of the big-wheel, social-climbing Catholic dads effortlessly flirted with all of the neighborhood moms, especially if they were attractive and Protestant. So, that's how I handled it.

Marcia called the first time to say how much she liked the story. It had "brevity," she said, a quality that her U/Mass professors were always trying to drill into their students. But you could still do a lot with brevity. There were all these little touches, she thought, that I had managed to work in.

"I mean, you know, you squeezed in that thing about 'highlights of sandy brown hair reflecting in the sun,'" she said. "That was nice."

"Well, your highlights *are* nice."

"Yeah, and I probably shouldn't tell you this, but they're fake. I got those highlights from the Lenox Beauty Salon."

"Big deal," I said. "They're still nice. The reader deserves to know that."

"Okay, okay," she said. "But I'd really like to know how you do those things. Maybe someday you'll show me."

"Well, that's up to you. But pretty much, you know, you've got to just go out and do it yourself."

"All right," Marcia said. "But, hey, can I ask a favor?"

"Sure. Try me."

"Well, the *Eagle* probably has a policy against this, but I wonder if I can get a negative of the picture they used. It's really a nice shot."

"For you?" I said. "They'll make an exception."

"Oh, great!" Marcia said. "I'm going to have it printed and then frame it for my husband. His birthday is coming up."

So, I dropped the negative off in an envelope one day when I was running through Lenox, but Marcia wasn't around and I left it behind the screen door. After that, she called a couple of more times just to chat, and then she invited me down for dinner one night when her husband was away. She'd just finished a term paper for communications arts and thought that I might be able to help her make it even better.

I'd always been a sucker for this kind of work, helping the babe with her homework. Compared to most of them, however, Marcia was pretty easy to work with, because I didn't have to start from scratch. She was actually a decent writer and her term paper, about how a large tobacco farm on the Connecticut River had complied with new EPA regulations on spraying pesticides, was pretty good. I made a few routine suggestions about how she could bring some material up from the middle and paraphrase some longer quotes. Marcia was very happy with the results, and it was enjoyable for me too because she was full of all kinds of loose compliments and an exaggerated sense of what I was really doing for her.

After that, Marcia invited me down to Lenox a few more times. There was always a good reason for me to be there—to peruse the "final draft" of her paper, for example, or to read a grant application for her tutoring program in the Springfield schools. I enjoyed going down there. Marcia cooked me all these great dinners—chicken curry, Hungarian goulash, and so forth. She was interesting and lively, and there was a frisson of illicit behavior being together in the pretty faux-Tudor house in Lenox, laughing and goofing around with a slightly older Jewish beauty dressed in tight jeans and a sleeveless knit blouse. After dinner, we'd retreat out to the small screened-in porch facing the back lawn, listening to the crickets screech and the distant hum of car tires rolling through Lenox, drinking wine and talking.

Marcia seemed hungry for companionship, anxious to talk about herself and to pry things out of me. I was naïve about this at first, mostly because I'd become accustomed to people naturally opening up to me as a reporter, volunteering a lot more about themselves than I needed for my story. Over the winter, while we were logging together, Bonnie had prodded me to accept this about myself. It was more than being a reporter, she thought. I had a knack for drawing people out and getting them to talk about themselves, Bonnie said, and I should just learn to enjoy it. So, now I was with Marcia. I felt very relaxed around her and enjoyed hearing her story.

Marcia's big interest that year was "cycling through" some of her personal issues with a local psychiatrist—well, actually, he was just a marriage counselor, she said. This was something great about living in the East, Marcia thought. You were practically a "social klutz" if you didn't have a shrink to talk about at cocktail parties. Therapy was just so self-indulgent and relaxing, as good for the soul as buying a puppy or a new car. But it could be also be uncomfortable, just another excuse to be bitchy. With the marriage counselor, she and her husband were supposed to be working on their problems together, but she was frequently annoyed with her husband because he'd cancel their joint appointments to make a business trip.

I welcomed hearing about all this because marriage still seemed mysterious and unobtainable to me. Marriage was intimidating, and the details seemed unfathomable, because I didn't see how I could ever accomplish such things as fidelity, buying a house, or keeping regular hours. Now Marcia was sharing all these fascinating secrets with me.

Marcia explained to me, for example, that she had entered her "myself and me alone period." Whenever her husband got back from a trip, it took her three or four days to acclimate to having him in the house again. Then, just as she got back into her marriage again, he took off for another business trip. She felt alone most of the time, even when her husband was around, but she also loved him and this aspect of their relationship.

"Oh, it's such a contradiction, you know? I *love* Robert for working so hard. He's so happy. Serious. And cute, you know? Just really cute and high school–boy earnest when he works so hard. I'm so in love with him. But then he's either gone all the time or distracted by his work. I'm a part of his life, but I'm *not* a part of his life."

When Marcia was done talking about herself, she turned her guns on me. She was very curious about my dating life and probed me for details about that, because she hadn't enjoyed a long period of dating before she got married and wanted to know what that was like. Loosened up by the wine and her own candor about herself, I felt willing to talk, but mostly Marcia goaded me into saying things by the sheer audacity of what she was willing to risk. For example, Marcia considered herself an "expert" on Catholic boys. Back in Michigan, she had dated a few Catholics during high school. She actually liked them a lot because they never pulled a lot of sexual moves without first being encouraged—Catholic boys, Marcia said, were "classic noninitiator types"—but they were also repressed and "fucked up." Marcia was certain that she had correctly diagnosed this problem with me.

"Okay, like how did your mother fuck you up about your body?" she asked me one night. "She hated your body, right? What did she say about your ass?"

Goddammit anyway. It always pissed me off when women knew, *just knew*, that they had the goods on me this way. How the hell would she know what my mother thought about my ass?

"Marcia, what makes you think that my mother would have an opinion about my ass? Why would my mother care about my ass?"

"Oh, see? I love this. She *did* say something about that, right? But you're going to hide it from me."

"All right, since you asked. My mother didn't like my ass. She said that it was too big for the rest of my body. Are you satisfied now? I'm sitting here on your porch, drinking your wine, and telling you that my mother told me all the time that my ass was too big. I hope you're happy now."

"Oh, this is good," Marcia said. "What were you supposed to do? Get a new ass? Get surgery?"

"No. Better posture. That's what my mother said. If I had better posture, my ass would look smaller."

"Oh my God. Better posture. That is so *Catholic*, you know? So what happened every time a pretty girl walked by? You listened to your mother and practiced better posture, right?"

"Yeah, better posture," I said. "I stood up straight and sucked in my ass. Every time I met a new babe, I sucked in my ass."

"Oh, how pathetic. You spent your whole, fucked-up Catholic childhood sucking in your ass."

"Yeah! You got a problem with that? I sucked in my ass a lot. That doesn't necessarily make me fucked up."

"No," Marcia said. "That's not what's pathetic about it. What's pathetic about it is that you have a great ass."

"Oh, Christ. Here we go. I've got a great ass. Thanks, Marcia."

"No! I'm serious. You've got a great ass! It's this cute, little boy's ass. So don't suck it in, okay? I like it."

"Thanks, Marcia. I really appreciate that. I came all the way over here tonight to learn that I've got a cute, little boy's ass."

"Oh, see? That's exactly my point. Jewish girls will think, 'Okay, he's got a cute ass, so I can tell him that,' and Catholic boys will think, 'God, I hope she doesn't notice my ass, because my mother told me it's too big.' But you just don't want to face that."

"Yeah, well, you know, thanks, Marcia. I guess my mother had to be wrong about something."

"Okay, good. By the way, your face is turning red. It's

really cute the way you get embarrassed when I drag you into dirty-girl talk."

At this point, all the warning lights were going off on my panel. *Eject! Eject! Eject! Disengage Sex Talk! Depart House! Eject!* I needed to get home anyway.

"Hey," I said, standing up to go. "Thanks for dinner. I better shove off, because I've got work tomorrow."

"Yeah, okay," Marcia said. "I've got classes at U/Mass."

At the door, when she gave me a good night smooch, I noticed that her cheeks were very smooth and she used facial cream that other women didn't use. A couple times, just to show her that I wasn't as pent up as she thought, I kissed her hard, and she kissed me hard right back.

"See ya, cute ass," she said.

.   .   .

Through friends in Hadassah, Marcia had met a young couple who owned a small bungalow down on Lake Buel in Monterey. They were a "culture vulture" couple from Westchester County in New York who occasionally used their cottage on weekends while taking in Tanglewood or Jacob's Pillow, and they were more than happy to have Marcia looking after it when they weren't around. The bungalow sat on a hill along the secluded, eastern shore of the lake, and staying there overnight while her husband was away became a big part of Marcia's journey that year. The cottage on the lake was private and pastoral, a "zone for me alone," Marcia called it, a place away from the rest of her life.

Lake Buel was peaceful and romantic. In the evening the sun fell behind Mount Everett to the west, casting a wash of yellow and purple light against the mist condensing off the water, and at night a string of soft lights rigged in the birch grove and out on the dock softly lit the black surface of the lake. A colony of otters slapped in and out of the water, and loons screeched from the marshes nearby. Marcia set up her typewriter on the table in the front room and worked on her U/Mass papers there, and then spent the afternoons reading out on the dock. When she invited me down there a couple of times, I saw and felt the mood that she was in, and I recommended Edward Weston's *Daybooks* and the letters of Fanny Kemble, and felt a rush of satisfaction when she enjoyed them.

Marcia had made a personal vow that year. The "holes in the relationship" with her husband Robert were partially her fault, she thought. When he was around, she was always either off at U/Mass or tied up with her Hadassah projects. So, that summer, she drastically curtailed her volunteer work and decided to do some extra nesting for her husband. At yard sales and cheap antique stores in Hudson, New York, she had bought some furniture to decorate their screened porch in Lenox, and now she was refinishing the pieces. She'd keep it all at Lake Buel and then surprise him with the finished job some night when he returned from a trip.

"God, it's so fulfilling, you know? Presto! The big surprise for Robert. Hey, honey, let's sit out on the porch. I can't wait to see the look on his face when he sees all this stuff."

Marcia had called me at the *Eagle* one day and asked if I knew anything about refinishing furniture. I'd done my share of that kind of work over the years, and it was enjoyable getting down there on a Wednesday or Thursday night, setting up an old pine cupboard or rocker on the dock, then dousing it down with paint stripper or varnish remover, showing Marcia how to get the edges and the trim right with an old toothbrush and triple-X steel wool. While I stripped and sanded away, Marcia made hamburgers on the outdoor grill and carried down a salad. We drank a lot of cheap wine together and the head buzz from that, mixed with paint thinner, was quite good.

I came to love Lake Buel and my times down there with Marcia. Nothing was more delightful than working hard all day in the *Eagle* newsroom or roaming the Berkshires on my new environmental beat, then driving down to south county in the evening to meet her. She was a very safe, convenient relationship for me. Marcia was tanned from reading out on the dock all afternoon, tight-waisted from taking hikes around the lake, hungry for conversation after a long day alone. Our relationship had a pleasing familiarity now, and I liked the suggestive, minimarriage simulation of her tone of voice when I arrived.

"Oh, hi, sweetie. God, it's so nice you're here. Are you all right? I can't believe how hard they work you at the *Eagle*. Here, have a wine. I love you and you need a wine."

Marcia was convinced that I was a pop-culture neophyte. I didn't know anything about the latest hot bands and I didn't go to enough movies. My head was always stuck in my work or a new book. One of the hot films that summer was *Alice Doesn't Live Here Anymore*, with Ellen Burstyn, and Marcia called me at the *Eagle* one Thursday afternoon and suggested that we take it in together at the movie theater in Great Barrington. Happy to be jumping the line on the weekend, I drove down to Lake Buel that evening. When I pulled in beside the birches in the yard, Marcia was waiting for me on the porch, sexy and radiant in her tight jeans and silk blouse. As she slipped into my car, we both felt a little self-conscious about it.

"The big date, huh?" Marcia said. "I feel like a teenager again, driving off in a car with you like this."

"Yeah," I said. "I promised your Dad to have you back by eleven."

When we came out of the theater after the movie, a low, angry thundercloud was unloading on town, so I left Marcia there and ran around the corner to Railroad Street for my car. Great Barrington is a moody, romantic place. Good blackplate peaks rise on three sides, so that there's always a pleasing prospect from the turn-of-the-century brick and granite facades. When I came back around the corner with my car, Marcia was standing alone under the marquee of the Mahaiwe Theatre, with mist condensing off the warm sidewalks from the rain. She looked lovely and detached, a figure out of an Edward Hopper painting.

When she jumped into the car and slammed the door behind her, Marcia did this enticing, sexy-babe default on the passenger seat, pulling her legs up underneath her and staring over at me with a smirky-smile.

"Hey, let's go somewhere," she said. "It's too boring to go home. Have you ever been to this place called Mundy's Bar?"

"No," I lied. "I've heard of it, but I've never been there."

"Okay! It's supposed to be a great dancing place. It's a big lesbian hangout, they say. It might be fun."

"All right. But I have to warn you. I'm a terrible dancer and I'm bashful around strangers. I don't know any lesbians."

"Fine. That's my only complaint about you. You're so serious. All you do is work and read books. Maybe you *should* meet some lesbians."

"Okay, okay! Let's go meet some lesbians."

So, we roared up my favorite blackplate road, Route 41. As we plunged weightless over the dip past Division Street, Marcia coyly looked over and opened this linen shoulder bag that she always carried.

"Hey, you don't mind, do you? I don't mean to be shocking you."

No, I didn't mind. It was always more a surprise than minding, observing just which women reached into their shoulder bags or purses and pulled out the stash of dope. I didn't do a lot of drugs myself, but I made a point about never being square about it. Over the winter a couple of the ski bunnies and one of the Everything Girls made a habit of always going to bed on a weekend after a nightcap smoke of reefer, and I liked sharing one of those and enjoying the turbocharging effect it had on martinis. One night somebody had even given me codeine, and boy, that stuff is really beautiful. So, Marcia expertly rolled one up and explained to me that she and Robert weren't exactly potheads, but they did marijuana a lot on weekends, and she was hooked on it for this kind of night. We shared the reefer riding up through the oxbows. The thundercloud from Great Barrington chased us north and I had the windows closed, so the car really filled up with smoke.

We were high, pulling into Mundy's, laughing at each other, and telling jokes as we crossed the lot.

Mundy's was mellow and fun on Thursday nights. The weekend crowd wasn't there yet, and everybody seemed to know everybody else. Bonnie and Helen weren't there that night, but a lot of their friends were, and when we came through the door they all started giving me these knowing winks and furtive little thumbs-up signs because it was unusual for me to show up with someone other than Rachel or one of the Everything Girls. I got Marcia settled at a table, and Randy, Rachel's friend, came over and started to chat her up. I went to the bar for some drinks.

At the bar, a bunch of my friends there started giving me long lesbian smooches and just generally goofing off. When I looked over my shoulder and caught Marcia's eye, she was smirky-smiling back at me, dropping her hand to the table with a look of exasperation, enjoying meeting Randy, and laughing at herself. Good, I thought. I knew she'd have a sense of humor.

When I got back to the table, Randy was making a date to dance with her a little later and then he greeted me with a hug and left.

Marcia cocked her head sideways, took a sip of her drink, and then slugged me on the shoulder.

"Hello, shithead," she said. "You are such a little rascal, you know? I can't believe I fell for your sarcasm on this."

"Sorry. It was just too easy a setup. I couldn't resist."

"Yeah, the joke's on me, ha-ha. You're a shithead. So, you practically live here, right?"

"No. Just on weekends."

"Yeah, right. So, what's the appeal? You dance with lesbians. Why? They're safe, right?"

"Nah. They're just better dancers than regular white girls, I guess."

"Oh bull. It's so obvious. You're a classic commit-o-phobe. It's written all over you. The big commit-o-phobe."

"Oh, shut up, Marcia," I said. "Stop psychoanalyzing me. If you like me, we'll stay here and dance. If you don't, I don't mind driving you home."

"Okay, okay. God, you're so sensitive."

When we got out to the floor there weren't a lot of other couples dancing, and the band just seemed to feel lazy and played several slow numbers in a row. Marcia pulled me close.

"Hey, don't be afraid to touch me now," she said. "I was terrified that you'd be afraid to touch me."

"Yeah, well, I think we're doing that now."

"Yeah it's just that I trusted you with my brain. You gave me all those books to read and I wondered if you would ever let me touch you."

"Okay. I'm just trying not to push it."

Marcia reached up with her hand and dug her nails a bit into the back of my neck and played with my hair, and did this lips to neck and lips to cheek deal, not a kiss really, just dry lips to neck and lips to cheek and chin, and pushed against me with her belt. It was a nice night at Mundy's and through the open door at the end of the bar I could see mist rising off the oxbows. So, I pulled her closer and enjoyed the dance.

Later, when the band stopped and they put the recorded music back on, Randy came over for his dance-date with Marcia, and she was very good and natural with him. It was a turn-on, watching the woman I was with dance with someone else, even a gay guy, and from a distance I noticed what a good tan she had now. I had a couple more drinks while I talked with some friends up at the bar.

We blew out of there feeling just fine and Marcia rolled herself another joint and smoked it while we rode south through the peaks for Lake Buel.

I was deliberately withdrawn during that ride. For my own satisfaction I had to resist her and not push the situation. Marcia and I felt close now. We'd done slutty-girl talk together, danced, and been physically close, but it could all end right there and be fine. Just an overt flirt was enough for me. Mind-fucking her was as good as sex, I thought. Pull back the power now, Rinker, and don't bend those wings. Back at Lake Buel she'd give me the big Pretty Mom smooch good night and then I'd go home.

When we pulled up to the bungalow, Marcia asked me not to leave just yet, because she'd be lonely if we didn't talk. She got us two wines and we sat on the screened porch on a wicker couch, looking down to the fog rising off the lake.

"Ooooooooooo," she said. "The mist. So romantic."

"Yeah. I like the way fog shuts off the world. I can wallow in it all night. It's melancholy."

"Melancholy you. Here. Mmmmmmmm. Yeah. Touch me there. You weren't going to do that, were you? Mmmmmm. That's so nice."

Lips to lips, as gently as fog at first, then moistly and hard, and then she reached up with the hands that had placed mine on her breasts and cupped me by the neck and ears, lips to chin and ear lobe and temples and hair, lips all over my face, a refreshing cleansing, the prolonged sexual tension between us finally broken by hard kissing. I wasn't going to pretend that I was resisting her. It was a fantasy of mine, even. I'd dreamed about doing her in a certain way. The married woman, the way her husband was familiar with her, how he enjoyed access to her every part and orifice. The firming of her nipples and her kissing injected adrenaline into me and my heart raced. Boldness, natural, libidinous boldness. I reached down and gently unbuttoned her jeans, took her belt off, and with exquisite pleasure from her moistness and the shivering of her pelvis I slipped my fingers into her vagina and enjoyed the slippery softness there, her quivering and spongy nest of hair as I reached softly but deep, then found purchase on her clitoris and just serviced, serviced, serviced her there, loving her for enjoying it so much, for responding so hard and kissing me almost painfully now. Marcia was very gratifying as a partner, amazing, even, because she suddenly and quickly enjoyed a very sharp orgasm and dug into my neck and shoulders with her nails and screamed out loudly. I flashed to that crazy mind-wander I'd had the first time with Rachel, the sorority of women, who seemed to be calling back to Marcia now from the mists out on the lake. I wasn't thinking about puerile concepts like my own orgasm or personal satisfaction or anything else, just enjoying her for responding so quickly and being happy. Doing her that way and well rushed me with feelings of power and sexiness. I could feel my ability to keep her going forever, just gently applying massaging pressure there and kissing her back lightly is all that it took, just maintain her and let her push back, and she came and came and came. With Marcia that night, with the fog all around, it was the perfect sexual experience. Serve her, do her, worship her, immerse yourself in her response, and don't ask where the sorority of women came from. It could be the drugs layered on top of alcohol, but the sisterly embrace could also really be there.

Marcia leaned back onto the couch and exhaled, pulling my hands back onto her breasts.

"Christ. You fantasize about something like that, and then it happens. No one's ever done me that way. Thank you."

I wasn't in the mood for pretending or playing games with her, and I unbuttoned my work shirt and took if off, then finished undressing her while Marcia arched up with her pelvis against me and took my clothes off and then we lay cupped together on the couch, slowly feasting on each other's bodies and talking. I need another sip of wine at this point, and then I hoisted her body up into my arms and carried her across the bungalow to the bedroom and we kissed and talked on the bed in there, and we just seamlessly fell together for the rest of the night like that, sleeping for an hour or two, then waking and making love again, and then talking and sleeping. At dawn we performed another one of these cycles together and then a couple of hours later Marcia woke up and made us breakfast, and then we fell into each other's arms again and made love and slept some more out there. We were insatiable, irresponsible, unplanned together, and existed in a sort of dreamlike euphoric exhaustion until I finally left for work. I enjoyed the confusion and uncertainty of losing control, surrendering completing to physicality and desire, and having no particular thoughts about it. I was a prisoner of desire now. My heart raced all the time around her and I had lost control, which was both exhilarating and confusing.

So, that is how the long, hazy end of the summer and the early fall played itself out. The pastel Berkshires, down near the water. I enjoyed spiraling out of control with Marcia, deluding myself that an affair with a married woman was safe, protected, free of strings. Being with Marcia made me feel mature, sophisticated, furtively sinful in ways that I had never allowed myself to be before. Most of all I enjoyed the loss of initiative that I was experiencing now, my total submission to someone else's schedule and needs. I made it a rule to never call her or initiate. She had to renew the advance every time, but she did, often, calling as soon her husband left on another trip. *Oh you poor, poor thing. Are they working you hard again? Oh, Rinker, we have to talk. Let's go play and dance. We'll go down to the lake.*

Marcia was very deliberate and open about one aspect of our affair. She was emotionally and sexually bored in her marriage, frustrated by her inability to break through the "communications block" with her husband. This was something that she'd been working on with her counselor, and long before we became involved, I had emerged as a sort of sexual stimulus and object of fantasy for her. I could tell from the shrink-wrap bouncing back to me that an aura of permission now surrounded our relationship. Marcia was indulging her fantasies for me for reasons that went beyond just us.

So, I was part of a triad now. Down on Lake Buel, or occasionally in the guest room of her house in Lenox, Marcia and I indulged long, luxurious sessions of oral sex, we experimented wildly and hard with every position, we spent hours together drinking wine and smoking pot, talking and touching and feeling. Then, when Robert returned from one of his business trips, Marcia would get him all toked up on dope and try all this new stuff out on him. I was entranced by the dynamics of being their sexual go-between.

Week by week, infidelity by infidelity, our proxy conjugation progressed. Robert was less squeamish about oral sex now, she told me. If she got him high enough on dope, he initiated different kinds of sex. They talked and laughed together more, she said, they just wasted time together around the house. She didn't feel so alone when she was with him now.

I knew that it was crazy to continue with Marcia, that it was dangerous to be falling deeper and deeper in love with her, but one other aspect of the affair amazed me and kept me addicted to her. After being with her, I was astonishingly productive for the next few days in the newsroom. I liked living crazy like this. I would have a story or two to finish on deadline, and perhaps I was late on a book review, but the emotional swirl of crazy-fucking with Marcia, and then maybe a night or two later being with Rachel, energized me, liberating me creatively. I could get monstrous amounts of work done, very efficiently and joyfully. The nexus of fucking and work. Fuck her and be crazy, roar through a pile of work the next day, and then Rachel would come chasing after me next, and we'd fuck and be crazy too. Rachel had a new man down in New York now, I was pretty sure of that, so there was an intense sensation of all of us mind-wandering to the other while we crazy-fucked all the time, passing each other along and doing relay sex, uninhibited by commitment and enjoying the exaggerated emotion and physicality of all that. I felt omnipotent now, for days and days on end.

Besides, I was learning so much. Marcia was exploding with change, exhilarated by the thrill of having good sex with two men at once, joyful about her improving marriage. When we sat out on the dock at night, drinking wine and watching the fog condense off the lake, she shared everything with me.

"Hey, little boy, my weird but good? Sorry. It's my weird but good for the night."

"Sure. Your weird but good."

"The more I see you? Each time?"

"Yeah?"

"The more I love Robert."

.　　.　　.

While all of this was going on down on Lake Buel, I'd established another important relationship, back in the *Eagle* newsroom. In a lot of ways I learned more from Nicole than anyone else.

Nicole was a Pittsfield girl. She was almost exactly my age that spring and had spent her first three years out of high school bumming around and working odd jobs in the West and California, where an older brother lived. She'd finally "found herself," she later told me, through a six-month relationship with a "very bad guy" in New Orleans, and then decided to return home to finish off her education. Nicole came from a third-generation, blue-collar GE family in town and had just defaulted to the natural course for a Pittsfield girl when she was back in town, enrolling in Berkshire Community College out on West Street. When I met her, in February or March 1974, she was in the middle of her first year at BCC, supporting herself by working nights at a convenience store and the Friday night shift in the sports department at the *Eagle*, compiling all the box scores and results from the high school games called in by the sportswriters and coaches.

Nicole was tall and effortlessly sensual, with long, strawberry blonde hair, a Nordic face, large, sexy breasts, and almost preternaturally skinny hips. She always wore the same outfit, faded and worn bell-bottom blue jeans, flip-flops or cheap sneakers, and a stone-washed denim work shirt. Some Fridays she was bra-less and didn't have any underwear on, so that I could see right through her tight jeans to the crack in her ass, and other weeks she came in all dolled up, with makeup on and combs in her hair, maybe because she was going out afterward on a date.

But attire didn't matter with Nicole. She was always just *there*, languid, sensual, and blunt.

"Hey, guy. Don't let me get bored tonight, okay? I'll go for coffee and then you can hit on me. Got it?"

Nicole carried her possessions in a see-through satchel, a Greek fisherman's net made into a shoulder bag. I loved watching her breeze through the double doors on Friday night. Whatever her life was that day or week—her Tampons or an old faded bathing suit, the books she was reading, or some dope paraphernalia—was tossed in there together as a tangled mass. Great. Nicole's here. I could look right through her bag and see her life.

I liked Nicole's sexy, bad-girl androgyny, and I was very attracted to her, but I deliberately avoided staging events toward a date. She wanted something from me that was extremely gratifying to deliver, and I was afraid that romance would spoil it.

Nicole was very ambitious and told me several times how she wanted to "get a better education and blow this town." She seemed to have read all of the articles I had written for the *Eagle* and was amused by the pile of books on my desk, stacked up and waiting for reviews.

"Look, I don't know anything, all right? I only started to read books last year. I don't know what to read. You can show me."

Those book chat nights with Nicole were delightful. Charley Bonenti generally worked the desk on Friday nights, and he couldn't have cared less how long I dawdled with Nicole as long as the copy he needed—the weather, a car wreck, a "local angle" feed for a national story—got done. When she had a pause between games Nicole would wander over, pull up Peter Scheer's chair, and cross her legs, plunging down with her open work shirt as she leaned on a knee with her elbow.

"Hey, what's this? Leo Tolstoy. We read his stories in English class."

It was Henri Troyat's massive biography of Tolstoy.

"Ah, I don't know Nicole," I said. "It's awfully long."

"Oh, so I wouldn't read a long book? Fuck you. I'm interested in this. I'm going to read it."

She was insatiable about it, glowing all over at age twenty-three from the pleasure of losing herself in books. When she returned a book, she often stuffed a short note inside, or slid it back across my desk with a wise-ass quip.

"Count Tolstoy, huh? And I thought *my* family was fucked up."

I was amused, too, by Nicole's obsession with social class, something I hadn't dwelled on very much before. I shared many typical assumptions of my college-educated generation. America was a free, democratic state with an open economy, and almost anyone could succeed. But Nicole showed me that it wasn't really economics that mattered most. People were trapped by class emotions and family baggage. Nicole seemed stuck there, almost compulsively driven to denigrate herself by confessing embarrassing truths about her family.

"God, my brothers and my cousins are all such losers. They only want to work at GE or become cops. It's so freaking depressing, you know?"

Nicole desperately wanted to escape all this, but her own tentative steps at social climbing had not worked out well. She'd dated a few Williams College boys and felt terribly insecure around them—they were always talking about rock groups or resorts in the Caribbean that she'd never heard of before. I knew that Nicole felt comfortable around me. I knew that she liked me. Still, I had graduated from college and then walked into a job at the *Eagle*. To her, that qualified me as just another "rich boy."

One Friday night in the newsroom, I was aimlessly dawdling away my time in between working on a couple of stories, thumbing through the L.L. Bean and Orvis catalogues that had piled up on my desk. When she came over to flirt and borrow a book, this really set Nicole off.

"God. You're such a dumb rich boy. What are you doing now? Buying clothes?"

"Sorry to disappoint you, but nobody who grew up in a family of eleven children is a rich boy."

"Oh, I just love rich boys. 'My Daddy really struggled to put me through Williams College. He had to sell his boat.'"

"Yeah, well, we didn't have any boats, Nicole."

"Oh no? Well how many cars and motorcycles, then? And your house. How many bedrooms in your house?"

"Oh Christ, Nicole. Who cares about bedrooms? We had a big family."

"Oh sure. Who cares about bedrooms. My uncle has seven kids stuffed into two bedrooms. I know plenty of families in Pittsfield with eight kids, bunked up in two or three rooms. So, how many bedrooms in your house, rich boy? You're afraid to tell me, aren't you? You're such a rich fuck you probably don't even know."

Crap. She really had me here. In fact, I didn't know. Who the hell counted the bedrooms in their house?

Nicole started to laugh when I began mentally calculating the number of bedrooms in the house I'd grown up in, counting them off on my fingers. I loved her for it too, the way she shitted on me like that. While I counted up the bedrooms in my boyhood home, she sat there with this gorgeous smirky-smile on her face, covering her laugh with her hand, her arms folded across her breasts, a biker babe who just couldn't wait to put me down.

"Okay, bitch," I said, looking up. "Counting the rooms up in the attic where my brother and I slept, there were ten fucking bedrooms. Are you satisfied now?"

"Oh! Your poor family. Eleven kids and only ten bedrooms. Who had to sleep on the couch?"

"Nobody. My older sisters were already away at college, all right? Now scram. Get lost. You're pissing me off tonight."

"Okay, rich boy. Thanks for the info. But just give me a book, wil'ya? I need a fucking book to read."

One Friday in late August that year I was enraged by an incident involving Nicole. When she breezed in through the double doors of the newsroom that night, Nicole had Erica Jong's *Fear of Flying* stuffed into her Greek fisherman's bag. The only thing unusual about Nicole's reading that book was that she was a year behind the curve of everyone else. She must have just heard about Erica Jong that week. After the first sports scores came in and she had her first lull of work, Nicole pulled the book out of her bag and started reading.

Sports departments at newspapers are generally staffed with lugheads, mostly dumb Irishmen, and of course it wouldn't occur to them that maybe Nicole was reading Erica Jong because the book was the big literary sensation that year, something everybody else had already read. To them it was just a sex book and that's why Nicole was reading it.

While she read *Fear of Flying* at her desk, Nicole lounged back in her chair and smiled, laughing at the funny parts. As soon as she started doing that, the men in the sports department started razzing her, making comments, and laughing, and one of them walked over to the copy and wire departments and got some folks there involved in the act. Half of the newsroom was laughing at Nicole now.

"Hey! *Fear of Flying*. Nasty Nicole."

"Nicole! What's your favorite *part?*"

As the ripple of laughter spread through the newsroom, Nicole turned red-faced and looked embarrassed. Generally Nicole could handle the men in the sports department just fine, matching them quip to quip, but I could tell that she felt overwhelmed this time. She turned her face sideways several times before stuffing the book back into her bag.

Like a fool, I went charging over there to defend Nicole. I was furious for her sake, but completely lacked the subtlety and guile required of the situation. I called one of the sports writers a "fucking retard" and a wire editor an "uneducated fart."

It was the wrong tactic, of course. Everything I said just got piled back onto Nicole.

"Oh, Nicole. Your lover boy is here. Rinker is *very* upset that you're reading this book."

Nicole was now begging me with her eyes and pouting, turning even more red in the face. *Rich boy, please, go away. You're making it worse.*

I didn't want to appear to be intimidated by those sportswriters, so I dawdled there for a while longer, asked Nicole if she wanted a coffee, and then went out for that. When I got back, Nicole seemed to be recovered, and she wasn't afraid to give those guys in sports the finger herself. A few minutes later she strolled over to my desk, just to show everyone that she wasn't embarrassed to talk with me.

"Good work, dumbo," she said. "You fucked that one up beautifully. But it's okay. You meant well."

"Yeah, well. I guess I don't do jerks very well. Sorry."

"No prob. Hey, I guess I need another book. Can I go through your pile?"

One day that week, when I came in from lunch and picked up my messages from the receptionist downstairs, there was an envelope from Nicole in the pile. She'd gone up to the Hallmark store on the Berkshire Commons and picked out one of these dorky, theme cards, "Just Thinking of You" and written me a short note.

"Hey. Thanks again for Friday night. You're an idiot, but cute. Luvya, N."

CHAPTER SEVENTEEN

LIVING HARD all week built toward the sweet exhaustion of working the Friday night shift. On Thursday, I often worked late to stage an extra feature and a book review for Pete Miller's big "Saturday read" for the weekenders, and then on Friday evening I enjoyed the pressure of churning out a half dozen stories at once—obits, the weather, cops, a local angle on a national story. In the sweltering heat of the newsroom, the percussive tapping of my old Royal typewriter merged with the metallic rumble of the freight trains going by outside on the Penn Central tracks. My shirt moistened with perspiration as the deadline neared. Then Nicole would slink over in her work shirt and grungy jeans, kick-starting the arousal feelings of the weekend with her spunky, bad-girl talk. If there were no big stories happening, Charles Bonenti would let me leave by ten o'clock. I exited the newsroom with an edge, feeling spent, sexy, competent. Then I'd cruise down through the peaks for the Red Lion Inn or Mundy's Bar.

One Friday night in late August that year, I lined up a bit more fun than I thought it was possible to have.

Rachel was supposed to go down to New York that weekend but had canceled at the last minute. She called me while I was working on a bunch of stories and sounded kind of low. Our relationship had reached a nice level of candor and mutual support, and I enjoyed being able to read her moods now.

"So, what happened to the guy in New York?" I said. "You didn't go."

"Oh, it's not important," Rachel said. "He couldn't make it tonight, so I ditched the city. New York's no good on a night like this. Too hot, you know?"

"Yeah, right. So you just called me to shoot the shit."

"Shut up," Rachel said. "I bought food at Nejaimes. I can feed you."

"All right, I'll be down. You can cry on my shoulder, little woman. But look, I've got to leave on the early side. I promised Peter that I'd pick Judy up from the late bus in Lee. Her car is in the shop again."

That happened to be bullshit, a necessary lie. Judy's yellow Maverick was fine. But Marcia Weiss had already called and told me that her husband was attending some GE golfing event out of town. We were looking forward to a weekend goof-off together on Lake Buel, and I'd made a date with her to drive down there after work tonight. But I knew that I could fit Rachel in first. It was more or less just a matter of stalling Marcia for an hour or two by telling her that I had to work late, and then I'd tell Rachel that I had to leave her place early enough to fetch Judy at the bus stop. This training in journalism—coming up with good stuff on deadline—was really proving quite useful.

So, I dialed down to Marcia and told her that I might be late. All kinds of big stories were breaking out all over the place, I told her, and I might have to slave away in the newsroom until midnight.

"Oh, you poor, poor thing!" Marcia said. "God, I hope those editors there appreciate what they have in you. You work so *hard* at your job."

"Yeah, well, you know, Marcia," I said. "A man's gotta do what a man's gotta do."

So, it was all set up. Two babes in one night. I didn't feel particularly guilty about this. First of all, the event wasn't my fault—Marcia and Rachel had called me, I hadn't called them.

Second, I'd always had just this tiny little fetish for serial sex, and I knew that if the opportunity ever presented itself I would go right ahead and do it.

The fantasy dated back to events during my college years. I was chasing around then with this fun-fun group of rich girls from Bennington and Skidmore Colleges, many of whom were going through their freshman- or sophomore-year slut phase. At parties, they loved to torture me with their indifference, and then disappear for a couple of hours to play around with some dirtball druggie or biker, come back to the party for a while, and then leave again with a graduate student or a big-name writer-in-residence. They called it "safari sex," bagging more than one guy a night, and I talked about it with a couple of them with whom I'd become close friends. Bagging more than one a night was thrilling and exotic, they thought, and they enjoyed the manipulation and deception involved, the eroticism of being passed from man to man. There were variations, of course—doing your female roommate first, and then hitting the bars to find guys, was reasonably popular as well. In England, where I studied later, safari sex was also pretty big among the European and American foreign-exchange students I met and dated over there. In addition to their dates with college-age boys like me, they all seemed to have an extra married art professor or history don on the side. Arrangements could get complicated, and they'd often sleep with both their guys during a single afternoon-to-evening cycle. But I'd only been the prey once or twice in safari sex, never the hunter.

So, now my big night had arrived, and everything was set up. I'd finally be able to get this little rascal out of my system.

Then Nicole walked into the middle of this and really complicated the logistics.

I'd been aware for a couple of weeks that Nicole was nudging in for a closer relationship. At the beginning of August she'd finally found a place of her own, a hippie shack way out in the hemlock forests along the Alford–West Stockbridge line. She and her grandfather had driven all the way down to the Pier One store at a mall in Springfield to buy furniture and wall hangings, and now, with the place all set up, Nicole was pestering me to visit. I knew that this was important to her. She was proud to finally have a place of her own and wanted to show it off. Her house out in the woods expressed her independence, her ability to break away from her family in Pittsfield. However, my arms were pretty full with romance already, and I didn't want to spoil our book-turding by making love with her too soon. But I knew that I couldn't put her off much longer. Nicole would just interpret that as the rich boy refusing to visit her reconditioned chicken coop.

That night, when Nicole walked over, I was reading at my desk and I didn't look up right away.

"Hey, book-boy, what are you up to?" she said. "You got any plans tonight?"

When Nicole said that, her voice was chalky and breaking and I could hear her nervously cracking her knuckles behind my back. When I swiveled in my chair and looked up, her face and neck were blushing bright red. The tension between us, which had been building for months, was very palpable at that moment.

Oh boy, I thought. Here we go. Until I figured out what she was up to, I'd better be noncommittal.

"Nah, no big plans tonight," I said. "Just the usual."

Nicole leaned down and spoke close to my face, almost whispering to avoid being overheard by Charley Bonenti nearby and the ladies working on the copy desk. Her arms were pony-shivering just a bit, and she had this coy, seductive way of biting her lip.

"Good," Nicole said. "Because I'm propositioning you. You're coming back to my place in Alford and giving me a zip-less fuck."

Jesus. Erica Jong was back in my life. Where the hell did all these critics get off, accusing her of being a great feminist writer? The only thing Erica Jong was doing that year was getting guys like me laid. I needed to start sending the author regular thank-you notes.

As soon as Nicole said that, she looked terribly embarrassed, but also relieved. Her eyes rolled in their sockets and she smiled vulnerably with a self-mocking expression. She had on this lip gloss that night that made her irresistible. *Go ahead, rich boy. Turn me down. Treat me like shit.*

But I wasn't going to do that and I knew it. I was powerfully smitten by Nicole at that moment and knew that I'd been conning myself about resisting her. Besides, safari sex was safari sex; nobody ever said that there had to be a legal limit. Nicole had simply added herself onto the night, and I knew that I didn't have the discipline to say no. It was her right to choose and she just happened to pick tonight.

So, what the hell. I liked living crazy and the night could be fun.

"Nicole," I said. "I'm game. But just for the record, you're the one who asked."

"Shut up. I've been hitting on you for months and you're such a fucking retard. I can't stand waiting around for an idiot like you to ask me out."

"Okay, okay. Jesus. Let's not fight about it. But look. I've got to pick up Peter's Judy at the bus stop in Lee, so let me make some calls and set things up."

"Cool," Nicole said. "Let's leave early if we can. Nothing's happening in sports."

So, I dialed down to West Stockbridge and gave Rachel a load of bull about being slightly delayed because of all the stories that were breaking in the *Eagle* newsroom, and then I called Lake Buel and repeated this fictitious scheduling information for Marcia, and both of them told me what a poor, poor thing I was and that I was far too dedicated to my freaking job.

Now I only had Charley Bonenti to deal with, but all of my stories were done, and he was usually a piece of cake about things like this. Walking over there, I decided not to lie to him because he was too good a guy.

"Hey, Charley. Mind if I duck out early? I've got a slight possibility of some babe action tonight."

"Oh please, Rinker, go," Charley said. "That's much more important than this place. By the way, do you mind if I say something?"

"No, go ahead."

"Rinker, I really appreciate the way you pump out all these stories on Friday night," Charley said. "Everyone notices. Thanks for the hard work."

Jeez. The whole damn world was just going my way tonight. Here I was sneaking off the job early to commence a twenty-four-mile, serial lay across Berkshire County, and everybody just couldn't get over how *hard* I worked. My personal motto was working overtime. Fuck up, be a hero.

As I was finishing up with Charley, Nicole was delivering a story from sports over to the copy desk and she stopped on her way back around.

"So?"

"We're blowing this place, lady."

"Good. Give me five minutes so it doesn't look too obvious, and then I'll meet you in the parking lot. You can follow me down to Alford."

Back at her desk, Nicole straightened out a few papers, threw on this floppy ball cap that she wore, and smiled sideways as she headed off. She tossed her Greek fisherman's bag over her shoulder, and it gently bounced against her skinny hips as she cruised through the double doors.

When I got down to the parking lot, Nicole was leaning against the door of her car, which was this great old slant-six Plymouth Valiant, a two-tone green, that her grandfather had fixed up for her. She was bright-eyed and more relaxed now, laughing at herself.

"Sorry," she said. "I'm such a jerk for the way I said that back there. Nervous, you know? Really nervous with you."

"Nicole. It's all right. I'm actually glad you were less bashful about it than me."

"Okay, but I'm nervous. Let me just say it. I know I'm not your type."

I reached out with my finger and poked her in the ribs and then, on impulse, just because I felt so comfortable with her, let my hand slide up underneath her breast. We briefly kissed.

"Nicole. I wouldn't be here if I didn't want to be. You're the one always calling me an idiot. Stop being one yourself."

"Okay, okay. I'm chilling. I'm working on that. Let's go. Follow me."

It was a nice drive out through town and down West Street past the airport, and then leaving the lights of Pittsfield behind for the moody, shadowy ravines of Richmond. All the way out past Card Lake and then Williamsville, the smell of marijuana being smoked wafted back to me from Nicole's car up front.

I liked Nicole's little hippie shack buried deep in the Alford woods. The craggy brow of a Taconic summit rose above the trees, and the yard was spongy and soft underfoot with a thick mesh of pine needles, wet from recent rains. The place was an old skeet-shooting lodge converted to a rental bungalow. Inside, Nicole had the place all dolled up after her Pier One and Salvation Army scavenger hunt. There was a yellow formica dinette set in the space designated for the kitchen, a lava lamp borrowed from her brother on an antique sideboard over in the corner, and the bright Indian rag rugs on the floor had that new smell of freshly manufactured textiles.

It was fun, cruising around the place, oohing and ahing over all the furniture and decorations that she'd bought. I turned over a rocker to see if I could figure out where it came from. This wasn't an act on my part. I was genuinely impressed with the way she'd gussied up her digs.

"Hey, Nicole, this place looks great. Congratulations."

"Thanks, rich boy. You're probably shitting me, but I don't care. I like it myself."

Nicole had bought two things for me, two small gifts, but they touched me a great deal and helped set a tone for the night that was not simply one of lust. She knew that I liked bourbon and the man at the liquor had told her to buy Jack Daniels, which was more money than she had to spend on me, but I liked the suggestion of forethought that it carried. She had planned this night, what would happen after she propositioned me in the newsroom. Also, she'd found this painted-pine magazine holder in an antique store, put a ribbon around it, and attached a card for me on it.

"Nicole, gee, you didn't have to do something like this. It's really nice. I always wanted one of these jobs."

"Yeah. It had your name on it. I couldn't resist."

I made a bourbon for myself in a 7-Up glass that was right there in the dish strainer, and Nicole poured herself a wine, and we sat outside on rickety chairs set up on this half-porch by the front door, listening to the wind in the trees and the deer spooking just beyond the pool of light on the lawn.

Nicole smoked another joint out there. I didn't know whether she always tried to get this high or was just reefering away her anxiety about me. But I didn't care. She was seducing me perfectly. It was foreplay, what she was doing. A woman going overboard on alcohol or drugs like that, it seemed to me, was advertising her sexual availability. I don't want to remember much, she seemed to be saying, I don't want to be restrained or in control. Just do me any old time you want now, guy, and please dispense with the usual protocol of being bashful and polite about this, because I'm getting high. And Nicole was very sexy about it, smirky-smiling as she smoked her joint and draping one of her legs over mine from her chair, lounging back so that her work shirt settled seductively on her breasts. *Shut up and kiss me, you idiot.*

As soon as we started doing that and touching each other I just loved Nicole, a whole lot, right away. Gorgeous, spongy, aggressive bad-girl Nicole, with the flat and opalescent stomach flesh and the automatic dig-in nails. She pushed me hard and invited me to push her back, taking my whole upper lip in her teeth and gently biting. Two fistfuls of my hair were in her hands as she perched up on my chair with one knee and forced my head back hard against the clapboard siding on the porch. I liked her this high, her spunky, bad-girl way of kissing. Lunge deep with the tongue, dig in hard with the nails, don't be afraid of your bad-girl talk. *Fuck, that's nice. I'm finally kissing you.* When she wanted my shirt off, so she could dig her nails in all over my chest and bite and kiss my stomach and hips, she took it off as frankly and nonchalantly as if she was undressing a little boy.

Christ. So skinny. Didn't your mother ever feed you?

Whatever happened now was fine with me, and I loved her rugby style of handling me so far. When I went into the kitchen to get another bourbon I just hoisted her up with a handful of work shirt and half-carried and dragged her in there behind me, poured my drink one-handed while I held her around the waist with the other, and the whole time she just kept lunging back for my mouth and my neck with her aggressive kissing. Somehow from there we ended up completely undressed on the floor, and she was the sexiest woman I ever disrobed because she didn't have any underwear on and one minute there were jeans pressing hard up against my groin, and then the next minute I was aware of her naked and riding on my chest. She was just great, Nicole, horsing around on top of me and lunging down with her mouth and knees to rough-sex me up a bit, her breasts so athletic and full, erotic to feast on, and we were uninhibited together and laughing a lot, she pushing me and doing all this rough-sex stuff with her arms and me pushing her back and laughing some more. When I went for my drink she tried to stop me. So I flipped her over and forced some of the bourbon down her throat.

We were both wild now, not worrying about where any of this would lead, or thinking beyond the present rough kiss. There were nice pauses during which we quietly talked while we pushed out far with our arms, interlocked them, and squeezed each other's hands.

"Hi, bastard. It's really nice you're finally here. You can just take me however you want. I'm into you just taking me however you want."

Nicole saying that, and perhaps just the spontaneous and crazy agenda for the night, reminded me that there was this one tiny little flu symptom of a sexual fantasy that I did have. I'd always wanted to take a woman from behind on the floor, and maybe rough her up a bit while I was at it. I pretty much knew where this image came from too, insofar as the provenance of sexual desire can be established that well. When I was a boy, my father would go on horse-buying sprees down in Lancaster County, Pennsylvania, and he had an old friend down there, Ivan Martin. Ivan was an Old Order Mennonite farmer and a big horse breeder in the county. He and my father were engaged in an eternal quest to breed the perfect pair of matched "general purpose" horses, a Percheron and Standardbred cross. Whenever we went down there, Ivan would trot all of his mares out to the barnyard and line them up, then call for his son Rufus to fetch the stallion, a big gray Percheron named Jack. Jack was a handsome beast, tall and beefy necked, with a long black mane and high-stepping front hooves. He was a wonderfully out-of-control horse, and it was fun, watching him do it. Jack was thoroughly inconsiderate and very rough with his sexual partners, pummeling the mares with his front hooves, biting their necks, and whacking them with his legs, as he fucked his way down the line of vaginas. Between the ages of eight and fourteen, I watched Jack and his successors mount at least a hundred mares, and pretty much, they always did it the same way. Rough her up, take her from behind. This was my first sexual imagery, and I guess I can't be blamed for letting my head run away with it, just a little. I'd always wanted to take a woman from behind, hard, on the floor. I could never do anything with this enduring desire, however, because the kind of girls I was usually with would be concerned about the damage that kind of treatment might do to their Bergdorf pajamas. So, I had behaved myself. The Smith College Goddesses had never had to worry about Rinker giving them rough sex.

Tonight was the night, however, to put all that altar boy crap behind me. Nicole had urged me to do her any old way I wanted, and that's how I was going to handle it.

So, it was glorious. I flipped her over and grasped up through her armpit to her neck with a half-nelson grip, clasping a thick knot of her hair in my hand, and then pushed her down hard on the rag rug and splayed out her other arm, interlocking it in mine. Her body was muscular and white, thin, very thin, with these pretty and distracting fringes of wispy blonde hair between her shoulders and on the soft lovely skin beneath her ears. It was all one liquid, flowing movement, flipping her over, clasping her in the wrestler's grip, and then experiencing the enormously erotic sensation of being received by her vagina, and not being able to distinguish between the moment when I was still outside of her and then in. Her ass pushing back up against me cupped my groin in the most comfortable way and we just fit, fit, fit together and we were rough with each other and laughing and talking. Nicole fought to get her left arm free and then reached back over the top of us to dig her nails into my neck and grab a handful of my hair herself. She forced our faces together and we locked our lips and teeth into more hard kissing, and with my grip on her neck I bent her forward to my face, very hard. We were just rough, very rough on each other until I didn't think we could do more, but we did, but then there were all these slow and patient pauses where we relaxed head-to-head together and just talked and affectionately kissed and I was desperate to feel her womanly, spongy, generous breasts and it was comforting holding those while I enjoyed her moistness, joined to me by ass-to-groin fusion. I enjoyed her variety, her protean sexual personality. Rough, rough, animal sex, then kiss her gently, be affectionate and talk in a whisper, bringing her down from bad girl to Pretty Mom, then rough-rough again and ramp her back up to bad girl. *Oh, you're such a bastard. You're taking me, you bastard.* We were gentle and then rough with each other after that some more, but it didn't matter because we couldn't feel it changing, either way. It was just one glorious long screw and fusion now, surreal and distorting time, like a dream, or a long flight in a plane over changing terrain, where hours grow into a span that seems to be weeks or years. Finally we lost patience beyond all impatience and just forced-loved-abandoned ourselves into orgasms, with dug-in nails and wrestler's grips to prolong them. Energy became spiritual. With Nicole that night I just mind-wandered right up through to pure sky.

Afterward we lay on the floor together and I liked the sensation of her perspiring breasts on my chest and the pearls of sweat beading up on her blonde hair.

"Ooooooooo. Sorry. I keep calling you an idiot but I mean it in another way. I knew you'd be such an idiot for love."

"Yeah, well. It's not as if you're a total loser yourself."

"No, no. I know. I mean it's just that when you came over that night when I was reading *Fear of Flying* in the newsroom I knew you were an idiot who would do anything for me. I wanted to bring you home, make you dinner, and then sleep with you."

"Yeah, well, I was an idiot. But I didn't know what else to do."

"That's my point, idiot. You weren't afraid to be mocked by those guys for me. Most boys I know would just join in. Even if I cry, it doesn't occur to them that I have feelings."

"Yeah, but just so you know. I didn't do that to get invited here tonight."

"I know! You're such an idiot! You're the only person in the newsroom who even seems to know I'm alive, and I'm like hitting you over the head five thousand times being grateful for that and you never do anything. I mean I had to practically drag your ass out here. You're such a fucking idiot, it's unbelievable. I mean I'm totally in love already with you, I'll probably just get hurt because I'm not your type, but I had to get the idiot out here and just do him. You know? I mean, I'm an idiot myself to fall for you."

"Yeah, I know what you mean. But why don't you knock off this stuff about not being my type? If you weren't, why do we spend so much time together?"

"I don't know. I'm just saying, I understand if you don't feel obligated. I asked *you*."

"Shut up, okay?"

Our unconventional first coupling had aroused in both of us a need for more conventional sex. We were just naturally curious about how that would be together and were feeling around now with our hands and kissing, inching toward that.

I was enjoying feelings of omnipotence that night, not simply because of the additional two dates still waiting for me down the road. Being desired by more than one woman at once is ego boosting enough, but it wasn't only that. It was the merging of my life already and this night of sex. I had logged hard all winter and then kept myself fit through the spring and summer hiking the peaks. Two hundred–pound logs just weren't a problem for me at all, and this wasn't so much a vanity of mine as a thing I simply enjoyed about myself. Good sex, of course, contributes mightily to body image and personal elan, and so when I couldn't resist sex with her anymore, I just hoisted Nicole up onto my waist with one arm and carried her into the bedroom, grabbing her wine jug with my free hand as we passed the formica table.

And it was beautiful in there too, laughing and kissing on the bed, enjoying very conventional and gentle sex with a woman who was so open and frank with her body. When she wanted my hands on her breasts or gently clasping her ears, she put them there with her hands, and when she wanted me inside her she placed me there. When we paused, and Nicole stepped up to get some wine glasses from the kitchen and glided through the doorway, I couldn't believe how slender and beautiful her body was.

Afterward we lay on the bed together and drank wine. Nicole was looking forward to the weekend. Her grandfather was installing new windows on his house, and she was going to help him. He was teaching her carpentry.

When it was time to go I took a shower in her bathroom, soothed by the warm water on my back and the sweet exhaustion of lengthy sex, and by the fragrances of her shampoo and body creams in there. They were all lined up on the cheap shelves of the bungalow bathroom, with no doors hiding the bottles and tubes. This was one of the best parts of meeting a new woman, I thought, the olfactory sensation of her bathroom. The immersion feelings of that shower seemed to resolve my confusion about that night, and I suddenly felt comfortable about the merging of romance and place that I was experiencing, the sorority of women I was sharing. I knew that I could transition quickly to a new zone for Rachel, but I was also surprised by my feelings for Nicole. I was a lot more interested in her than I expected to be. Changing into my clothes, I was determined not to leave without alerting her to my desire for a next step.

"Hey, what's your night off this week?"

"Tuesday."

"All right. We're going to dinner. We'll go to Alice's or somewhere like that, somewhere nice."

"Oh, okay. I didn't expect you to say that. I mean I thought I'd cook you dinner here."

"No, no. That's later. Let me take you out first."

"Okay. But you're just so different. You're really different for me."

"Yeah, well, get used to it then. We'll have to be different, I guess."

"I'm working on it," she said.

"Yeah, and lay off the dope too. Get some sleep when I leave."

"Yeah, I'm going to. Tomorrow, I'm my grandfather's little gofer."

I scooped up the magazine rack that she'd bought for me, and before I crossed the spongy lawn for my car, we embraced on the half-porch. Nicole was dressed in her work shirt, nothing else. Lips to lips and lips to hair and temple, frankly but gently, and I loved the feel of her buttocks in my hand.

"Hey, thanks for coming," she said. "I was terrified of you, but now I'm not."

"Good," I said. "Get used to it. I'm taking you out now."

"Okay, okay. Okay."

That particular drive was one of my favorites—out through the deep hemlock forests, then skirting the tornado district up along the Williams River into West Stockbridge. The road along the river was very reliable for seeing owls. And it was a unique night, with the air very pregnant with humidity before the thunderstorms blew through. Heat lightning tessellated to the east behind the peaks, making them glow with electric blue and orange flashes.

. . .

Rachel had a very nice meal set up when I got to Card Lake—a curried chicken dish, tabouli and flat bread, and a salad niçoise. For us, food had become a medium of our maturing love. Rachel was going out with all these new men in New York now, a process that I was encouraging, and she knew about and drew great amusement from all of my flings. So, often, we sat around at night enjoying the sort of dishes that could be bought at the better delicatessens in Stockbridge or Great Barrington, talking about our love lives and problems. Some nights this led to sex, other nights it didn't. We loved each other and liked being together, and now we were enjoying the process of exchanging raw passion for a deeper, lasting friendship.

Rachel taught me one important thing about relationships, which is that reversion is the basis of love. I'd concluded by then that people arrive in your life fully formed and they're not going to change that much, so you'd better like the package you see right now and fall in love with everything, including the faults that would return again and again. Comfort Halsey was the loveliest person in every way, but she was never going to be comfortable with my need to escape into the woods with Linscott and then prowl the bars. Rachel was entertained by that side of my character and so our relationship worked better. And I loved her reversions, the way her beautiful brown face puzzled up and she reached across the table for my hand.

"Okay. This is like the third time he's made a date and then canceled on me at the last minute. But I'm hooked on him now. It hurts. I admit it."

"Fine," I said. "You're going to be unhappy for a while with this thing. You know how I handle that, what I've decided to do? I'm just going to be unhappy for the longest time until I'm suddenly happy, and then it's going to feel amazing, by comparison."

"Yeah, yeah, fine, but that's you," Rachel said. "You can get away with being unhappy, because you're basically stable. I mean you're acting out all the time and being crazy, but you can make that work because you're stable. I'm really not. I have to be happy, right now."

"Well you can be happy right now. You're allowed to go out

and meet these guys and see if they're right, before you fall in love. You're supposed to be sampling the market."

"Yeah, yeah. I mean partial lightbulbs are going off here. I'm identifying a strong relationship as the thing that will get me out of here."

"Yeah, and that's wrong," I said. "You can get out of here without a relationship. You're permitted to live just for your-self."

"Exactly. And this guy has already shown me all I need to know about him. It's time to move on."

"Well, maybe it's okay to have these crushes all the time," I said. "But that doesn't necessarily make him right for you. Look at my ridiculous life."

"Yeah, well, it is ridiculous, your life. Completely. But it's also you."

My enduring fantasy about Rachel was that I would, after all, end up marrying her. Yes, we had done all the bars and the dance halls together and ridden back and forth over the mountains on romantic, snowy nights, but mostly I enjoyed her domesticity and the comforts of her farmhouse on Card Lake, her ability to smother me in warmth and love, and the satisfying role I had played in her therapeutic quest. We would settle down and live happily ever after in the quiet house in the country that I mind-wandered to when we were having sex. After a busy week at work, I would return to her on a Friday night and eat a meal like the one we had just had, relax, and enjoy some very conventional sex with her, then sit around and watch a ballgame or read together on the couch before we returned to bed and slept in each other's arms. With Rachel I would escape to the settled and con-tented life that I knew that I had to find someday. It was over-powering that night, the urge to escape to a new and quiet life through the comforts of sex with Rachel.

I had always been careful with her, because of her needs, to wait for a signal and never be aggressive about sex. But I could see now that she was relaxed from dinner and our talk, and dreamy from two glasses of wine, so I scooped her up in my arms and carried her into the bedroom. I would appease myself with her. I was allowed to be selfish. On the bed I placed her comfortably so that her head rested where it belonged on the pillow, gently removed her skirt and her underwear, stripped off all of my clothes, and then without foreplay or the elaborate permissions I generally sought I just entered and enjoyed her, particularly aroused by the fact that she still had her blouse and bra on, the fantasy of married sex being ever so much richer for the image of taking my wife while she was still partially clothed.

This moment of sex was unusual for me because I felt so strongly the need to speak with her, and not wait for her words first. I was liberated to speak and say exactly what I thought. *Rachel, I'm doing you this way because I always wanted to. You're so beautiful. I love you and we're never going to marry, but I love you so much. You're beyond perfect.* And she was relaxed and enjoying herself, reaching back with her hands for the headboard, glossy nails against antique maple, and I could last forever then because I had already expended myself with Nicole. And then the nicest, calmest thing happened. Standard coition, the routine vaginal approach, gentle sex just the way I wanted it, and she came and came and came, very steadily and soundly, as reliable as the Staten Island ferry coming in. I could maintain her a long time because there was nothing left in me except for muscle, a very satisfying conclusion for both of us. Toward the end I flashed powerfully with a dozen thoughts, more than my brain could ever retrieve, but mostly that sex wasn't about sex, that it was simply a medium delivering two people to communication. Sex, *the* universal language. I was also going to stop apologizing to myself about my behavior, even tonight. I had fucked and loved and laughed my way to heaven and back with so many women up in those mountains, and tonight, by ridiculous accident and promiscuity, I'd broken through with Rachel to a new place. It all seemed worth it.

"Wow," Rachel said. "I can't believe that just happened like that. Where did that come from?"

"Oh, heaven, I guess. Who knows?"

"Yeah, well, it was amazing enough, but also what you said. I've always known that about us. I love you for everything, but it's all for up here. I can't imagine us together somewhere else. Long-term."

"That's why I said it, I guess. I meant it."

"Okay, and now I'm completely going to shock you. What you said? It's perfect. I don't have anything more to say about it. For once in my life I am completely talked out."

"Okay, okay," I said.

Rachel wanted to sit on the porch and watch the lake and the lights of the village below for a while. The nonexistent bus that Judy wasn't really on was not scheduled to arrive for almost an hour. Rachel put on the men's pajamas that were so attractive on her, and I changed back into my clothes, and we drank some more wine out on the swing couch. Moths and mosquitoes buzzed around the porch lamp, and Rachel, lounging back on the couch, was lovely under the soft light. The whoosh of cars and the voices of the late-dinner crowd leaving the Westbridge softly moved up the hill.

I loved watching Rachel this time of night. She accepted sleep so graciously, with a sigh and a gentle smile.

"Hey, put me to sleep. I love the way you do that."

So, I picked her up in my arms and carried her into bed and helped her arrange the light quilt so she was comfortable, and then I stroked her hair and chin for a while and told her all the stories about myself and my family that she liked. When her eyes began to flutter and close I turned off the light, and then I just rested my hand on her head until I knew that she was asleep.

I finished my wine alone on the porch, enjoying the moonlight down on the lake, just to make sure she was all right. Then I quietly pulled shut the front door and left, coasting my car down the hill before I started the engine.

It felt as if this was the last time that I would see her, but it wasn't really. I was driving away from her, climbing the hill beside West Stockbridge Mountain, filled with both sadness and happiness for her and for me. I'd done all I could just knowing that girl.

. . .

Marcia had fallen asleep on the couch out on the screened porch when I got down to Lake Buel, but she woke up, stretched her arms, and drowsily smiled when I arrived. I loved her for her gullibility that night, for seeing in me what she wanted, not what I had really done. I was exhausted but energized by my night of spectral sex with Nicole and Rachel. Marcia had her own thoughts about the source of my fatigue.

"God, you poor thing. It's almost one o'clock. I can't get over how you work your ass off for the *Eagle*."

"Ah, it wasn't that bad, Marcia," I said. "I really like working for a newspaper. It's fun, burning on empty."

I felt insatiable now, limitless. Bagging more than one a night was supremely egotistical and interesting. My self-image was soaring, I liked the way my muscles and my stomach felt—sinewy and overworked, as if I'd been logging all day—and my mental powers were peaked. Deception was such fun, getting away with sin very satisfying, and the nocturnal passage from one woman to the next very erotic. And the talk, the talk that arrived with intimacy. Talk, talk, talk, immerse yourself in her issues. Everything about this night was thrilling.

As Marcia stood up and embraced me, I looked out to the lake and was overwhelmed by a desire to swim. Losing myself in the water seemed like the most desirable thing I could do right now.

"Hey, let me take a swim first, okay? I just want to wash that newsroom out of my hair."

"Oh sure, sure," she said. "It will be relaxing. Can you eat anything?"

"Sure," I said, because I was hungry as hell that night too.

So, it was lovely, that swim. I walked up to my car and retrieved my bathing suit, changed and switched on the dock lights, and then walked down and dove in, swimming out fifty or sixty yards with long strokes, cleansed and refreshed by the water streaking over me and the sudden, chilling sensations of swimming through the spots of colder water. On the way back in I sounded low several times, swimming a breaststroke underwater. The sensation of the plants at the bottom of the lake brushing against my chest felt clingy but fleeting, as if I had distanced myself from all life in a strange dream.

When I got back to the porch, Marcia had made sandwiches and put a bottle of wine out. We ate and talked, flirting a lot as we drank the wine and enjoying the effect we had on each other. After a while Marcia reverted to a familiar subject, her relationship with Robert, which filled my chest for a minute or two with pangs of jealousy but then, too, a feeling of calm satisfaction. I just liked women so much, I liked ruminating over their issues and talking to them about their lives. Marcia had used me as an amorous and physical sounding board to work on the issues of her marriage, and I loved her for it. I loved her improving marriage. Our life together had sent out spokes of love that helped other people. Jealousy. How worthless. And, of course, it was preposterous of me to be complaining about the amount of love I was receiving on that particular night.

When we got into the bedroom, I was supremely lazy about making love to her. But Marcia performed beautifully, fulfilling another fantasy that I had about lovemaking. Be done by her. She services you. The minimarriage simulation that prepares me for a future with my own little lady someday. *Oh God, you're so tired. Just relax and let me do the work here.* After I collapsed onto the bed with just my shirt off, she gently undressed me the rest of the way, began smothering me with kisses and long, feathery strokes of nails on my chest and hair, progressively undressing herself along the way and then just fluidly rising astride and placing me inside her. It was slow, gentle, and relaxing, effortless for me, what sex should be. All thoughts of male performance were erased from my head, and I felt that I experienced that night, for the first time, the true essence of masculinity, which was not dominance and control, but instead submission to the sexual prowess of a woman. And she was so beautiful and sensual that night, with her full, firm breasts, narrow waist, and rich, flawless complexion. It was immensely pleasurable, submitting, gently lifting up my head to kiss her breasts, enjoying the rhythm of her thin but fleshy torso on mine, the chips of moonlight on her shoulders and arms. She was controlling her own pleasure now, coming and repeating that. Out through the curtains there were streaks of yellow light from lamps on the far-off docks and a purple aura of horizon against the peaks.

I don't remember falling asleep. She caressed me there with her gentle rocking and her arms on my body, so that there was no separation between the sex and my sensation of welcoming sleep.

A big thunderstorm blew through very late, sending divine crashes echoing down from the peaks and reverberating across the lake outside. Marcia and I woke and held each other and then made love again. We made an early breakfast and watched the rain fall on the lake until the sky cleared.

I had expected to rise exhausted, all tuckered out, and then Marcia and I would begin a very pointless and lazy goof-off weekend. But instead I was rushed with energy that surprised me, so we drove over to Sheffield, rented a canoe, and followed the Housatonic River oxbows south to Ashley Falls.

We paddled down past the Sheffield Plain, then through the muddy horseshoe turns as the river flowed over the state line at Canaan. Marcia was brown from sunning on the dock all summer, sexy in her black tank top, khaki shorts, and hiking boots with big, woolly socks. A fallen willow, sprouting new roots in the river and lush-green, framed her full-bodied profile as she paddled up front in the canoe.

"Hey boyfriend. You're my boyfriend guy, you know? It's so nice having a boyfriend."

I felt lazy under the sun. The meandering oxbows, with the willow and ash trees dropping their boughs to the water, created a tunnel vision effect, dreamy and soporific. Last night's exertions were finally catching up with me, so we pulled over to the banks and I fell asleep in Marcia's lap.

"Oh, my little guy," Marcia said, stroking my hair. "My little guy. I love being here with you. It's so peaceful."

Bayonets flashing, charging downhill. I probably should have remembered that as a night of living sexually, but really it always felt more like a night of soul and pure sky.

CHAPTER EIGHTEEN

THAT FALL, as I combed the hollows in search of stories on my environmental beat and resumed my weekend hikes with Roger Linscott, a new and refreshing sensation filled my days. I was calm now, at rest. My night of lyrical sex in late August had a lot to do with this. I didn't feel that I had as much to prove anymore and grew a lot less manic about women, which eliminated a large distraction from my life. In those mountains that I loved, I had pushed the envelope of passion about as far as it could go. Now I didn't feel that I had to be as compulsive, and I could concentrate on one relationship at a time. That same restraint carried over to my other pursuits. Writing, hiking, or weekend flying didn't have to be so hell-bent now. Life felt more disciplined, but still quite full.

Besides, the winding down of those relationships left behind a residue of goodwill. Rachel calmed down and seemed to be taking her lumps in the New York love market a whole lot easier now. One night in September Marcia Weiss and I sat down out at Lake Buel and agreed that our affair had become sexually addictive, and that her need for thrills outside her marriage had run its course. I was breaking up with women all over the place now, but finally understanding the reasons. Nicole and I dated for about eight months after our big hookup in August, enjoying a very relaxed, mutually supportive relationship. With Nicole, I learned to enjoy the three-or-four-day interlude between dates, the comfort of knowing just her, the familiarity of our routines. Up in Hancock, we mowed the grass together, and then in the fall we raked leaves. God, what a concept. One babe at a time. I actually had time to catch my breath now.

I always liked the way my friendship with Pete Miller played out too. That summer and fall we had one big fight and then one last, gorgeous time.

In 1972, just as the Sexual Revolution was spooling up, America briefly lost its head over a pornographic film called *Deep Throat*. The film, a steamy and generally tasteless ode to oral sex, featured a porn star named Linda Lovelace and the penis of a fellow named Harry Reems. Interest in *Deep Throat* intensified after the New York tabloids caught Jackie Onassis slipping into a Manhattan movie theater to watch it. By the summer of 1974, *Deep Throat* had "gone mainstream" and was enjoying modest success as it was distributed as a summer rerun in smaller markets, usually as a double billing at drive-in movie theaters with another porn classic, *The Devil in Miss Jones*. At the time, American movie-viewing habits were changing, and drive-in theaters were slowly dying. But the national release of *Deep Throat* briefly provided a last commercial hurrah for the big outdoor screens.

One Friday night in August, when *Deep Throat* and *The Devil in Miss Jones* reached the Lanesboro Drive-In, just north of Pittsfield, Peter Scheer and I drove out to take in the show. We arranged to have an *Eagle* photographer cover the event, just in case we decided to do a story. It was an interesting experience for both of us, mostly because neither of us had ever seen pornography before and didn't know what to expect. We both found the rancid production values and lousy acting thoroughly boring, and I soon dozed off, sleeping right through Linda Lovelace's famous oral performance.

Still, we were amazed at who we found there. During the intermission, before *The Devil in Miss Jones* began, Peter and I wandered around and interviewed the audience in the grassy amphitheater of the drive-in. There was a wealthy industrialist from town whom we knew, a bunch of week-enders from Lenox and Stockbridge, and several GE executives and their wives. The manager of the drive-in told Peter that "all the social pillars of Pittsfield are here," which was probably stretching the truth, but it seemed to confirm what we'd seen. *Deep Throat* had attracted mostly an upper-middle-class, educated audience, hardly a profound cultural interpretation, but something to write about all the same.

Peter and I raced back to the newsroom after that and cobbled together a story on *Deep Throat* at the drive-in, one of our few joint by-line pieces. The editors that night were glad to have it because there was a big hole on the local page and the picture of the drive-in manager was pretty good. Because we liked it so much, the "all the social pillars of Pittsfield" quote was staged near the top of the piece. We left the newsroom congratulating ourselves about the "national story told locally" that we'd hastily put together and drove home. Judy was there by then and she gave us a big earful for wasting our time at a filthy movie like *Deep Throat*, but we promptly fell into our usual weekend routine together and forgot about it.

Pete Miller was livid about that story. He had always refused to accept advertising for X-rated films, a puritanical streak that earned him a lot of respect, but also periodically involved him in squabbles with the local movie theaters, which would pull their advertising schedules after the *Eagle* selectively refused to advertise one or two films. Now, two of his favorite and most pampered reporters had bypassed his ban on pornography, devoting a huge amount of space to what Pete regarded as a free ad for filth.

On Monday morning, dispensing with his usual habit of passing a note up through the editors, Pete stormed up to the newsroom and confronted Peter and me. He was red-faced and fidgety, thumbing the note cards in his pocket and furiously scratching his elbows, even stumbling over his words. I had been warned about Pete's occasional flashes of temper, and he was particularly venomous toward me that day. Because all his emotions were so well hidden, Pete could explode uncontrollably when his feelings finally emerged.

"All the social pillars of Pittsfield, huh?" Pete said, his high-pitched voice cracking. "Hah! Well, *I* wasn't there, young man, and neither was anyone I know. You've used my newspaper to promote filth. Rinker Buck, I am very disappointed in you. Is this how you express gratitude for the opportunity we've given you?"

After he was done with me, Pete turned on Peter Scheer and screamed at him for a while, and then stalked out of the newsroom. Both of us knew that it was useless to say much when Pete was that angry.

Intellectually, I was very tough about it. I knew Pete was wrong and was overreacting. Slimy as it was, *Deep Throat* was an unimportant but somewhat revelatory cultural event sweeping the country, and we had merely delivered to the readers the somewhat interesting spin that the audience was surprisingly educated and upscale. Emotionally, however, I was crushed. By that time my whole self-image was tied up in devotion to Pete and his *Eagle* mission. The Millers ran a smart paper, with smart stories devoted to important issues and interesting people, all of it wrapped up in a carefully designed package that was nationally recognized for its quality and taste. Everything I had worked for had been chucked out the window by this silly junket out to see *Deep Throat*.

My self-image was also tied up in my friendship with Pete. I took a lot of ribbing from the other reporters in the newsroom about going out all the time with Pete. They were more professional and intent on carefully building their careers, but I was a romantic and just wanted to be wild a lot of the time. It was fun being with Pete and a bit of a risk, and I wanted to live irresponsibly for a little while longer before I settled down somewhere and got boring. I was pathologically afraid of aging too quickly and growing smug, and my times up in the mountains and in the bars with Roger and Pete seemed like an emotional lifeline to me. But now I'd thrown that out too.

Pete kept me in the doghouse for a couple of weeks after that, glowering at me whenever we passed in the hall, scratching his rump with annoyance, and muttering under his breath as he walked by in his jerky gait.

"Hah. All the social pillars of Pittsfield. We'll see."

After a few days, however, I realized that I was enjoying my contretemps with Pete. It was secretly thrilling to have the publisher of the paper rampaging about me, and I rose to the challenge of winning him back. Instinctively, I knew that the foundation of our friendship was too strong for him to stay mad very long. I also knew exactly what to do, because I'd carried forward from adolescence a merry, bantering style of dealing with my father's tirades. Whenever Pete goaded me, I abused him back with relentless good cheer.

"So, there he is again, the publicist for *Deep Throat*," Pete would say, encountering me around the building. "All the social pillars of Pittsfield were there. Hah! *You'll* never be a social pillar of Pittsfield."

"Hey, Pete!" I would reply. "How are you doing, good buddy? Having a good day?"

Pete would never admit that my technique was working. If he had an emotional life, it wasn't shared with anybody. But he did give up. A few weeks after the *Deep Throat* incident, Pat Faucett called me at my desk.

"Okay, Rinker" she said. "I think he's finally ready to say Uncle. Pete wants to know if you'd like to go to lunch."

So, Pete and I went out together across the state line, to the Queechy Lake Inn, where the martinis were exceptionally potent and large. If we ever discussed the *Deep Throat* piece, or resolved our feelings about that, I certainly wasn't in a state to remember it. After lunch, we drove south into Austerlitz and then crossed back into the Berkshires through Alford and Great Barrington, pretending to be engaged in the lofty pursuit of exploring the land-preservation possibilities of the Taconic range. This was bull, of course. All we did for a couple of hours was drive around in circles in Pete's creaky VW Bug, goofing off and hitting a couple of bars. After arriving back at the *Eagle*, Pete took his afternoon nap and I drove back up to Hancock for a long, long sleep. We were back on track.

I never really could identify a "last time" with Pete, mostly because there wasn't one. Even after I left the *Eagle*, I would drop in on him in his office, on my way up through to Vermont, or while visiting for a weekend to hike with Linscott, and we remained in touch other ways, speaking on the phone and occasionally exchanging letters over the years. But there was one last event with him that I associated with my *Eagle* years. It seemed to symbolize his determination to take in everything happening within his world—the confines of Berkshire County—and also to have fun.

That year, 1974, a spasm of public nudity was sweeping American college campuses. It was called "streaking." Groups of students, a little bit high on dope, giggling between themselves, would strip off their clothes and gallop together across the grassy quadrangles or through crowded lecture halls, interrupting the day and generally embarrassing college administrators with a spirited display of nakedness. There was not much to it really, except that attractive co-eds running hand-in-hand across the Mount Holyoke or Antioch campus were highly photogenic, a welcome media antidote to the somber images of Richard Nixon crying while he resigned from power, and then the comedic Gerry Ford taking over as president and bopping bystanders on the head every time he visited a country club and sliced another golf ball. Streaking was pretty useful that way. The transition from the self-important acting out of the late 1960s to the more forthright hedonism of the mid-'70s "Me Decade" had to be symbolized somehow, so college girls stripped off their leotards and dungarees and ran around naked for a while. Now, having worn itself down at the Ivy League schools, streaking had trickled down and was enjoying a last throb at community colleges.

One warm Indian summer afternoon that fall, Nicole called me from the Berkshire Community College campus. A group of students were going to stage a streak across the campus lawns when classes let out that day. Nicole suggested that I cover this for the *Eagle*, but I told her that I wasn't interested. I didn't think I could get the concept past Morton and Bell, and besides, the story just wasn't that important.

"Oh, you're such an idiot, you know?" Nicole said. "The book boy. So *serious*. And you're chicken too. You know you can't get a picture of BCC kids streaking in *The Berkshire Eagle*, so you're not even going to try."

"All right, woman," I said. "How much are you going to bet that I can pull this off?"

"Dinner anywhere you want," she said.

"That's okay for starters," I said. "What about entertainment afterward?"

"Oh, God. You're such a horny jerk. But yeah. I'll throw that in too. Are we on?"

"We're on. I'll see you down there at three."

I didn't trust myself to take the picture, so I arranged for an *Eagle* photographer to follow me down there, and we agreed to keep the story a secret until we got down to BCC and saw what we had, because Morton and Bell would just kill the idea if we asked for clearance first. In the middle of all this, Pat Faucett made one of her regular afternoon calls to find out if anything was happening in the newsroom, so I told her about the streaking event. She called me back a few minutes later.

"Okay," Pat said. "Pete wants to see the streakers. So do I. Can we come? It'll be fun for Pete."

Yeah, what the hell. I told her to round up Pete and meet us down in the parking lot in fifteen minutes.

So, we did that dumb-ass thing, leaving the *Eagle* lot in a caravan of cars and squealing past the Berkshire Commons toward the community college on West Street, with Pete and Pat bringing up the rear in his wobbly VW Bug. When we got down to the college, I staged Pete and Pat at a good viewing position on the lawn, with a group of students waiting for the streak to begin, and Pete stood around with them, happily scratching his rump and smirking, chatting up the small group of students. I strolled across the grass to the opposite side with the photographer because he wanted to shoot the scene with the rim of mountains framing the image. I took out a notebook and began interviewing a few students, and then Nicole slinked over in her jeans and a sexy white T-shirt, snuggling up beside me to enjoy the show.

The streak itself was anticlimactic. Up front there was a group of skinny boys with tattoos, then a group of lumpy girls, none of them really worth looking at, dressed or nude. But behind them there was one tall girl with the best kind of body—broad, strong shoulders, skinny hips and waist, large melon breasts flopping in the air, and thin blonde hair blowing back as she ran. Her gentle smile as she glided by was confident and unembarrassed. It was a balmy day. Up on the peaks the birch and maple had turned to yellow and fiery orange, and a bank of cirrus had merged with the summit rim to form a horizon of lavender and gray. She was lovely, that thoroughbred girl, racing by with her figure profiled against the pastel sky.

When I got down to the college parking lot, Pete was chortling all over, enthusiastically scratching his rump, a very pleased man.

"Hah! Streaking," Pete said. "How'd you like that young filly at the end? Very athletic, wouldn't you say?"

"That's the kind of look that turns you on, huh Pete?" I said.

"Now, now, now, young man," Pete said. "It's not that at all. I'm merely observing that she had very classic lines."

"Oh, I see," I said. "It's a question of aesthetic appeal. Your artist's eye."

"Exactly! She had very classic lines. Now. Thank you very much young man. I feel that I have now seen a bit more of what's happening on campus these days."

The next morning, when the photographer's proofs reached the newsroom, Pete Miller and Pat Faucett were in every single frame. The photographer had shot from across the lawn and caught Pete in the background as the streakers gamboled by. Pete wasn't particularly large in the photos, but noticeable, and he had a look of benign amusement, with his hand resting on his chin. The best shot was the nude profile of the young blonde "filly" running past Pete.

Bill Bell surprised me by getting the biggest charge out of this and laughing hysterically, and then he carried the proof sheet over to Tom Morton, who smiled impishly, dabbed his forehead, and called me over.

"Hell's bells, Rinker," Morton said. "The publisher of this

newspaper is in every one of these damn shots. How the hell did you arrange that?"

"Hey Tom. *I* didn't take those shots. How was I supposed to know Pete would be standing there?"

"Yeah, right," Morton said. "And I was born in a manger in Bethlehem. You've pulled another stunt on me, Buck. I mean Pete is leering at this girl. He's staring at her tits. And he's the publisher of this damn newspaper. Christ."

"Tom, c'mon," I said. "Can't we have a sense of humor around here? Besides, this will get him back for all the crap he gave me on *Deep Throat*."

"Oh Lord," Morton said. "My sanity in hiring practices really has to be questioned. But, what the hell. We'll do it."

When the paper came out that afternoon, I went downstairs to see how Pat Faucett liked the streaking shot. Outside Pete's office, everyone who worked in classified was howling about the picture of the naked girl running by, and Pete's voyeuristic grin. The commotion drew Pete out of his inner sanctum and he put on a pair of spectacles, stared at the shot on the Local Page, and then looked over to me.

"Young man, whose idea was this? I'm in the paper, staring at a naked girl. Did you set this up?"

"Pete, no," I said. "This was Tom Morton's idea. You need to talk to him."

"Well, dammit, I will," Pete said, nervously scratching an elbow. "Jeez. Wait'll Amy Bess sees this. I'm really going to be in Dutch tonight."

"Ah, chill, Pete," I said. "She'll get over it."

In fact, Amy Bess didn't mind. She called into the *Eagle* as soon as the paper reached the Shaker Village that afternoon, speaking first with Pat, and then me, and she was laughing her pretty face off.

"Rinker Buck, that's *my* Pete Miller in that picture," she said. "He's staring at a naked girl. I'm holding you responsible for this."

"Ah, c'mon, Amy Bess," I said. "Pete was having fun."

"Oh, I know, I know! Listen, we're having guests Friday night. Will you come?"

That particular night out in Melville Land was one of the best martini sloshes ever, and that fall, as I grew even more comfortable with Pete, I realized something new about him. I was never going to figure him out. Accomplished people often arrive in complicated packages, their methods of working and their personalities ineffable. Pete had turned the *Eagle* into a standard of excellence, and he had infused others with his enthusiasm for preserving open lands, but nobody could really say why they responded so avidly to his leadership. It might simply have been that he was a lot of fun, and that was more than enough for me now.

·   ·   ·

Over the winter of 1974–1975 I began receiving a lot of job offers, some of them from newspapers in neighboring areas, which I wasn't particularly interested in, and some of them resulting from job applications I'd filed with magazines in New York almost two years earlier, while I was sitting around waiting to see if the *Eagle* would hire me. I could have been a fact-checker at a magazine, or a reporter-researcher at a newsweekly, but these positions offered me a lot less satisfaction than the *Eagle* slot I already had. Besides, whole months would pass during which my weekend regimen of wandering the bars and snowshoeing the peaks filled me with immense pleasure, and there were times when I suspected that I would never leave those mountains. Up on Perry's Peak or Mount Everett, as I took in the views of the distant, craggy Catskills with Roger Linscott, he would listen to me describe these prospects and then prod the snow with his boot, scowling.

"Gad. You suffer most egregiously from a young-man-in-a-hurry complex. Where does this obdurate mania for success come from? None of these offers are good enough for you, and speaking purely selfishly, I wish that you wouldn't go yet."

Late in the winter of 1975, however, one promising job offer did arrive. Now that Watergate was over, one of the big national stories was the economic decline of the so-called Frostbelt states of the Northeast and New England, and the concomitant rise of the Sunbelt. Hugh Carey, the incoming Democratic governor of New York, had symbolized both these shifting demographics and the end of Nelson Rockefeller's sixteen-year reign in New York by making his famous "the days of wine and roses are over" speech. That winter, the financial collapse of New York City seemed imminent, and with it, the nation's largest and wealthiest state was also imperiled. Nothing like this had happened since the Great Depression and I was enormously drawn to the story. When a small foundation-supported magazine offered me a job in Albany, the state capital, with a specific mandate to cover the crisis, I leapt at the chance.

My move to the urban backwater of Albany proved both maladroit and opportune. The fellow who ran this magazine was a graduate of Harvard, but most definitely not its business school. The foundation money soon dried up, and the job didn't last much more than a year. But by then I was ferociously plying the New York freelance market and had managed to place a long series of Sunday stories in the Week in Review of *The New York Times*. That circulated my name around New York, and within two years I had managed to find a good position as a staff writer under two wonderful editors, Michael Kramer and John Berendt, at *New York* magazine. All week, I churned out my stories for them, and then on weekends or during long vacations I junketed up to New England or out west. I found New York's ecumenical mix of women to be irresistible, and everything went pretty well as long as I was disciplined about following my motto of working hard and drinking martinis.

·   ·   ·

I knew that the Berkshires had already laid a marker on me for life, and it was hard saying good-bye, letting go.

When she heard that I was leaving town, Marcia Weiss called me in the newsroom and said that she wanted to get together over the weekend. There was one last thing, she said, that she wanted to do.

"Now listen here, Mister Buckaroo," she said. "I am taking you shopping for clothes."

"Oh Christ. Here we go. Marcia, I don't need any clothes."

"No! No. I know you. You'll show up at a press conference with the governor in your logger's pants. I am taking you shopping and you can't wiggle out of this."

So, we drove over to the Northway Mall in Albany together, and for the next several hours at Macy's and Bloomingdale's Marcia dressed me up like her Ken doll. It was extremely gratifying to be doted over like that, but still, I found it embarrassing. On the way home, we stopped at Les Pyrénées in Queechy Lake and had dinner.

"Oh, that was *so* fulfilling," Marcia sighed over dinner. "So fulfilling. God I just love shopping for a man. Especially when it's somebody like you, who really needs it."

"Fulfilling? Marcia, we're both broke now. We blew our money on clothes. What's fulfilling about that?"

"No, no. Please don't mess it up with your future girl-friends, okay? They want to shop for you. Please. Trust me. Let them do it because it's *so* fulfilling."

Roger Linscott had his own way of handling my departure. One afternoon during my last couple of weeks at the *Eagle* he ambled in toward my desk, placed his oxford on my typewriter stand and looked down with his expressive brown eyes.

"Say, it's egregiously sentimental to have to say good-bye to someone, and I would rather not do so with you. I have what you might regard as a sensible proposal."

"Sure, Roger. Shoot."

"Well, you will most assuredly need a suitable weaning period from our hikes together and will only be an hour or so away in Albany. So, I suggest that we continue our weekend jaunts for a respectable period, until you're adjusted over there. This is a perfectly selfish suggestion on my part. You're an insufferable bore, but I concede that I shall miss you."

"Roger, that's really nice. Thanks. We'll continue our hikes. That way we don't have to say good-bye."

"Precisely. Bravo."

As it happened, there was good snow all the way through to the end of March that year and Linscott and I did some of the northern peaks up by Greylock, and then one weekend we made a last run of the winter up behind his place, our old circuit over Perry's Peak and then down the pipeline route into New York State. When we got back to his house on Rossiter Road, Linscott paused to talk near the carved owls at the end of his drive.

"Say, there is one thing I had meant to say to you, but I'd rather express it out here, so that Lucy doesn't think I've gone off my rocker," Linscott said. "It comes more or less without explanation, so I shall just say it."

"Roger, sure."

"I have the utmost of confidence in you. I just wanted to say that. I have the utmost of confidence in you. Perhaps someday you'll recall that I said that."

"Okay, Roger. Thanks. I'm not sure I know what you mean, but thanks."

"'Tisn't much meaning to it, really. It's just the utmost of confidence in you. Should we ever lose touch, or not talk for several years, please never be afraid to call. I'll always want to hear from you."

Then we went into his house, made a fire, and drank bourbon and played backgammon until midnight.

. . .

That spring, Peter, Judy, and I were all unsettled by how quickly our old weekend threesome had broken up. As soon as I got over to Albany, I fell in love with the most beautiful Irish girl in America, and on weekends I was usually off visiting new places with Suzanne, and Judy almost never came out to the Berkshires, because she was studying so hard at Harvard Law School. Peter would follow Judy to Harvard Law in the fall and was commuting to Cambridge most weekends to be near her. For almost two years we had all lived intensely, spending almost every weekend together, and now we'd hardly seen each other for four or five months. In the middle of the day I would be overcome by these sudden, intense pangs of missing both of them, and I particularly regretted that my Saturday morning chats with Judy around the kitchen table had come to an end. We had never really said good-bye.

One warm Saturday in late May that year I was out in the Berkshires to hike with Linscott, and he passed along a message from Peter. Judy was finally visiting the mountains that weekend, and Peter thought that it would be a nice idea if I surprised her by stopping by their place. So, late in the afternoon, I left Linscott by his barn and then drove over Lenox Mountain to find the cottage that Peter had rented overlooking the October Mountain State Forest. When I got there, Peter was out running errands and Judy was alone in the house.

It was good to see Judy at last. In the kitchen, she was cooking up some great dinner for Peter, the house smelled of freshly baked challah, and the pine table in there overflowed with all of this stuff that she cluttered up her weekend with—plant projects and plant holders, dead cattails and glass vases, and all these artsy-crafty little projects that she would buy for herself at Jennifer House. Judy had on her old purple leotard and her Arcadia Shop hiking shorts. After so long a separation there was a rush of familiarity about seeing her, the skinny-hipped, sexy-brainy Smith College Goddess who was so lovely to know.

"Oh, Rinker, you're finally here. God, this is so difficult. I'm warning you, okay? I'm going to cry. We're all getting this divorce from each other and I don't want it to happen."

"Yeah, well, you know, Judy. It had to happen eventually. I missed you."

"Ditto. I don't know why I'd miss a wise-ass like you, but I do."

We cleared a space at the table, shared some wine, and debriefed each other for a while. I was excited because my new girlfriend came from the same sort of large, insane Irish Catholic family that I was from, and it was a delight being with someone who understood me so well. Judy told me all about how tough but rewarding law school had been, and what was going on with her and Peter. We made all the usual promises about staying in touch. But I could sense how emotionally fragile we were about saying good-bye, and I knew it would be too painful if I stayed much longer.

We walked arm-in-arm down the sloping lawn to my car. I got in and rolled down the window, and we talked for a few more minutes there.

"Okay, okay," Judy said. "This will sound like it's rehearsed, but it really isn't, I mean there are just two things I wanted to say to you. They are things you might forget about yourself. But you can't be sarcastic, okay?"

"All right, I won't be sarcastic. I won't forget anything you say until tomorrow."

"Shut up. Okay, now look, I'll just blurt it out. Rinker, everybody loves you. Everybody loves you and you don't have to be—"

"Oh Christ. Here we go. Everybody loves me."

"No! C'mon, listen. Rinker, you don't have to be macho-man all the time and pulling all these stunts and, you know, crazy-boy. People love you and you can just be yourself. I mean just try it for a change, just try it, if not for anybody else than for me, okay? I mean it."

"All right, all right. Everybody loves me. I'll try and get better about that. What's the second thing?"

"Oh, you know, I'm just studying in the middle of the afternoon and this thought about you pops in my brain. Or Peter mentions you. And I say, 'God, if he would just write like he talks.' Rinker, I really think it can be easier for you than you think. Just write like you talk."

Probably because of the intense emotions of the moment, or the sense of my time up in those mountains winding down right there, the suggestion sank in and proved very useful, and I never forgot what Judy Lesser said.

"All right," I said. "Everybody loves me and just write like I talk. It sounds like a program. Now. Just keep working your ass off at law school, okay? You're going to be great at this someday. I just know it."

"Me too. I mean, thanks. It's a lot easier now that the first year is over."

When she leaned down to kiss me on the cheek through the open window, Judy was whispering.

"Okay. Go now. Unless you want to watch me cry."

Judy stepped back from the car a bit and raised her hands to her eyes to catch some of the moisture forming there, and then she did this cute little Jacob's Pillow Girl knee bend and leaned back through the car window and we kissed very hard, lips-to-lips, as if the pent-up feelings of two years could be released while we simultaneously made good our parting. When we broke off I started the car and put it into gear.

"Hey, woman. Have a good life. Really."

"You too. God, you too."

She was crying now, her hands together high on her cheeks, and she waved once as I bumped down the drive, a strong, smart woman in her leotard, a purple splash receding against the lush green of October Mountain in the spring. The image of her through my rearview mirror seemed to leave a marker forever. For what felt like a decade we had group-groped on the couch at night, flirted and book-turded in the kitchen in the morning, and we'd done Alice's Restaurant and Mundy's Bar with the little sisters. She and it and everything else had transformed me. Now, as I looked back through my mirror, her figure had disappeared, and I knew that I finally had to face leaving those mountains.

I didn't want the moment to pass too quickly and I longed to see the Stockbridge oxbows one more time, so I drove south through the mansion district, screamed up past the Musgrave and Clark estates, past Mundy's and then down over Card Lake in West Stockbridge, exiting the range through the tornado district. I hit the New York Thruway driving hard, pushing my car as fast as it would go over the last foothills of the Taconics. Then the peaks, turning porphyry and black in my rearview mirrow, also disappeared. Strange emotions of regret and anticipation, of events telescoped together, gripped me as I drove, and I felt like crying. I had a new life now, new friends and work, a lovely girlfriend

I would be with that night, and I knew already that I would soon reach a promising future in New York. But the life I was racing toward would never be as intense as the one I was leaving behind.

EPILOGUE

THE CALL USUALLY arrives early on a Friday or Saturday evening, those quiet, satisfying hours after I've come in from flying or chain-sawing in the woods. I've laid a fire in my den, poured some bourbon, and put on the David Wilcox and Shawn Colvin tapes. My daughters won't have to be delivered to the ski slope or their babysitting jobs for another hour, and then my wife will drag me off to a party or we'll spend a quiet night together at home.

There's a nice constancy to the calls from my old friend. The conversations from one year to the next merge and get confused, expressing the passage of time.

"Say, whenever I get egregiously lonely like this, my friends suggest that I commence a program of regularly seeing mooovies. I consider this a satisfactory idea. From among the current billings, do you have a suitable recommendation?"

"Sure, Roger. The movie that I'd check out right now is a thing called *As Good As It Gets*. It's got Jack Nicholson and a great acting job by this total babe named Helen Hunt. You'll like it."

"Bravo. *As Good As It Gets*. I shall sample this and give you a report."

Roger Linscott is eighty-two now, and I'm just past fifty, more or less the same age he was when I first met him. I like the sense that we have now of still pulling in harness together as we age.

Several years after I left *The Berkshire Eagle*, Lucy Linscott was diagnosed with Alzheimer's Disease. Roger spent a very noble and selfless fifteen years shepherding her through that, coming out of retirement to work at a trade publishing company to pay for her home-nursing care. On weekends, with a curmudgeonly but loving sense of humor, Roger shuttled Lucy around to restaurants and museums so that she could enjoy what remained of her years. Occasionally, when I visited, Roger, Lucy, and I would sit out on their deck, watching the songbirds flock in to the feeders in the backyard. Observing this distinguished Pulitzer-winner dote over his wife was actually quite pleasant and very moving. Lucy, even as she grew increasingly remote and forgot who I was, was enormously fun to be around. She wandered freely back and forth through time, told marvelous stories about her childhood, and, with amazing accuracy, quoted passages from Shakespeare. Roger never despaired, never complained, and never lost track of the complex details of her care. I'm not sure that I'll ever again witness love this pure and brave.

I played a small, uncomfortable role at first, but one I gradually accepted. I refused to believe that Roger's old-age devotion to his wife should exclude our need to get out into the woods together. A few times a year, I called ahead and insisted that Roger hire weekend nurses for Lucy, and then I drove up from New York and yanked him out of his house for hikes up on the peaks, and we shared some very enjoyable evenings too, hitting the pool halls together. It was a good lesson for me in other ways. The needs of one established marriage—mature, facing its last big challenge—helped inform the learning curve of a new, fresh union. By then I'd met and married an exquisite Danish-American beauty, Amelia de Neergaard, and in those early years before our daughters came along, it was enjoyable to occasionally get away with my own set of friends, while Amy raced around New York for the weekend, keeping up a busy schedule of "art date" visits to the museums and galleries with her crowd.

It became a lot easier to see Roger seven years ago, after Amy and I decided to put New York and its suburbs behind us forever by moving north. We wanted to finish raising our daughters in a quiet country setting, and my wife was tired of hearing me complain that I didn't have a suitable place to chop wood. So, we found a big old rambling manse on sixteen acres of Little Berkshire land just south of the Massachusetts line, a short drive away from my old haunts in Great Barrington and Stockbridge. Lucy Linscott died that same year and I didn't sit around waiting for a suitable period of mourning to pass. I called Roger right away and made a hiking appointment for a week or two away, and that night we played pool over in Lebanon Springs. There was therapy involved for both of us. Roger had been confined in the house caring for Lucy for almost fifteen years, and I had been making good money but was unhappy living in New York. Now we were busting out together on weekend nights, being irresponsible and insulting each other all the time, just the way we could always do it in the past.

In 1998, when Roger was almost eighty, we ascended Perry's Peak for the last time, on snowshoes. At the top, the distant Catskill rim was lavender and moody and we sat on the snow and talked. My memory played a nice trick on me that day, because I realized that the spot where Comfort Halsey had once stood and been so breathtakingly beautiful was the same place, five years later, where my wife had paused on her snowshoes too, and in the sunlight that day she'd had this wonderful Scandinavian glow. It suffused me with pure sky just being up there again with Roger, appreciating the way that his companionship had connected me to my own years and loves.

The next summer, on a warm, clear day, we did Monument Mountain together. Just below the summit, Roger was too winded to continue, but he urged me to go on alone. So I scrambled up the last rock faces to the top, enjoyed the sun and the views up there, and then rejoined Roger below. I was pleased by the way that Roger dawdled from there, resting and amiably telling stories along the gently curving logging road that descends to the bottom. Our slow pace allowed me to absorb the feelings evoked by the familiar spots we passed—the old gnarled oak where Linscott got into a cerebral spat with the poet Heather McHugh one day, the stand of birches where he'd told Marcia Weiss a funny story, and then Marcia had whispered into my ear as he walked off, "*Hey, Linscott is so sexy!*" The collision of past memory and present tense was difficult, and I tried to hide my feelings from Roger. I knew that it was the last time that we'd do Monument Mountain together. Indeed, it was our last mountain forever.

Now, when Roger and I are together, we take a leisurely stroll down the road to Bartlett's Orchard or amble up View Drive. Afterward, we linger on Roger's deck, which faces north to the mountains. Donald MacGillis, an old *Eagle* friend, came by with his son a few years ago and took out the big ash that was blocking Roger's view, and I hauled away the wood. During the summer Roger and I often sit out there in the evening, drinking martinis and gin and tonics, watching Greylock turn porphyry and yellow under the setting sun.

Our favorite hangout now is a restaurant and bar in Great Barrington, 20 Railroad Street. It's a good, '70s-era hippie kind of place with a long wooden bar, ponytailed potters and gay guys, and, in the winter, lots of attractive and laughing ski bunnies. The waitresses there are mostly college students. They wear tight, clingy black leotards for the full bosom look and sleek blue jeans, and they always seem to enjoy it when Roger is around because he tips well and jokes with them a lot. There is something dear to every American barmaid about a fun and cranky geezer.

To a certain degree, our roles are reversed now. A quarter century ago, Roger listened to the ravings of the twenty-three-year-old with the maxed-out brain. Now I am receiving an education about old age. We've agreed that his compulsion to work well into his eighties is probably good because it has kept him mentally fit and surrounded him with the young. Roger seems to enjoy describing his various, brief hospitalizations. A daughter needs a new car, and Roger is giving her his own, late-model sedan. He solicits my advice about which new model to buy for himself and then ignores it. We continue to talk about books a lot and exchange favorite titles and authors. He'll be moving into an assisted-living community soon, and I reassure him that I'll continue to visit.

Most people, as far as I'm concerned, have got it all wrong about aging, what's happening to their relatives and old friends. The passage of years generally increases candor, and the occasional slipping of the mental transmission is a lot of fun to share.

"Say, have you noticed lately just how egregiously lewd the movies have become?" Linscott asked me one night. "It's an industry maniacally devoted to filth."

"No, not particularly, Roger," I said. "What are you talking about?"

"Well, some infernal jackass friend of mine, except that I can't remember which one, recommended that I go see something called *As Good As It Gets*. It was ghastly, this film. The language was obscene, it was full of all these sexual obsessions that people have these days, and the makeup department, I surmise, has been eliminated due to budget cuts. Goddamn movie should have been named *As Awful As It Gets*. I wish I could remember the egregious baboon who suggested that I take in this trash."

"Yeah, well, you know, Roger. You have to pick your friends carefully, I guess. But look. When you remember who sent you? Let me know. I don't want to take that guy's movie picks either."

"Precisely," Linscott said. "When I remember who it was, I'm going to throttle the bastard."

Outside, on Main Street, we say good night by his car. I'm occasionally struck by the contrast of knowing him now. Back then, when we first met each other, he was so tall and debonair, ruddy-faced from being outside so much of the time, leaning nonchalantly against his red Duster and saying the most outrageous things. Now, he's got a modest Subaru sedan, and his legs and arms are thin.

"Say, thanks again for spending time away from your family to visit me. I enjoy the things we talk about."

"No problem, Roger. You know that. I seem to remember a time when you would neglect your family for me."

"I suppose. Still, I'm grateful. It is rather touching in a way that we've made the effort to remain friends."

Leaving him there, or at his place in Richmond, I drive my Jeep south, slowly, enjoying my Shawn Colvin tapes. Route 41 is still reliable for owls and I like the places illuminated by my headlights—our old pullout for Perry's Peak, the grove of hemlocks where we walked in with fishing poles for the Williams River, the bridge over the Green. Down along the Sheffield Plain, if there are no cars coming the other way, I can see silver oxbows in the moonlight.

At home, I make a fire, pour a nightcap, and stare into the flames for a while, dreamy about my afternoon with Linscott. He allows me to appreciate the things I've achieved. When I first knew him, Linscott seemed to be the man who had it all, and I was terrified about the challenge of someday making a home and building a stable life as good as his. But now I've got the big pad in the country, two daughters who are the best Book Turds in their class, the ultimate Pretty Mom wife. When Amy comes in from her painting studio on a night like that, I am often struck by her beauty and her well-preserved figure. Still, it seems amazing that the old Berkshire County hell on wheels has practiced fidelity for twenty-four years. I get carried away then and have to tell her how I feel.

"God, Amy, you are just so egregiously beautiful sometimes. I love you in that outfit."

"Dear, thanks. But listen. Every time you come back after being with Roger Linscott? You drink too much and you use that stupid word again. 'Egregious.' Can't you watch it?"

"Yeah, yeah, yeah, dear. Okay. I'll try and become a better person for you."

"No. It's all right. Sorry. I'm just saying that with Roger you drink too much and say that word 'egregious.' But it's all right. I know how much he means to you."

So, she heads up for bed, ascending the stairs by the brick chimney, still the gorgeous tightwaist after so many years. I finish my drink and stare at the fire. What the hell. It's been a good day with Linscott and that's all that I need.

Don't ever give up on friendship like this. Seek it, find it, embrace it, immerse yourself in this baptismal font. Get that weekend dose of soul-mate love. Without it, life is but a pale facsimile of existence, and though you may climb high some-day and reach that purple-black rim, you'll never see and feel and pulse with all the colors, or know yourself fully suffused with sky.

ACKNOWLEDGMENTS

So MANY FRIENDS and former colleagues were unstinting in their help with this book that I sometimes felt that I was merely the collector of information, not the writer. All of them were aware that I would apply my habitual caustic humor to the events described and cheerfully contributed all the same. I am fortunate to enjoy such a wide circle of loyal companions.

A year before he died of cancer in the spring of 2001, Tom Morton sat down with me for two interviews in his house in Pittsfield, astonishing me with his memory for detail and his humorous approach toward my tragicomic years underneath him as a cub reporter. Pat and Frank Faucett, Bill Bell, Abe Michaelson, Mary Jane Tichenor, Milton Bass, Charles Bonenti, Rory O'Connor, Mike Meserole, Nick King, Donald MacGillis, Helen Southworth, Joel Librizzi, Steve Moore, Grier Horner, Betsey Kittredge Little, Susan Merrill, Helen Du Pont, Alex Timchula, and Billy Kie also shared their recollections, confirmed important details, and generously provided photographs and documents that I needed. No one can ever say enough good things about George Wislocki. David Scribner, the present editor of *The Berkshire Eagle*, and librarian Grace McMahon opened the paper's archives for my use. Richard and Judy Davies, Alistair Highet, and Alexandra Chalif provided valuable smarts and support. Irene L. Tague generously allowed me to use several photographs from the archive of her late husband, the superlatively gifted William Tague. Two wonderful and loyal friends from my *Eagle* years, Donna and John Mattoon, constantly made themselves available by e-mail and phone to answer my queries and fact-checks. Dianne Blick and Rhonda Bezio at my local business center were indispensable and cheerful partners.

After Harvard Law School and stints as an editor and publisher in Washington and San Francisco, Peter Scheer remains as fun loving and perceptive as he was before, and made himself available for phone interviews and frequent e-mail queries. I regard it as a lifetime achievement that we've remained such good friends. My debt to Roger Linscott has been made abundantly clear in this book and need not be repeated here.

Perhaps the biggest delight of finishing this book was briefly reuniting with Comfort Halsey Cope and Betty Sudarsky, who filled in many of the gaps in my memory about the winter we spent together in Richmond. Judy Lesser, now Dr. Judith Lesser Nelson (yes, after law school, she went on to medical school), has been an enormously helpful and witty e-mail correspondent and fact-checker, despite a busy medical practice and teaching schedule at the Mount Sinai School of Medicine in New York.

A number of other friends and relatives helped simply by insisting that I continue to write and by sharing their own memories of their first job years. They include Bill Carmean and Nancy Ross, Peter Paden, Michael Moschen, Cathrine de Neergaard, and Daniel Fetterman. My sister McNamara Rome offered useful critiques of some of the family material in this book, and my father-in-law, William F. de Neergaard, tirelessly promotes my interests. Danielle Mailer is a dream girl whose spunky wisdom helps sustain me.

I am particularly grateful to Cindy Rousseau, whose frequent readings of portions of my manuscript and joyful, prodigious e-mail correspondence proved vital while I was finishing this book. George Rousseau knows airplane parts very well and correctly pointed out that anal-retentive is hyphenated.

My agent, Sloan Harris, never lost his enthusiasm for this

project, and his cheer and attention to detail is in every respect what a writer needs in a publishing partner, and Teri Steinberg and Susan Kaufman at ICM have also been wonderful.

PublicAffairs has more than lived up to its stated ideal of performing as an idea-driven, boutique publishing house. Peter Osnos and Geoff Shandler were extremely gracious and supportive when acquiring this book, and Paul Golob not only displayed admirable patience between revisions but goaded me to improve structure in the places where the narrative required additional help. David Patterson and Gene Taft are tireless and make publishing almost too much fun.

My wife, Amelia, should have dumped me years ago. Her willingness to put up with not only my working hours but also the content of this book speaks volumes about her devotion to my purpose. My daughters, Sara and Charlotte, are too loving and supportive, and intellectually precocious, to describe here with words.

PHOTOGRAPH CREDITS

PublicAffairs is a publishing house founded in 1997. It is a tribute to the standards, values, and flair of three persons who have served as mentors to countless reporters, writers, editors, and book people of all kinds, including me.

I. F. Stone, proprietor of *I. F. Stone's Weekly,* combined a commitment to the First Amendment with entrepreneurial zeal and reporting skill and became one of the great independent journalists in American history. At the age of eighty, Izzy published *The Trial of Socrates,* which was a national bestseller. He wrote the book after he taught himself ancient Greek.

Benjamin C. Bradlee was for nearly thirty years the charismatic editorial leader of *The Washington Post.* It was Ben who gave the *Post* the range and courage to pursue such historic issues as Watergate. He supported his reporters with a tenacity that made them fearless, and it is no accident that so many became authors of influential, best-selling books.

Robert L. Bernstein, the chief executive of Random House for more than a quarter century, guided one of the nation's premier publishing houses. Bob was personally responsible for many books of political dissent and argument that challenged tyranny around the globe. He is also the founder and was the longtime chair of Human Rights Watch, one of the most respected human rights organizations in the world.

.　　　.　　　.

For fifty years, the banner of Public Affairs Press was carried by its owner Morris B. Schnapper, who published Gandhi, Nasser, Toynbee, Truman, and about 1,500 other authors. In 1983 Schnapper was described by *The Washington Post* as "a redoubtable gadfly." His legacy will endure in the books to come.

Peter Osnos, *Publisher*